NATIONAL GEOGRAPHIC
TRAVELER

ireland

by Christopher Somerville

National Geographic
Washington, D.C.

CONTENTS

Pages 2–3: Medieval Blarney Castle, home of the famous stone, near Cork
Opposite: Beautifully embroidered designs based on ancient Celtic symbols adorn the dress of a young dancer in County Kerry.

TRAVELING WITH EYES OPEN

Alert travelers go with a purpose and leave with a benefit. If you travel
responsibly, you can help support wildlife conservation, historic preservation,
and cultural enrichment in the places you visit. You can enrich your own travel
experience as well.

To be a geo-savvy traveler:

- Recognize that your presence has an impact on the places you visit.

- Spend your time and money in ways that sustain local character.
  (Besides, it's more interesting that way.)

- Value the destination's natural and cultural heritage.

- Respect the local customs and traditions.

- Express appreciation to local people about things you find interesting and
  unique to the place: its nature and scenery, music and food, historic villages
  and buildings.

- Vote with your wallet: Support the people who support the place, patron-
  izing businesses that make an effort to celebrate and protect what's special
  there. Seek out shops, local restaurants, inns, and tour operators who love
  their home—who love taking care of it and showing it off. Avoid businesses
  that detract from the character of the place.

- Enrich yourself, taking home memories and stories to tell, knowing
  that you have contributed to the preservation and enhancement of
  the destination.

That is the type of travel now called geotourism, defined as "tourism
that sustains or enhances the geographical character of a place—its environment,
culture, aesthetics, heritage, and the well-being of its residents." To learn more,
visit National Geographic's Center for Sustainable Destinations at *www
.nationalgeographic.com/travel/sustainable.*

ireland

ABOUT THE AUTHOR

Christopher Somerville is one of Britain's best known travel writers, with
some 35 books to his name—including *National Geographic Traveler: Great Britain.*
He writes regularly for the travel sections of the *Times* and the *Irish Independent*
and also broadcasts on radio. His love affair with Ireland was kindled on his first
trip to the island, an 800-mile (1,280 km) walk through the rugged and romantic west. Since then, he has written four books and countless words of travel
journalism about the country, and returns whenever he can to hook up with old
friends, walk the mountains and coasts, play traditional music, and continue his
search for that place "just around the corner, now," where the *craic* is mighty
and the pub never closes.

Charting Your Trip

With its charming towns, cozy pubs, sheep-dotted hills, and friendly and quick-witted locals, it's easy to see Ireland only as depicted in the emerald-green pages of a tourist brochure. But Ireland is not all about soft-focus romanticism.

Alongside the donkey cart, sometimes overtaking it rather brashly, you'll see the 4x4 of modern progress and the sheen of a youthful, forward-pressing republic. This bracing, sometimes challenging, and always fascinating mix will be readily on show as you take in the justly famous sights and landscapes, even if you have only a short time to explore this rich and surprisingly complex land.

Ireland's extensive bus and rail systems make it easy to move about the country, but many people find the freedom and flexibility afforded by a car the best way to go. Car rentals agencies abound in all cities and most sizable towns. But remember to drive on the left.

How to Visit: If You Have a Week

Even if you have only a week in Ireland, spend a day or two in the capital city, **Dublin,** on the country's east coast. Join one of the guided walks for some flavor of this spellbinding place, a nursery for writers, artists, musicians, rogues, and rebels. **The National Museum of Archaeology and History** boasts dazzling ancient and medieval relics and an account of the nation's long road to independence from Britain. Other can't-miss attractions include the wonderfully illuminated **Book of Kells** (A.D. 800) at Trinity College and the grim but gripping tour of **Kilmainham Gaol,** essential to understanding Ireland's revolutionary history and spirit.

Then head to Ireland's **southwest**—the country's most iconic region—for two or three days. Travel by way of **Killarney National Park** (190 miles/300 km southwest of Dublin), a wonderfully preserved ring of lakes and mountains, on your way to explore the spectacularly wild shores and mountains of **Cork** and **Kerry,** where the restless Atlantic breaks up the seaboard into jagged green peninsulas—especially Iveragh with its famous **Ring of Kerry** drive (best out of season) and the green and hilly **Dingle Peninsula** in north Kerry.

Heading north two or three hours up the west coast from Kerry takes you through the bare gray hills of County Clare's **Burren** region, famous for its spectacular late-spring and early-summer carpets of wildflowers. An hour northwest of the Burren, make a day circuit of the large west Galway peninsula, better known as **Connemara,** the iconic heart of "wild Ireland." Then carry on north another hour into rugged

A statue in Cobh commemorates Irish emigration.

County Mayo for a night in the pubs of **Westport,** a peerless town for traditional musical sessions.

You could then return to Dublin (160 miles/260 km from Westport) across the vast **peat bogs** of the Irish Midlands, many now being conserved for their wildlife. You can also stop off en route to visit the round towers and beautifully carved buildings of **Clonmacnoise** on the banks of the River Shannon in County Offaly to cap off your week.

If You Have More Time . . .

. . . then lucky you! It's a great pity to rush through such a laid-back country. The suggested itinerary below follows some of the same route as the one-week version above, but ventures more off the beaten tourist trail and explores more of the island.

Around Dublin: There are several regions near the capital worth exploring. About 30 miles (48 km) north of Dublin in County Meath lies the extraordinary Stone Age necropolis of **Brú na Bóinne** with its great 5,000-year-old tombs, including **Newgrange.** The riding stable and famous horse-racing tracks of the **Curragh** of Kildare beckon 40 miles (65 km) west from Dublin; here you'll also find the eastern edge of the wide flat boglands. Then turn southeast to the **Wicklow Mountains** to stroll by the supremely beautiful twin lakes of **Glendalough,** about 40 miles (65 km) south of Dublin. With a 1,500-year-old monastery as part of the setting, a walk here–in the early morning or late evening to avoid the crowds–gives insight into the "Irish soul" as few places do.

NOT TO BE MISSED:

The beautiful Book of Kells at Dublin's Trinity College 54–55

Going for a dawn or evening walk at Glendalough 98–103

A boat trip to the Blasket Islands off the Dingle Peninsula 156

The spectacular wildflowers of the Burren 170

A music session in Westport 190

The views over Yeats Country from Knocknarea 210–211

Sailing down the River Shannon to Clonmacnoise 250–251

A Black Taxi tour of the murals of Belfast 284–291

Cruising to the islands in Lower Lough Erne 323

When to Go

Because there's no guarantee of either sunny or wet weather at any specific time of year, the question of when to visit Ireland depends on what you want to do once you arrive.

If you possess even a speck of Irish blood, you'll enjoy the celebrations on St. Patrick's Day, March 17, especially the massive parade and celebration in Dublin. In the months that follow, roughly April through June, everything looks particularly green, the wildflowers are out, the birds are singing, and tourist facilities are open again after the winter.

If you want to experience Ireland's great festivals (see p. 44 & Travelwise p. 342), then visit in July or August. Places are crowded then, and sometimes the rain falls as the prices go up. But at least the sea is a swimmable temperature.

There's often a burst of clear, if cool, weather in September and October, as the colors change and prices begin to fall, while winter is for fans of the outdoors—walkers and mountaineers out to enjoy crisp, frosty days on the hills—and for lovers of a cozy pub, a blazing fire, a warming whiskey, and a timeless session of talk.

Tipping

No one is entitled to a tip, and the only service providers who might mutter to themselves if one isn't forthcoming would be taxi drivers and waiters and waitresses in restaurants. For a taxi ride, tipping the driver 10 percent of the fare is plenty. In a restaurant, look to see whether service has been added to your final bill. If it hasn't, whether or not to leave a tip is entirely up to you. A tip of 10 percent of the final bill would be fine, 15 percent would be very generous. (See Travelwise p. 347 for more information.)

Southwest & Western Ireland: From Glendalough in the Wicklows, a 60-mile (95 km) drive south along the sandy, warm southeast coast brings you to to **Waterford**—the famous crystal factory no longer offers tours, but the showroom still exhibits and sells exquisite handcrafted glassware. From Waterford, it's another 80 miles (130 km) southwest to ring the **Bells of Shandon** on a tour of historic **Cork city.** Just outside Cork, you can guarantee yourself the gift of the gab by kissing the **Blarney stone** at Blarney Castle before heading a couple of hours west to the famed west Cork and Kerry coasts (see p. 8).

From the southwest peninsulas, travel north of the Burren and Connemara to the western Irish counties of **Clare, Galway,** and **Mayo,** each about 150 miles (240 km) west of Dublin. The west is a stronghold of great traditional music: Try **Ennistymon** and **Doolin** in County Clare, **Galway** city, and almost any town or village—just ask around. Hill-climbing and walking are also wonderful here, especially the **Twelve Bens** and **Maumturks** of Connemara and the remote **Nephin Beg** of Mayo. Mountains with a special spiritual significance are **Mullaghmore** in the Burren region of Clare and the famous pilgrimage mountain of **Croagh Patrick** on the shores of Clew Bay. And don't miss a trip out to the glorious **Aran Islands** to glimpse a more traditional way of life.

Central & Northwest Ireland: The flat central Midlands nestled between Dublin and the wild west, mostly bog and meadows, have their own understated charm. Take a cruise along the **River Shannon** from **Athlone** or **Carrick-on-Shannon,** or walk the bog roads and trails of **Longford, Offaly,** or **Laois** to appreciate it. In the northwest of the country, the shadows of the Yeats brothers, poet

What to Pack

Generally, dress in Ireland is quite informal. But, since the country lies right in the track of Atlantic weather patterns, its climate is notably damp. You will probably see everything from soft, freckling, pervasive moisture to good honest rain while you're here. So you'll need to bring a good waterproof jacket and pair of pants, footwear that will stand a soaking, a collapsible umbrella, and a good hat with a brim. These will make all the difference to your enjoyment of Ireland, no matter what time of year

you visit, and will prevent you having to search endlessly—and pay through the nose—for decent weatherproof gear.

If you plan on playing golf, don't forget your favorite shoes, and bring sturdy walking boots if you want to do any hiking. Small, light binoculars are a boon for admiring birds or the scenery.

Take some cards printed with your name and contact details to give to new friends, and pack a sense of humor and irony—the Irish deal in little else. (See Travelwise p. 342 for more information.)

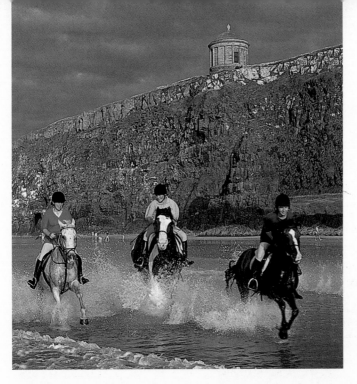

On the beach below Mussenden Temple in County Londonderry, Northern Ireland

William and painter Jack, lie long through mountainous **Sligo** (135 miles/215 km from Dublin), while an Irish-speaking, rugged atmosphere pervades the moors and lonely coasts of **Donegal** (about 50 miles/80 km north of Sligo). Here on the cliffs of **Slieve League,** or out in the **Rosses,** you will feel truly away from it all.

Northern Ireland: Don't neglect Northern Ireland, an unmissable part of your Irish experience. A walking tour of **Belfast** (100 miles/160 km or two hours by high speed train from Dublin) reveals the warmth of this vibrant city, while you'll get a full-strength account of recent history and politics on a **Black Taxi tour** to see the remarkable political murals. Then drive north up the **Antrim Coast,** a breathtaking display of volcanic cliff scenery, to the famed **Giant's Causeway** promontory of basalt. **Londonderry** (62 miles/100 km northwest of Belfast) has its walled city and gorgeous beaches, while in **County Fermanagh,** in Northern Ireland's southwest, you can cruise the island-dotted waters of Lough Erne. In the southeast, climb the noble hills—the mountains of **Mourne** in Country Down, South Armagh's **Slieve Gullion**—for mighty views before you head south again the 70 miles (115 km) to Dublin.

Visitor Information

Faílte Ireland *(www.discoverireland .ie)* is your one-stop center for travel information for Ireland, while the excellent **Northen Ireland Tourism Bureau** *(www .discovernorthernireland.com)* covers the North.

Information on bus travel within the Republic can be found at **Irish Bus** *(www.buseireann.ie),* and at **Ulsterbus** *(www.translink.co.uk/at ulsterbus.asp)* for Northern Ireland.

For rail schedules and reservations, contact **Irish Rail** *www.irish rail.ie* or **Northern Ireland Railways** *(www.translink.co.uk/nir.asp).*

History &
Culture

The penny whistle drives many
an Irish jig.
Opposite: Dublin's city center

Ireland Today

A leather-faced countryman in a cloth cap and an old patched jacket, pitchforking his hay in a tiny stonewalled field against a timeless backdrop of mountains and sea: That's Ireland today. His green-haired daughter striding out of a Dublin cappuccino bar, networking to the United States on her mobile phone: That's today's Ireland, too, on the move and on the change.

Romance with a Hard Edge

Romantics have no trouble at all finding what they're looking for in Ireland. Few countries project such a seductive image as this rainwashed little island off the northwest coast of Europe, and few fulfill their visitors' dreams so faithfully—the green fields, the soft rain, the quick-tongued and open-handed people, the Guinness-drinking and laughter against that eternal backdrop of irresistible Irish music.

But there is a hard edge, too, not far underneath the fun and fancy. During the past 15 years, no western European country has undergone such a profound economic and social change as Ireland. Everywhere people talk of the Celtic Tiger, the boom economy that saw business and optimism swell in the Republic in the 1990s. "Ireland of the Welcomes," the laid-back land where hospitality is

> **Romantics have no trouble at all finding what they're looking for in Ireland. Few countries . . . fulfill their visitors' dreams so faithfully.**

the watchword and no one's in a hurry, still flourishes, of course, as much in visitors' minds as anywhere. You can feel more relaxed, more welcome here than in almost any other country in the world. Ireland is famous for just this atmosphere, with good reason. But the signs of change are all around, too—money jingling in Dubliners' pockets, farmland sliced by superhighways built with European development grants, extravagant modern houses sprouting on remote hillsides, and a confidence in the attitudes of youngsters who no longer need to emigrate to find a decent job and some freedom to live their lives as they see fit.

The image of Ireland as a gently backward, rural, and mystical land, and of the Irish as a rustically humorous community of God-fearing, thrifty peasants (seeded with a few erratically brilliant novelists and poets), was deliberately fostered in the 1930s and '40s for nationalistic reasons by Eamon de Valera, prime minister of the newly and proudly independent Eire. It wasn't without a basis in truth. And it served the Irish tourist industry well, fixing southern Ireland in the world's mind as the ideal soft landing for an escape from reality. What it disguised, though, was an all-too-real rural poverty, economic and social, which drove young, vigorous men and women to emigrate in droves up to the mid-1990s. Now, at the beginning of the 21st century, many are returning to Ireland, or have never had to leave in the first place.

This new, shiny-faced, and thrusting young republic, transformed into one of Europe's most dynamic economies, has been built on a foundation of development money from the European Union and from the International Fund for Ireland. Agricultural and pharmaceutical chemicals and information technology have been particularly big players, with multinational companies settling in Irish towns on a featherbed of tax breaks, subsidies, and start-up grants. They like the Irish willingness to work hard for moderate wages and the brightness of motivated school leavers.

Dublin shines at dusk along the River Liffey.

Troublesome Tiger

All the same, the Celtic Tiger has turned out to be a troublesome and uncertain beast. Too many of these new high-tech industries have been found to flit out from under when times get tough or when the global market gives a twitch, with little sense of loyalty to their host country or workforce. Older homegrown industries such as textiles, car assembly, and agriculture haven't done so well. Some visitors find an un-Irish offhandedness and arrogance in the new breed of entrepreneurial young highflyers. Indeed, the Irish are not unquestioning Europeans. On June 12, 2008, they voted to reject ratification of the Treaty of Lisbon, which established a Europe-wide Constitution in everything but name. In October 2009, though, after reassurances on taxation and autonomy, the Irish reversed that decision.

Then there's the crude, often laughable effect of too bright and insensitive a spotlight being shone on Ireland's cultural heritage. Many think that Riverdance, for example, the internationally successful stage show that drew the world's attention to Irish dancing, cheapened this very formal, highly technical connoisseur's art by coating it in an alien, glitzy sexuality. And can you really find the true "crack," that absolutely and uniquely Irish version of a high old time, in Beastie O'Shagg's Irish Theme Pub in Salzburg or Bangkok?

The [2009] collapse of much of Europe's banking system . . . brought recession and enormous economic uncertainty to the Republic.

In 2009, worldwide economic overconfidence caused the collapse of much of Europe's banking system and brought recession and enormous economic uncertainty to the Republic. The Celtic Tiger had been footed on a boom in the construction industry, itself shakily propped up by unsustainable borrowing and economic aid. Building works halted overnight, and housing and business park projects stood unfinished. After two decades of prosperity, Irish youngsters once more prepared to emigrate in search of work.

New Hope for the North

The island of Ireland contains 32 counties. The six northernmost counties of Antrim, Derry, Tyrone, Fermanagh, Armagh, and Down make up the province of Northern Ireland, which remained politically a part of the United Kingdom when the other 26 counties of Ireland split away to form the Irish Free State in 1921 after the Irish War of Independence (see pp. 32–33). You may hear Northern Ireland called Ulster—the six counties formed part of the ancient Irish province of that name. Ancient Ulster contained three additional counties (Donegal, Cavan, and Monaghan), but these joined the infant Free State (later the Irish Republic) in 1921 and have remained politically apart from Northern Ireland ever since.

Fans of the Irish national soccer team celebrate a goal by the home team.

Almost everyone in Northern Ireland in the mid-1990s would have given their eyeteeth to enjoy an image as benign, if misleading, as the Republic's leprechaun winsomeness, instead of the dour and deadly reputation—equally false—that they had been cursed with through the activities of a few bitter bigots. Thirty years of being unwillingly strapped to the careering headless horse of sectarian and politically motivated terrorism made all moderate folk—and they constitute the majority of people in the North—heartily sick of being classified with extremists. They knew only too well the damage it was doing to their province's economy, with visitors and overseas investors reluctant to come to a place tarred with the deep-staining brush of violence and intolerance. The North's traditional heavy industry, following a pan-European trend, was in decline, the economy stagnant. Emigration of bright, ambitious youngsters, always seen as a purely southern Irish scourge, was getting a grip of Northern Ireland, too.

With all its flaws and uncertainties, the Good Friday Agreement of April 10, 1998 (see p. 289), brought about a new perspective on Northern Ireland. The outside world, looking in, began to see growing shoots of hope for peace and a settled society, rather than yet more uprooted aspirations. In 2005, the IRA declared its campaign over after 35 years of the "Troubles," during which the paramilitary republican group had sought to bomb and shoot the British Army out of Northern Ireland and to establish by violent means a reunification of the island of Ireland. Few onlookers could quite believe the cessation, and the subsequent process of decommissioning the IRA's arsenal of weapons was fraught with mistrust. Loyalist paramilitary groups took some time to follow suit. Since then a number of splinter groups have caused trouble and concern, but they are tiny and have no voter endorsement.

Peace on the streets of Northern Ireland depends on the existence of a credible form of devolved government for the North. The Northern Ireland Assembly, based at Stormont Castle just outside Belfast, has had a troubled genesis since first elected in June 1998—it has been suspended four times already in its short existence. Nothing did more to establish better relations between nationalists and unionists than the emergence of a wildly unlikely mutual regard between Democratic Unionist Party leader Ian Paisley, First Minister of the Assembly 2007–2008 (since replaced by Peter Robinson), and the deputy leader of Sinn Féin, Martin McGuinness, Deputy First Minister since 2007. Pho-

Old-fashioned traditions are still practiced in many isolated pockets of rural Ireland.

tographs of Paisley, iconic defender of the Union between Northern Ireland and the UK, grinning and joking with McGuinness, former hard-line IRA boss, had the pair quickly dubbed the "Chuckle Brothers." The spectacle caused as much grim amusement as it did incredulity and even hope.

Rural Charm & City Buzz

Few enough visitors yet know about Northern Ireland's gorgeous secret countryside or the warmth of the welcome in the music pubs and bed-and-breakfast houses of the province. Their expectations are vague, their image of the North distorted by the Troubles (see p. 35). But south of the border it's a different story. Three million visitors a year flock to the Republic, one tourist for every inhabitant. Tourism is big business here.

Visitors planning a trip to southern Ireland have a seductive image in mind—the beauty of the mountains and sea coasts of the west and southwest, the sophistication and humor of Dublin, outdoor fun on golf courses, horse tracks, and fishing lakes, and the laid-back pleasures of the talk, the music, and the general lifestyle everywhere. Famous beauty spots and tourist honeypots lie thick on the ground, and those who come to Ireland to find the fantasy Island of the Leprechauns don't go home disappointed. Buying shamrocks and shillelaghs in the crowded gift shops of Killarney, crawling bumper to bumper around the Ring of Kerry's overpopular scenic route, fighting for a table in a Kinsale fish restaurant, or watching stage Irishwomen at their spinning wheels in Bunratty Folk Park, you could be forgiven for thinking that all Ireland was out to sell itself lock, stock, and barrel to the tourist trade.

The real living country, you'll find, lies along the lane just off the main road, in the street behind the harbor, ten minutes' walk up the mountain track, out along the bog road. Explorers and wanderers get the best out of Ireland—so do talkers and listeners, hikers and drivers, laughers and quaffers, and those who like the odd angle and the elliptical way.

EXPERIENCE:
Take the Time to Yarn

"Every gateway holds a farmer, and every farmer holds a story." You'll find the truth of that old saw when you travel through backcountry Ireland—but not if you race through, cocooned in your rental car. Rent a bike for a day, or better yet, set out on foot. Irish folk are notably friendly and inquisitive, and the more rural the situation, the more they will be ready for a good chat. That's the best way to hear the stories, the legends, and the scandals, not to mention opinions both well-informed and "original." Find hundreds of downloadable walking routes, from country rambles to jaunts through Ireland's bustling cities, at www.discoverireland.ie/walking and www.walkni.com.

That easygoing image, of course, is only half the story. It's true that there are still thousands of small traditional farms in rural Ireland, especially out in the Irish-speaking Gaeltacht areas of the west, working their picturesquely tiny, intensely green stonewalled fields, with EU subsidies to prop up the businesses. Country towns still tend to be charming and sleepy in equal proportion, retaining their old-fashioned grocers' and butchers' shops and tiny dark pubs. But cities such as Galway and Cork, where many of the Celtic Tiger youngsters have injected a healthy dash of loud life, buzz with modern energy these days.

Keeping an Eye on Things

Irish politics, both local and national, have always been riven by scandal. Bribes, cronyism, and deals behind closed doors were so much the order of the day by the early 1990s that they were becoming an embarrassment to the Irish themselves, as well as an international talking point. An Ethics in Public Office Act was passed in 1998 to try to get a grip on this shady side of things, with mixed success to date.

During the same period, a very noticeable growth in concern for the environment, both built and natural, has led to lively debate about planning, development, and design, notoriously unchecked until recently. Traveling through rural areas you'll hardly fail to spot the much reviled "Irish hacienda" style of architecture—a sprawling ranch-style bungalow fronted by an enormous prairie of slate patio behind raw brick arches, usually posed on an otherwise pristine hillside. Around city streets the main culprit has been the use of garish plastic and eyeball-tingling paint. In areas of outstanding natural beauty and historical interest, European development money has paid for several interpretive centers of often obtrusive design. Few would have raised a murmur 20 years ago; now, thanks to the emergence of a better educated and more sophisticated electorate, the powers-that-be are obliged to take notice of objectors.

> Change is sweeping through Irish life, and nowhere is this more clearly shown than in the rise in status that women acheived during the last decade of the 20th century.

Perhaps the best example of this new consciousness is the growing protest over the destruction of the vast boglands by Bord na Móna, the Peat Board (see pp. 254–255). Seen until recently as barren wastelands fit only to be exploited for cheap fuel, the boglands are now regarded by many as a wonderful, strangely beautiful refuge for wildlife.

Women to the Fore

Change is sweeping through Irish life, and nowhere is this more clearly shown than in the rise in status that women achieved during the last decade of the 20th century. When Mary Robinson, a liberal-minded barrister with strong feminist allegiances, was elected President of the Republic of Ireland in 1990, she became an inspiration to many women, who were still taking pretty much a back seat in Irish political and business life, and they quickly became much more assertive and self-confident. Robinson proved an indefatigable traveler in her own country and through the wider world, keen to gain a hearing for unpopular or ticklish subjects such as unmarried mothers, drug abuse, gay rights, and religious intolerance. By her warm and genuine personality she raised the profile of the presidency and of Ireland, and especially of Irish women. In 1997, she was appointed United Nations High Commissioner for Human Rights, and another woman—Mary McAleese, a Roman Catholic law lecturer from Northern Ireland—took her place. Times had changed indeed.

A Church in Crisis

The business of who lines up on which side of the religious divide has come to mean less and less in the modern Ireland. In Eamon de Valera's backwoods Ireland of the 1930s, the Roman Catholic Church was king of the castle, dispensing welfare and education and laying down strict rules of behavior that the largely poor and rural populace disregarded at their peril. Anyone who crossed a priest in some country parish would become an untouchable. Respect for the Church and adherence to Christianity—Church of Ireland or Roman Catholic—was almost universal.

But social change, greater affluence, international travel, and a wider education have put an end to all that. These days, after a series of well-publicized sexual and financial scandals, the Roman Catholic Church is in a very reduced state. A parish priest no longer has the automatic respect of his flock: He has to earn it.

The "Old Faith"

What some call superstition and others name the "Old Faith"—belief in the power of holy wells and woods, offerings to natural gods, ceremonies at standing stones and circles—continues unabated, a powerful hidden tide still surging below the surface of modern life. Often it works side by side with Christianity, or is bound up with music and dance. You won't have to look too hard to find it. ■

The Roman Catholic faith struggles to maintain its influence at the center of community life.

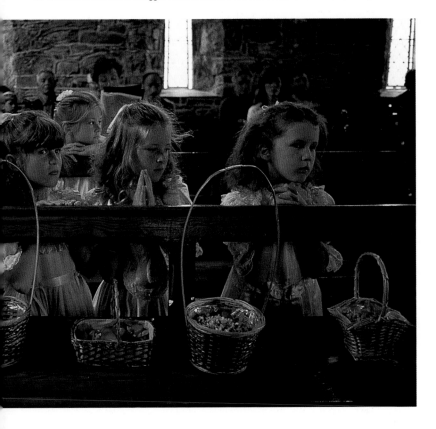

Fauna, Flora, & Climate

Ireland's climate is famously mild and wet, with rain falling somewhere almost every day of the year. In the west, on what locals euphemistically term "soft" summer days, it can seem as if most of it is falling on you. The prevailing damp westerly airstream off the Atlantic is what makes Ireland so beautifully green.

Ireland is like a great geological wheel, with a hub of carboniferous limestone filling the interior within a rim of ancient volcanic rock. You'll find schist and gneiss in western Connemara and parts of the far north, spectacular basalt formations along the Antrim coast, and granite along the north shore of Galway Bay, in west Donegal, and southwest of Dublin. The famed bogs that formed in the central region are still cut and milled for turf—as the Irish call their horticultural and fuel peat—but exploitation is in its final phase now (see pp. 254–255).

Ten thousand years ago the meltwaters of Ice Age glaciers heaped parts of the landscape with eskers (long ridges) and drumlins (round hillocks) of rubble, now greened over to form bumpy little hills and islets.

All of these areas support a variety of wildlife (famously lacking in snakes), though Ireland's four-legged creatures—wild goats, hares, deer—can be difficult to spot.

The spectacular seabird colonies of the west coast cliffs and islands are matched by tremendous gatherings of overwintering wildfowl on east coast estuaries such as Strangford Lough, east of Belfast, and the North Slobs mudflats and marshes near Wexford. It's the mountains and moorlands of Ireland that will give you the best opportunity to spot birds of prey, including hen harriers, peregrines, merlins, and wheeling buzzards. The boglands offer the chance to spot buntings and warblers, while along the hayfields around Killala Bay where Sligo meets Mayo, and in remote Inishowen in northern Donegal, you might just hear the grating *crex-crex* of the elusive corncrake.

As for wildflowers, you'll find beautiful pink bogbean, insect-eating sundews, and wonderfully colored rushes and grasses in the bogs, primroses in the narrow country lanes in springtime, and blood-red fuchsia in the hedges of the southwestern counties in summer. Ireland's showpiece for wildflowers, however, is the Burren in County Clare (see pp. 168–173), a unique environment of limestone pavement where acid- and lime-loving plants and arctic and Mediterranean flowers abound. ∎

EXPERIENCE:
Conserving Resources

Over the past half century, intensive farming, greenbelt development, and neglect have damaged wildlife and despoiled vast acreages of bogs. But things are improving as government agencies and private organizations across the island move to place conservation at the top of the agenda.

The **Irish Wildlife Trust** (*www.iwt.ie*) offers educational programs and volunteer activities for those wanting to pitch in. **Groundwork,** their affiliate group, organizes one- and two-week summer work camps for volunteers from all over the world—their primary project is a multi-year effort to remove invasive rhododendron species from Killarney National Park. See Groundwork's website at *www.groundwork .ie.workcamps.htm* for more information.

Blocks of turf, dug from the boglands of Achill Island, lay neatly in long rows to dry.

History of Ireland

Ireland's spiritual influence and artistic achievement reached their zenith more than a thousand years ago, bolstered by a rich mythic tradition and a flowering of passionate Christianity. Echoes of that magnificence sustained the Irish over the ensuing centuries and through the long, bitter struggle for independence from the British. The stories of Ireland and Britain, uneasy neighbors and bedfellows, have been intimately bound up together for the past ten centuries.

Immemorial myth, that potent source of national identity and pride, has Ireland's ancient inhabitants, the Firbolgs, being overcome by a race of mystical and magical conquerors known as Tuatha de Danaan, the People of Danu, Mother of the Gods. This version of the island's story gets off to a flying start with tales of wooings, betrayals, battles, feasts, and mighty deeds of derring-do by heroes and heroines such as Fionn MacCumhaill (Finn McCool), Diarmuid and Gráinne (see p. 262), Deirdre of the Sorrows, and Cúchulainn (see pp. 334–335).

More prosaically, it was a hardy bunch of fishermen and food-gatherers who first crossed to the Antrim coast from Scotland about 10,000 years ago, at the end of the last Ice Age. Little is known about this thin population who made their settlement by lakeside and seashore.

By the time the first Celts from central Europe began to arrive around 500 B.C., Irish culture had progressed through successive Stone, Bronze, and Iron Ages that left the landscape scattered with splendid chambered tombs, stone circles, and field systems. Irish became the universal language in a country divided among rival noble families who elected their own kings from among themselves. Families lived in wooden homesteads surrounded by earth banks, well strengthened with stone walls. Land was held in common; cattle became the main measure of wealth, with cattle-raiding endemic. Warfare between family "kingdoms" was a way of life. Balance and a sense of justice were encouraged by the liberal set of rules known as Brehon Law—the experts who codified the law were known as brehons—by which society more or less abided.

> The stories of Ireland and Britain, uneasy neighbors and bedfellows, have been intimately bound up together for the past ten centuries.

Coming of Christianity

Into this fertile, vigorous society came Christianity, brought to Ireland by the itinerant preacher Patrick in A.D. 432. By now Ireland had divided into the four major kingdoms, or provinces, of Ulster (north), Connacht (west), Leinster (east), and Munster (south),

each ruled by its own king. St. Patrick and the early Christian missionaries wisely
decided to work with, not against, the established druidic religion of the Irish Celts.
They built many of their churches and monasteries on sites already considered holy
and showed respect for the leaders of Irish society. Their reward was to see Ireland
embrace Christianity fervently.

Golden Age

Along with Christianity came literacy and a flowering of the arts. Monasteries became centers of culture, from which Irish monks went out to spread the
word all over Europe and far beyond. Poetry, song, stone-carving, and the arts of
jewelry and gold-working all flourished. The seventh and eighth centuries were
Ireland's golden age, culminating in the production of such glorious works of art
as the Ardagh Chalice and the Tara Brooch, both from the eighth century (now
in the National Museum of Archaeology and History, see pp. 56–59), and the

Around Lough Gur lie the remains of buildings that span 5,000 years of human occupation.

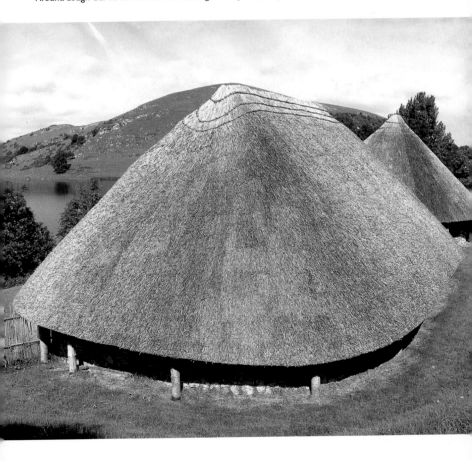

incomparable Book of Kells around 800 (now in Trinity College, Dublin, see pp. 54–55). The Vikings were unwelcome visitors from around that time onward; Brian Boru, High King of Ireland, finally defeated them and broke their power at the Battle of Clontarf in 1014. Another century was to pass before even more effective invaders began to cast their eyes across the Irish Sea.

Settlers from England

The Normans had occupied mainland Britain in 1066, but it took another hundred years for them to invade Ireland. They came to support Dermot MacMurrough, King of Leinster, who had been banished by Rory O'Connor, High King of Ireland (for stealing the wife of one of the king's friends). At first the Normans made a great show of force, building castles on land they seized. But after various military setbacks, with the passing of centuries and some intermarriage, they settled down—mostly in a strip of land around Dublin known as the Pale, defended with palings, or palisades—to a more or less neighborly accommodation with the Irish.

Oliver Cromwell earned an everlasting reputation for brutality for his savage repression of Irish insurgents.

Repression & Rebellion

Fearing a Roman Catholic invasion of the mainland from Irish soil, King Henry VIII of England and then his daughter Queen Elizabeth I set the fire under the cauldron of Ireland in the 16th century with a series of punitive taxes, confiscations, and legal exclusions of influential Irish Catholic families. In 1541, Henry had himself proclaimed King of Ireland and unleashed a wave of repression that in its turn bred resentment and rebellion. The Catholic countries of Europe, keen to blunt the supremacy of England on the high seas and to bring the newly Protestantized country back into the Roman Catholic fold, saw Catholic Ireland as a potential springboard for the invasion and subjection of the British mainland. A mixed Spanish and Italian landing on the Dingle Peninsula in 1580 was defeated with savagery by Elizabeth's Crown forces, and more repressions followed. Repression bred rebellions, each put down with the mailed fist. The last uprising of this period, an insurrection headed by Hugh O'Neill, Earl of Tyrone, and backed by 4,500 Spanish soldiers, was crushed in 1601.

By 1610, the leaders of the great families of Ulster had fled overseas, and in what was known as the Plantation of Ulster, Protestant farmers from Scotland and England were encouraged with grants of money and land to settle all over the north of Ireland in order to keep land and influence out of Catholic hands.

If things were bad for Irish Catholics, they got a great deal worse in the mid-17th century when ripples from the English Civil War ignited more trouble in Ireland. After ten years of confused fighting, Oliver Cromwell arrived with his battle-hardened Ironsides and instituted a repression that put even the Elizabethan brutalities in the shade. Towns such as Drogheda and Wexford were sacked; rebels were executed en masse.

Catholic landowners all over the country were stripped of their property and rights and driven west across the River Shannon "to Hell or Connacht," to the poorest land in the west, while "planters" took their place in the fat lands of the east and the midlands.

From Penal Times to Swaggering Dan

The infamous penal times continued through the late 18th century. After the Cromwellian repressions, there was a surge of Catholic hope when King James II, the Roman Catholic monarch deposed from the English throne, tried to gain support for his cause in Ireland. Though James was defeated at the Battle of the Boyne on July 12, 1690, his conqueror, King William III, seemed to hold out promise of better and more equal opportunities for Irish Catholics. But William soon went back on his word, and within a few years the miserable penal laws had been introduced.

The penal laws enshrined Catholic disenfranchisement; no Catholic was allowed to vote, to educate his children as Catholics, or to hold property. The intention of the penal laws was clear—to perform a kind of ethnic cleansing on the Catholic majority by squeezing them out of political, social, and economic life. The ban that really hurt, though, was that on celebrating Mass. Roman Catholicism became a clandestine faith, practiced in out-of-the-way places, its priests in fear of death, its adherents increasingly politicized through poverty and desperation. Risings came and went, each harshly suppressed. Rebel groups formed in secret, plotting insurrection. The United Irishmen mounted the final rebellion of the 18th century in 1798, bolstered by 1,100 Frenchmen who landed at Killala Bay on the Sligo/Mayo border. It started successfully, with a crushing defeat of the English at Castlebar, but ended, as all the other uprisings had, in defeat for the rebels and death for their leaders.

Heritage Sites

The best way to enrich your understanding of Ireland's long and extraordinary history is to relive it at the country's Heritage Sites. Ranging in date from the end of the last Ice Age to as recently as the 20th century, Heritage Sites include everything from Stone Age monuments and early Christian monasteries to looming castles and national parks.

Ireland's **National Monuments Service** (www.archaeology.ie) provides a guide to nearly 1,000 historical places and buildings around the country. To find out which sites are open to the public, visit **Heritage Ireland** (www.heritageireland.ie). There you can also purchase a Heritage Card, which allows for unlimited free admission to most of Ireland's Heritage Sites for one year from the date of purchase.

Intolerance of Catholics as a general practice had been softening toward the end of the 18th century. The penal laws were not being applied as rigorously as they had been at the outset. In 1782, a qualified parliamentary independence was granted, but the 1798 Rising put an end to all that. The new century opened with the 1801 Act of Union that abolished the Irish parliament and imposed direct rule from London. Discrimination against Catholics was tightened, not to be relaxed again until the forceful Kerry lawyer Daniel O'Connell won his famous long-drawn-out struggle to force Westminster to attend to the grievances of the Irish poor. "Swaggering Dan," or "the Liberator" as his followers styled him, finally gained a seat in Parliament as a Catholic MP (member of Parliament) in 1828.

The Great Famine

The history of 19th-century Ireland—and 20th-century Ireland, too—was shaped by the overarching tragedy of the Great Famine of 1845 to 1849. The potato fungus *Phytophthora infestans* struck a country with a population of nine million, the majority of them poor, illiterate peasants living in enormous families on tiny patches of rented land in remote regions, entirely dependent on the potato for food. When the fungus turned their potatoes to black slime in the ground four seasons out of five, they had no defense against the disaster.

The British government's response has frequently been condemned as cruelly indifferent, even deliberately so. Initially, in fact, measures were taken to relieve the famine. Food depots were established, corn was put on the market, hospitals were opened, and relief works started. But the authorities were soon overwhelmed by the scale of the catastrophe, the sheer numbers of people involved, the lack of infrastructure—hospitals,

During the famine, overcrowded workhouses and hospitals turned away the starving.

relief centers, port facilities, even roads—within rural Ireland, and the rapidity with which disease and death spread. A hard-hearted change of policy after the first year of the famine saw the government at Westminster throw much of the responsibility for dealing with the disaster onto the shoulders of local Poor Law Unions, charitable organizations, and individual landlords.

It is tempting to see all the landlords as absentee exploiters, feathering their own nests and harshly evicting those tenants who failed to pay their rent. Some certainly fitted that bill. Others, such as the Marquess of Sligo, however, suspended rents and sold their own possessions to aid their tenants. But it was the peasants of Ireland who paid the highest price for the government's past policy and present pragmatism. Workhouses and temporary hospitals were filled to overflowing. Sick and starving people were turned away. Typhus, cholera, relapsing fever, and diarrhea

> The history of 19th-century Ireland—and 20th-century Ireland, too—was shaped by the overarching tragedy of the Great Famine of 1845 to 1849.

spread like wildfire through the crowded cabins and hovels of the rural poor and through the unsanitary streets of the towns. Families died where they lay together, unattended by doctor or priest. It is impossible to collect accurate figures, but a million men, women, and children probably died during the five years of the Great Famine—either from disease or literally starving to death.

Emigration & Anger

Emigration, which had been a means of escape from poverty for the rural Irish for a century or more, swelled to a flood during and after the famine. Anyone who could scrape up the price of a ticket boarded one of the emigration ships—leaky, dirty old buckets as many of them were—in hopes of a better life elsewhere, especially in mainland Britain, the U.S., Canada, and Australia. The Irish diaspora spread all over the world during the following century, draining the young and active lifeblood of Ireland, especially in the poor rural west. Today the population of the Irish Republic is about three million—one-third its pre-famine level.

As the emigrants picked up the threads of strange new lives, powerful feelings of attachment to their homeland were mingled in many cases with bitterness and anger toward Britain, the country they held responsible for their plight. This mixture of sentiment and politics grew stronger as time went on. It was to fuel the activities of 19th-century anti-British organizations such as the Fenian Brotherhood, established in the U.S. in the 1850s, and sees its expression today in support among many expatriate Irish communities for extremist causes in Northern Ireland.

Land Reform & Home Rule

As for the movement for political change in post-famine Ireland, it continued down its well-worn track of clandestine groupings organizing boycotts, sporadic attacks on landlords and their agents, and a string of brief and unsuccessful risings. But the grievances of poor Catholic Ireland were coming more and more to the fore in mainstream politics. Michael Davitt's nonviolent Land League movement eventually forced a Land Act, passed in 1881, which ensured fair rents and security of tenure for tenants. And the ever more vociferous Home Rule movement found a powerful mouthpiece in one of the Land Act's keenest supporters, Charles Stewart Parnell (see sidebar), heir to Daniel O'Connell's crown as champion of the Catholic poor.

Parnell was brought down by a sexual scandal in 1890, but the impetus he gave to the Home Rule movement meant that the government could no longer consign the issue to the back burner. As the new century dawned, militant pressure for independence from Britain grew irresistible. Yet in Northern Ireland the Protestant people, descendants of the 17th-century planters with a clear interest in preserving the status quo, were lining up behind charismatic Dublin MP Sir Edward Carson to repudiate the notion of political severance from the United Kingdom. Their stance was made far worse in the eyes of many Northern Catholics by Carson's decision to agree to the establishment of an Ulster that excluded three of the nine counties of the historic province. Catholic voters were in a majority in Monaghan, Cavan, and Donegal, and Protestant dominance of those three counties looked uncertain. So they

"Uncrowned King"

Charles Stewart Parnell (1846–1891) was a wealthy Protestant landowner and MP. Although he had little in common with his Irish Catholic countrymen, Parnell was nevertheless a keen proponent of land redistribution, which he felt was the first step toward Irish self-government. His denunciation of the 1882 assassination of two British officials helped subordinate radical nationalist factions to his own more moderate fight for home rule. Under his leadership, the Land League became the wildly popular Irish National League, while Parnell himself was popularly known as Ireland's "uncrowned king."

were "let go" to the putative independent free state of southern Ireland. Their Protestant inhabitants were not happy to be included in what appeared to them a hostile and backward country. Home Rule–minded Catholics in Antrim, Derry (called Londonderry by Protestants), Tyrone, Fermanagh, Armagh, and Down, the Six Counties of the proposed Ulster, resented being severed from the political freedom that their southern brethren seemed about to enjoy. Seeds of cross-border bitterness and resentment were sown.

A compromise Home Rule Act, excluding the Ulster counties of Antrim, Londonderry, Tyrone, Fermanagh, Armagh, and Down, was passed in 1914. But this effective partition of Ireland was then immediately suspended upon the outbreak of World War I. This was the final straw as far as radical Home Rule advocates were concerned. They drew together under the umbrella of the Irish Republican Brotherhood (first formed in the 1850s in the aftermath of the Great Famine) and began preparations for an armed rebellion.

The Easter Rising

The Easter Rising of 1916 was planned by a small group of people dedicated to gaining independence from Britain. They were organized and led by socialist trade

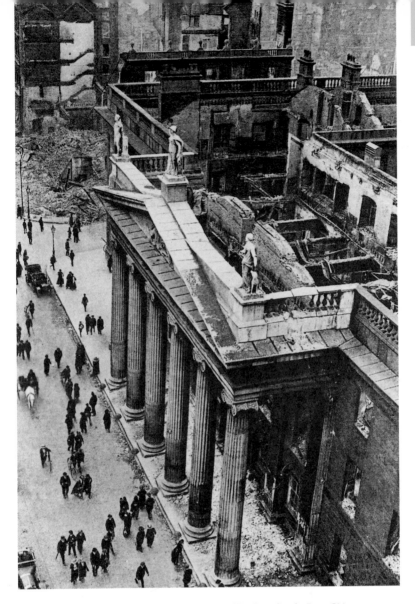

Dublin's post office building became a powerful symbol of freedom after the Easter Rising.

unionist James Connolly and Christian schoolteacher Padraic Pearse. They argued, philosophized, organized, and drilled their small bands of volunteers, looking for the right moment to act. "England's difficulty is Ireland's opportunity," ran the republican mantra. On the eve of the planned uprising, the activists dispatched Sir Roger Casement to Germany, looking for support. Casement's assessment was that they could expect no help and should call off the rising. But they went ahead anyway, hoping for simultaneous action from 10,000 sympathizers all over Ireland.

Owing to confusion, poor coordination, and lack of communication among widely scattered groups, only 2,000 rebels joined the rising, with almost all the action taking place in Dublin. The initial action that Easter Monday morning took the authorities by surprise, and about 1,000 armed insurgents installed themselves in various key administrative buildings across the city. Standing on the steps under the portico of the General Post Office (GPO) on O'Connell Street, Pearse read out the rebels' proclamation: "We hereby proclaim the Irish Republic as a Sovereign Independent State, and we pledge our lives and the lives of our comrades in arms to the cause of its freedom, of its welfare and of its exaltation among the nations."

> In 1919, . . . [Sinn Féin] forced Ireland to the top of the British government's agenda . . . by declaring independence.

Fine words and fine aspirations—which were soon crushed. The rebels had the bravery but not the resources to withstand the British Army for long, once it had recovered from its shock and rolled its troops and hardware into action. A week of bombardment, and many deaths on both sides, saw the GPO shattered by shellfire and the activists forced to surrender. If the British government had played it cool from then on, benefiting from a wartime public mood in Ireland that initially saw the rebels as misguided hotheads—if not downright traitors—rather than heroes, a lot of subsequent bloodshed would have been avoided. Instead they enshrined the insurgents as martyrs by shooting 15 of the leaders, drawing out the executions over the following weeks in a manner that outraged decent opinion.

Two Wars

Republican sentiment coalesced around Sinn Féin (Ourselves Alone), a small political sect that quickly grew to wield real power. Immediately after the end of World War I in 1919, with half its MPs in jail, it forced Ireland to the top of the British government's agenda again by declaring independence, forming its own parliament under Eamon de Valera, and making a demand that Westminster could not agree to: a withdrawal of all British troops from Ireland. There followed two years of war between the official military forces of Britain and the irregular battalions of the nationalists' Irish Republican Army (IRA), of bombs and ambushes, interrogations, and ransackings, during which the British paramilitary force known as the Black and Tans gained notoriety for its brutality, and the republican leader Michael Collins developed from a dashing, romantic Robin Hood–style guerrilla fighter into a charismatic political figure. In 1921, the Anglo-Irish Treaty put an end to the fighting, establishing an independent Irish Free State that excluded those six contentious counties of Northern Ireland.

Now came a split between followers of Collins, reluctantly prepared to accept the partition of Ireland—and even the prospect of basing some British troops there in time of war—and the less accommodating republicans behind de Valera, who held out for a united Ireland and denial of all military concessions to Britain. The Civil War that broke out between the two factions in July 1922 claimed the lives of thousands more Irish men and women, including Collins himself, generated internecine bitterness that lasts to this day, and ended in May 1923 with defeat for the hard-line republicans.

From Free State to Republic: Decades in a Rural Backwater

Eamon de Valera went to jail, and the brand-new Irish nation began to lick its wounds. In 1924, de Valera was released, and in 1926, he quit Sinn Féin and started his own Fianna Fail (Warriors of Destiny) party. Six years later, Fianna Fail came to power, and de Valera started a mammoth term as Taoiseach (prime minister) that would last until well after World War II. The Free State renamed itself Eire, a good indication of the folksy-nationalist direction in which it was heading—a direction inspired by de Valera's vision of "a land whose countryside would be bright with cozy homesteads, whose fields and villages would be joyous with the sounds of industry, with the rompings of sturdy children, the contests of athletic youths and

In the 1970s, IRA terrorist attacks (and the ensuing loyalist reprisals) rocked Belfast.

the laughter of comely maidens, whose firesides would be forums for the wisdom of serene old age." Fianna Fail abolished the oath of allegiance to the Crown and claimed sovereignty over the North (a bone of contention not resolved until the Good Friday Agreement of 1998, see p. 289). Meanwhile the Roman Catholic Church tightened its grasp on all aspects of life south of the border. In the North, Protestantism stayed in the ascendancy while the economy took a nosedive along with the rest of the industrial world.

Eire declared itself neutral for the duration of World War II, though thousands of men and women from both sides of the border volunteered to fight in the Allied cause. Belfast was badly bombed—in one terrible night in April 1941 more than 700 civilians were killed. In 1949, Eire—now calling itself the Republic of Ireland—left the British Commonwealth. Through the 1950s it stagnated, stuck in an agricultural and social backwater, with increasing censorship of books, films, and plays by a church and state unwilling to come to terms with the modern world. Emigration soared as younger Irish people left to find better-paid work and greater artistic, sexual, and moral freedom than small-time farming or backwoods town life in Ireland could provide.

From the perspective of Protestants north of the border, life in the Republic seemed backward and unappealing, although the slow and steady rundown of Ulster textile and shipbuilding industries was beginning to make itself felt. Northern Catholics were still enduring a position of economic and social inferiority cemented in place by the inbuilt majorities of Protestant local politicians.

Battle of the Bogside

On August 12, 1969, a group in Londonderry known as the Apprentice Boys held its annual parade to commemorate a 17th-century Protestant military victory. The parade route passed very near the Bogside, an impoverished Catholic neighborhood, where the confrontation between the two groups quickly erupted into violence.

Hampered by barricades and bombarded with stones and homemade bombs, the Royal Ulster Constabulary could do little to quell the riots. Fighting finally stopped after the British Army stepped in on August 14.

Yet the damage had been done. During the three days of rioting in Londonderry, similar conflicts had arisen in many other places, including Belfast. Northern Ireland soon found itself mired in decades of deadly confrontations that came to be known as the Troubles.

Progress in the Republic

In the 1960s, the Republic became a more energetic and outward-looking place under the leadership of Taoiseach Sean Leamass; Eamon de Valera, by now the grand and rather out-of-touch old man of republicanism, had been "moved upstairs" to occupy the presidency. In the 1970s, the country joined the European Union and began to benefit from a flow of economic development money and a healthy agricultural economy. The 1980s saw a faltering in progress and a rise in emigration, but the following decade became a gallop to economic glory on the back of the Celtic Tiger and a remarkable boom in tourism and popularity around the world.

Signs of hopeful new times: Former enemies Ian Paisley (left) and Martin McGuinness after being sworn in as ministers of the Northern Ireland Assembly in 2007

Northern Ireland Through the Troubles

As for Northern Ireland in the 1970s, '80s, and '90s, rarely can a country have undergone such a thoroughly publicized roller-coaster ride through such depths of misery and despair. Discrimination against Roman Catholics in the workplace, in housing, and in health, education, and social services had been enshrined since 1921—and for centuries before that, too. The civil rights movements of the late 1960s aimed to force change through popular protest, in as peaceful a way as possible. But with so much mutual mistrust and bitterness, contempt, and bigotry on hand, the marches became the flashpoint for full-blown civil strife. From the moment in August 1969 that British troops were deployed on the streets of Londonderry and Belfast (see sidebar, p. 34), the Troubles were on every television set and radio. They were to stay center stage, making Northern Ireland a byword for sectarian hatred and terrorism for almost 30 years (see pp. 286–289), until the historic paramilitary cease-fires and the signing of the Good Friday Agreement in 1998.

No one would claim that all the problems of the North have been solved, as witness the repeated suspensions of the power-sharing Assembly (see p. 18), but great changes for the better have taken place. People from all traditions and shades of political and religious opinion are learning to live with each other. Peace is catching and looks more secure with each passing year.

Above all, the people of Northern Ireland want to let the outside world know that they are not all like some of the opinionated sectarians who have grabbed headlines during the past 30 years or so of the province's difficulties. In fact, the absence of tourist overkill has left Northern Ireland and its people with a fresh, welcoming approach that every visitor can appreciate. ∎

Food & Drink

Irish food was once famous for its plainness, but affluence and tourism changed things. In the 1990s, the number of restaurants serving international cuisine—and fast-food outlets, too—witnessed phenomenal growth. Homespun Irish dishes fell into disfavor. Recently that trend has reversed with the onset of a new sophistication and a more demanding class of visitor.

A lunch out at MV Cill Airne—a ship-turned-restaurant moored in the docklands of central Dublin

Today's young chefs use the very best that Ireland has to offer, including wild Atlantic salmon, mountain lamb, shellfish, and organically grown vegetables and herbs. They take pleasure in adding a touch of modern magic to such traditional Irish fare as *champ* (mashed potatoes and scallions), *drisheen* (black pudding), *colcannon* (potatoes, cabbage, onions, and cream), *brack* (fruity tea bread), or the famous Irish stew that can have pretty much anything in it along with the four vital ingredients: neck of mutton,

potatoes, onions, and a pinch of serendipity.

Visitors with their preconceptions still intact are always surprised to learn that the Irish national drink is not Guinness but tea. God alone knows how much tea is drunk in Ireland every day, but it's plenty. In the cities these days you can also get a very respectable cup of coffee, from cappuccino to espresso with all the variations in between. As far as alcoholic drink is concerned, there is a smallish but good selection of Irish whiskeys (County Antrim's Bushmills and Jameson's of Cork head the smoother brands, generally sweeter than their Scottish counterparts) and a growing number of "real ales" or unpasteurized, unfiltered beers brewed by small, independent breweries and served from a hand pump.

INSIDER TIP:

While a cozy pub is the popular image of an Irish night out, the recent influx of renowned chefs has made Dublin a choice destination for world-class dining.

—RUTH MORAN
Tourism Ireland

But it's the famous strong black stout with its creamy head, poured with ritual slowness from a tap rather than a bottle, that rules the pub roost. Murphy's (favored in Cork) is sweeter, Guinness heavier and more bitter. What the Irish tell foreigners about Guinness is absolutely true: If you have tried it in your own country and disliked it, give it another go when you visit Ireland. Guinness drunk in an Irish pub is one of the world's most nectarous delights.

You can certainly come across the famed poteen or home-distilled spirit if you know where to look and how to ask—generally the farther west and the more remote you are. Poteen-distilling is illegal, but the tradition is strong. So is the liquor, which can vary from smooth to extremely rough. If badly distilled it could turn nasty or even fatal, but the good stuff is characterful with a very special effect—including impromptu music making.

Two emblematic symbols of Ireland meet: A pint of Guinness and a four-leaf clover

---

Top Food & Drink Guides

Time was, not so long ago, when Irish cuisine was the object of suspicion, if not outright derision. Bacon, cabbage, potatoes, and then what? But that's all in the past. These days Ireland is well-known for its great food and drink, and there are plenty of resources to guide you to the best the country has to offer.

One of the most reliable is **Georgina Campbell's Ireland** *(www.ireland-guide .com)*, an online guide to Ireland's restaurants, pubs, and hotels. Search for places to eat by location, budget, and dietary needs. Join **The G Club** *(www.thegclub.ie)* for savings on meals at top-rated restaurants and hotel stays.

The cosmopolitan editors of **Bridge-stone Guides** *(www.bestofbridgestone .com)* offer punchy reviews of some of the trendiest restaurants in Ireland. For a more personal touch, try **Been There: Ireland** *(www.ivebeenthere.co.uk/places/ ireland)* to find out what locals and other tourists recommend.

Arts & Culture

Novelists, playwrights, poets, short-story writers; rock bands, fiddle players, opera stars, traditional singers; TV soap stars and comedians; film directors and actors; dancers, painters, street performers . . . Ireland has them all, in numbers and of a quality that would be the envy of a country ten times the size. James Joyce, W. B. and Jack Yeats, U2, Enya, and Riverdance merely scratch the surface.

The oral tradition of Irish folk tales dates back 2,000 years or more and is embedded deeply in the national sense of identity. It's not by random selection that the influential traditional music group De Danaan named itself after a mythical race of magic makers or that the cultural activities center in Mullaghbane in County Armagh is named Tí Chulainn, the House of Chulainn, after the legendary blacksmith of nearby Slieve Gullion mountain. Such names, and the tales that are associated with them, still carry considerable power.

The Mighty Deeds of Fionn MacCumhaill

The best known of Irish heroes must be Fionn Mac-Cumhaill—Finn McCool—not in fact a giant, although his mighty deeds make him seem one. Stories were beginning to be made up about him in the fourth and fifth centuries. Fionn's most famous act was to establish the band of knightlike heroes known as the Fianna, the Warriors. Entry requirements were tough. Anyone who wanted to join the Fianna had to be able to defend himself against nine spears hurled simultaneously, while buried up to his waist in the ground and armed only with a hazel stick. Candidates also had to prove themselves capable of escaping a band of the Fianna while running through the woods, without cracking any twig or having any of their hair dislodged from its braid. While running full tilt they must also leap over a head-high stick, duck under a knee-high one, and pick a thorn out of the sole of their foot. And, of course, each aspirant member had to show himself brave and honest, while also producing perfectly polished poetry. There were not many Fianna.

Perhaps the best tale of all concerns Fionn MacCumhaill's love in old age for the beautiful Gráinne, daughter of Cormac, the High King of Tara (see p. 262), and his pursuit of her after

> **The oral tradition of Irish folk tales dates back 2,000 years or more and is embedded deeply in the national sense of identity.**

she eloped with handsome young Fianna member Diarmuid. This is a great chase saga, and you'll find rocks and hollows known as "Diarmuid and Gráinne's Bed" all over Ireland. Fionn got his woman in the end, but only after wreaking his revenge on the dying Diarmuid (see pp. 214–215) on Benbulben Mountain.

From Telling to Writing

Tales like these were the bedrock on which Ireland's long-standing tradition of fireside storytelling was based. Literacy, education, and modern ways of entertainment have all but eclipsed such domestic tale-spinning, although it is reviving in a new generation of "ceilidh houses" in which people gather to swap songs and stories.

Musicians take the floor at An Púcán bar in Galway in west Ireland.

But when this lyrical talent with words hits the page, it deepens into a characteristic Irish magic. Ireland has produced four winners of the Nobel Prize for Literature— William Butler Yeats (1923), George Bernard Shaw (1925), Samuel Beckett (1969), and Seamus Heaney (1995)—a truly astonishing accolade for such a small country. The writer whom most regard as the greatest of the lot, James Joyce (1882–1941), never won a Nobel Prize: His output was far too controversial. But it was Joyce with his dense, convoluted, and brilliant 1922 masterwork *Ulysses*—unbelievably daring with its sexual frankness and open challenge to the "Celtic Twilight" quaintness of most Irish writing of the time—who set the stage for the modern novel.

James Joyce may head Ireland's roll call of 20th-century literary genius, but it bulges with other talent, too. Among short-story writers of note are Liam O'Flaherty (1897– 1984), Sean O'Faolain (1900–1991), Corkman Frank O'Connor (1903–1966), with his superb stories of the 1919–1921 War of Independence such as "Guests of the Nation," and the Kerry pub owner and gentle humorist John B. Keane (1928–2002). Older-guard novelists who have caught the nuances of Irish life include Brian Moore (1921–1999), Edna O'Brien (born 1932), the wonderfully subtle John McGahern (1934–2006), and the masterfully funny and erudite Brian O'Nolan (1911–1966), who wrote under the names Flann O'Brien and Myles na gCopaleen.

The Irish Renaissance

Alongside the political struggle for self-government that defined the late 19th and early 20th centuries, Ireland witnessed the flowering of a movement that came to be known as the Irish Renaissance or Celtic Revival. Inspired by the folktales, legends, and mythology of ancient Ireland, poet W. B. Yeats and young dramatists like Sean O'Casey and J. M. Synge revitalized popular interest in traditional Irish culture and language and sparked the development of a distinct national identity. Dublin's famed Abbey Theatre, which produced plays that helped establish Ireland's literary reputation, was inaugurated by Yeats and playwright Lady Augusta Gregory in 1904.

Struggle for Literary Freedom

These groundbreakers did not have it easy in the repressive cultural atmosphere of the Ireland in which they were trying to get their work published. Edna O'Brien's 1960 novel, *The Country Girls,* was banned for encouraging immorality, while John McGahern's second novel, *The Dark,* treating as it did homosexual child abuse, was likewise banned in 1966. James Joyce himself wrote and published *Ulysses* abroad in self-imposed artistic exile— publication in its home country of what many regard as the most influential novel ever written would have been unthinkable. When Joyce died in 1941, his countrymen were still unable to buy his masterpiece in Ireland; they would have to wait until the 1960s.

Later writers to benefit from the freedom of expression won by these trailblazers include Roddy Doyle (born 1958) with *The Commitments, The Snapper,* and *The Van,* his sharp working-class Dublin trilogy; Eoin McNamee (born 1960) with the dark Troubles novel *Resurrection Man;* Frank McCourt (1930–2009), awarded the Pulitzer Prize in 1997 for *Angela's Ashes,* his searing account of a sad childhood; John Banville (born 1945), whose novel *The Sea* won the 2005 Man Booker Prize for Fiction; and Anne Enright, another Booker winner in 2007 with *The Gathering.*

The biographies of three native Irish-speakers from County Kerry's remote Blasket islands—Tomás O'Crohan's *The Islandman* (1929), Maurice O'Sullivan's *Twenty Years*

A-Growing (1933), and Peig Sayers's *Peig* (1936)—represented an astonishing flowering of talent within a tiny, culturally isolated, and largely illiterate community.

Poetry—From Yeats to Heaney

As for poetry—the line from William Butler Yeats (1865–1939) through Patrick Kavanagh (1904–1967) to Seamus Heaney (born 1939) glints with genius. Much of Yeats's poetry is undergoing a recession in popularity at present, part of a natural cycle; many see him as important as much for his catalytic effect on the Gaelic Revival of the late 19th century, and his articulation of an Irish sense of independent nationhood, as for his actual verses. In fact, the poet's painter brother Jack (1871–1957) is seen nowadays as far more of an innovator, with his vivid expressionist art so profoundly influenced by the landscapes of Sligo where the Yeats boys spent much of their childhood.

Oscar Wilde: a searing, flamboyant wit

Kavanagh's poetry, expressive of the back-breaking work and rural poverty—financial and spiritual—of his native County Monaghan, cut away the myth of the dignified, happy peasant Ireland so dear to Eamon de Valera's heart and opened the way for the uncomplicated yet profound insights of Heaney's work.

Heaney, a Northerner from Bellaghy in County Derry, found ways of exploring the tensions and anxieties of the Troubles without climbing onto an overtly political soapbox; but it is his cameos of rural life and his journeys through the nature of faith and humanity that distinguish him as Ireland's poet laureate and foremost living poet.

The Stage . . .

Among Irish playwrights to have influenced the world stage (often from positions of cultural exile) are household names such as Oscar Wilde (1854–1900), George Bernard Shaw (1856–1950), Sean O'Casey (1880–1964), with his great trilogy *Shadow of a Gunman, Juno and the Paycock,* and *The Plough and the Stars,* and the man who became James Joyce's secretary in 1932 before finding one or two things to say on his own account—Samuel Beckett (1906–1989), author of the world's least understood famous play, *Waiting for Godot.*

. . . and the Screen

The classic early Irish film documentary, Robert Flaherty's (1884–1951) *Man of Aran,* came out in 1934. But it wasn't until the establishment of the Irish Film Board in 1981 that Ireland really came into its own as a filmmaking country. Neil Jordan (bron 1950) has triumphed with a tale of an IRA man tormented over his execution of a hostage (*The Crying Game,* 1992), an account of the life and death of a War of

Independence leader (*Michael Collins*, 1996, starring Liam Neeson), and an adaptation of Patrick McCabe's fable of small-town oppression (*The Butcher Boy*, 1998).

Meanwhile, Jim Sheridan's (born 1949) star rose to international acclaim with his version of Christy Brown's *My Left Foot* (1989), starring Daniel Day-Lewis; John B. Keane's sardonic rural parable *The Field* (1990), filmed in the spectacular mountains around Killary Harbour on the Mayo/Galway border; and *In the Name of the Father* (1993), the story of the unjust imprisonment of the Guildford Four for an IRA bombing they did not commit, also starring Day-Lewis and partly set in the grim surroundings of Dublin's Kilmainham Gaol (see pp. 74–79).

Three sprightly, very funny films were made of Roddy Doyle's Barrytown trilogy, *The Commitments* by Alan Parker in 1991, and *The Snapper* (1993) and *The Van* (1996), both by Stephen Frears Meanwhile Hollywood has not forgotten the photogenic nature of Ireland's landscape—Mel Gibson filmed some wild "Scottish" scenes for his 1995 Anglo-bashing *Braveheart* around Trim in County Meath, while the beaches of County Wexford took a pounding during the making of Steven Spielberg's 1997 D-Day epic, *Saving Private Ryan. The Wind That Shakes the Barley* (2007), starring Cillian Murphy, won the Palme d'Or at Cannes.

Irish As She Is Spoke & Played

The Irish language, after a post-famine decline to the point where barely one in ten could speak it, has undergone a revival thanks to being allotted a place in the school curriculum. These days, while only 3 percent of people in the Irish Republic use Gaelic as their first language, more than 10 percent are fluent, and most educated people have at least a smattering. The language's strongholds—including west Donegal, northwest Mayo, Connemara and the Aran Islands, and west Kerry—are termed Gaeltacht areas and receive subsidies to prop up their Gaelic-speaking communities. That's where you are most likely to hear Gaelic, although you'll read it all over the Republic in the form of place-names on bilingual road signs. Radio na Gaeltachta and Teilifís (TV) na Ghaeilge, both based in Connemara, cater specifically to Gaelic-speakers.

The revival of the language is one symbol of pride in Irish nationhood. Another is the huge popularity of traditional Irish games such as hurling and Gaelic football, administered by the powerful, and chiefly Catholic, Gaelic Athletic Association. You'll see children playing with hurley (wooden stick) and sliotar (leather ball) in most town parks on weekends. However, this traditionalism hasn't prevented soccer from becoming a ruling passion throughout Ireland, with the Republic's team reaching the World Cup quarterfinals of 1990, 1994, and 2002, and only failing to qualify for the 2010 tournament because of a disputed goal by France.

Pronunciation

á (bodhrán) = "aw" ("bow-rawn")
ane (cloghane) = short "an" sound ("cloch-an")
bh (cobh) = "v" ("cove")
ch (Achill) = "ch" as in Scottish loch
dh (bodhrán) is silent
eagh or **eigh** (Glenveagh, Glenbeigh) = "ay" ("Glenvay, Glenbay")
gh is silent at the end of a word, and softer than the "ch" sound in "loch" in the middle of a word—almost "h," but slightly harder.
h is slightly harder than "h," slightly softer than lo**ch**.

Blood, guts, and determination: Hurlers battle for glory in one of Ireland's most popular sports.

Another very popular pastime around south Armagh and in rural County Cork—to name it formally a "sport" might be stretching a point—is road bowling, in which players have to project an iron ball along the road for an agreed distance (up to a couple of miles in some cases) using as few throws as possible. If, on your travels, you find an informal roadblock set up, the chances are that one of these keenly contested matches is going on. Take the opportunity and hop out of your car to see a very Irish bit of sport.

On the Horses

Big bets can be laid at a road bowling match, but not as big as when thousands of people are gathered together for horse racing, Ireland's grand sporting passion. The Curragh in County Kildare is the place to go (see p. 94), but throughout the country you have your pick of nearly 30 courses and dozens of meetings, from the unique thrill of Laytown Races on the beach near Drogheda and the genial holiday atmosphere of Galway Races to the "dukes-and-dustmen" democracy of the Irish Derby at the Curragh in June.

There's a great sense of democracy at these occasions, as the drink and bonhomie flow. One word of warning: Keep your wits about you, or you may find you have been

A Festivals Sampling

Specific dates can vary from year to year. Contact *www.festivals.travel.ie* for details.

Public figures are satirized during a parade on Ireland's famous St. Patrick's Day.

January
Lord Mayor's New Year's Day Parade— Marching bands from around the world convene on Dublin. *www.visitdublin.com*

March
St. Patrick's Day, March 17—The world's favorite party throughout Ireland, but Dublin hosts the biggie: *www.stpatricksday.ie.*

April
City of Belfast Spring Fair—Magnificent floral displays. *www.belfastcity.gov.uk.*

May
Fleadh Nua, Ennis, late May—The cream of Irish traditional music and dance. *Tel 065 684 0406, www.fleadhnua.com.*

June
Bloomsday, June 16—A literary Dublin pub crawl in commemoration of Leopold Bloom, hero of *Ulysses. www.jamesjoyce.ie*
Cork Midsummer Arts Festival, late June— Two weeks of arts, dance, drama, music, film. *www.corkmidsummer.com*
Irish Derby, late June—Lords and layabouts rub shoulders at the Curragh for Irish racing's Big Day Out. *Tel 045 441205, www.curragh.ie.*

July
Orangemen's Day, July 12—with flute and drum, Protestants in Belfast and throughout Northern Ireland celebrate the victory of "King Billy," William III, at the Battle of the Boyne in 1690. *www.gotobelfast.com.*

July/August
Galway Races *(tel 091 753870, www.galway races.com)* and **Galway Arts Festival** *(tel 091 509700, www.galwayartsfestival.com)*—Fun at the track spills over into music, theater, films, and literary events around the city.
Connemara Pony Show, third Thursday in August—Buying, selling, and exhibiting ponies at Clifden, County Galway. *www.cpbs.ie.*

September
Matchmaking at Lisdoonvarna, County Clare—A chance for single men and women in the west of Ireland to get together. *Tel 065 7074005, www.clare-tour.com.*

October
Kinsale Gourmet Festival, mid-October—A celebration of food in a beautiful County Cork coastal location. *www.kinsalerestaurants.com.*

November
Wexford Festival Opera, late October/ early November—Some of the great names of opera perform in front of a highly enthusiastic audience. *Tel 053 22144, www.wexfordopera.com.*

December
Downpatrick Christmas Festival, early December—Crafts, song, and good cheer in County Down, Northern Ireland *Tel 02844 612233, www.downdc.gov.uk.*
Dingle Wren, December 26—Boisterous fun in Dingle, with extravagant costumes and wild music. *Tel 066 9151188, www.dingle-peninsula.ie*

sold a spavined nag by the friendly man in the greasy plus fours. If you really do want to buy a horse, try the Clifden Show in August for a Connemara pony (see p. 183).

Traditional Music—Alive & Kicking

Of all branches of art, it's the country's traditional music that most ostensibly carries the flag for Irish culture today—that infectious, irresistible forward rush of tunes that were originally created simply to help dancers keep in time but proved to have a joyful life of their own as performance and "all-join-in" pieces.

The Dubliners and the Clancy Brothers promulgated Irish songs and ballads in the 1960s, the Chieftains burst onto the scene with brilliant musical dexterity in the early 1970s and still play to worldwide acclaim, and younger bands such as De Danaan, Planxty, the Bothy Band, Dervish, Lunasa, Danu, and Patrick Street found they could make a living by playing their native music all over the world. Masters of their craft such as uillean pipers Liam O'Floin and Davey Spillane, singers Dolores Keane, Mary Black, Cara Dillon, and Cathal McConnell, and fiddlers Tommy Peoples, Kevin Burke, and the dynamic Martin Hayes command a reverence among aficionados of the music. And young musicians such as brothers Bréanainn and Cormac Begley and their cousins Niall and Eoin Begley from west Kerry, fiddler Caoimhin Ó Raghallaigh and piper Seán McKeon, and bands like Gráda and Teáda are carrying on the tradition in tremendous form.

The astonishing international rise of interest in Irish traditional music in recent years has a lot to do with the sheer size and geographical spread of the Irish diaspora. Modern media have been enormously influential, too. Like it or not, slick shows such as Riverdance and Lord of the Dance have made a huge impact, drawing worldwide attention not only to the costumes and dancing but also to the wild music that drives the whole thing along. And when listeners and watchers decide to come over to Ireland to see where it all started, they find that the music has never been more alive.

EXPERIENCE: Storytelling at Tí Chulainn

Ireland's storytellers may be less well-known than the country's rich tradition of singers, musicians, poets, and writers, but they are just as important to the island's cultural heritage. South Armagh especially cherishes its traditional Irish roots. The **Tí Chulainn Cultural Activity Centre** (tel 028 3088 8828, www.tichulainn.com), in the village of Mullaghbane, gives a stage and an audience not only to the musicians and poets of the area but also to those with a talent for "telling the tale." The storytellers of Tí Chulainn are just as likely to put a hilarious spin on some recent event as they are to recount heroic feats of the mythological past. For news of proper old-fashioned storytelling sessions in other parts of Ireland, consult **Storytellers of Ireland** (www.storytellersofireland.org).

Pleasures of the Session

Well-honed music by professional troupes is laid on at Bunratty Castle and other such commercial venues that cater to the tourist trade. You may also find some of the big names in concert in the main towns and cities. But you'll find the best and most enjoyable traditional music—rough edges, occasional blemishes, and all—in the sessions that take place in pubs all over the country.

Anyone in the town or village can tell you where and when you'll find a session. They tend to start around 9:30 in the evening and go on till 11:30 (or much later); they may be entirely spontaneous but will probably be based around one or two musicians that the pub landlord has asked to turn up. The instruments will tend to be some combination of fiddle, flute, squeezebox, *bodhrán* (round goatskin drum), tin whistle, traditional uilleann (literally "elbow") pipes, guitar, bouzouki, and banjo. Anyone is welcome to join in, provided they have the courtesy to ask first and as long as they are skilled enough not to spoil the tune. Session music is rarely humdrum; frequently it touches great heights. Occasionally it goes into another dimension altogether, giving birth to a roaring beast of a medley that gathers its own unstoppable momentum, or a heart-meltingly emotional song or air that produces a pin-drop silence in a crowded bar. At such moments you wouldn't want to be anywhere else in the world.

Ireland seems an inexhaustible breeding ground for rock and pop performers—superstar Van Morrison from Belfast, boy bands Boyzone and Westlife, powerful women singers such as Mary Black and Sinead O'Connor, pop acts from the Corrs to Snow Patrol, rock bands from Rory Gallagher's R&B outfits to world-straddling U2 and outsiders Fight Like Apes, and maverick wildman rock poets like Shane MacGowan of the Pogues and Phil Lynott of Thin Lizzy. Great things can happen, too, when innovators mix traditional music with rock (The Pogues, The Waterboys), jazz (Moving Hearts), ambient (Enya), or more classical influences (Michael O'Súilleabháin). ∎

Riverdance lives on as a tribute to traditional Irish culture.

A thought-provoking introduction to the country's history, fabulous collections of national treasures, or just a roaring good time

Dublin

Georgian door knocker, Dublin

Dublin

The best thing about Dublin is that there is no one best thing. Each of a hundred aspects of Ireland's agreeable national capital helps to build a picture of a city that has seen a lot of history—hard times and prosperity, dignified consolidation and brash expansion—while somehow retaining a manageable pace and scale.

Molly Malone, or the Tart with the Cart, as Dubliners call this statue of their city's heroine

Those who remember Dublin "in the rare old times" will tell you that it has lost the cozy intimacy and humanity that inspired James Joyce. Certainly Ireland's wild turn-of-the-millennium ride to economic boom time on the back of the Celtic Tiger has transformed the center of the once sleepy city on the River Liffey into a place rattling with new money and businesses and stiff with the chic kind of eateries, wine bars, and dance clubs that young go-getters love to frequent.

Equally, there is still poverty in parts of the city where the new money doesn't reach and the tourists don't go. But those who come to Dublin as first-time visitors will be delighted to discover a city bustling with confidence and energy, yet still conserving its time-warp pockets of peace in traditional backstreet pubs and out-of-the-way gardens.

One of the key factors in Dublin's favor is that everything around the city center is built low, with the great Georgian and Victorian civic buildings such as the General Post Office, the Custom House, and the buildings of Trinity College dominating the scene, rather than anonymous modern office buildings. This helps put visitors in the mood for the mythic Dublin that so many expect to find—the Joycean old city where there's always time for another pint and a bit more chat.

Another advantage the city enjoys is its relationship with the River Liffey. They used to tell you that the superiority of Guinness over other porters and stouts was due to the use of Liffey water in its brewing. You might even believe it if you have never seen the muddy waterway—rather more turbid than limpid. However, the Liffey is close to Dubliners' hearts, and it makes a fine spectacle as it flows through the heart of the city, between handsome old

NOT TO BE MISSED:

Marveling at the intricate decoration of the Book of Kells   54–55

Ireland's Golden Age artifacts in the National Museum   56–59

The General Post Office, symbol of the 1916 Easter Rising   61

Exploring the unrivaled collection of Oriental and religious art at the Chester Beatty Library   65–67

A literary pub crawl with the shades of Joyce and Behan   68–69

Enjoying a session of traditional music at the Cobblestone Bar   72

Touring grim and atmospheric Kilmainham Gaol   74–79

Area of map detail

Belfast

Dublin

CENTRAL IRELAND
p. 233

6 kilometers

3 miles

◁6

Balscaddan

N1

Balbriggan

R122

R127

Rockabill

Naul

M1

Skerries

St. Patrick's Island

R127

R128

Shenick's Island

Garristown

R130

Delvin

Loughshinny

◁5

R108

Ballyboghil

N1

Lusk

R128

Rush

Oldtown

R122

Broad Meadow Water

Portraine

Irish Sea

Killsallaghan

Ward

Donabate

Lambay Island

CENTRAL IRELAND
p. 233

Swords

N1

Malahide

Malahide Castle

◁4

St. Margaret's

Dublin Airport

Cloghran

N2

Kinsaley

Portmarnock

D U B L I N

M50

M1

N32

Ireland's Eye

Corduff

Tolka

Santry

Coolock

Howth Harbour

N3

Mulhuddart

Blanchardstown

Glasnevin

Killester

Sutton

Howth

National Botanic Gardens

Marino

Casino

ST. ANNE'S PARK

Clontarf

North Bull Island

R105

◁3

Royal Canal

Liffey

PHOENIX PARK

See map pp. 50-51

Lucan

N4

DUBLIN

Isle of Man

Holyhead, Liverpool

Grand Canal

R131

Dublin Bay

Clondalkin

M50

Rathgar

R118

Booterstown

Holyhead

R120

Newcastle

N7

R113

N81

Rathfarnham

N11

N31

Dun Laoghaire

James Joyce Museum

Rathcoole

Tallaght

Ballyboden

Sandycove

Dalkey

Archibald's Castle

Saggart

Ballinteer

R113

153m Killiney Hill

Dalkey Island

N81

Dodder

R113

Stepaside

M50

N11

Killiney

Killiney Bay

◁2

Brittas

R115

Golden Ball

R119

Shankill

582m
Glendoo
Mountain

THE WICKLOW WAY

R116

Glencullen

R117

M11

to Bray

648m
Seahan

618m
Corrig
Mountain

EAST IRELAND
p. 87

◁1

752m
Kippure

△
A

△
B

△
C

△
D

Visitors and locals alike enjoy conversation over a pint in Dublin's wonderful pubs.

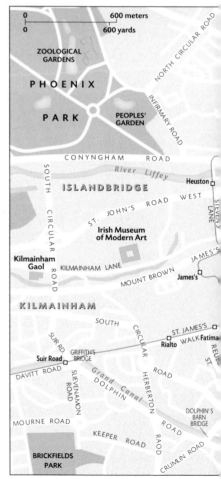

quays and beneath a series of fine bridges on its eastward journey to Dublin Bay. Favorite meeting places, Dublin's bridges are more like lively thoroughfares than mere river crossings.

Central Dublin is small enough to visit almost everything on foot or using the LUAS light railway, and most of its celebrated attractions—Trinity College, St. Stephen's Green, St. Patrick's Cathedral, shops and cafés on Grafton Street, the trendily renovated quarter of Temple Bar—lie south of the Liffey. North of the river you can enjoy the sassy market vendors of Moore Street and Mary's Lane.

East of the city center, the Liffey quays take you into an area that boasts a number of fine eating and drinking places with wonderful views of the river. To the west, you come to the great national monument of Kilmainham Gaol—a must-visit place—and Europe's largest urban green space, the magnificent open miles of Phoenix Park, a marvelous place to relax when the pace of city life gets to be too much.

Although the city of Dublin is far and away the main attraction, the Irish capital is not the be-all and end-all of County Dublin. The DART, Dublin's swift suburban railway, will take you out of the city center to Dublin's outer pleasures. To the north, you can enjoy walking in St. Anne's Park at Killester or around the promontory of Howth Head—the Howth Head walk in particular is a beauty, with very fine views over miles of mountains and green countryside as well as far prospects out to sea. Rhododendron season at Howth Castle is a famous day out for Dubliners.

Driving on northward, you'll find the handsome town of Malahide, well-known for good restaurants. Malahide Castle, home of the Talbot family for nearly eight centuries, is a romantic dream of battlements and turrets, on a core of late Norman work. Northward again is Skerries, a pretty fishing town where you can enjoy more brilliant sea views.

South of the city, the DART runs through some handsome Georgian and Victorian seaside towns. Dun Laoghaire, Dublin's main ferry terminal, is a pleasant place to idle, while Dalkey, with its narrow streets, still retains something of an old-fashioned village air.

Other delights of south County Dublin are visiting the James Joyce Museum at Sandycove and spotting the millionaire residents of exclusive and expensive Killiney from the top of Killiney Hill. At the end of the DART you can pick up the flavor of a traditional Irish day by the sea at the old resort of Bray. ■

Trinity College

Trinity College claims not only the finest set of university buildings in Ireland but also a roll call of alumni that embraces fierce polemicist Jonathan Swift and Ireland's first female president Mary Robinson, satirical humorists Oscar Wilde and Brian O'Nolan (Flann O'Brien), rebel leader Wolfe Tone and statesman Edmund Burke, and writers Bram Stoker and Samuel Beckett. It also houses the Book of Kells, judged by many to be the most beautiful book in the world.

Undergraduates mix with tourists in the courtyards of Dublin's university, Trinity College.

Dublin

🅰 49 B3–C3

Visitor Information

✉ Dublin Tourism Centre, Suffolk St., Dublin 2

☎ 01 605 7799

www.visitdublin.com

Trinity College faces College Street, its entrance a low doorway far more modest than the grand buildings beyond. After the buzz of modern-day Dublin, everything just seems more peaceful inside the cobbled quadrangles and university buildings spanning four centuries.

Queen Elizabeth I founded Trinity in 1592. Her aim was "to civilize Ireland with both learning and the Protestant religion, for the reformation of the barbarism of this rude people." Although in practice Catholics have studied at Trinity from the early 19th century, the Roman Catholic Church did not officially approve until the 1960s. The admission of women undergraduates as long ago as 1903, however, shows that the university was far from hidebound over gender discrimination.

University Chapel

On your left as you enter the first quadrangle is the university chapel, a peaceful paneled church with beautiful painted windows under a stucco ceiling of subtle grays and greens. The chapel was built in 1798, the momentous year when the United Irishmen launched their doomed rebellion (see p. 27).

The Old Library

On the far side of the quad you pass a 100-foot-high (30 m) Victorian campanile before heading right into the Old Library, a fine early 18th-century building. Inside, on the first floor, a permanent exhibition, **Picturing the Word,** explains the technicalities of how religious manuscripts were written and illustrated, preparing you for the kernel of the exhibition, the **Book of Kells** (see pp. 54–55).

On the upper floor of the Old Library is the truly impressive **Long Room,** a vast shadowy tunnel some 200 feet (60 m) long under a barrel-vaulted roof whose pillars turn out on close inspection to be huge stacks of books—about a quarter of a million in all. Aside from the books, two items here claim attention. One is an ancient harp of dark willow wood; it has been dated from 1400, although legend makes it 400 years older and places it in the hands of Brian Boru, the High King of Ireland who was killed as he led his men to victory over the Danes at the Battle of Clontarf in 1014.

The other historic treasure here is an evocatively tattered

and roughly printed poster, a rare original copy of the Proclamation of the Republic of Ireland, pasted up around Dublin by the rebels during the Easter Rising of 1916 (see pp. 30–32): "The Provisional Government of the Irish Republic, to the People of Ireland. . . .We declare the right of the people

INSIDER TIP:

While admittedly austere, the Trinity College dorms offer unique accommodations as well as a jump-start on the line for the Book of Kells the next day.

—ROBIN CURRIE
National Geographic author

of Ireland to the ownership of Ireland, and to the unfettered control of Irish destiny, to be sovereign and indefeasible. . . . We hereby proclaim the Irish Republic as a Sovereign Independent State, and we pledge our lives and the lives of our comrades in arms to the cause of its freedom, of its welfare, and of its exaltation among the nations."

Campus Architecture

The buildings of Trinity College, throwbacks to an era when craftsmanship was prized above functionality, are worth careful inspection. Don't miss the weird and wonderful flora and fauna carved in the Victorian stonework of the **Museum Building** on New Square. ∎

Trinity College

- Map p. 51
- College St., Dublin 2
- 01 896 1000 (central switchboard)
- All cross-city buses

www.tcd.ie

Book of Kells

- Trinity College, College St., Dublin 2
- 01 896 2308
- $$

www.tcd.ie/Library/ heritage/kells.php

Trinity College dorms

- 01 896 1177
- $$$$$

www.tcd.ie/ accommodations

Book of Kells

This glorious 680-page book of the four Gospels was crafted by monks at Kells Monastery (see p. 260) in County Meath around A.D. 800, at the height of Ireland's golden age of monastic talent and influence. It is the world's first example of an illuminated manuscript—a handwritten text beautified with handcolored illustrations.

The monks who created the Book of Kells used dozens of natural sources of color to complement their exquisite artistry.

Viewing the Book of Kells

The Book of Kells lies under glass in its own special display area at the heart of the Picturing the Word exhibition in the Old Library at Trinity College (see p. 53). In 1953, it was rebound in four volumes, of which two are always on display—one open at a sumptuously illuminated page, the other at a page of text. The pages chosen for display are changed every few months to prevent the illuminated script from fading from overexposure to light. But in fact the egg-white fixative employed by the monks 1,200 years ago has proved remarkably effective in keeping details sharp. On summer holiday weekends it's a good idea to plan your visit as early in the day as possible to avoid a tedious half-hour's wait in line.

Unmatched Artistry

Whichever page is displayed when you visit, you can't fail to be dumbstruck by the beauty, humor, and force of imagination that come shining through the patina of the centuries. The Kells illustrators must have been strongly influenced by the artistic brilliance of the monks of Iona (a monastery established off the west coast of Scotland in about 563), because the freedom of line and intricacy of detail so characteristic of Iona work of that era are all present here.

Each of the illuminated capital letters looks at first sight like an inextricable riot of circles, rectangles, and curlicued bits of foliage in gold, red, and blue. But as you stare you begin to see more—beasts with open mouths, misshapen devils, little domestic cameos, men passionately embracing, huge-eyed angels, heavenly flowers and fruit, all cunningly sneaked into uprights or packed into round spaces. The single page becomes an admonitory or encouraging sermon on the pitfalls and pleasures of life in the real world. What infinite pains the monks of Kells took in making their wonderful masterpiece—and what evident delight, too.

For colors, they used what they had on hand or could get by barter, purchase, or gift—gold leaf, chalk for white, copper verdigris for green. Red came from lead, black from charcoal, blue from either ground-up lapis lazuli or woad, a European plant. How much eyesight the Book of Kells consumed, and how many monkish migraines the crafting of its minuscule details provoked, one can only guess.

Other Books on Display

After admiring the unmatched artistry of the Book of Kells, take some time to admire the other superbly beautiful ancient Gospel books on display. The eighth-century pocket-size **Book of Mulling** was intended for an unknown

missionary monk. Another Gospel on display was made by Dimma the Scribe around the same time, while the **Book of Armagh** was made in 807 for Torbach, Bishop of Armagh. And the oldest decorated Gospel book in existence, the **Book of Durrow,** was created around 675.

Illustrations in the Book of Kells reveal both allegorical tableaux as well as a variety of scenes from life in eighth-century Ireland.

National Museum of Archaeology and History

Inside Dublin's splendid National Museum is gathered the majority of the nation's most significant archaeological finds, brought here from the peat bogs, fields, and hillsides where they have been dug up or stumbled across over the years by turf cutters, plowboys, and amateur archaeologists. The best of Ireland's treasure trove of religious art is here, too. The museum itself was built in 1890, its grand entrance hall floored with a giant mosaic of the zodiac.

The early 18th-century Royal Barracks, renamed Collins Barracks, is now an annex of the museum.

National Museum

- Map p. 51
- ✉ Kildare St., Merrion Row, Dublin 2
- ☎ 01 677 7444
- 🕐 Closed Mon.
- 🚌 Bus: 7, 7A, 10, 11, 13 (O'Connell St.); Rail: Pearse Station, DART

www.museum.ie

The Exhibitions

The National Museum has seven permanent exhibitions. The Treasury (the museum's chief attraction), Prehistoric Ireland, Ór—Ireland's Gold, and The Road to Independence are sited on the ground floor in the Great Hall, while the first-floor gallery and its side halls contain Viking Ireland and Ancient Egypt, along with The Church.

Prehistoric Ireland

On entering the Great Hall you will find the Prehistoric Ireland exhibition directly in front of you. Exhibits that catch the imagination are the **Lurgan log-boat,** 52 feet (19 m) long, fashioned from a tree trunk nearly 5,000 years ago; the tiny **Knowth mace head** crafted of flint with whorls shaped like an astonished human expression, which came from Knowth burial chamber at Brú na Bóinne (see p. 264); and the **wood and leather shields** with which Stone and Bronze Age Irishmen protected themselves.

Chalice Cheat

In the 1860s, a west Limerick man named Quinn was in the habit of planting his potatoes in the soil inside Reerasta ring fort at Ardagh. One day, in 1868, while digging, he unearthed an astonishing treasure hoard—the Ardagh Chalice, four brooches, a wooden cross, and a bronze cup that he smashed by mistake with his spade. Quinn had only a hazy idea of the true value of his find and sold the lot to a sharper-eyed neighbor for £50 ($75)—an enormous sum to an Irish peasant back then, but a raw deal all the same. Eight years later, the hoard was on display in Dublin, its worth having risen many hundredfold. Quinn's widow campaigned furiously for compensation. In 1878, a payment of £100 ($150) was made—not to the Widow Quinn, but to the Bishop of Limerick, on whose land the potatoes had been planted. It was left to the bishop and his conscience to deal fairly with Mrs. Quinn. To his credit, he handed over half his windfall to her.

Ór—Ireland's Gold

Beyond Prehistoric Ireland, in the center of the hall, is Ór—Ireland's Gold, a wonderful exhibition of gold ornaments made in Bronze Age Ireland between about 2000 B.C. and 700 B.C. One of many peaks of skill comes in the form of the **Gleninsheen Gorget**—a heavy, many stranded gold collar with circular shoulder pads found near the Gleninsheen wedge tomb in the Burren, County Clare.

The Treasury

The right-hand side of the hall contains the fabulous Treasury exhibition. Perhaps the three most famous exhibits here are the Tara Brooch, the Broighter Hoard, and the Ardagh Chalice.

The shape of the bejeweled eighth-century **Tara Brooch,** with its circular gold clasp and long pin, is familiar as the inspiration for countless pieces of modern Celtic jewelry. The brooch was found by chance in 1850 on the seashore at Bettystown near Drogheda, just south of the mouth of the River Boyne. The museum has it displayed above a mirror so that you can see the exquisite gold filigree work on both sides.

Another wonderful collection of treasures is the **Broighter Hoard,** discovered in the 1890s near Limavady in County Londonderry. This is pre-Christian goldwork at its finest—leaf-thin hollow necklace balls, disks with hammered indentations, crescent-shaped lunulae to wear round the neck, and a model boat of sheet gold so thin it looks as if a touch would break it.

The **Ardagh Chalice**—a wide-bowled, two-handled cup of softly glowing silver-copper alloy banded with finely chased gold and set with crystal, enamel, and amber—was made in the eighth century, Ireland's golden age. The story of its discovery near Ardagh in west Limerick (see sidebar above) is one that tells plenty about 19th-century society and its values.

The other glories of the Treasury exhibition include the **Derrynaflan Hoard,** which contains a silver chalice, paten, and other treasures of the eighth and ninth centuries found as recently as 1980 by casual seekers wielding a metal detector at Derrynaflan in County Tipperary.

Among the Treasury's extensive collection of reliquaries and shrines is the bronze **Shrine of St. Patrick's Bell**, ornamented with crucifixes, gold, and gemstones. It was made around 1100 to hold the sturdy iron bell (ca 406) also on display.

Other wonderful reliquaries include several gem-encrusted shrines to hold the crosiers of 11th-century bishops, the eighth-century **Moylough belt-shrine** of bronze plated with silver that was found near Tobercurry in County Sligo, and an assortment of book-shrines that includes one made to hold a psalm-book said

The shrine that housed St. Patrick's bell for centuries

INSIDER TIP:

Look for the design on the underside of the Ardagh Chalice. The intricate interlace would only be seen by worshipers when the priest drank from the chalice.

—ROZ HOAGLAND
Private guide, Hoagland Art Travel

to have belonged to St. Columba. Strangest of all to modern sensibilities are the shrines for such objects of veneration as St. Lachtin's arm, St. Bridgid's shoe, and St. Patrick's tooth.

The Road to Independence

The fourth exhibition on the ground floor, occupying the left-hand side of the Great Hall opposite the Treasury, tells the story of Ireland's struggles to break political ties with Britain in the early 20th century (see pp. 30–33), from the Easter Rising of 1916 through the guerrilla warfare that followed, the 1919–1921 War of Independence, and the disastrous Civil War of 1922–1923 between the army of the newly born Irish Free State, backed by the British government, and the forces of the IRA. Of all the deaths in the Civil War, none was more poignant than that of Michael Collins, charismatic young commander-in-chief of the Free State Army. The exhibition includes the uniform that Collins was wearing when he was shot by an IRA sniper near Bandon in County Cork on August 22, 1922.

Viking Ireland

Upstairs you'll find Viking Ireland in the gallery on the right side, directly above the Treasury. Giving the lie to the Vikings' enduring image as bone-headed philistines intent only on plunder and slaughter, this fine exhibition reveals them as sensitively skilled artists in metal—particularly the decorative pins and brooches swirling with interlacing patterns.

Medieval Ireland

Alongside the Viking Ireland display is this fascinating exhibit that explores the era when power shifted from the Irish to English kings, when the land was settled by English lords. A unique collection of artifacts, many never before on show, illustrates the lifestyles, trades, and activities of the people of Ireland—kings, lords, and warriors in the Power Gallery; farmers, artisans, and townspeople in the Work Gallery; and bishops, priests, and their parishioners in the Prayer Gallery.

Ancient Egypt

At the front of the upper gallery, next to the curve of the Rotunda, is the last of the permanent exhibitions, Ancient Egypt, containing everything you'd expect on this theme from painted mummy cases to jackal-headed gods.

National Museum of Decorative Arts and History

Collins Barracks, just north of Wolfe Tone Quay on the River Liffey, 1.5 miles (2.4 km) west of the parent museum, is home to a decorative arts collection. The impressive building was built in 1704 (when it was known as

Leinster House

Next to the National Museum stands massive Leinster House, housing the Irish Parliament, Dáil Éireann. The house was built between 1745 and 1748 as the Dublin seat of the Earl of Kildare. Twenty years later, when the earl became Duke of Leinster, its name was changed. It became the seat of the Irish Parliament in 1922, after the War of Independence, when the Free State Government established itself there.

You must be part of a guided tour to see the workings of Irish democracy firsthand, so plan ahead (tel 01 618 3781; e-mail event.desk@ oireachtas.ie).

Royal Barracks) to house 3,000 men and 1,000 horses. These days it holds a fine collection of Irish ceramics; silverwork, from elaborate 17th-century goblets to swirly modern jewelry; costumes through the ages; weapons; and a range of furniture, from ancient carved chairs to the latest contraptions. ∎

National Museum of Decorative Arts and History

- Map p. 51
- Collins Barracks, Benburb St., Dublin 7
- 01 677 7444
- Closed Mon.
- Bus: 25, 25A, 66, 67, 90 (Aston Quay); Rail: Heuston Station; Museumlink bus from National Museum of Archaeology and History; LUAS Red Line: Museum stop

Leinster House

- Map p. 51
- Kildare St., Dublin 2
- 01 618 3000
- www.irlgov.ie/ oireachtas

Walk: Through Central Dublin

This stroll through the heart of Dublin leads from the bustling riverfront to the leaf-green oasis of St. Stephen's Green and on through the trendy quarter of Temple Bar. From there it runs along the characterful quays of the Liffey to reach the city's grandest and most handsome Georgian building, the Custom House.

The base of the Monument of Light (the Spire) on O'Connell Street in central Dublin

Starting on **O'Connell Bridge,** walk south to cross the River Liffey. Keep straight to pass **Trinity College ❶** and the Book of Kells (see pp. 52–55). Bear east along Nassau Street, then turn right on Kildare Street to pass the **National Museum of Archaeology and History ❷** (see pp. 56–59). At the end of Kildare, bear right through the gardens of **St. Stephen's Green ❸** (see p. 63), then turn right up Dublin's prestigious shopping thoroughfare, **Grafton Street.** Stop at **Bewley's Oriental Café ❹** *(78 Grafton St., tel 01 672 7720)* for a cup of coffee.

At the top of Grafton Street, bear left along Suffolk Street, past the old church that houses the **Dublin tourism center,** and left again along

NOT TO BE MISSED:

Trinity College & the Book of Kells • Ór—Ireland's Gold exhibition in the National Museum • Chester Beatty Library & Gallery of Oriental Art • General Post Office

Dame Street to reach **Dublin Castle** and the **Chester Beatty Library and Gallery of Oriental Art ❺** (see pp. 64–67). From here, steer northeast through **Temple Bar** (see p. 62) until you hit the river. Bear left along the water to the end of Merchant's Quay. Cross the

Liffey on **Father Matthew Bridge** to find the
Georgian dome and facade of the **Four Courts**
facing you to the right. The building still houses
Dublin's High Court and Supreme Court.

Turn right to make your way back to the
south end of O'Connell Street, setting for
the great colonnaded portico of the **General
Post Office** or **GPO** ⑥ *(O'Connell St., tel 01
705 7000),* where the Proclamation of the
Republic was read during the Easter Rising of
1916. Nearby soars the **Monument of Light,** a
390-feet (120 m) stainless-steel needle known
to Dubliners as "the Spire."

Return down O'Connell Street. Near the
bottom, turn left along Abbey Street Lower to
find the **Abbey Theatre** ⑦ *(tel 01 878 7222,*

- ⓜ See area map p. 49 C3 & p. 51
- ► O'Connell Bridge
- ⇄ 4 miles (6 km)
- 🕐 From 2 hours to a whole day, depending on which attractions you decide to explore
- ► Custom House

Dublin Walking Tours

**The best way to get to know Dublin is
on foot. The city's official tourist office
maintains lists of guided walking tours
($) to suit every taste. Themes include
Georgian Dublin, culinary culture,
the 1916 Rebellion, and much more.
Explore everything on offer by visiting**
www.visitdublin.com.

*box office closed Sun., theater open for performances
only–due to relocate to St. George's Dock in the near
future),* Ireland's national theater, founded by
poet W. B. Yeats and his patron, Lady Gregory.

Head back to the water and walk a block
downriver to see the **Custom House** ⑧
*(Custom House Quay, tel 01 888 2000, closed Mon.
& Tues. Nov.–mid-March),* built between 1781 and
1791, Dublin's grandest building.

Temple Bar

If you had mentioned to a group of Dubliners 20 years ago that you were going to hang out in the neighborhood of Temple Bar, a lot of funny looks would have come your way. These days all you'll get is advice as to where to shop and which street has this great little restaurant, and there's this Georgian dance group on at the Arthouse . . .

Temple Bar Cultural Information Centre

- Map p. 51
- 12 East Essex St., Temple Bar
- 01 677 2255
- Bus: All city-center buses; Rail: Tara St. Station, DART

www.templebar.ie

Not so long ago, Temple Bar (named after a local landowner, Sir William Temple, whose property included a sand bank, or bar, on the south side of the river) was due to be flattened to make way for a bus depot. The area just west of Trinity College had become so run down and seedy that no one wanted to live or work there, much less visit for pleasure. Then Group 91, a group of young architects, came up with some radical plans for the district. They designed a

compact mix of galleries, theaters, and an arts center around a market square. Rooflines became fun, sprouting twisted rods like punk hair; balconies curved and snaked; buildings lost their drab brick and whitewash in favor of hot orange or Mediterranean blue.

Temple Bar suddenly became the trendiest place in Dublin. New boutique and lifestyle shops proliferated. Artists, photographers, and filmmakers began to frequent the area and exhibit. And at night a tide of young people spilled between dance clubs and pubs.

This is the place to come during the day for a good cup of coffee or a meal in an ethnic restaurant, shopping, or people-watching. Noisy, rowdy crowds descend at night.

Flashy decor in Temple Bar

Meeting House Square

The heart of Temple Bar is Meeting House Square, scene on Saturday mornings of an open-air market, a great place to stock up on fabulous olives, cheeses, sushi, homemade bread, and sausages. Around the square are an acting school and a children's activity center, **The Ark,** along with a gallery and center for photography, **Temple Bar Music Centre,** the **Arthouse** arts center, and the **Irish Film Centre and Archive.** ∎

St. Stephen's Green

At the far end of Grafton Street from Trinity College lies St. Stephen's Green, 22 acres (9 ha) of gardens at the heart of southside Dublin. Generations of Dubliners have come here to sunbathe, stroll, and flirt among the flowerbeds and under the trees.

The fountains and lawns of St. Stephen's Green exhibit the timeless elegance of Georgian Dublin.

You'll find monuments here to heroes of Ireland's long struggle for Home Rule—notably the 1798 leader Wolfe Tone and Constance Gore-Booth, Countess Markiewicz (see pp. 212–213), who fought like a tiger against British rule and was imprisoned for her activities during the 1916 Easter Rising.

Georgian buildings surround the Green, including the pedimented **Royal College of Surgeons** on the west side, where, in 1922, the constitution of the new Irish Free State was drafted under the chairmanship of Michael Collins. The big hotel on the north side, with its sculptures of princesses lording it over bond maids, is the **Shelbourne,** a mid-Victorian extravaganza.

More of Dublin's handsome Georgian architecture graces **Upper Merrion Street** and **Merrion Square** just northeast of St. Stephen's Green, and **Harcourt Street** to the south. Take plenty of film on your stroll—it's impossible to resist the famous double doorways, side-by-side entrances to neighboring houses, flanked by columns, with elaborate semicircular fanlights above. ■

St. Stephen's Green

 Map p. 51

Dublin Castle

For seven centuries the prime symbol of English dominance over Ireland, Dublin Castle has long had its medieval grimness dressed up in mellow Georgian brick. There are the elaborate 18th-century State Rooms, an undercroft, and various towers to explore. The castle's Clock Tower is home to one of the world's great collections of Middle Eastern and Oriental manuscripts and art.

For centuries, Dublin Castle was a symbol of British power at the heart of the Irish capital.

Dublin Castle

⛰ Map p. 51

✉ Dame St., Dublin 2

☎ 01 677 7129 (prearranged tours: 01 645 8813)

🚌 Bus: 77, 77A, 56A, 49 (Eden Quay), 123 (O'Connell St.) stop at Palace St. Gate; Rail: Tara St., DART

💲 $$

www.dublincastle.ie

The castle was built in the early 13th century as the seat of power for the English rulers of Ireland, a function it served for the following 700 years right up until the establishment of an independent Irish Free State in 1922.

There were at least two sieges of Dublin Castle. "Silken Thomas" Fitzgerald made an attempt in 1534, but his forces were driven off when the garrison made a gallant sortie. The other attempt was

made in 1916, a hopelessly brave attack by the republican rebels of the Easter Rising, who succeeded for only a few hours in penning up the British Army soldiers.

Not much remains of the original castle, which was redesigned internally in good Georgian style with a range of buildings added at the elegant height of the 18th century. Down in the **Undercroft**, you can inspect the ancient footings of the Norman castle's Powder Tower, bedded on walls that the Vikings raised around a fortress of their own three centuries before, along with ancient segments of city wall and moat—a real sense here of a hidden past under your feet

The main focus of a tour around the castle, though, is a circuit of the opulent 18th-century **State Rooms,** still sometimes used to entertain foreign dignitaries. The tour has to be taken with a guide, who follows a fixed route. It includes **St. Patrick's Hall,** almost 100 feet (30 m) long and festooned with banners of the long-disbanded Knights of St. Patrick under a fine painted and paneled ceiling. Other highlights are the gorgeous powder-blue **Wedgwood Room,** the great **Drawing Room** entered between gilt Corinthian columns and barred with light from tall windows, and a **Throne Room** stiff with gold and lit by golden chandeliers.

Chester Beatty Library & Gallery of Oriental Art

The real treasure of Dublin Castle, however, resides in the gardens at the back of the castle beyond the State Apartments *(enter by the Ship Street gate),* home to the incomparable Chester Beatty Library and Gallery of Oriental Art. Dublin is lucky to have this fabulous collection, put together over the best part of 60 years by the agents of Canadian mining tycoon Sir Alfred Chester Beatty (1875–1968). Beatty moved to Dublin in 1953 and donated his collection to the Irish nation in 1956.

Beatty was primarily interested in Oriental art and in religious manuscripts—he owned more than 300 copies of the Koran—and eventually amassed some 22,000 manuscripts as well as thousands of paintings, printed books, maps, and carved objects.

The **Clock Tower** displays, occupying two floors of the tower, are arranged in seven exhibitions that pick and choose among the highlights of this huge mass of material. They are so absorbing that you will certainly want more than half a day to appreciate them. You'll find a good magnifying glass enhances your enjoyment, too, since there is so much delicate detail in the Oriental work.

INSIDER TIP:

Dublin Castle's grounds offer galleries and museums in an unbeatable city-center location. Picnic in the shadow of the castle with the locals.

—ALEXANDRA BURGUIERES
National Geographic contributor

Gallery Floor 1: On entering Gallery Floor 1, you'll find an exhibition outlining the life and work of Sir Alfred Chester Beatty. Beyond this, the gallery is simply but effectively laid out. Most of the material on this floor comprises manuscripts and printed books, bindings, calligraphy and typography, miniature paintings, prints, and drawings.

Chester Beatty Library & Gallery of Oriental Art
- Dublin Castle, Dublin 2
- 01 407 0750
- Closed Mon. Oct.–April
- Bus: 50, 51B, 54A, 56A, 77, 77A, 78A, 123; Rail: Tara St., DART

www.cbl.ie

On the left side of the gallery are exhibits from the **Western and European traditions.** From the Egypt of 1160 B.C. a papyrus screed has somehow survived; love poems, said to be the most important example of ancient Egyptian poetry in existence, are written on it in Hieratic text. There's also a wonderfully illuminated 15th-century Book of Hours. In the center is the Islamic material—Arabic, Persian, and Turkish. Here is a unique treatise written by a medieval Iraqi expert on engineering, the use of artillery, astronomy, and geometry. On the right, you'll find treasures from India and East and Southeast Asia. They include Tibetan ceremonial swords and a magic dagger with a carved deity on the pommel, along with many Indian paintings and examples of jeweled work.

This section also contains decorative **arts from China and Japan.** Because of the miniature size of much of the work, you'll benefit from taking plenty of time to explore these collections. From China are cups carved from rhinoceros horn, lacquered boxes, finches painted on silk, and a number of tiny snuff bottles in jade, lacquer, porcelain, and mother-of-pearl.

The Japanese items form the cream of the Chester Beatty Gallery's nonmanuscript displays. Notable are dozens of **netsuke**— toggles made to weigh down the ends of a kimono cord—little men, animals, trees, and birds carved from ivory, wood, or jade.

But it is the Japanese paintings that may fascinate, intrigue, and inspire you most. Here are dozens of hand-painted scrolls of paper

A detail from "Snow at Night," one of the Chester Beatty Library's exquisite Oriental paintings or silk, dating from the early 17th to the late 19th centuries, telling stories or recounting courtly and military history. Some are up to 80 feet (29 m) long, with each scene rendered in incredible detail—a young girl daydreaming on a rock, a poets' meeting at which everyone is trying to look wiser than the next man, the courtesan Konami gripping her handkerchief between her pearly little teeth in a carefully staged flood of emotion.

Then you come across a whole selection of prints—the tranquil "Plum Garden at Karneido," the actor Sawamura Sojuro caught pulling a face in 1794. Such works of art form a bridge between cultures and ages across which it is a breathtaking privilege to step.

Gallery Floor 2: Upstairs, on Gallery Floor 2, the great spiritual traditions of the world are explored. The layout is the same as on the floor below. To the left are items illustrating the **Western and Christian traditions**—pre-Christian texts, Judaic scrolls, and early Old and New Testament manuscripts. Here Christian treasures include a double papyrus page of St. Luke's Gospel, copied early in the third century, and a segment of the Book of Revelation of around the same date, the oldest fragment of the final New Testament chapter yet discovered. Even more astonishing is the version of St. Paul's Epistles written around 200—only three or four generations separated scribe and author. Out of the Middle Ages come wonderfully

Islamic Treasures

In the Islamic section on the second floor of the Chester Beatty Gallery are illustrated manuscripts of the Koran, miniature paintings of the life of the Prophet, and Islamic history and traditions within the Arab, Persian, Mughal Indian, and Turkish worlds. The Arabic calligraphy of the richly gilded Koran texts is of stunning beauty as an art form, as are the ancient jeweled Koran stands and the tiny gold cases inlaid with enamel that were made to hold miniature copies.

illuminated bibles and a copy of St. Augustine's *City of God,* dated from around 1100.

The second floor also houses art of the **Eastern religions**— Buddhist, Hindu, Jain, Sikh, Daoist, and Shinto. In Southeast Asia, Sir Alfred Chester Beatty collected Thai paintings of the life of Buddha, including one of the saint as a golden elephant in flight, and gilded lacquer statues from Burma. Tibet yielded elaborate prayer wheels as well as a Thanka painting on cotton cloth of the four-armed Avalokitesvara.

A good tip to help ensure maximum enjoyment of this unique and remarkable collection: Don't try to see it all in one day. Set aside two half days and give your senses time to recover in between. ■

Literary Dublin

If there's one art above all others for which Dublin is celebrated, it is the city's astonishingly rich literary heritage. The old saying that there's the making of a great novel on the backseat of every Dublin cab has some truth to it. Dubliners seem to be born with a feel for rhythms and cadences of language. Conversations in the bars and on the street corners of the city are rich in imagery and imagination to the eavesdropping outsider. In such fertile ground, many seeds of genius have flourished.

This statue of poet Patrick Kavanagh receives less than its due respect from a young Dubliner.

The Writers

James Joyce (1882–1941) towers over literary Dublin. His shadow has hardly diminished in the 80 years since his 1922 masterpiece and love-letter-in-exile to the city, *Ulysses*, was first published.

These days, Joyce fanatics from all over the world descend in fancy dress on Dublin each "Bloomsday"—June 16, the date on which all the action in *Ulysses* takes place—and embark on a James Joyce Trail that faithfully follows the perambulations of the novel's hero, Leopold Bloom, around the city's streets and pubs. You can join in *(get details from Dublin Tourism)*, but

make sure your digestion is in good shape; along with the pints of Guinness and the *Ulysses* readings, one ritual is immutable—the reenactment of Bloom's lunch of a Gorgonzola and mustard sandwich and a glass of burgundy in **Davy Byrne's pub** on Duke Street. Alternatively, enjoy the trail at any time of year and at your own pace by following the bronze plaques set into the sidewalks of central Dublin.

Dublin carries the mark of a host of literary giants besides Joyce. Dean Jonathan Swift (1667–1745), author of *Gulliver's Travels*, *Tale of a Tub*, and other furiously indignant polemic and political satire, lies buried next to his platonic lover, Esther Johnson, "Stella" (1681–1728), in the nave of St. Patrick's Cathedral.

The Abbey Theatre on Abbey Street Lower saw historic opening nights of plays by Nobel Prize winners W. B. Yeats (1865–1939) and Samuel Beckett (1906–1989). Near Baggot Street Bridge, a sculpture of Monaghan-born poet Patrick Kavanagh (1904–1967) contemplates the turbid water of the Grand Canal, as Kavanagh himself loved to do while recuperating from lung cancer operations in the 1950s.

The Pubs

So much of Dublin's literary life, high and low, has been conducted in the city's pubs. Patrick Kavanagh frequented **McDaid's,** whose Moorish frontage looks out on Harry Street, a pedestrian-only lane off Grafton Street. Acid-witted columnist and novelist Brian O'Nolan (1911–1966), writing like an avenging angel with a great sense of humor under the pseudonyms Flann O'Brien and Myles na gCopaleen, also drank in McDaid's, as did rambunctious playwright Brendan Behan (1923–1964).

Nearby, on Lower Baggot Street, is **Toner's.** North of the River Liffey are the working-class estates whose life and speech have been brilliantly captured by Roddy Doyle (born 1958) in his "Barrytown Trilogy"—*The Commitments, The Snapper,* and *The Van.*

The Museums

A couple of literary museums are well worth visiting. The **James Joyce Centre** *(35 N. Great George's St., tel 01 878 8547, closed Sun.–Mon., www.jamesjoyce.ie, $$)* has an excellent reference library, first editions, memorabilia, and tapes of the great man reading from *Ulysses* and other works. Joyce-themed walking tours leave from here.

The modest birthplace of Nobel Prize–winning playwright George Bernard Shaw, at **33 Synge Street,** is evocative of (outwardly) stiflingly respectable Victorian life. You'll find the strands of many of these literary Dublin lives pulled together in the displays, portraits, and memorabilia in the **Dublin Writers' Museum** *(18 Parnell Sq. North, tel 01 872 2077, www.writersmuseum.com, $$),* just north of the top end of O'Connell Street.

Or you could opt for one of Dublin's organized Literary Pub Crawls *(contact Dublin Tourism, $$$)* and make a round of half a dozen pubs where actors bring Dublin writers to life.

EXPERIENCE: Literary Festivals & Events

Dublin is justly famous for Bloomsday, its annual celebration of James Joyce's novel *Ulysses* (see p. 44). But the city plays host to so many other literary festivals and events that you are bound to find something that interests you no matter when you visit.

Celebrating the best in contemporary Irish literature, the **Dublin Book Festival** (www.dublinbookfestival.com) takes place over three days in early March. See your favorite authors in person, write verses with a practicing poet, and learn about new and exciting things to read. The festival is free and includes workshops, book launches, and plenty of events for kids.

In early June, the **Dublin Writers Festival** (www.dublinwritersfestival.com) draws Irish and international poets and authors to the famed Abbey Theatre and other venues around the city. The weeklong celebration includes intimate readings and jaw-dropping performances, personal discussions with leading writers, and forums about writing and publishing. See website for details and ticket information.

For other literary events taking place around the city, including public lectures and classes, consult the **National Library of Ireland** (Kildare St., Dublin 2, tel 01 603 0200, www.nli.ie).

St. Patrick's Cathedral

St. Patrick's Cathedral is a beautiful, uncomplicated building, much of it dating back to the 12th century, with a west tower and spire that soar to 225 feet (69 m). It was built on the site of a well where St. Patrick is said to have baptized converts, and there was probably a church on the site from the fifth century onward.

The spire of St. Patrick's Cathedral soars into the Dublin sky, a landmark and symbol to the city's Roman Catholics.

St. Patrick's Cathedral

🅰 Map p. 51

✉ Patrick's Cl., Dublin 8

☎ 01 453 9472

🚍 Bus: 49, 49A, 49B, 50, 54A, 56A, 65, 65B, 77, 77A (Eden Quay); Rail: Pearse Station DART

💲 $$

www.stpatricks cathedral.ie

Inside, you'll find the graves of Dean Jonathan Swift and his companion, "Stella." They lie under the floor of the nave just beyond the entrance. On the south wall opposite hangs Swift's self-penned Latin epitaph, "laid ... where fierce indignation can no longer rend the heart. Go traveller, and imitate, if you can, this earnest and dedicated Champion of Liberty." In the north transept is a little Swift exhibition.

The cathedral's splendid tombs include the enormous 17th-century **Boyle Monument,** with its three tiers of Westons, Fentons, and Boyles. There are some fine 16th-century brasses in the aisle

south of the choir, as well as a feeble likeness of Ireland's most revered musician, the blind harpist Turlough O'Carolan (1670–1738). Arrange in advance if you wish to make brass rubbings *($$$)*.

Don't miss the old wooden door with its central panels missing. In 1492, this was the door of the cathedral's chapter house, behind which the Earl of Ormond

INSIDER TIP:

For an unbeatable and atmospheric musical experience, try to visit St. Patrick's Cathedral during a choral service. Check the website for service times.

—ÁINE KAVANAGH
Dublin Tourism

barricaded himself against his enemy, the Earl of Kildare. Ormond refused to come out, even though promised safe passage, so Kildare hacked a hole in the door with his spear and stuck his unprotected arm through in a brave gesture of trust. Ormond grasped the hand, the feud was ended, and the expression "chancing one's arm," meaning taking a risk, entered the language. ∎

Guinness Brewery & Storehouse

Half of all the beer drunk in Ireland is brewed in the sprawling Guinness Brewery at St. James's Gate on the Liffey's north bank. Altogether some 2,500,000 pints of the black stout with its creamy white head are drunk daily in 120 countries in all parts of the world—not bad for the little family brewery that Arthur Guinness established on the site in 1759. They are still black-roasting the malt here, and the popularity of Guinness continues to grow.

The brewery itself is not open to the public, but the company's **Guinness Storehouse** attraction nearby will tell you all you want to know and then—fulfilling Guinness's proud boast—serve you the best pint and the best view in Dublin.

The Guinness company has always excelled at marketing itself through clever advertisements. They engaged some of the best commercial artists, who produced masterpieces of the genre for the company—the ostrich with the Guinness glass stuck halfway down its neck, the pelican with its bill crammed with bottles of stout, the toucan balancing a pint of Guinness on its orange bill ("See what Toucan do!"). All of these and more, many in full street-hoarding size and color, are displayed in the Storehouse.

Guinness Storehouse

- Map p. 51
- St. James's Gate, Dublin 8
- 01 608 8000
- Bus: 51B, 78A (Aston Quay), 123 (O'Connell St.); Rail: Heuston Station
- $$$$

www.guinness-storehouse.com

The fruits of the Guinness company's labors can be enjoyed in many venues around town.

INSIDER TIP:

The Gravity Bar at the top of the Guinness Brewery offers panoramic views of the city, plus you get a free pint with the price of the tour. Cheers!

—WILL HALICKS
National Geographic contributor

Inside one of Guinness's former fermentation and storage plants—a handsome 1904 building in cast iron and brick—the company has developed a six-story exhibition based around a giant atrium shaped like a pint glass. Here you'll find out exactly how the black nectar is made—ingredients, techniques, plant, and manpower—in a replica brewery with a giant *kieve* or mash tun, a big gleaming copper fermentation vat, and displays on the malting process and hop growing. Fascinating 19th-century photographs of the brewery show heavily moustachioed men hauling casks into tottering mountains. The casks were mostly handmade especially for the brewery until after World War II. There is also an exhibit of the cooper's art.

You can shop in the retail store, which offers a huge range of Guinness merchandise, or enjoy a meal in the restaurant. And then there's the pint itself—after the tour you'll be offered a taste of the Black Stuff in the viewpoint Gravity Bar on the top floor. ■

EXPERIENCE: Discover the Great Pubs of Dublin

Dublin and pubs . . . now why would they come to mind together? Ireland is justly famous for its pubs—not as drinkers' dens, but as centers of social life, conversation, information, music, and fun. Here's a handful of suggestions to get you started.

At 8 Poolbeg Street, between Trinity College and the River Liffey, you'll find **Mulligan's;** the Guinness is superb. East of Grafton Street are **Davy Byrne's** at 21 Duke Street (see p. 68), **McDaid's** (see p. 69) at 3 Harry Street, and the traditional **Kehoe's** at 9 Anne Street South.

West of St. Stephen's Green lie three contrasting pubs. On Lower Baggot Street you'll find **Doheny & Nesbitt,** a popular spot-the-politician pub at No. 5, and the plain-fronted **Toner's** (see p. 69) at No. 139, the only pub, reputedly, that W. B. Yeats ever brought himself to enter, considering himself too refined for such places; and at 15 Merrion Row is a traditional music pub, **O'Donoghue's.**

In Temple Bar you'll get tourist tunes in the **Oliver St. John Gogarty** at 58–59 Fleet Street. The modern **Porter House** at 16 Parliament Street brews its own delicious beer, while the **Stag's Head** in Dame Court off Dame Street has a cozy atmosphere.

At 3 Great George Street South, the **Long Hall** is another pub full of character. Eastward, two great traditional music pubs face each other across Bridge Street Lower, **O'Shea's Merchant** and the **Brazen Head.**

North of the river is a splendid trio of pubs with music: the **Cobblestone Bar** on King Street North and **Hughes** at 19 Chancery Street for traditional sessions, and **Slattery's** at 129 Capel Street for rock and ballads.

Phoenix Park

Phoenix Park—the green lung of Dublin—is a vast oasis of trees and grassland with nature trails, bike paths, polo fields, and other attractions for Dubliners looking to enjoy a bit of fresh air. It has been open to the public since the 18th century.

Dublin's Phoenix Park is the largest urban green space in Europe.

Surprisingly few visitors to Dublin get out to Phoenix Park, although it lies only just over a mile (1.6 km) upriver of the city center and conveniently close to the national monument of Kilmainham Gaol. The park never feels crowded—this is the largest walled city park in Europe, with 1,750 acres (700 ha) of open space enclosed by 7 miles (11 km) of wall.

Displays in the **visitor center**, near the northern edge, trace the history of the park through its various monastic and aristocratic owners and use as a hunting ground to its 18th-century landscaping and eventual opening to the public in 1745.

Attractions

The President of Ireland lives in the park in a mansion called **Áras an Uachtaráin;** the residence of the U.S. ambassador is here, too. There's also a zoo and a hospital.

By far the best thing to do in Phoenix Park is to bring a picnic and wander through woods and over grassland, watching for fallow deer and stopping to enjoy the spectacle of Gaelic sports such as hurling and Gaelic football that are played on weekends. ∎

Phoenix Park

🅰 Map p. 50

✉ Main entrance on Parkgate St., opposite Heuston Station

🚌 Bus: 25, 26, 51, 66, 67, 69, 69X from city center; Rail: Heuston Station

Phoenix Park Visitor Centre

☎ 01 677 0095

🚌 Bus: 37 from Abbey St. to Ashtown Gate, 38, 39, 70

Kilmainham Gaol

For anyone who wants to understand what has shaped modern Ireland, anyone with the smallest interest in Irish history and the centuries of strain and strife between Ireland and England, a tour of the country's most famous jail is a must. The young guides have a passionate interest in their subject. Once you have walked its cold, echoing corridors, stood silently in one of the tiny, chilly cells, and stared around the blank-walled execution yards, you will appreciate why this national monument was a keystone in the building of independent Ireland.

The claustrophobic facade of Kilmainham Gaol killed the hope of every prisoner who entered.

Symbol of Struggle

Certain dates resonate around Kilmainham—1798, 1803, 1848, 1867, 1881, 1883. These were the years of abortive uprisings and rebellions in an Ireland ruled from mainland Britain: Wolfe Tone's United Irishmen and their French allies in 1798, Robert Emmett's short-lived rising of 1803, the quickly crushed Young Ireland rebellion in the famine year of 1848, the Fenian rising of 1867 backed by American money. Leaders and activists of all these revolutionary groups, along with suspects and innocent parties, were held in this prison; so were Charles Stewart Parnell and Michael Davitt, leading lights during the "Land War" of 1879 to 1882.

But 1916 is the most poignant date in Kilmainham's history because, in May of that year, 15 leaders of the Easter Rising were shot for treason in the prison yard. The General Post Office on O'Connell Street, scene of the first proclamation of the Irish Republic and the subsequent weeklong siege of the Easter rebels, is one icon of the Irish struggle for independence. Kilmainham is an even more potent symbol; its story goes back more than two centuries and represents the continuing struggle.

Building of the prison started in 1786, on open fields to the west of the city center, and it was designed to look as grimly forbidding as possible. That's the impression you still get as you approach the looming gray bulk of the complex and come to the thick entrance door with its spyhatch, set in a massive stone surround. Above the door are carved the Five Devils of Kilmainham, five hissing snakes chained by the neck to represent evil under strict control.

Prison Museum

Kilmainham Gaol was not built purely to house political prisoners, but as an all-purpose prison for general malefactors. The guided tour begins in the prison museum with an introduction to Georgian and Victorian Dublin, a place of crowded, unsanitary slums, mass unemployment,

rampant disease, ignorance, alcoholism, child abuse, and early death. Most of the inmates of Kilmainham Gaol were debtors and petty thieves, with a sprinkling of sheep stealers, prostitutes, rapists, and murderers. This was where the flotsam of Dublin life ended up, often for many months or years. Neglect was the norm, beatings commonplace. Executions took place week in, week out, in the prison or before large public crowds out at Blackrock on the southern arm of Dublin Bay.

INSIDER TIP:

On the gaol tour, listen for the heartbreaking story of Joseph Plunkett, who married his sweetheart in the prison chapel hours before his execution.

–ÁINE KAVANAGH
Dublin Tourism

Central Hall

With such scenes in mind, you move off from the museum, along the gloomy corridors of the east wing, to emerge into the frigid light of the prison's enormous Central Hall, a horseshoe-shaped structure built in 1862. With its 100 cells stacked in four tiers and looking inward to a cats' cradle of iron walkways and stairs, it is the embodiment of control. The wardens muffled the walkways with carpet so that the prisoners never knew when they were being observed.

Kilmainham Gaol
- Map p. 50
- Inchicore Rd., Kilmainham, Dublin 8
- 01 453 5984
- Prearranged tours only
- Bus: 51B, 51C, 78A, 79 from Aston Quay; Rail: Heuston Station
- $$

Central Hall
(19th-century cell block)

Exercise yard

Main entrance

The guide shows you a cell decorated with a mural, the "Madonna of the Lilies." It was painted in 1923 by Grace Plunkett while she was held here as a republican prisoner during the Irish Civil War. Seven years earlier, as Grace Gifford, she had married Joseph Plunkett in the chapel of Kilmainham Gaol at 1:30 a.m. on May 4, 1916, with 20 British soldiers as witnesses. Two hours later her bridegroom was dead, shot for treason as one of the leaders of the Easter Rising. Thinking of this, you can't help but be moved as you inspect the chapel. A carpenter who was serving a seven-year sentence made the altar: His crime was stealing a cart wheel.

Exercise yard

18th-century
cell blocks

Kilmainham Gaol is one of the largest
unoccupied prison facilities in Europe.
Access is by guided tour only and is
well worth it. The tour lasts one hour
and includes an informative audio-
visual presentation.

Exercise yard

Exercise yard

Outer wall

Central courtyard

Exercise yard

Kilmainham Gaol

Bleak dark corridors lead to flights of steps, their granite treads hollowed by convict feet. The guide tells of the Williams family, sentenced to one month's imprisonment in 1850 for fare-dodging on the railway; they all had to serve the sentence, including the youngest, a boy of six.

Easter Rising Rebels

The cells where the Easter Rising rebels were held are in the older part of the prison, in a particularly chill and dark passage. You can have yourself

Famine Refugees

Kilmainham Gaol in mid-Victorian times was as grim a place as could be imagined. Even so, to many desperate and starving men and women during the Great Famine (see pp. 28–29) it seemed a refuge. They would break windows or steal fruit in order to be sent to Kilmainham and qualify for a straw bed in a cold cell and a spoonful of the prison's anemic gruel.

shut into one of these stark, claustrophobic boxes where the insurgents were held while the authorities decided their fate. The cells had their final use during and just after the Civil War of 1922–23, when Sinn Féin leader Eamon de Valera—later in life to become Taoiseach (Prime Minister) and President of Ireland—was

incarcerated here. The guide points out the cell from which de Valera was released on July 16, 1924, Kilmainham's last prisoner. The prison was abandoned until the 1960s.

INSIDER TIP:

Close to a Dubliner's heart, a visit to Kilmainham Gaol can be a powerful and moving experience. Many Irish rebellion leaders were imprisoned here.

—TOM JACKSON
National Geographic Society

Invincibles' Yard

Outside, you walk through a grim, gray enclosure walled with stone—the "Invincibles' Yard," named after members of a secret organization who were hanged in the yard in 1883.

And so you move on to the most resonant, most chilling place on the whole tour—the high-walled prison yard, once used as a place for convicts to break stones in hard labor, where 15 of the Easter Rising leaders were executed by firing squad for treason. The signatories of the original Proclamation of the Republic—Padraic Pearse, James Connolly, Joseph Plunkett, Sean MacDermott, Thomas MacDonagh, Eamonn Ceannt, and Thomas Clarke—were shot, along with eight others, in ones and twos over the long week

Thanks to the defining drama that the Easter Rising prisoners played out within its walls, Kilmainham Gaol has become a symbol of Irish independence and national pride.

between May 3 and 12, 1916. Connolly could not stand, his ankle having been shattered, so he was shot sitting tied in a chair.

When details of these long-drawn-out executions began to emerge, the public mood in Ireland swung behind the rebels. The British had succeeded only in creating martyrs out of men whose actions the majority of ordinary Irish men and women had been inclined to view with bafflement or contempt. Standing in the cold shadow of the execution yard walls, you can almost hear the echoes of history.

The Poorest Prisoners

In among all the clangorous reverberations of Ireland's turbulent history, one still small voice is heard above all—the voice of the poor. Under the tide of great events, it is the stories of Dublin's poor and dispossessed that stay with you the longest—the young boy brutalized and hanged for stealing a loaf of bread and the starving girl who broke a window so that she could be sentenced to a few months in Kilmainham Gaol, where the thin, watery prison gruel never ran out. ■

Walk: Hill of Howth

Feel like taking a break from the city and getting a lungful of fresh sea air? This half-day stroll around a beautiful coastline is a favorite with Dubliners and easily reached by suburban DART train in less than half an hour from the city center.

Sea and coast views under huge skies enhance the bracing walk around Howth Head.

Disembark the DART *(tel 01 850 230 330)* at Howth Station. Turn left out of the station along **Howth Harbour ❶**. In a third of a mile (0.5 km), turn right up Abbey Street. **Ye Olde Abbey Tavern ❷**, on the right, serves good lunches. Take the steps beside the pub to reach the ruined shell of **Howth Abbey ❸**, famous throughout medieval Europe for the brilliance of its monks. The view from here over Howth Harbour is excellent.

Spies from Paris University once landed at Howth, intending to entice away the abbey's students. But the abbot, forewarned, posted monks disguised as dock laborers on the harbor. The spies returned to France empty-handed, saying that it was useless to bring offers of education to a place where even the dockers conversed in Latin!

Return to Abbey Street and continue uphill, then turn right along St. Lawrence's Road. In about 100 yards (90 m), continue along Grace O'Malley Road, then turn left up Grace

NOT TO BE MISSED:

Howth Harbour • Ye Olde Abbey Tavern • View from Howth Abbey ruins • Shielmartin summit • View of Baily Lighthouse

O'Malley Drive. Where the road bends to the left (by a phone booth), keep walking straight up the path, and then follow the road to the top. Turn right at the top. A ramp next to house No. 53 leads to a grassy slope; climb it to go through trees and on up a steep bank to a golf course. At the top, bear right along the top edge of the course and follow the path under craggy Dun Hill. Cross the golf course and climb the slope ahead (aim for red-and-white striped poles) to the top of **Shielmartin ❹**.

Offering the best view of the walk, this summit takes in Dublin Bay, the city, and the Wicklow

Mountains. Follow the path seaward off the hill, descending to turn left on Carrickbrack Road. In about 300 yards (250 m), cross the road and go through a gate, ignoring the ominous "Dangerous Cliffs" sign as the cliffs are perfectly safe. Take the footpath down to the shore. Turn left here and follow the **cliff walk ⑤**. Narrow in places, it runs for about 5 miles (8 km) around the bulbous nose of the Howth Peninsula.

You will pass by the 1814 **Baily Lighthouse ⑥**. Continue walking along the coast path

⚑	See area map p. 49, D3
▶	Howth DART railway station, a 25-minute run from Connolly Station, central Dublin
⟷	7 miles (11 km)
⏱	3–4 hours
▶	Howth Harbour

among seabirds and wonderful sea views until the path deposits you safely back at Howth Harbour.

Attractions Out of Town

By far the best way for visitors to get a feel for what lies beyond O'Connell Street and St. Stephen's Green is the DART—Dublin Area Rapid Transit. These little green trains are not just cattle trucks for commuters; they bring the pleasures of outer Dublin within easy reach of the city center. The DART is punctual, quick, and handy, with city-center stations north of the River Liffey at Connolly and south at Tara Street and Pearse Street.

Bathers launch themselves into the sea at Sandycove.

North Bull Island, often known as Dollymount Strand, has an east-facing coast of fine sandy beaches where you can swim in a bracingly fresh sea. It is also a great favorite with bird-watchers. Its location is a good spot for migrating birds to descend and rest midjourney, and many species of northern ducks, geese, and waders come to spend the winter here. Bring your binoculars for a stroll along the beach, and if you want to find out more about the wildlife, visit the interpretive center.

The terminus of the DART lies farther along the coast at **Howth**—the start point for a superb 7-mile (11 km) walk (see pp. 80–81).

South of Dublin

Southward from the city center, the DART reaches **Booterstown Station** on the shores of St. George's Channel. Here at low tide you can hop over the sea wall and enjoy a superb bird-watching beach stroll on a great scimitar of sand. Farther along is **Dun Laoghaire** (pronounced "Dun Leary"), a lively port town well-known for its ferry services to Holyhead (Wales) and Liverpool (England), with handsome Georgian terraces and fine granite harbor walls.

North of Dublin

Ride the DART north of the city center to reach **St. Anne's Park** *(Killester or Harmonstown Station).* On the west side of the park, a footpath dips through a wooded valley, past a number of eccentric architectural follies, before reaching the coast and some fine views across North Bull Island to the rounded peninsular hump of Howth Head.

INSIDER TIP:

The picturesque sea-side town of Howth is best visited on a Sun-day, when the bustling local farmer's market is in full swing.

—CHIARA CECCHINI
National Geographic contributor

Next comes **Sandycove,** where the granite-built Martello tower now known as the **James Joyce Tower** is an object of pil-grimage for fans of *Ulysses*. It was in this fortification, built in 1804 against the threat of a Napo-leonic invasion of Ireland, that Joyce stayed with Oliver St. John Gogarty in 1904. Joyce set the opening scene of *Ulysses* here, with Buck Mulligan (Gogarty) at his early morning toilet on top of the tower. Views from up there

are wonderful, and there's enough Joyceiana collected in the little museum to make this an enjoy-able side trip.

Beyond Sandycove, the DART reaches the nicely preserved old seaside town of **Dalkey,** with its stubby fortified house called Archibold's Castle. Flann O'Brien made merry with Dalkey's genteel atmosphere in his bitingly funny book *The Dalkey Archive*. Dalkey lies around the foot of **Killiney Hill** *(Killiney Station),* worth climbing for its stunning views around the giant curve of Dublin Bay to far-off Howth Head.

In the well-heeled village of **Killiney** itself there's always the sport of celebrity spotting; plenty of rock stars, writers, and TV notables have migrated here. Farther along the coast you can enjoy some great clifftop and beach walks around the resort town of **Bray.** ∎

DART information
☎ 01 836 6222

James Joyce Tower & Museum
Ⓜ 49 D2
✉ Sandycove Point, Dublin
☎ 01 280 9265
🕐 Open April–Oct., by appt. rest of year
🚌 Bus: 59 from Dun Laoghaire, 8 from Eden Quay
💲 $$

EXPERIENCE: Swimming at Sandycove

For generations, Dubliners have learned to swim at the **Forty Foot.** Located out at Sandycove on the southern curve of Dublin Bay, the Forty Foot is a fortified headland whose name commemorates the 40th Regiment of Foot, which was stationed here around the turn of the 19th century to resist any invasion attempt by Napoleon Bonaparte.

With its stone-cut steps and slippery rocks, the Forty Foot was, by tradition, reserved exclusively for men, while its relatively secluded position meant that skinny dipping was the rule rather than the exception. These days, things have changed at the Forty Foot; both sexes now swim here, suitably attired.

If you have a love for Irish literature, make for the neighboring **Martello tower** *(www.dun-laoghaire.com, $$)* once you have toweled off. The tower is now a museum dedicated to James Joyce, who lived there briefly in 1904. The action in Joyce's greatest novel, *Ulysses,* takes place on June 16, 1904, and the book's opening scene is set in and around the tower.

To reach the Forty Foot at Sandycove, take the N11 from Dublin city center to Dun Laoghaire. From there, follow the coast road past the East Pier. Turn left at Sandycove. Be sure to bring with you a bathing suit, sunscreen, and a good towel. Be aware that the water around the Forty Foot is notoriously chilly.

More Places to Visit in & Around Dublin

Casino at Marino

This 18th-century folly must rank as Dublin's oddest building. It is famed as the masterpiece of leading Scottish classical architect William Chambers (1726–1796), who designed it for the Earl of Charlemont. The casino was built between 1758 and 1776 as a miniature palace of pleasure, its three stories of harmonious rooms, with their stucco ceilings and inlaid floors lit cleverly by concealed sources of light, all hidden away inside what seems from the outside to be a single-roomed Greek temple. The corner columns are hollow, concealing rainwater pipes; funerary urns on the roof disguise chimneys; curved windowpanes act as one-way mirrors, concealing those inside from passersby. All is trickery, conceit, and *trompe l'oeil,* a rich man's fantasy that eventually bankrupted the earl. *www.heritageireland.ie*

 49 C3 Off Malahide Rd., Marino, Dublin 3 01 833 1618 Open daily, May–Oct. Bus: 20, 20A, 27, 42, 42C, 123; Rail: Clontarf, DART $

Christ Church Cathedral

Christ Church was stone-built in the late 12th century, replacing a wooden church founded on this site in 1038 by the splendidly named Norse king Sigtryggr Silkenbeard. In the enormous crypt that runs the full length of the church, you'll find carvings and statues and the grisly tableau of the "cat and the rat"—their mummified corpses were found in an organ pipe, where they had become trapped during their last chase. *www.cccdub.ie* Map p. 51 Christ Church Pl., Dublin 8 01 677 8099 Bus: 49, 50, 51B, 54A, 56A, 65, 77, 77A, 78A, 123; Rail: Tara St., DART $$

A Dublin girl dressed up for the magnificent Victorian glasshouses of the National Botanic Gardens

Chilling Churches

Dublin has several churches with more or less macabre items on display. The mummified corpses in St. Michan's Church (see p. 86) are well-known, but there are others to seek out. Two interesting ones are the bones of that patron saint of lovers, St. Valentine, and the cast of Jonathan Swift's skull.

St. Valentine's remains are contained in a handsome black-and-gold chest under an altar in the **Carmelite Church Whitefriar Street** *(56 Aungier St., tel 01 475 8821; buses 16, 16A, 19, 19A, 122 from O'Connell St., 83 from College St.,*

65B, 65C from Eden Quay). They were given to Father John Spratt by Pope Gregory XVI as a reward for Spratt's excellent preaching when the Dublin priest visited Rome in 1835.

In **St. Patrick's Cathedral** (see p. 70), the Jonathan Swift display in the north transept features a plaster cast of the writer's skull. The original skull was removed from Swift's grave in the 1830s and started a bizarre 100-year circuit of the drawing rooms of fashionable Dublin as a conversation piece. It was reburied in the 1920s.

Irish Museum of Modern Art

Here you can see stimulating, sometimes baffling exhibitions from a big collection of Irish and worldwide modern art. They are housed in part of the finest 17th-century building in Ireland—designed in the 1680s as a colonnaded, courtyarded retirement home for old soldiers and only decommissioned from that role in 1927. www.imma.ie
🅰 Map p. 50 ✉ Royal Hospital, Military Rd., Kilmainham, Dublin 8 ☎ 01 612 9900 🕐 Closed Mon. 🚌 Bus: to James St. (5-minute walk via steps to Bow Lane onto Military Rd): 123 (from O'Connell St./Dame St.), 51B, 78A (from Aston Quay); Rail: Tara St.

Iveagh Gardens

This quiet green enclave in the heart of southside Dublin, a five-minute walk from St. Stephen's Green, is never overcrowded. There are sunken lawns and gravel paths beneath mature trees, secluded little arbors, and a beautiful fountain whose basin is held aloft by winged angels.
🅰 Map p. 51 ✉ Clonmel St., off Harcourt St., Dublin 2 ☎ 01 475 7816 🚌 Bus: 14, 14A, 15, 15A, 15B, 15C, 48A 🕐 Closed at dusk (6 p.m. in summer)

Malahide Castle

Out to the north of Dublin, in the seaside town of Malahide, this old castle sits on 250 acres (100 ha) of parkland. The Talbot family lived here from 1185 until 1973, and the whole place—with its fully restored interior—is steeped in strong, rather cranky atmosphere. In the Great Hall, a huge painting by Jan Wyck depicts the Battle of the Boyne on July 14, 1690; 14 Talbot cousins were killed. Be sure to stroll the grounds and their prized gardens. www.malahidecastle.com
🅰 49 C4 ✉ Malahide, Co. Dublin
☎ 01 846 2184 🚌 Bus: 42; Rail: Northern Commuter rail from Pearse, Tara St., or Connolly Station to Malahide, DART to Malahide 💲 $$

National Botanic Gardens

These gardens have limestone pavements, an arboretum, decorative beds, and more than 20,000 plant species. The impressive glasshouses contain ferns, alpine and tropical water plants, and much more. www.botanicgardens.ie 🅰 49 C3 ✉ Botanic Ave., Glasnevin, Dublin 9 ☎ 01 804 0300 🕐 Closed at 6 p.m. (winter at 4:30 p.m.) 🚌 Bus: 4, 13, 19 (from O'Connell St.), 134 (from Middle Abbey St.)

City-goers take to the water aboard the good ship *Viking Splash.*

INSIDER TIP:

Explore Dublin by land and water on a *Viking Splash* tour [*www.vikingsplash.ie*]. The amphibious World War II craft offers the best and most fun way to see the city.

—ALLY THOMPSON
National Geographic contributor

National Gallery of Ireland

Highlights of the National Gallery's wonderful collection include some of J. M. W. Turner's watercolors, a vigorous, dark "Taking of Christ" by Caravaggio, a Rubens "Annunciation," Irish landscapes and portraits that form a kind of history of Anglo-Irish Ireland, and a number of Dutch masters and French and English Impressionists. A room is devoted to the blurred, hallucinatory work of Jack Yeats (see pp. 208–209). *www.nationalgallery.ie*
🅰 Map p. 51 ✉ Merrion Sq. West, Dublin 2 ☎ 01 661 5133 🚌 Bus: 5, 7, 7A from Burgh Quay, 10 from O'Connell St.,

44, 48A from Hawkins St.; Rail: Pearse St., DART (5-minute walk); LUAS Green Line: St. Stephen's Green

Royal Canal & Grand Canal

These two canals were built in the 18th century (Grand Canal started in 1765, Royal Canal in 1789) in a fantastically ambitious move to connect Dublin by water with the northwest and west of Ireland via the Shannon system, and with the southeast by way of the River Barrow. They ring the center of the city, the Royal to the north, the Grand to the south, and these days are used for fishing, boating, and strolling. 🅰 49 A3–C3

St. Michan's Church

St. Michan's, on the north side of the Liffey, contains two remarkable features—a gloriously carved organ case and, in the vaults, a macabre collection of "mummified" bodies, including those of crusaders that date from the 12th century. They have been preserved by the water-absorbing qualities of the magnesian limestone foundations.
🅰 Map p. 51 ✉ Church St., Dublin 7 ☎ 01 872 4154 🕐 Closed Sun. 🚌 Bus: 34, 83 💲 $ (tour)

From green Tipperary farmlands and the horse-racing plains of
Kildare to the Wicklow Mountains and the sandy coast of Wexford

East Ireland

An eastern Irish horse

East Ireland

East Ireland takes in the mountains, grassy plains, sandy coasts, and rich green farmland that make up the southeast part of the island. It is instantly likeable, its pleasures easily accessible. All you'll need is plenty of time to take the narrow back roads, explore the little country towns, and bask in the good weather of Ireland's driest, sunniest region.

Kildare is the most celebrated county for horse racing and breeding in Ireland. If you are a horse fanatic, the county town of Kildare will entrance you with its National Stud and Horse Museum and its world-famous racing and training ground of the Curragh. But even if you do not care for horses, these characterful places will fascinate.

To the east is County Wicklow, where the rugged, heather-clad mountains—crossed by a fine network of footpaths—hide the beautiful old monastic settlement of Glendalough in their heart. Yet most visitors content themselves with Glendalough and never get out of the hills and down to the uncrowded coast.

Two rivers cross the rolling farmland of little County Carlow—the Barrow in the west and the Slaney in the east. To the west, County Kilkenny has the finest medieval town in Ireland as its capital. South is County Wexford, with its fine sandy coast and superb winter bird-watching on the marshes, as well as the old-style county town of Wexford, full of music, from traditional

NOT TO BE MISSED:

Admiring the beautiful racehorses at the Irish National Stud **92–95**

The monastic site of Glendalough in the Wicklow Mountains **98–100**

Wandering the streets of medieval Kilkenny town **108–112**

Dressing to the nines for a night at the Wexford Festival Opera **114**

Taking part in one of Ireland's popular walking festivals **121**

to opera, and Enniscorthy, with its stirring evocations of the Rising of 1798.

Farthest west are County Waterford, with its rugged cliffs and well-preserved old county town where they make the finest crystal glassware in Ireland, and inland Tipperary, whose ecclesiastical sites culminate in the wonderful assembly of churches, monastic houses, and round towers on the Rock of Cashel.

Area of map detail

Belfast

Dublin

CENTRAL IRELAND
p.233

M4

Maynooth

Carbury

Castletown House

M4 Lexlip

Celbridge

DUBLIN
p.47

Grand Canal

Bog of Allen

R403 Clane

Liffey

Irish National Stud,
Horse Museum, St. Fiachra's
Garden, & Japanese Garden

Russsborough
House

Enniskerry

Bray

Powerscourt

Powerscourt
Waterfall

Kilmacanoge

Naas

Kildare

M7

Newbridge

Blessington

Monasterevin

Kilcullen

The
Curragh

R413

Pollaphuca
Res.

Sally Gap

501m
Great
Sugar Loaf

R759

Grey-
stones

R761

Dan Donnelly
obelisk

N78

Hollywood

WICKLOW
MTS. N.P.

R756

Roundwood

Newtown Mt.
Kennedy

N9

KILDARE

N81

Wicklow Gap

R115

R755

Ashford

Glendalough

Devil's Glen

Vartry

Rathnew

Athy

R418

Barrow

Slaney

Laragh

Avonmore

Wicklow

R752

R750

Wicklow
Head

Baltinglass

Wicklow
Mountains

925m
Lugnaquilla

Rathdrum

Brittas
Bay

Mizen Head

Castledermot
high crosses

R418

WICKLOW

Ow

Avonbeg

Meeting of
the Waters

Vale of Avoca

Avoca

N11

Avoca
Handweavers'

Carlow

Graiguecullen

Browne's
Hill dolmen

Hackestown

R747

Arklow

CENTRAL IRELAND
p.233

Castlecomer

Tullow

CARLOW

R747

Kilmichael
Point

Ballyragget

M8

Freshford

Ballyfogle

Black
Castle

Leighlinbridge

Derry

Bunclody

Gorey

N11

Courtown

Urlingford

Dunmore
Cave

Ballymoon
Castle

N10

Bagenalstown

Slaney

Bann

R741

Cahore
Point

Nore

Kilkenny

Kells

Borris

793m
Mount
Leinster

Blackstairs Mts.

Borris House

R742

St. George's Channel

Callan

N75

KILKENNY

N9

Thomastown

Graiguenamanagh

Urrin

National 1798
Visitor Centre

Knocktopher

Kings

N10

Graiguenamanagh

St. Mullin's

Enniscorthy

Vinegar Hill

Fethard

Jerpoint
Abbey

Nore

WEXFORD

N11

Ahenny
high crosses

R697

N9

New Ross

N30

Irish National
Heritage Park

Wexford
Wildfowl
Reserve

Clonmel

Ormond
Castle

Mullinavat

N25

Wexford

Carrick-on-
Suir

Barrow

R734

Rosslare

WATERFORD

Waterford

Ballyhack

Wellingtonbridge

N25

Fishguard, Pembroke

St.

Waterford
Crystal

R731

Fethard

Rosslare
Harbour

Roscoff, Cherbourg

Kilmacthomas

Guillamene
Cove

Waterford

Waterford Harbour

Slade

Kilmore
Quay

Carnsore
Point

Madon

Tramore

Dunmore
East

Hook Head

SALTEE
ISLANDS

N25

N72

Dungarvan

Celtic   Sea

Ardmore
monastic site

Ardmore

Ram
Head

0   20 kilometers
0   10 miles

6

5

4

3

2

1

C   D   E   F

County Kildare

County Kildare holds a splendid variety of treasures: a fine cathedral in a friendly town, the Irish National Stud with its flawless Japanese garden and Horse Museum, and the Curragh—hundreds of acres of grassland to run wild. You'll see horses everywhere, because the Curragh is the home of Irish horse racing and a world-renowned bloodstock breeding center.

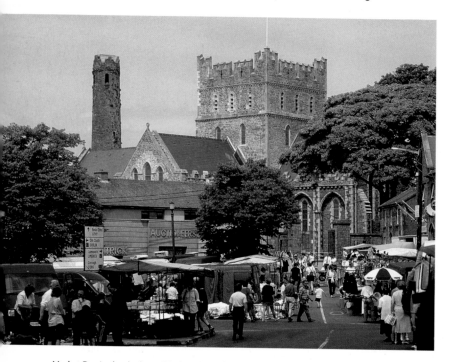

Market Day in the shadow of St. Brigid's Cathedra in the town of Kildare.

Kildare town

🏛 89 D5

Visitor Information

✉ The Square,
Kildare,
Co. Kildare

☎ 045 521240

Kildare Town

Kildare is a friendly little town with a storied history. Christianity—courtesy of St. Patrick—had been in Ireland for less than 60 years when, in 490, St. Brigid founded a mixed-sex monastery here on the wide plains of the Curragh (see p. 94), 30 miles (50 km) from Ireland's east coast.

St. Brigid's Cathedral: You can get an idea of what the Curragh must have looked like from the **scale model** of the walled settlement that stands in the present-day St. Brigid's Cathedral—thatched round wattle-and-daub huts for the monks and nuns, dining and kitchen buildings, and a big wooden church in the middle.

A handsome gray stone cathedral stands on the monastery site today. It dates from the 13th century, although it was heavily restored in 1875. Some

INSIDER TIP:

Try getting a bird's-
eye view from one of
Ireland's ecclesiastical
landmarks: the Round
Towers. St. Brigid's in
Kildare and St. Canice's
in Kilkenny [see p. 111]
are open for the public
to climb.

—TOM JACKSON
National Geographic Society

amusing modern gargoyles adorn
the corbel table—they include two
bespectacled men, one with a cow
across his shoulders, the other
clutching a pair of moneybags.

Along with the monastery
model in the south transept is the
fragmented but beautiful **tomb of
Bishop Walter Wellesley** (died
1539), with stone carvings that
include a very poignant figure
of Christ stripped for scourging,
sitting with hands bound, his head
bowed in sorrow and exhaustion.
Under the eaves of the tomb,
sharp-eyed explorers will spot a
sheela-na-gig dancing with her legs
lasciviously astraddle—and maybe a
similarly unabashed sister, too.

The guard/guide will show
you a so-called **pardon stone**
with a penitential prayer carved
on it. The carving also features a
rare depiction of two angels holding jars to catch streams of the
crucified Christ's blood.

The cathedral **font** is a tremendous piece of work, a crude
and plain upright stone rectangle
with a recessed top that might

have been created anytime over
the history of Christianity—and
possibly long before that.

Round Tower: Beside the
cathedral rears Kildare's impressive round tower (*tel 045 441
654*), 108 feet (33 m) tall, an
orange-gray finger of stone
now shaggy with innumerable
clumps of grass. Some date it
to the 10th century, some to
the 12th. The fine recessed
Romanesque doorway—unusu-
ally ornate for a round tower—
was set into the tower 15 feet
(5 m) above ground level to
secure it against Danish attack.
Inside, you ascend wooden

EXPERIENCE:
Riding Horses

Fancy a trot after a day at the races? The
Curragh may be the nerve center of Irish
racing and riding, but there are stables
open to the public throughout Ireland.

Stables around the Curragh include:
Kill International Equestrian Centre
*(Kill, Naas, Co. Kildare, tel 045 877 333 or
877 208, www.killinternational.ie)*; **Leinster
Lodge Equestrian Centre** *(Old Carton,
Maynooth, Co. Kildare, tel 087 912 0579,
www.leinsterlodgeequestriancentre.com)*;
Kildare International Equestrian Centre
*(Winterdown Stud Farm, Rathmore, Naas, Co.
Kildare, tel 085 727 8043, www.kildareinter
national.ie)*; **Osberstown Equestrian Cen-
tre** *(Enoville House, Osberstown, Co. Kildare,
tel 045 879 074)*; and **Littlehill Stables**
*(Boleybeg, Ballymore Eustace, Co. Kildare, tel
087 204 7911)*.

The **Association of Irish Riding Establishments** *(tel 045 850 800, www.aire.ie)*
maintains a list of hundreds of other registered riding stables across the country.

Castletown House

The finest country house in County Kildare is undoubtedly Castletown House *(at Celbridge off R403, www.castletownhouse. ie)*, built between 1722 and 1732 for William Conolly, Speaker of the Irish House of Commons, as a piece of Palladian splendor. The enormously long colonnaded facade is a breathtaking sight. Much of the interior—the hand-blown Venetian chandeliers in the pale blue Long Gallery, the elaborate stucco on the staircase walls—reflects the exuberant 18th-century

taste of Lady Louisa Lennox. Aged 15, she married Conolly's great-nephew, who inherited the estate, in 1758. More intimate are the black-and-white prints that Lady Louisa herself selected and pasted on the wall of the Print Room. The follies in the park—the piled domes and curly exterior staircase of the Wonderful Barn and the 140-foot (40 m) obelisk on tiers of arches that commemorates William Conolly—were the contribution of Conolly's wife, Katherine.

Irish National Stud, Japanese Garden, St. Fiachra's Garden, & Irish Horse Museum

🗺 89 D5

✉ Tully, 1 mile (1.6 km) E of Kildare, Co. Kildare

☎ 045 522963/ 521617

🕓 Closed mid-Nov.– mid-Feb.

💲 $$$

www.irish-national-stud.ie

ladders (103 steep steps, so not for the unfit) to reach the tower's **original cap,** a shallow ribbed cone inside inauthentic 19th-century battlements. The view is tremendous, 30 miles (48 km) across the plain of the Curragh and north over the vast Bog of Allen.

If you find the cathedral and the round tower closed during the lunch hour *(1–2 p.m.),* a great place to sit it out is **Top Nolan's** *(tel 045 522241, www. topnolans.com),* a pub established in 1870 near the churchyard gates. Ancient wooden shelves behind the bar sag under their freight of vintage Guinness bottles and rolls of long-deleted brands of toilet paper, as if some past landlord had stocked up against nuclear war—a peculiarly Irish view of how to survive the apocalypse.

Irish National Stud

In 1900, Col. William Hall-Walker selected the village of Tully, a mile (1.6 km) east of Kildare, as the ideal place to start a stud farm—mainly

because of the high levels of calcium carbonate (good for bone strength) in the waters of the River Tully and in the Curragh grass. Colonel Hall-Walker was phenomenally successful, so much so that when he gave the stud to the British Crown in 1915, he was created Lord Wavertree for his generosity with such a valuable asset.

A guided tour around the Irish National Stud (state property since 1943) makes for a fascinating hour, even for non-horse-lovers. Among the attractions are the **Foaling Unit,** with its intensive care stable, and the **Stallion Yard,** with ten roomy boxes for the stallions whose fertility is the real business of the National Stud (covering fees can top $500,000 for a single impregnation). Mating takes place in the **Covering Shed.** The **Oak and Tully Walks** pass the railed paddocks where the beautiful creatures graze contentedly—mares and foals in small groups, the naturally aggressive stallions with a private paddock each.

Along the way, you learn plenty: that the Irish National Stud offers its breeding service to small-scale breeders at special cut-rate prices; that 90 percent of foals are born at night; that stallions work hard during the January to June breeding season, covering four mares a day (and being photographed while in action to prove paternity), six days a week. You'll also become acquainted with Colonel Hall-Walker's notions about astrology—he designed the stallions' stalls with special skylight roofs so that the moon and stars

could infiltrate their beneficial influences, and he ordered all foals with inauspicious birth horoscopes to be sold, no matter how successful their bloodline.

The Gardens: Between 1906 and 1910, Colonel Hall-Walker engaged one of Japan's top gardeners, Tassa Eida, to lay out a **Japanese Garden** to reflect a "Journey through Life." From the Stallion Yard, you enter the garden by way of the Gate of Oblivion and make your way along the narrow Path of Life

Bog of Allen
89 D5

EXPERIENCE: Bog of Allen Nature Centre

The peat bogs of Ireland are unique, both in their iconic status within Ireland and in the way they have been industrially exploited. Learn all about these treasured resources at the Bog of Allen Nature Centre in Lullymore, about 12 miles (19 km) northwest of Kildare.

The Bog of Allen, Ireland's largest expanse of raised bog, spills over the borders of nine midland counties and covers an area of nearly 285,000 acres (115,000 ha). Like many boglands across the country, harvesting and development have wreaked havoc on its fragile ecosystem. The most devastating effects were felt in the last 50 years, when mechanized harvesting allowed for the swift destruction of mile after mile of bogland in order to feed power stations, agribusinesses, and urban consumers. Today, less than 10 percent of the bog remains unspoiled.

With the aim of returning the bog to wetland wilderness and preserving it for the enjoyment of future generations, the Irish Peatland Conservation Council (IPCC)—a national charity that campaigns for the conservation of the country's peat bogs—established the **Bog of Allen Nature Centre** (Lullymore, Rathangan, Co. Kildare, tel 045 860 133, www.ipcc.ie/BOAorientation.html) in 2003.

Visitors to the center learn all about the delicately balanced ecosystems of these fascinating and fragile places. The insects that feed on the bog plants, for example, are themselves fed on by

insectivorous plants, other insects, and small songbirds that in turn provide nourishment for larger birds, namely raptors. Frogs, otters, badgers, and red deer, wallowing away their parasites, also live in the bog, as have centuries of humans. Remarkable archaeological finds include ancient tools, wooden boats, leather shoes, and even preserved human bodies.

The IPCC—which conducts nature surveys of the area—runs bog trips, family nature days, and conservation work camps so that you can experience the bog in a hands-on way and contribute personally to its preservation.

Horses & the Curragh

What is it with the Irish and horses? Set up a horse race anywhere in the world and there'll be an Irish interest, and presence, more knowledgeable and intense than that of any other nation.

Horses thunder down the final stretch—another exciting day at the races!

Sales of Irish Thoroughbred horses in Ireland alone approach 160 million dollars annually, and hundreds of millions more change hands each year in covering fees at Irish studs. Attendance at classic horse races swells year by year, while down at the other end of the scale you'll find ragged men with rusty old trotting rigs competing on country roads while onlookers bet as if money and common sense were going out of style.

The origins of good relations between the Irish and horses go back into pre-Christian times, with evidence that horses had been domesticated—perhaps for the table as much as for transport—as far back as 2000 B.C.

Steeplechasing had its origins in north County Cork in 1752, when Lord Doneraile staged a 4.5-mile (7 km) race between the two church steeples of Buttevant and St. Leger. By

the mid-19th century, there were nearly 30 flourishing racetracks in this small and poor country. Today, Irish men and women from all walks of life are as bound up as ever with the fortunes of horses, and Ireland still has the same number of racetracks.

Little of the elitism generally associated with racing obtains in Ireland—top hats mingle with cloth caps, morning coats with greasy anoraks, at meetings as prestigious as the Irish Derby or the 1,000 and 2,000 Guineas. These three premier races all take place at Ireland's best known racetrack, the Curragh (*cuirrech*, in Gaelic, means a racecourse), just outside Kildare. The track is iconic among race-goers, and the broader expanse of the Curragh proper—6,000 acres (2,400 ha) of unfenced, gently rolling grassland around Kildare town—is the very heartland of Irish racing.

through gorgeous flower banks and trees, both dwarf and full size. There are childhood's Tunnel of Ignorance, the Bridge of Engagement (broken in the middle!) and Bridge of Marriage, the mazelike Hill of Ambition, and the scarlet Bridge of Life to negotiate before you walk the smooth lawns of the Garden of Peace and Contentment in old age.

A recent addition to the attractions at the Irish National Stud is **St. Fiachra's Garden,** opened in 1999 by President Mary McAleese. In its way, this is as artificial as the Japanese Garden, with mock-ups of hermit huts and a "drowned forest" of imported bog oak. It lacks the subtlety of its senior cousin, but it still makes a pleasant stroll under silver birch and conifers.

INSIDER TIP:

On a sunny day, the Japanese Garden outside Kildare town is a beautiful setting for a stroll. For horse lovers, the National Stud is on the same grounds.

—SUSAN JOHNSTON
National Geographic field researcher

The Irish Horse Museum:

There is also the Irish Horse Museum to enjoy—the prize attraction here is the large but fragile preserved skeleton of Arkle, Ireland's great steeplechaser of the 1960s, a rather bizarre but impressive item. Other exhibits include ancient

Dan Donnelly, the Curragh Bruiser

In a hollow on the south side of the R413 road, 3 miles (5 km) west of Kilcullen, stands a railed obelisk. It commemorates a bare-knuckle fight that took place in 1815 between Curragh-trained Dan Donnelly and the "famous English pugilist" George Cooper. Donnelly won, after a tremendous battle. In 1818, after another victory, he was dubbed "Sir Dan" by the Prince Regent. Less than two years later, Donnelly died, penniless. His body was exhumed and sold to a surgeon, who preserved the fighter's phenomenally long right arm.

pieces of horse equipment, a portrait of Colonel Hall-Walker with stiffly upswept moustache alongside one of his horse horoscope books for 1914, an enjoyable gallop through the history of the horse, and an entertaining account of the "pounding matches" of the 18th and 19th centuries. These challenges between country gentlemen—proxy dueling, in fact—involved each man in turn choosing a difficult or dangerous obstacle to jump, the other contestant being obliged to follow on behind. Needless to say, much money was wagered and many necks broken in pursuit of such macho honor and glory. ■

County Wicklow

If you have been exploring Dublin, you will almost certainly have seen the Wicklow Mountains already, rising enticingly in tall blue humps right on the southern doorstep of the capital. Inevitably, the mountains see a lot of visitors; they are Dublin's country playground, after all, being less than half an hour's drive from the south of the city.

A hiker contemplates the day's route as she looks toward the high peaks of the Wicklow Mountains.

Wicklow Mountains
 89 E4

Wicklow Mountains

Most day-trippers make for only a handful of Wicklow destinations, the "must-see" sites: either the beautifully located monastic site of Glendalough, the picturesque village of Avoca with its photogenic handloom weavers, or the two great Anglo-Irish houses of Russborough and Powerscourt with their stunning gardens.

Once clear of them, however, you will find great tracts of upland and hillside, valley and coast, where you'll have only the birds—and maybe the occasional hiker or two—for company.

Getting There: There are several ways to drive into the Wicklow Mountains from Dublin, all of them increasingly beautiful the farther into the hills you go, all becoming steeper, slower, and more twisty. This is definitely not country for speed demons. The main coast road to Wexford, the N11, skirts the Wicklow Mountains on the east. Side roads from the N11 include the R755 from Kilmacanoge, under Great

INSIDER TIP:

The Wicklow Way's [see sidebar below] picture-perfect waterfalls and scenic views are perfect for both Sunday walkers as well as seasoned hikers venturing farther out.

—CHIARA CECCHINI
National Geographic contributor

Sugar Loaf, and the R765 from Newtown Mount Kennedy—these both reach Roundwood on the shore of Vartry Reservoir.

Another beautiful way into the hills is via the R763 from Ashford near Wicklow town, which goes west to Laragh and Glendalough. Three miles (5 km) west of Ashford you can take a narrow side road on the right that leads to the entrance to the **Devil's Glen,** a spectacularly rugged cleft threaded by a footpath from which you can see the Vartry River tumble 100 feet (30 m) into the agitated pool called the Devil's Punchbowl.

Alternatively, you could take the R115 from central Dublin through Rathfarnham and up over the wild **Sally Gap pass;** here the road divides, with the R759 swinging off to the left and down to Roundwood, while the R115 wriggles on down to Laragh and Glendalough. Or you could start out southwest from Dublin on the A81 Baltinglass road and follow it down to Hollywood, where the R756 cuts off eastward to Laragh over the **Wicklow Gap** in superb hill-country scenery of bare, heathery moorland rising to mountain ridges and peaks.

A lovely alternative to this last route is to leave the A81 at **Blessington,** 5 miles (8 km) north of Hollywood, and make your way on a minor road over narrow bridges and around the north

EXPERIENCE: Walking in the Wicklow Mountains

The Wicklow Mountains are wonderful country for hill walking. The usual precautions about keeping an eye on the weather and taking proper hiking gear and a good map need to be observed. They may look small in comparison with other mountain ranges—Lugnaquilla, the highest, reaches only 3,038 feet (927 m)—but the Wicklow Mountains and their notoriously changeable weather should be treated with proper respect. The **Wicklow Way** (www.wicklowway.com) is well marked, and any number of paths cross and climb the mountains.

Hill Walkers Wicklow by David Herman (Shanksmare Publications) is widely available locally; it details 30 full-day walks in the area (wear good walking boots). Irish Ordnance Survey 1:50,000 sheets 56 and 62 (available at www.osi.ie) also cover the mountains. The **Wicklow Mountains National Park** information point between Glendalough's Upper and Lower Lakes *(closed Oct.–May)* has details of walks, or you can get books and maps from the visitor information offices at Glendalough *(tel 0404 45325, see p. 98),* Wicklow town *(tel 0404 69117),* or Arklow *(tel 0402 32484).*

Glendalough

St. Mary's Church

⛰ 89 E5

💲 $

Visitor Information

✉ Entrance to
Glendalough,
Bray, Co.
Wicklow

☎ 0404 45325

shore of the Pollaphuca
Reservoir to join the R758,
then the R756.

Glendalough

Whichever route you choose,
all roads in the Wicklow Mountains seem to lead inevitably to
Glendalough. This remarkable
monastic site, tucked down in
its lake valley among steep
mountainsides, well repays half
a day's exploration. St. Kevin, its
patron saint and lodestar, was
an awkward young monk of the
early sixth century, so embar-
rassed at his unwanted fame as
a miracle worker that he gave
up monastic life to live in a
hollow tree in the utter seclusion
of Glendalough, the Valley of
the Two Lakes.

In 570, Kevin became abbot
of the slowly growing monastic
community in the valley, which
had consolidated into a sizable
fraternity by the time he died,
about 617. The lonely valley was
not immune from outside attack,
however; the community was
plundered by Danes in 922 and
again by Norman adventurers
in 1176, but as a counterbalance there was a great period of
rebuilding under Abbot Lorcan

Round Tower or
Bell Tower

St. Kevin's Cross

The Cathedral

Gateway

The Priest's House

St. Kevin's Kitchen
(Church)

St. Kieran's
Church

**Glendalough monastic site,
reconstructed in the 12th century**

O'Tuathail (St. Laurence O'Toole, 1128–1180). In 1398, a party of English soldiers razed the monastery, but the church continued in use. By then, pilgrimages to Glendalough, attracted by St. Kevin's piety, had become a fixture. Similar pilgrimages continue to this day.

It is not just the beautiful enclosed setting that makes Glendalough so special; equally remarkable are the number and density of the monastery's dozen or more 10th-, 11th-, and 12th-century buildings. A well-marked footpath leads through a sturdy granite double arch—the only surviving monastic gateway in Ireland, with a big sanctuary cross just inside—and runs around the riverside site. Here you will find

Avoca Weavers

The village of Avoca, a scenic hamlet of whitewashed houses under slate roofs with wooded hills rising at its back, lies a mile (1.6 km) or so downstream from the Meeting of the Waters. Located on the banks of the River Avoca, the old mill here—the oldest still operating in Ireland—has been working since 1723. Inside you can see weavers clacking and shuttling away at their rattly hand-looms, though these days the mill also relies on power looms to keep up with demand. The mill shop (Millmount Mills, Avoca Village, Co. Wicklow, tel 0402 35105, www.avoca.ie) **offers a good variety of rugs, blankets, and throws in natural fibers such as lamb's wool, cotton, mohair, and linen. You will also find a selection of gloves and scarves, as well as a line of tweed clothing for women.**

INSIDER TIP:

Brittas Bay is a fantastic golden beach with impressive dunes (great for hide-and-seek!), but avoid visiting on the last weekend in August when Dubliners descend on it in droves.

—ALLY THOMPSON
National Geographic contributor

St. Kevin's Kitchen, a cramped little oratory that might perhaps date as far back as the time of St. Kevin, with a round 11th-century belfry. Nearby, among the remains of other buildings and a forest of graveslabs, are the shell of a ninth- or tenth-century cathedral, a 12th-century priest's house whose east wall contains a fine dogtooth arch, and a splendid tapering rocket of a tenth-century round tower, built 110 feet (33 m) high to give the Glendalough monks a good lookout, its stairless door some 12 feet (3.5 m) above the ground to keep besiegers at bay.

Toward the Coast

From Glendalough's neighboring village of Laragh, take the R755 to Rathdrum, the snaky road threading its way through the lovely tree-lined Vale of Clara. Then continue south on the R752, stopping 4 miles (6 km) south of Rathdrum to enjoy the spectacle of the confluence of the Avonbeg and Avonmore Rivers, an often crowded beauty spot known as the **Meeting of the Waters.**

EXPERIENCE: Staying on a Working Farm

If you want to experience the rhythms of life outside the city, consider spending a night or two on a working farm deep in the beautiful Irish countryside. Greet the dawn without an orchestra of cars, and breathe in the hay-scented air rather than traffic fumes and cigarette smoke.

Just across Dublin's southern doorstep sits the hilly county of Wicklow, temptingly near the capital but emphatically not spoiled by the close relationship. Leaving Dublin, travel south past the mountains of northern Wicklow to reach the region of south Wicklow around the village of Tinahely. There is great walking here, beautiful hilly country on the skyline, and best of all, **Kyle Farmhouse** (Tinahely, Co. Wicklow, tel 059 647 1341, www.kylefarm.com), a working sheep and

dairy outfit run by the extremely hospitable Margaret and Hugh Coogan. Help milk the cattle or gather the sheep, go for a country walk under Hugh's guidance, or just relax with a nice cup of tea and a plate of Margaret's great home baking.

Elsewhere, **Waterford Farm Accommodation** (www.waterfordfarms.com) lists a dozen working farms in County Waterford that offer a wide variety of experiences, from dairying to horses and sheep. Or try Northern Ireland's **Heathfield Farm** (Coleraine, Co. Derry, tel 028 2955 8245, www.heathfieldfarm.com), an award-winning beef and sheep farm, very convenient for County Antrim's Causeway Coast.

Search for other farm opportunities online at www.irishfarmhouses.com and www.irishfarmholidays.com.

From the town of Avoca (see sidebar opposite), the R752 and R747 lead southeast down the Vale of Avoca to Arklow, a quiet little town situated on the Wicklow coast.

The coast of County Wicklow stretches north for 40 miles (64 km) from Kilmichael Point, a few miles below Arklow, to the jaded but enjoyable seaside resort of **Bray,** just south of Dublin. Generally overlooked by visitors in favor of the mountains, this is a coast for connoisseurs of moody, lonely shores and seascapes.

The old R750 road along the coast from Arklow to Wicklow town, followed by the R761 a mile or so (1.6 km) inland all the way up to Bray, has long been superseded by the fast N11, but offers a largely traffic-free saunter up the coast for those in no hurry.

Mizen Head and **Wicklow Head** are two fine promontories, and the harbor town of **Wicklow** makes a good place to stop for a cup of tea. As for the beaches, they are mostly sandy as far as Wicklow, with **Brittas Bay** the pick of them, and mostly pebbly from there on up. Any side road to the right from the R761 will land you after a more or less potholed mile (1.6 km) on the low cliffs of the northern Wicklow coast, the perfect place to gaze at the sea and daydream with not another soul to bother you. St. Kevin himself could not have asked for more.

Russborough & Powerscourt

Two tremendous Palladian houses flank the northern Wicklow Mountains: Powerscourt
(continued on p. 104)

Walk: Glendalough & the Glenealo Valley

This is an easy, level walk among the remains of monastic and mining activity in Glendalough, with an upward climb into the upper Glenealo Valley. The first part of the walk is very popular. To avoid crowds, set off in early morning or wait until late afternoon.

St. Kevin's Kitchen could date back to the time of St. Kevin, in the early sixth century A.D.

Before you start, make sure that you look around the excellent display on St. Kevin and the Glendalough monastery in the **visitor center ❶** *(tel 0404 45325)*. From the visitor center parking lot, cross the river by a footbridge and turn right along the track. In about 300 yards (300 m), recross the river to view **St. Kevin's Kitchen ❷**, the **round tower ❸**, and the other features of the main monastic site (see pp. 98–100).

Return across the river, where "Green Road to Upper Lake" signs guide you along the south side of the **Lower Lake ❹**. Walk for 1 mile (1.6 km), admiring the mountainside and white

NOT TO BE MISSED:

Visitor center display • St. Kevin's Kitchen • Round tower • Kevin's Bed View • View down Glenealo Valley from waterfall above the old mine workings

houses reflected in the lake, until you reach the ground between the Lower and Upper Lakes.

Just past the **Pollanass Waterfall ❺**, where the track swings right to cross between

INSIDER TIP:

Lose yourself in the mists of time with a stroll at dawn through Glendalough—the "glen of the two lakes"—site of a medieval monastic settlement.

—JUSTIN KAVANAGH
National Geographic International Editions

the lakes, continue to the **Reefert Church** ❻ ruins among weathered crosses and gravestones. Just beyond here, well signposted, is the semicircle of stones on a little promontory that marks the site of **St. Kevin's Cell** ❼. Return to cross between the lakes and bear left on a path between tall pine and larch trees along the north shore of the **Upper Lake** ❽. A sign, "Kevin's Bed View," leads to a viewpoint that looks across the lake to the tiny square black mouth of a partly man-made cave known as **St. Kevin's Bed** ❾.

Continue beyond the lake end, through the ruined buildings and spoil heaps of 19th-century **lead-mine workings** ❿.

You can retrace your steps from here back to the visitor center, but if you have water-proof footwear and sufficient energy, continue

Saintly Slayer

St. Kevin, good with wildlife, was hopeless with women. When an over zealous female follower came too close, the pious saint stung her cheeks with nettles to warn her off. Another story (probably a Victorian invention) tells how St. Kevin, meditating in the coffinlike cave (now called St. Kevin's Bed) above the Upper Lake, fell asleep and dreamed that one of his female acolytes, Kathleen, was standing between him and the Gates of Heaven. Waking to find Kathleen bending over him, and taking her to be a temptress sent by the devil, he plunged her in the lake and drowned her.

forward to reach the zigzag track up beside the **waterfalls** ⓫ of the Glenealo River. The path leads to a memorable view back over the Upper Lake.

🅰 See area map p. 89 E5
▶ Glendalough visitor center
↔ 6 miles (10 km)
🕐 Allow 3 hours
▶ Glendalough visitor center

Russborough House

A 89 E5

✉ Blessington,
Co. Wicklow

☎ 045 865239

🕐 Open daily,
May–Sept.; Sun.,
April & Oct.

$ $$$

www.russborough.ie

near Bray to the east and Russborough near Blessington on the west. Built in the mid-18th century, they trumpet the wealth and power of the Anglo-Irish gentry of British origins who owned great tracts of Ireland. Some were absentee landowners who rarely set foot in Ireland. Others lived on their Irish estates and would move mountains—literally, in some cases—to get the landscape effects they wanted. The interiors of the grandest Anglo-Irish houses, too, reflected what money, sophisticated taste, and influence could achieve.

Powerscourt House, never as grand as Russborough, was burned out in a fire in 1974, while Russborough's grounds were always intended to be wild and green rather than meticulously organized, so it is the house at Russborough and the gardens and grounds at Powerscourt that are the main attractions today.

Russborough House:

Russborough was built in the 1740s for Joseph Leeson, Earl of Milltown and heir to a brewery fortune. He spent his money on creating one of the most impressive-looking houses in Ireland. Its immense **facade,** 900 feet (275 m) long, is topped with heraldic lions and features a twin sweep of curving colonnades.

Inside, all eyes turn to the richly unrestrained plasterwork. Italian brothers Philip and Paul Francini, the leading exponents of plaster ornamentation at the time, were commissioned to do the work

The upper terrace at Powerscourt House overlooks the formal gardens and the sunken Triton Lake.

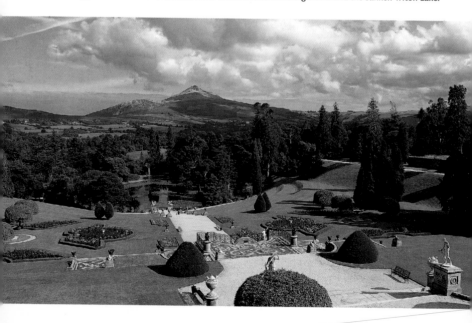

and filled the house with intricate floral sprays, swags, fruit, faces, and foliage. Another artist, less delicate but more fantastical, created the hounds enmeshed in sprays and flowers who career up the main staircase.

The house contains an astonishing **art collection**—Vermeer, Rubens, Goya, Velazquez, Thomas Gainsborough, Hans Hals. Sir Alfred Beit, cofounder of the De Beers diamond mining empire, initially put it together. The Beit collection has suffered two high-profile robberies: in 1974, 16 paintings stolen to raise funds for the IRA were quickly recovered; in 1986, several pictures were removed and have not yet been retrieved.

Powerscourt: The glory of Powerscourt is its setting, best seen from the uppermost of the five terraces that drop away to the **Triton Lake** and its 100-foot (30 m) fountain in the valley below. From here you look out over the lake, cradled in tall trees, to the peak of the 1,643-foot (501 m) **Great Sugar Loaf** 2.5 miles (4 km) away across a patchwork of farmland. The "wildness" of this prospect only enhances the artistry of the 50 acres (20 ha) of gardens.

The steeply sloping terraces were designed in the 1840s by Daniel Robertson, a martyr to gout who stimulated his genius with copious drafts of sherry while being trundled from one vantage point to the next in a wheelbarrow. Walking down the terraces between formal gardens, you pass a superb mosaic pavement featuring the planets, created with colored pebbles and enclosed by elaborate cast-iron screens. Beautiful Austrian cast-iron work appears beyond the upper terrace, too, in the 18th-century Bamberg Gate. The peaceful, terraced **Japanese Garden**, screened from the Triton Lake by bamboos and shapely conifers, contains delicate temples and bridges.

INSIDER TIP:

The gardens at Powerscourt make a wonderul stop between Dublin and Glendalough. The Japanese Garden with its picturesque foot-bridge is a favorite.

—ROZ HOAGLAND
Private guide, Hoagland Art Travel

After all this artifice, a visit to the **Powerscourt Waterfall,** a signposted 3.5-mile (6 km) walk or 3-mile (5 km) drive from the gardens, is refreshing. At 425 feet (130 m), this is the highest waterfall in Ireland—although "the longest" might be more accurate, as the River Dargle tumbles from one ferny rock face to the next. This is a great place to picnic, especially on a sunny afternoon, a day or so after heavy rain, when the fall is at its most spectacular. ∎

Powerscourt

◪ 89 E5
✉ Powerscourt Estate, Enniskerry, Co. Wicklow
☎ 01 204 6000
$ $$$
www.powerscourt.ie

County Carlow

Tiny County Carlow is landlocked and surrounded on all sides by more glamorous counties—horse-mad Kildare, Kilkenny with the finest medieval town in Ireland, Wicklow and its mountains, and Wexford's sandy coast and superb bird-watching. Carlow tends to be overlooked. Yet there's plenty in this easygoing agricultural county to please you, if you are content to wander at a slow pace and listen to some fairly elastic local tales.

The capstone of Browne's dolmen stands propped precariously on its supporting stones.

Carlow town

🗺 89 D4

Visitor Information

✉ Tullow St.,
   Carlow,
   Co. Carlow

☎ 059 913 1554

www.carlowtown
.com

Carlow Town

The town of Carlow, up near the county's northwest border, was for centuries a frontier town between the Norman English of the Pale (the defended area of British influence around Dublin; see p. 26) and the troublesome Irish "beyond the Pale."

From certain viewpoints, Carlow's sturdy 13th-century stone castle still looks impregnable. However, closer inspection reveals a solitary castellated wall suspended between two towers, all that was left after a local doctor blew it up in 1814. He was trying to reduce the thickness of the walls, with the intention of turning the place into a refuge for psychiatric patients.

Carlow also boasts a handsome **courthouse** from 1828–1830. Small wonder if the Ionic columns of the portico look as if they should be gracing some Greek temple—they are modeled on the Parthenon.

On May 25, 1798, about 640 "Croppy," or Catholic, rebels supporting the United Irishmen's rebellion were massacred on Tullow Street. Their mass grave (the Croppy Grave), marked by a Celtic cross, lies across the River Barrow at **Graiguecullen.**

Father John Murphy, a priest who led a contingent of the rebels, was hanged in the market square at **Tullow**, 9 miles (14 km) east of Carlow; a memorial commemorates him there.

Near Carlow

Two miles (3 km) east of Carlow, **Browne's Hill dolmen** is signed from the Hacketstown road. This is a wonderful site, the 4,500-year-old burial place of some leader important enough to have his tomb sealed with a capstone that weighs many tons. The weathered capstone lies propped on three of its original curbstones.

The threat of unrest and even insurrection in this frontier region led to the building of several castles in County Carlow. You can find the ruins of the 12th-century **Black Castle** at Leighlinbridge, in the lovely valley of the River Barrow, and, near Bagenalstown, the ruggedly massive ruins of **Ballymoon Castle**. Later, when things became quieter in County Carlow, symmetrical plantation villages were built, each with its dominating "Big House."

The Blackstairs Mountains

County Carlow tapers southward from Borris toward the rolling heights of the **Blackstairs Mountains**. These bleakly beautiful hills, straddling the border country between Carlow and Wexford, rise to the 2,600-foot (793 m) peak of Mount Leinster. A great way to enjoy the Blackstairs is to stroll along the well-marked **South Leinster Way,** a long-distance footpath that skirts Mount Leinster on its way northeast to link up with the Wicklow Way.

The River Barrow forms all but a snippet of the western boundary of County Carlow. There is great coarse fishing (fishing for any freshwater fish other than salmon or trout) and good towpath walking along the **Barrow Way.**

Everything leads more or less southward to **St. Mullin's,** 3 miles (5 km) north of the Wexford/ Kilkenny border, where remnants of a monastery founded in the late seventh century lie around the village's present-day church. ∎

Ballymoon Castle
🔼 89 D4

Borris House
🔼 89 D3
www.borrishouse.com

Borris House

Borris House, near the Blackstairs Mountains of County Carlow, is an impressive manor house dating from the late 18th century. Its owner in Victorian days, Arthur MacMurrough Davanagh (1831–1889), was a determined and courageous man. Born with only stumps of arms and legs, he nevertheless succeeded in becoming not only an excellent shot and horseman but also a career politician—quite a feat for someone with such handicaps in mid-19th-century Ireland. The house can be visited by appointment in groups of ten or more.

Kilkenny Town & Around

County Kilkenny lies to the west of County Carlow, with its county town, Kilkenny—by far the most complete medieval city in Ireland—at its heart. This is a small-scale town, a place with character stamped on its old buildings and narrow lanes.

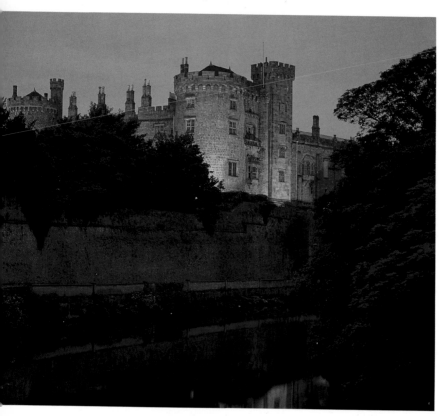

Kilkenny Castle occupies a site that's both strategically superb and scenically outstanding.

Kilkenny Castle

✉ The Parade,
Kilkenny,
Co. Kilkenny

☎ 056 772 1450

$ $$

Kilkenny Castle

Set on the west bank of the River Nore, Kilkenny town lies between its two chief landmarks, the castle and the cathedral. Most visitors make straight for Kilkenny Castle, dominant on its bend of the river. This three-sided fortress (Oliver Cromwell's men knocked down the fourth in the 1650s) is built of local gray limestone, with castellated battlements and drum towers at the corners. Richard de Clare, the Norman baron better known as Strongbow, first built a wooden fort on this site in 1172 to guard the river crossing; his son-in-law, William le Mareschal, built the stone castle.

When the Butler family, Earls of Ormond, bought the castle and the lordship of Kilkenny in 1392, the city was already an important place, a fortified stronghold where parliaments were held. The parliament of 1366–1367 passed the famous Statutes of Kilkenny, aimed at keeping the Anglo-Norman heritage free from taint by the Irish. Their prohibitions on marrying Irish partners, speaking Irish, or playing Irish games or music were honored more in the breach than the observance.

The Butlers lived in Kilkenny Castle for nearly 600 years, suffering all the vicissitudes of fortune that flowed from being stubbornly loyal to the royal house of Stuart. They lost wealth and influence by backing the deposed king, James Stuart, in his defeat at the Battle of the Boyne in 1690, and when the second Duke of Ormond supported a Stuart-inspired plan in 1714 to invade England with Spanish troops, he was attainted for treason and lost his earldom. It took the rest of the 18th century for royal memories to fade sufficiently to allow the Butlers to resume their ancient title.

A tour around the castle takes in the Victorian library and drawing room, the bedrooms with their hand-painted wallpaper and beautiful Georgian furniture, and the showpiece **Long Gallery.** Here, Butler portraits frown down darkly below a delicately carved 19th-century hammerbeam roof (braced with arches), painted with trails of foliage in pre-Raphaelite style and furnished with a central skylight to admit the daylight.

Outside there are terraces, gardens, and walks by the river and through woodland.

Across the road from the castle entrance are the handsome 18th-century stables that now house the **Kilkenny Design Centre** (tel 056 22118), a showcase for good modern design in textiles, jewelry, furniture, and ceramics.

INSIDER TIP:

Every summer, Kilkenny hosts the Carlsberg Cat Laughs Comedy Festival (www.carlsbergcatlaughs.com), featuring many of Ireland's top comics.

—STEPHANIE ROBICHAUX
National Geographic contributor

Kilkenny Town

From the castle, cross the top of Rose Inn Street to enter **High Street,** the first part of a crooked old road that changes its name to Parliament Street and then Irishtown as it runs north through the heart of the city. On the right, you'll see the **Tholsel,** or toll stall, with its octagonal clock tower and round-arched arcade projecting into the roadway. It was built in 1761 as an office where traders and others could pay dues and tolls, and it is still in use as the offices of Kilkenny's city council. The Tholsel is only one of Kilkenny's many medieval buildings, rare survivals in Ireland.

Follow the narrow "slips"

Kilkenny Town
89 C3
Visitor Information
Shee Alms House, Rose Inn St., Kilkenny, Co. Kilkenny
056 775 1500
www.kilkenny tourism.ie

Rothe House Museum

✉ Parliament St., Kilkenny, Co. Kilkenny

☎ 056 772 2893

$ $

or alleyways, some of them so steep they require steps, to seek out these remnants of historic Kilkenny, from humble cottages to churches and merchants' houses. The one with the best story attached is the 13th-century **Kyteler's Inn** (tel 056 772 1064) on St. Kieran's Street, which runs in from the right to join High Street at its juncture with Parliament Street. It was in this house that Alice Kyteler, the famed

---

EXPERIENCE:
The Many Sides of Kilkenny Castle

Kilkenny Castle is not just a superb historic building, it's also the focus of dozens of events, exhibitions, concerts, and art displays throughout the year. Take a look at the castle's events calendar (www .kilkennycastle.ie/en/NewsEvents), and plan your visit to take in a food market or a gourmet feast in the Great Hall. Lovers of veteran and classic cars will adore Kilkenny Motor Club's rallies; or you could slow things down with a horse and carriage ride around the grounds. Music fans are offered concerts ranging from music in the gardens to operas; there are family-friendly "Prams & Proms" events, and family treasure hunts, too.

Witch of Kilkenny, was born. Alice was charged with being a witch in 1324 after she had been overheard offering peacocks' eyes and nine red cocks to her familiar, a sprite named Robin Artysson whom she would meet at the crossroads. She was also reported to have gone through the streets of the city at night with her

broom, sweeping the dirt toward her son's house while chanting: "To the house of William, my son, Lie all the wealth of Kilkenny town." Dame Alice was convicted, but pardoned. Sentenced to death after reoffending, she escaped and left her unfortunate maidservant Petronella to be burned at the stake as a substitute. The Tholsel was later built on the place of execution on High Street.

Farther along Parliament Street are two notable medieval buildings. On the west side is **Rothe House Museum,** another arcaded building with a tall central gable, linked by tiny courtyards to two other houses. Built in the 1590s as a rich merchant's dwelling, the whole complex operates these days as a museum of Kilkenny history.

On the east stands **Grace's Castle,** built as a fortified tower in 1210, a prison since Tudor times and a courthouse from the late 18th century to the present day. United Irishmen, supporters of the failed Rising of 1798, were executed here.

Like every prosperous medieval city, Kilkenny had several monastic houses. Along Abbey Street (running west from Parliament Street) you'll find the well-restored church of the 13th-century **Black Abbey,** with some beautiful medieval glass.

Toward its northern end, Parliament Street becomes Irishtown. In Norman times, the native Irish were confined to this ghetto outside the city walls, an area already sacred to them because of its holy well dedicated to St. Kenny or Canice, the founder of

Kilkenny's first monastery in the sixth century.

St. Canice's Cathedral: On a rise of ground at the top of Irishtown you'll see the squat bulk of St. Canice's Cathedral *(tel 056 776 4971),* built in the 1250s on the site of St. Canice's monastery. It's a massive building, its central tower pulled down low into the roofs like a square head tucked into hunched shoulders.

Beside the cathedral rises a slender 101-foot-high (31 m) **round tower,** built by the monks some time between 700 and 1000. You can climb its wooden ladders (weather permitting; $) to enjoy a stunning panorama over Kilkenny town.

When Oliver Cromwell's troops captured the city in 1650, they used the cathedral as a stable, broke the font while letting their horses drink out of it, shot guns into the roof, and smashed stained-glass windows and other furnishings. Despite this, most of the church's glories survived, including its wonderful collection of carved memorial slabs and effigies in the shiny local limestone known as Kilkenny Marble.

The tombs of the ruling Butler family in the south transept are wonderful examples of the carver's art, particularly the smiling effigies of Piers Butler, Earl of Ormond and Ossory (died 1539), in his domed helmet and elaborate breastplate, and his wife, Margaret Fitzgerald, with billowing

The thick stone walls of Rothe House guard treasures of antique furniture and fine paintings.

Dunmore Cave

⚠ 89 C4

✉ Ballyfoyle,
Co. Kilkenny

☎ 056 776 7726

💲 $

**www.heritage
ireland.ie**

Jerpoint Abbey

⚠ 89 D3

✉ Thomastown,
Co. Kilkenny

☎ 056 772 4623

🕐 Closed Dec.–
March, except
pre-bookings

💲 $

sleeves and horned headdress.

The dozens of humbler memorials, many of their images rubbed smooth and shiny by centuries of hands and feet, include the graveslab of Jose de Keteller (died 1280), probably the father of Dame Alice the Witch; slabs showing the tools of trade of a cobbler, a weaver, and a carpenter; and the slab to Edmund Purcell

INSIDER TIP:

Sculpture is the real high point at Jerpoint Abbey. Look for the tomb carved with images of the disciples, each identifiable by what they are carrying.

—ROZ HOAGLAND
Private guide, Hoagland Art Travel

(died 1600), the captain of the Earl of Ormond's mercenary army, whose carving includes the tiny image of a bird perched on the rim of a cauldron—the cock that crowed twice as St. Peter denied Christ for the third time.

When you have had enough of sightseeing, pop into a pub for a pint of Kilkenny ale. This fine beer, brewed in town, owes its reputation to its creamy texture. Be patient—it takes almost as long as Guinness to settle in the glass.

Dunmore Cave

A steep descent on foot takes you into this well-lit cavern, located 7 miles (11 km) north of Kilkenny town and reached via the N77

and N78. It contains several rock formations—including the **Market Cross,** at 23 feet (7 m) reckoned to be the tallest stalagmite in Europe.

Dunmore Cave has a dark history. In 1973, spelunkers found the skeletons of 46 women and children who had taken refuge in the caves during a Viking raid in 928 in which their menfolk—more than a thousand of them—were slaughtered. There were no signs of violence on the bones, suggesting that the victims either starved to death or were suffocated with smoke from fires lit by the attackers.

Jerpoint Abbey

Ten miles (16 km) south of Kilkenny town via the N10 then the N9 eastward are the finest Cistercian abbey ruins in Ireland. Donal MacGiollaphadruig, King of Ossory, founded the Jerpoint Abbey in 1158; its first abbot was Felix O'Dulany, founder of St. Canice's Cathedral in Kilkenny.

O'Dulany's tomb lies in the barrel-vaulted choir of the abbey, the carving showing his bishop's crosier being swallowed by a snake. More finely carved tombs of the 15th and 16th centuries can be seen in the transepts; one carries effigies of fiercely staring and heavily bearded Apostles.

Carving is also rich on the inner and outer faces of the double pillars in the cloister arches. Here you will find beasts and soldiers, a grinning knave, a woman in a long gown, and St. Christopher with a long staff, his face as meditative as an Easter Island statue, raising one hand in blessing. ∎

Wexford Town & Around

Stretched out behind its long quays beside the Slaney Estuary, Wexford town has no glamour, but its lack of hurry and worry and the friendliness of its people draw visitors back time and again. Not that the town is uncrowded—narrow, undulating, and winding Main Street, parallel with the river, is usually thronged with customers of the old-fashioned stores. The sweet whiff of turf smoke from domestic fires hangs around the streets, and pubs such as Tim's Tavern, Kelly's, and Simon's Place make cozy, cheerful watering holes.

The quays of Wexford

Vikings founded Wexford town down in the southeast corner of County Wexford in the ninth century, and their street plan survives in the narrow covered alleyways, such as Keysers Lane, that run down from Main Street to the quays.

Wexford's history has been spectacularly bloody. When Oliver Cromwell captured the town in 1649, his men destroyed the 12th-century Selskar Abbey (its fine red stone ruins still stand off Abbey Street) and slaughtered 1,500 citizens—three-quarters of Wexford's population. In the 1798 Rising (see p. 27), there were many brutalities on both sides. A heroic statue of a peasant pikeman in the Bullring commemorates the United Irishmen rebels. You can learn more in the **Wexford Experience** exhibition in the Norman-era Westgate Tower, or take your time over the small 1798 display in the beautiful and peaceful late 17th-century

Wexford town

🅰 89 E2

Visitor Information

✉ Crescent Quay,
Wexford,
Co. Wexford

☎ 053 91 23111

**www.wexford
tourism.com**

EXPERIENCE: Enjoy Opera

Opera lovers in the tens of thousands come to Wexford town in the autumn for the three-week **Wexford Festival Opera** (*27 High St., tel 053 91 22400 or 053 91 22144, www.wexfordopera.com*). The festival generally runs from mid-October until the first week in November and offers three full-length operas staged in the Theatre Royal, as well as fringe events and other kinds of music ranging from blues and jazz to traditional concerts and informal sessions.

At Wexford, you're more likely to hear some seldom-performed opera than the famous old favorites. In fact, the festival prides itself on rescuing and reviving these neglected pieces, so it's something of a connoisseur's treat. But there's no snobbery about Wexford Festival Opera. The town's shopkeepers dress up their front windows, performers and festival-goers drink elbow-to-elbow in the bars, and there's music in and out of the pubs.

Wexford Wildfowl Reserve

▲ 89 E2
✉ Visitor center, North Slob, Co. Wexford
☎ 053 912 3406

www.wexford wildfowlreserve.ie

Irish National Heritage Park

▲ 89 E2
✉ Ferrycarrig, Co. Wexford
☎ 053 912 0733
💲 $$

www.inhp.com

Church of St. Iberius on High Street, parallel to and one block higher than Main Street.

Wexford Wildfowl Reserve

Tidal wetlands are known in Ireland as "slobs," and those along the estuary of the River Slaney northeast of Wexford town are internationally famous as breeding and wintering grounds for ducks, geese, and waders.

The North Slob, some 4,500 acres (1,800 ha) of marsh reclaimed for agriculture during the Great Famine, is the site of the Wexford Wildfowl Reserve, where you can spot mallards, black swans, goosanders, greenshanks, and redshanks, as well as reed warblers and reed buntings in the extensive reed beds. Winter has the best bird-watching, when 10,000 Greenland white-fronted geese (about 35 percent of the world population) overwinter here, along with light-bellied brent geese and large flocks of lapwings and pochards.

Leave the visitor center at dusk and perch yourself on the seawall with a pair of binoculars; you'll never forget the extraordinary sight and sound as several thousand white-fronted geese rise into the air all at once with a mighty roar of wings and gabble of voices and fly low overhead to their nighttime sea roosts.

Irish National Heritage Park

This 30-acre (12 ha) open-air park, created on the marshes of the Slaney Estuary just west of the Wexford Wildfowl Reserve, recounts Irish history up to medieval times by way of reproduced sites—a Stone Age encampment and stone circle, a *rath* (ring fort) and a *crannóg* (lake island stronghold) from the native Celtic culture, a Viking shipyard (complete with longboat moored on the river), a Norman castle, and more. Trails connect the sites, and a guided tour is available.

Enniscorthy

Fifteen miles (24 km) north from Wexford along the N11, the

lively small town of Enniscorthy holds the **National 1798 Visitor Centre,** an excellent and detailed exhibition about the United Irishmen's 1798 uprising. This attempt to win independence for Ireland by force of arms was fueled by widespread resentment of the oppressive penal laws (see pp. 26–27) and carried along on a wave of revolutionary fervor that was sweeping Europe.

The rising started in mid-May of 1798, when rebels and government forces set about slaughtering each other. Thousands were maimed, raped, and killed in Wexford, Carlow, and Kildare, as they were all over the country, before the insurrectionists in the southeast of Ireland were finally crushed on June 21 at the Battle of Vinegar Hill on the east bank of the River Slaney outside Enniscorthy. Five hundred people were killed there, many of them the wives and children of the fleeing rebels. The punitive measures that followed served only to stoke up more bitterness and resentment.

All this is told graphically with animated and static displays, light and laser effects, contemporary accounts, and cartoons. You can drive up to the battle site on **Vinegar Hill** (signposted from the town), where there is a round tower, a memorial plaque, and a fine prospect over Enniscorthy.

South of Wexford

The N25 leads south from Wexford to **Rosslare,** a busy harbor town with ferry connections to Fishguard and Pembroke in Wales. Beyond here, minor roads lead to the coast. The thatched cottages of **Kilmore Quay** look out to the **Saltee Islands.** From March to June, the islands are home to a quarter of a million puffins, kittiwakes, gannets, razorbills, and other seabirds. Boat trips are available from Kilmore Quay. ∎

National 1798 Visitor Centre
- 89 E3
- Millpark Rd., Enniscorthy, Co. Wexford
- 053 923 7596
- $$

Rosslare
- 89 E2
- 053 913 3232

Glorious light and sound at a Wexford Festival Opera church concert featuring choir and orchestra

Drive: The Old Coast Road from Dublin to Wexford

You can dash from Dublin to Wexford in an hour and a half by the fast N11, or you can saunter along the old coast road through quiet towns and villages, flirting with a coastline of low cliffs, lonely pebble strands, and splendid sandy beaches. This is real back-country travel—motoring just for the pleasure of it.

Courtown Bay and its sandy beach make a popular family resort.

Setting off from central Dublin, head east along the south bank of the River Liffey to Ringsend, where you pick up the R131 for Dun Laoghaire. This is the old coast road, easing south for 12 miles (19 km). Rediscover the pleasures of back-country driving by getting out of the car every so often and exploring the seaside towns along the way.

Pass through Sandymount to join the R118 at Merrion, continuing through Booterstown past the vast, low-tide sand and mud flats in Dublin Bay. Then join the N31 to head through Blackrock to the bustle of **Dun Laoghaire ❶**, with its Georgian terraces and busy ferryport.

NOT TO BE MISSED:

Great Sugar Loaf • Brittas Bay • Arklow • Courtown • Wexford Wildfowl Reserve

Continue on the R119 through Sandycove (see p. 83), past Dalkey and under the seaward flank of Killiney Hill, to reach Ballybrack and Bray. Stretch your legs with a walk along the coast path between Bray and Greystones, returning by DART railway.

Take the R761 south past the eastern outliers of the Wicklow Mountains. There's the first exciting sight of sharp-peaked **Great Sugar Loaf ②**, with the rounded flanks of 2,380-foot (725 m) Djouce beyond. Past Greystones, a former fishing village whose charming harbor and old cottages are now surrounded by modern housing projects, the road enters flattish, well-wooded country. Just four side roads lead to the sea between here and Wicklow; each will land you on a bleak strand of red, gray, and yellow pebbles. Turn left at Killoughter and get out for a peaceful stroll down to the shore.

At Rathnew, you join the R750 through Wicklow town and on along the lovely sandy curve of **Brittas Bay ③**, where duckboard trails through the dunes around Mizen Head may tempt you to stop for a breath of salt sea air.

Arklow ④ *(tel 0402 32484)* is a pleasant, slow-paced little town, just right for a cup of coffee and a hazelnut slice from the Stone Oven bakery on Lower Main Street. From here, head south from the harbor on a minor road, aiming for Castletown and the fishing harbor of tiny **Courtown ⑤**. Here you pick up the R742 and follow it for 25 miles (40 km) to Wexford.

The pretty fishing village of **Curracloe ⑥**, 5 miles (8 km) short of Wexford, is now spoiled by a hotel monstrously out of sympathy with its surroundings. If you're after seashore peace and quiet, take the side lanes to coastal hamlets such as Cahore Point, Morriscastle, or Blackwater Harbour. Or pack a picnic for a stroll along the half-mile duckboard walk that forms a nature trail through the Curracloe dunes.

Before plunging into Wexford town, follow signs from the R742 to the **Wexford Wildfowl Reserve ⑦** (see p. 114). The numbers of wildfowl are especially spectacular at dusk.

▲ See area maps pp. 49 & 89
► Central Dublin
⊕ Half a day
↔ 85 miles (136 km)
► Wexford town

Waterford Town & Around

Looking at Waterford town from the quays that line both banks of the River Suir, many visitors feel a sense of disappointment. They don't expect a place with such a varied history to look so workaday. But that is part of the charm of the chief city of southeast Ireland—the gritty bustle of shipping along its river and the old streets and buildings of its historic heart hidden away just behind the southern quays.

Quayside pubs and houses are enticingly lit by night and reflected in the waters of the River Suir.

Waterford town

 89 D2

Visitor Information

 The Granary,
41 The Quay,
Waterford,
Co. Waterford

☎ 051 875788

Waterford Town

The Vikings, no mean judges of a decent anchorage, settled Waterford town in the mid-ninth century, calling it Vadra-fjord, the Weather Haven. Their three centuries of occupation, and their leather boots, dinner bowls, jewelry, and daggers, are displayed in the splendid **Waterford Museum of Treasures** next to the Tourist Office. Not confined to the Vikings, the museum also gives a comprehensive account of Waterford's dramatic history. The Vikings

built walls around the town in 1000 A.D., and many fragments still stand. The best stretch leads from the Watch Tower, where Castle Street meets Parnell Street at the apex of the old city's triangular layout.

The cylindrical **Reginald's Tower** (tel 051 304220), founded by Ranguald the Viking in 1003, stands a little way from here, at the waterfront end of the Mall. In the adjacent Reginald's Bar is an arched section of the old city wall. Boats entered the city here along a waterway now replaced by the

Join the chilly swim-
mers at Guillamene
Cove outside of
Waterford town. The
views are spectacular
and the locals friendly
and welcoming.

—ALEXANDRA BURGUIERES
National Geographic contributor

Mall. The bulk of the tower is Norman, built shortly after these new
invaders had captured the city in
1170. They revamped the city walls
and added a string of watchtowers,
many of which still stand today.

In medieval times, Waterford
became the most prosperous city
in Ireland, and Georgian money
built the fine houses along the
Mall and O'Connell Street, as well
as the **Roman Catholic Holy
Trinity Cathedral,** lit by Waterford
crystal chandeliers, on Barronstrand
Street. East, on Bailey's New Street,
another addition was the **Protestant Christ Church Cathedral,**
with its rich stucco ceiling; the
morbid effigy of James Rice, seven
times Lord Mayor of Waterford
in the 15th century, is shown as a
sunken corpse being burrowed by
toads and worms.

Today, the city of Waterford has
a buzz about it, perhaps because of
the student population, the commercial activity of the port, and the
light industry around the outskirts.

Ardmore Monastic Site

Down in southwest County
Waterford, the resort of Ardmore
boasts a superb monastic site.
On the hillside above the town,
with wonderful coastal views,
you'll find a 12th-century round
tower standing 97 feet (29 m)
tall next to ruined **St. Declan's
Cathedral,** dating from the 10th
to 14th centuries.

The chief attraction is the
stone tableaux, probably ninth
century, on the outside of the
cathedral's west wall. Framed in
a double row of arcades, they
include a winged Archangel
Michael weighing souls in his
scales, Adam and Eve being banished from Eden, and St. Declan
converting the heathen Irish.
The eighth-century oratory of
the saint—he came from Wales
sometime between 350 and
420—stands nearby. ∎

St. Declan's Holy Well & Stone

While at the Ardmore
monastic site, follow the
path toward the cliffs of
Ram Head, where, beside
the ruins of Dysert Church,
you'll find St. Declan's
holy well guarded by
rough-hewn crosses. Also
down at this southern
end of Ardmore beach
is St. Declan's Stone,
on which his bell and
vestments are said to
have floated to Ireland
from Wales. It is said that
rheumatics who manage
to squeeze under the stone
on the Feast of St. Declan,
July 24, will gain a miracu-
lous cure—even if they hurt
their back in the process.

Waterford Museum of Treasures
✉ The Granary,
   Merchant's
   Quay,
   Waterford,
   Co. Waterford
☎ 051 304500
$ $$
www.waterford
treasures.com

Guillamene Cove
🗺 89 D2

Ardmore
🗺 89 B1
Visitor Information
✉ Seafront parking
   lot, Ardmore,
   Co. Waterford
☎ 024 94444

Walking in Ireland

Although Ireland has come to embrace recreational walking only recently, you will find ample opportunity to get out on foot.

The Dingle Peninsula in County Kerry offers excellent walking tracks.

Historically, people in Ireland had access to private land only with the permission of the landowners, many of whom were absentee landlords, who could withdraw permission at any time. A dependent peasant population and the lack of a confident, well-educated middle class able to stand up for its rights meant that, until recently, Ireland had few established public rights of way.

For the past couple of decades, interest in country walking and other outdoor pursuits has grown, fueled by greater mobility and prosperity, a desire to become fit, and the influence of enticing television and magazine images. Many visitors to Ireland expressed surprise and disappointment at the lack of opportunity to go walking on legally permitted

routes. In response, Ireland established a network of around 40 marked ways—long-distance routes of varying lengths, some of several days' duration. Eight waymarked paths were also established in Northern Ireland. But the lengths of these trails limited their appeal only to those people with enough time and energy to enjoy them.

In the last few years, serious efforts have been made on both sides of the border to cater to the needs of all walkers. The Republic's domestic tourist organization, Failte Ireland, and the Department of Community, Rural, and Gaeltacht Affairs, working with the national forestry organization Coillte, have jointly developed a large number of signposted and maintained loop walks. These walks emanate out from designated trailheads and range from easy strolls of an hour's duration along flat terrain to rugged mountain hikes. At the time of writing, there are nearly 200 looped walks across the country, with more in development. To find a walking route that suits you, along with lists of nearby accommodations and attractions, visit *www.discoverireland.ie.*

Until recently Northern Ireland boasted only one long-distance path, a 600-mile loop called the Ulster Way. The route was too long, primarily along roadways, badly maintained, and poorly waymarked. Today, the Ulster Way has been relaunched in 16 "Quality Sections"—which are primarily off road and well signposted—and 10 "Link Sections," unmarked trails along often busy roads. Read about the Ulster Way and many other walks in Northern Ireland by visiting *www.walkni.com.*

You never know who you'll meet around the next bend when walking the Irish countryside.

EXPERIENCE: Ireland's Walking Festivals

A marvelous way to enjoy walking on either side of the border is to take part in one of the numerous walking festivals held each year. Before the creation of today's popular walking routes, these festivals represented the best chance for many people to enjoy a new part of the country on foot and under the guidance of local experts. That is still their chief attraction, along with the chatter, fun, and partying that festivals of all kinds invariably generate.

Walking festivals typically last from one to three days and can draw thousands of participants of all ages. Many also feature multiple routes, with something suitable for every level of fitness and interest. Three grades of walk cater for most abilities. Gentle "C" Grade walks follow mostly level ground for a distance of about 7 miles (11 km), or 3–4 hours. "B" Grade routes usually take in ridges and peaks at a moderate pace. They are usually around 8 miles (13 km) in length,

include a climb of about 3,000 feet (900 m), and last 4–5 hours. "A" Grade walks are strenuous, covering several peaks at a good pace (7–8 hours of walking). These routes can extend up to 13 miles (21 km) and climb 4,000 (1,200 m) feet or more. Family-friendly and educational routes are also usually offered.

Ireland's popular walking festivals include the brilliant **Glen of Aherlow Walking Festival** *(tel 062 56 153),* held every year in January and May; the **Ballyhoura International Walking Festival** *(tel 063 91 300, www.ballyhouracountry.com),* which explores the hills of North Cork, East Limerick, and West Tipperary; the **Slieve Bloom Walking Festival** *(tel 086 278 9147, www.slievebloom.ie),* in April/May, which shows off the hilly country of Tipperary and Laois; and the **Mourne International Walking Festival** *(tel 028 4175 2256, www.mournewalking.co.uk),* a wonderful introduction to County Down's Mourne Mountains held each June.

County Tipperary

Tipperary is often glossed over by travelers racing through impatiently to get to the dramatic coasts and peninsulas of the southwest. But there are plenty of hidden delights hereabouts, just off the beaten track, for those who take the time to slow down.

Dark Age symbol of the power of Munster kings, the Rock of Cashel dominates the Tipperary plains.

Rock of Cashel

Your first sight of the Rock of Cashel rising out of the Golden Vale of Tipperary, its domed top tightly packed with towers, spires, and pointed gables, will be unforgettable. During the first millennium, the Rock was indeed a kind of secular and spiritual capital, the seat of the Kings of Munster and a rival to the power of Tara, where the High Kings of Ireland held sway. Great and grim history clings to the Rock, and there's a resonance about the place that is enhanced even more at night

when floodlights throw it all into brilliant relief.

The limestone outcrop on which the walled citadel stands is 200 feet (60 m) high. Legend has it that the devil, who had just taken a bite out of the Slieve Bloom Mountains (they still call the place Devil's Bit), saw St. Patrick about to build a church in the Golden Vale. In disgust, he spat his mouthful out and it landed at Cashel. But this rock was already fortified in the fourth century, when it was known as "Cashel of the Kings." In the fifth century, it was the coronation place for the

Kings of Munster, and St. Patrick came here to baptize King Aengus in 450. During the ceremony he inadvertently jabbed his crosier through the king's foot, but stoical Aengus, thinking the saint was testing him, did not flinch.

By the 11th century, Cashel was held by Brian Boru, High King of Ireland, but in 1101, King Murtagh O'Brien gave it to the Church, after which the great buildings that now crowd the summit were erected.

You enter the complex through the **Hall of the Vicars Choral,** built in 1420 for the choristers of Cashel's cathedral. It houses an exhibition and the weathered 12th-century high cross of St. Patrick.

Cormac's Chapel: Outside, you pass a reproduction of the cross en route to Cormac's Chapel (1127–1134), built by King Cormac MacCarthy. This sturdy little building under a steeply pitched roof, its pinkish stone contrasting pleasantly with the dour gray of the great cathedral looming behind, is considered the earliest and finest surviving Romanesque church in Ireland.

Outside is a **corbel frieze** of the heads of men and beasts, and more of these look down from the pillar capitals of the arcade inside. The round Norman **chancel arch** is studded with heads, too, and there are highly colored fragments of the original **frescoes** in the chancel. At the west end stands a **sarcophagus,** probably that of King Cormac.

Even more impressive is the carving in the **tympanum** over the north doorway. It shows a wild scene of a grinning monster, its clawed feet trampling two unidentifiable animals, while a centaur in a Norman helmet (complete with noseguard) twists his upper body back to fire an arrow at it.

INSIDER TIP:
Visit Tourism Ireland's website at *www.discover ireland.com* for a wide array of excellent planning tools and ideas on things to see and do all around Ireland.

—LARRY PORGES
Editor, National Geographic Books

St. Patrick's Cathedral: The cold, echoing shell of the 13th-century St. Patrick's Cathedral stands roofless and loud with jackdaw cries. Cobbled onto its west end is the fortified palace of the archbishops of Cashel.

The cathedral was burned in 1495 by the Earl of Kildare, who excused himself to King Henry VII by confessing with much honesty, "I thought the archbishop was in it." Cashel's prelates were as powerful and unpopular as any monarch. Archbishop Myler Magrath (1523–1622), whose tomb is in the choir, held one archbishopric, four bishoprics, and 77 other livings, making him extremely wealthy.

Tragedy came in 1647, when up

Rock of Cashel
- 88 B3
- Cashel, Co. Tipperary
- 062 61437
- $$

Athassel Priory

⚑ 88 B3

✉ Golden,
Co. Tipperary

to 3,000 people were sheltering from attack by Cromwell's army under "Murrough of the Burnings," Lord Inchiquin. The attackers piled bricks of turf against the outside of the cathedral and set

priory for Augustinian canons in 1192, only a few years after the Normans had arrived in Ireland. His tomb lies inside. Irish marauders burned the priory in 1319 and again in 1329 and 1447.

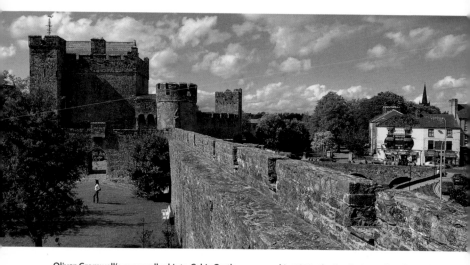

Oliver Cromwell's men walked into Cahir Castle unopposed in 1650—that's why its walls still stand.

Cahir

⚑ 88 B2

Visitor Information

✉ Castle parking lot, Cahir, Co. Tipperary

☎ 052 74 41453

Cahir Castle

✉ Cahir, Co. Tipperary

☎ 052 74 41011

$ $

them ablaze, killing everyone who had sought refuge inside.

Beside the cathedral rises a round tower, 92 feet (28 m) high, of the 11th or 12th century.

Athassel Priory

The substantial ruins of what was once the largest priory in Ireland occupy a very peaceful location beside the River Suir. Rising above trees on the riverbank are the tall gray walls of the abbey church, pierced with lancet windows, and its shattered 15th-century tower. Other remains include the priory gatehouse, the cloister ruins, and the stump of the chapter house.

William Burke founded the

Cahir

The main site to see in Cahir is **Cahir Castle,** one of Ireland's most impressive—and most complete, having surrendered to Oliver Cromwell's forces in 1650 before they could set about battering it to pieces. It stands on a rock in the River Suir, a natural defensive site, first built on by Conor O'Brien in 1142. The fortified tower he erected is incorporated into the inner ward of the present castle, a two-stage rebuilding—first in the 13th century, when the Anglo-Norman keep was built, and second by the Butler family, Earls of Ormond, once they had acquired the site in 1375. In the middle ward stands the keep, complete with its portcullis, and a chilling prison cell.

Swiss Cottage: A stroll along the river, 1.5 miles (2.5 km) south of Cahir's town center, will bring you to the Swiss Cottage, designed in 1810 by celebrated English Regency architect John Nash for Richard Butler, 12th Baron Cahir. Nash used the *cottage ornée* style, then extremely fashionable, to suggest that this crooked little hunting and fishing retreat, with its rustic timbering, artfully asymmetrical windows, and roses round the door, had somehow been engendered by the spirit of the surrounding countryside.

Carrick-on-Suir

One building distinguishes this quiet market town—the splendid ensemble of **Ormond Castle** and its satellite mansion, the finest Tudor domestic building in Ireland. The castle was built in 1309 and contains a brace of 15th-century fortified towers as proof of turbulent times in medieval Ireland. But when Black Tom Butler, tenth Earl of Ormond, built a new mansion onto his ancestral castle in 1568, he felt confident enough to dispense with any fortifications. The castle is lit by an almost continuous run of mullioned windows under the gables and is glorified inside by a tremendous carved fireplace and some wonderful ornate plasterwork in the Long Gallery.

Mitchelstown Caves

This 2-mile-long (3 km) cave system, the longest in Ireland, is the one to visit if you abhor "touristification" of such natural attractions. Mitchelstown Caves are not overburdened with tourist developments or gimmicks—you simply walk through the three enormous caverns and admire the extraordinary mineral formations of stalactites, stalagmites, and calcite flows.

Although the caves lie in the sandstone Galtee Hills, they themselves are part of an intrusive band of limestone. Rain and stream water burrowing along cracks and fault lines in the rock have hollowed out the caves, and its chemical interaction with the limestone has formed their pinnacles and flows over countless million years. ■

Swiss Cottage
- Kilcommon, Cahir, Co. Tipperary
- 052 74 41144
- Closed Nov.– mid-April; Mon. in Oct.
- $

Ormond Castle
- 89 C2
- Castle Park, Carrick-on-Suir, Co. Tipperary
- 051 640787
- Closed Oct.–May

Mitchelstown Caves
- 88 B2
- Burncourt, Cahir, Co. Tipperary
- 052 74 67246
- $$

Ahenny High Crosses

Two of the oldest ringed high crosses in Ireland stand in Ahenny churchyard, near Carrick-on-Suir. Dating from the eighth and ninth centuries, the sandstone crosses— each about 13 feet (4 m) tall—are covered with intricately carved decoration. Both feature beautiful geometric Celtic designs, and on the base of the northern cross, you will find an image from the biblical story of David and Goliath. The crosses came from the nearby monastic site of Kilclispeen.

To reach Ahenny Church (see map p. 89 C3), take the R697 north from Carrick-on-Suir for 3 miles (5 km). Turn left at Scrogh Bridge, then turn right. The church is located a little more than a mile (2 km) down the road on the right-hand side. Look for the crosses in the field to the right of the church.

More Places to Visit in East Ireland

Castledermot High Crosses

These two tenth-century high crosses, standing near a lovely Romanesque arched doorway and a 67-foot (20 m) round tower, are carved with biblical scenes. *www.high crosses.org/castledermot.com* 🄰 89 D4 ✉ Off the N9, 10 miles (16 km) SE of Athy via the R418, Co. Kildare

Hook Head

The circular 30-mile (48 km) Ring of Hook Drive is reached via the Passage East to Ballyhack car ferry, 7 miles (11 km) east of Waterford. You'll find yourself driving down a lovely peninsula of green farmland and dark cliffs. Attractions include the gaunt gray shells of two 13th-century monasteries, Dunbrody Abbey and Tintern Abbey. You'll enjoy the vast sandbanks of Bannow

---

EXPERIENCE:
Irish Crystal

The manufacture of Irish crystal—a very particular kind of heavy, lustrous glass—is a specialty pursued in several places in the Republic and Northern Ireland. You can visit several factory showrooms to admire the skill and craftsmanship. Buy pieces directly from the factories, at select retailers, or online.

While **Waterford Crystal** (see entry, right) no longer conducts factory tours, a large new retail outlet and visiter center will be opening there in June, 2010. Besides Waterford, several other crystal manufacturers have shops at their factories where you can purchase glassware, including **Galway Irish Crystal** (*Heritage Centre, Merlin Park, Dublin Rd., Galway, tel 091 757311, www.galwaycrystal.ie*) *and* **Duiske Crystal** (*High Street, Graignamanagh, Co. Kilkenny, www.duiskeglass.ie*).

Bay, the big star-shaped Tudor fort at Duncannon, and the craggy ruins of Slade Castle. All roads eventually lead south to the **lighthouse** on Hook Head's dusky red sandstone cliffs. The modern light sits atop a 100-foot (33 m) tower built in 1172, making it the oldest lighthouse in Ireland. Enjoy sensational views from the top (*tel 051 397055 or 397054, Mar.–Oct., daily, $$). www.thehook-wexford.com* 🄰 89 D2 ✉ SE of Waterford via the R737, the R734, and minor roads, Co. Waterford 🕐 Seasonal **Waterford visitor information** ☎ 051 875788

Lismore Castle

Lismore, a huge, impressive castle on a hill above the River Blackwater, is mostly 19th-century but based on a 12th-century stronghold. Elizabethan adventurer and pioneer American colonist Sir Walter Raleigh owned it from 1589 to 1602, and physicist and chemist Robert Boyle was born here in 1627. The castle is private, but the 800-year-old Yew Walk, the Pleasure Grounds with their flowering rhododendrons (*May–June*), and the other gardens are open. *www.lismore castle.com* 🄰 88 B2 ✉ On the N72, 15 miles (24 km) W of Dungarvan, Co. Waterford ☎ 058 54424 🕐 Castle not open; grounds closed Oct.–Easter 🄢 $$

Waterford Crystal

Waterford sets the standard to which all other glassmakers aspire. The process here hasn't changed much since the 18th century—litharge (lead monoxide), silica sand, and potash are blended in furnaces. The molten crystal is then blown into shape and smoothed. When the crystal has cooled, a master cutter engraves intricate designs: leaves, faces, even a foxhunt or a garden. *www.waterfordvisitorcentre.com* 🄰 89 D2 ✉ Kilbarry, Cork Rd., Waterford (2 miles/3 km from city center) ☎ 051 332500 🄢 $$

Small-scale pastoral landscapes, the historic water-girdled city of Cork, and the five stunning peninsulas of west Cork and Kerry

Southwest Ireland

Southwest magic: Kings in the wood

Southwest Ireland

Three counties make up southwest Ireland: Cork, Kerry, and Limerick. Hereabouts, the landscape begins to break up and the edges of the land become ragged, splitting apart into five great peninsulas that push out into the Atlantic. These fracture further into headlands and islands, giving the map of this region the appearance of blobs of liquid streaking out from some central spillage.

The city of Cork has plenty of Dublin's zip and zing, and not too much of the capital's impatience and glitziness. Eastern County Cork is well wooded with wide farmlands, cut into on the south by the great lagoon of Cork Harbour with its historic town of Cobh.

The farther west you go, the more appealing County Cork becomes, its gorgeous south coast indented with bays and dotted with villages. The three southernmost peninsulas— Mizen, Sheep's Head, and Bear (Beara)—break away and spear out to sea between their inlets of Roaringwater, Dunmanus, and Bantry Bays.

The southwest has one other big city, Limerick, a place with a vivid history that somehow can't quite match the warmth and intimacy of Cork. But the rest of County Limerick makes

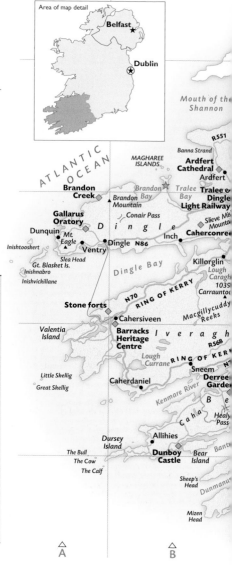

NOT TO BE MISSED:

up for what its capital lacks, with charming picture-book villages, fine houses, and a swath of underdiscovered country out west.

County Kerry shares the Bear (Beara) Peninsula with County Cork and boasts two more of its own—Iveragh, whose mountainous spine is formed by Macgillycuddy's Reeks and whose beautiful coast is circled by the spectacular Ring of Kerry road, and rugged, otherworldly Dingle, with the remote Blasket Islands at its outermost tip. Kerrymen are the butt of jokes for their supposed backwoods gullibility. Don't let that fool you—the Kerrymen themselves make the same jokes about Corkmen.

WEST IRELAND p.163

EAST IRELAND p.87

◁5
◁4
◁3
◁2
◁1

Castleconnell

Shannon

Limerick

Carrigafoyle Castle

Ballylongford

Ballybunnion

Adare

Patrickswell

Rathkeale

N69

N21

N24

Lough Gur

Listowel

L I M E R I C K

R523

Deel

Maigue

Newcastle West

R515

Kilmallock

Abbeyfeale

N20

N21

R515

Charleville

N69

Feale

...alee

R576

Castleisland

Newmarket

R522

Buttevant

Mitchelstown

...lennerville Windmill

Kanturk

N73

N8

K E R R Y

R577

Mallow

N72

Fermoy

N22

N72

Blackwater

Ross Castle

...isfallen

Killarney

Millstreet

C O R K

R628

R627

...ough Leane

Muckross Estate

R582

N20

N8

...adies' View

Torc Waterfall

KILLARNEY NATIONAL PARK

N22

Blarney

Blarney Castle

Fota Wildlife Park & Arboretum

Jameson's Distillery

Youghal

N25

Kenmare

Macroom

Midleton

N71

Lee

CORK ✈ ✪

Cobh

...ountains

Béal na Bláth

R585

N22

Carrigaline

Swansea

◁2

Glengarriff

R584

Dunmanway

Bandon

N71

Franciscan friary

Kinsale

Charles Fort

Roscoff

Whiddy Is.

Bantry

R586

Birthplace of Michael Collins

Courtmacsherry

Timoleague

...arinish Is. ...ay

Durrus

Clonakilty

Seven Heads

Seven Heads Bay

Celtic Sea

...ally dehob

N71

Skibbereen

Ross Carbery

Ceim Hill Museum

Drombeg Stone Circle

Roaringwater Bay

Sherkin Island

Clear Island

...stnet ...ock

Cape Clear

0   30 kilometers
0   15 miles

◁1

C   D   E   F

Cork City

Although the most important city in the southwest of Ireland, Cork wears a relaxed air. The best way by far to get the most out of this civilized place—and its "softly sharp" people with their distinctive roller-coaster intonation—is to take your time and stroll about, letting the city under your skin by slow degrees.

The bridges and fine old houses along the River Lee lend dignity and character to the city of Cork.

Cork City

🔺 129 E2

Visitor Information

✉ Áras Fáilte, Grand Parade, Cork, Co. Cork

☎ 021 4255100

www.corkcity.ie

The physical shape of Cork is easy to grasp. The city center occupies a long island in the River Lee that is connected by numerous bridges to 19th-century suburbs on the steepish hills to north and south.

History of Cork City

The low-lying land in the Lee Valley was a good spot to settle. St. Fin Barre established a mon-astery at Corcaigh, the "marshy place," in 650, and once the

Vikings had ceased plundering the monks, they too settled and established a town during the ninth and tenth centuries.

With its fine river frontage and its great natural harbor just to the southeast, Cork prospered on trade in Norman and medieval times, and it developed an inde-pendent political spirit based on this mercantile confidence. Wisely, the city admitted Oliver Crom-well's forces in 1649; not so wisely, it backed the deposed King James

II during his unsuccessful comeback bid against King William III in 1690 and had its town walls and many of its buildings flattened when the Protestant army broke in.

The 18th century brought prosperity to Cork—not least thanks to the industry of French Huguenot refugees, who settled here at a time when newly dug canals were bringing improved trade. In the 19th century, the city became a refuge for Home Rule activists, while in the 1919–1922 War of Independence, it was a hotbed of IRA plotting and action—a period brilliantly caught in *Guests of the Nation,* a selection of short stories by Cork's great writer, Frank O'Connor.

In 1920, the Black and Tans, a brutal paramilitary British regiment, murdered the mayor in front of his family and later burned and ransacked much of Cork. Some of what you see in the city center today is a rebuilding of what was burned in 1920, but many of the fine Georgian houses remain.

English Market & South

Cork's chief thoroughfare and shopping street is **St. Patrick's Street,** which curves south from the North Channel of the river and then westward through the center before resuming its southward course as Grand Parade to reach the South Channel.

As a base for a walk around Cork, off Grand Parade you'll find the **English Market** *(www.corkenglishmarket.ie),* a handsome Georgian covered hall on the site of a 400-year-old market where people still go to meet, greet, and eat. Sounds and sights are on the vivid side around stalls such as the Real Olive Company, the Meat Centre, and On the Pig's Back (a French deli stand), as well as at the vegetable stands, joke stores, and clothing booths, while smells are a rich jumble of bread, fish, apples, spices, leather, and earthy potatoes.

INSIDER TIP:

For event guides and pretty much anything else you might want to know about Cork, visit the online phenomenon *www.peoplesrepublicofcork.com.*

—TOM JACKSON
National Geographic Society

Plunge in, then climb to the first-floor balcony and look down on the bustle below as you enjoy a meal at the outside tables of the Farmgate Restaurant.

Going south from English Market along Grand Parade, take a right turn down Tuckey Street and a left on South Main Street to pass a Cork institution on your way to the South Channel of the River Lee—**An Spailpin Fánai,** one of the best pubs in the city for sessions of traditional music (generally a 9:30 p.m. kickoff). Don't worry a bit if you can't play or sing—just sit back and enjoy the craic and the tunes. If you can play, ask to join in; the musicians will be delighted to welcome you. You are in for great atmosphere, great Guinness, and music you won't forget in a hurry.

St. Fin Barre's Cathedral

🅐 Map p. 135

✉ Dean St., Cork, Co. Cork

☎ 021 496 3387

💲 $

http://cathedral
.cork.anglican.org

Crawford Art Gallery

🅐 Map p. 135

✉ Emmet Pl., Cork, Co. Cork

🕐 Closed Sun.

☎ 021 490 7855

www.crawfordart
gallery.ie

Church of St. Anne & Bells of Shandon

🅐 Map p. 135

✉ Church St., Cork, Co. Cork

☎ 021 450 5906

💲 $ (bells)

www.shandonbells
.org

St. Fin Barre's Cathedral shows off extravagant Victorian Gothic decor.

Cross South Gate Bridge and turn right along the river to find the gray rocket tower of **St. Fin Barre's Cathedral,** its exterior walls carrying statues of saints, angels, and demons. The medieval cathedral was shattered during the siege of 1690, and this church, dating from 1878, is an exuberant example of high Gothic exterior and something more artsy-craftsy within. It has walls of blood-red Cork marble, a beautiful rose window on the theme of Creation, a finely colored mosaic floor in the choir, and glorious gold, blue, and red angels in the roof of the sanctuary. Lift the seats of the choir stalls to enjoy the carved grasshopper, butterfly, stag beetle, and dragonfly under the misericord ledges—on which choristers can recline while seeming to remain upright.

North of English Market

A walk north from English Market would start with a right turn along St. Patrick's Street, from which Carey Lane and French Church Street lead north into the old **Huguenot Quarter.** Now a chic part of the city, it's a peaceful area of high stone walls, small 18th-century houses, and brick-paved pedestrian

Talk & Tipple at the Hi-B

South of English Market, down Grand Parade, a left turn on Oliver Plunkett Street will take you east all the way to the tip of the "island." If you are in search of a drink, there's no need to go farther than the General Post Office, for above the chemist's shop opposite, you'll find the wonderful Hi-B bar up a flight of steps. The Hi-B is everything you look for in an Irish town pub—cheerful, friendly, comfortable, firelit, and a bit old-fashioned—a place where regular folk and connoisseurs can pass a pleasant hour trying to decide which is better, the talk or the ale. Both are among the very best in town.

alleys. The heart is **Rory Gallagher Square,** honoring the Stratocaster-wielding bluesman (who spent his young days in Cork) and featuring a sculpture of a twisted guitar with Gallagher's words and music streaming out of it.

North of the Huguenot Quarter, Paul Street runs east to pass the **Crawford Art Gallery.** Don't be surprised to find more people eating in the gallery's café than looking at the pictures—the fabulous food is provided by the Ballymaloe Cookery School (see sidebar). Once you have had your fill, the paintings are definitely worth a look—among them an icy 1955 portrait of writer Elizabeth Bowen by Patrick Hennessy, a sentimental Victorian "Letter from America" by James Brenan, a thoughtful Barrie Cooke study of modern Irish poet John Montague, and a blazing yellow-and-blue "Rice Field" (1989) by William Crozier.

Shandon

Just north of the gallery, Christy Ring Bridge crosses the North Channel of the River Lee to reach the northern suburb of Shandon. From its perch high on the hillside, the tall tower of the **Church of St. Anne** calls you up twisty, steep old lanes. Here, for a small fee, you can ring the famous **Bells of Shandon.** Make up your own composition or "read" a tune off a crib card.

At the foot of the tower stands the **Butter Exchange,** built in 1770 to cope with the grading of hundreds of thousands of casks of

prime Cork butter. It now houses Shandon Craft Centre, where you can watch makers of fiddles and fishing flies, crystal goblets and ceramic mugs—and buy their products, naturally.

A half-hour walk west of Shandon leads to Sunday's Well and the former **Cork City Gaol.** It houses a chilling exhibition about the harsh conditions in the jail and the even harsher social conditions in 19th-century Cork that drove prisoners such as Mary Sullivan to steal the twopence-worth of calico that earned her a seven-year sentence, or that sentenced Edward O'Brien to gaol and a twice-weekly lashing for stealing brass—his 52nd offense, and he was only nine. ∎

EXPERIENCE:
Cooking at Ballymaloe

With the country's culinary reputation on the rise, there's never been a better time to enjoy an Irish cooking class. Run by Ballymaloe House, one of Ireland's best known hotels, **Ballymaloe Cookery School** *(Shanagarry, Co. Cork, tel 021 464 6785, www.cooking isfun.ie)* offers one-day courses devoted to fabulous finger foods, Irish breakfasts, and even foie gras. No one will rap your knuckles if you make a mess or get it all wrong. This is how cooking is supposed to be—informative, lighthearted, and enjoyable.

For cooking classes outside Cork, try **Belle Isle School of Cookery** *(Co. Fermanagh, tel 028 6638 7231, www.irish-cookery-school.com),* which offers gourmet cooking in a beautiful location, or **Ballynocken Cookery School** *(Co. Wicklow, tel 0404 44627, www.thecookeryschool.ie),* featuring a wonderful blend of Irish and Italian cuisines.

Butter Exchange
- Map p. 135
- Shandon, Co. Cork

Cork City Gaol
- Convent Ave., Sunday's Well, Cork, Co. Cork
- 021 430 5022
- $$

www.corkcitygaol
.com

Walk: Around Cork City

Although Cork is Ireland's "second city," and by far the largest conurbation in the south-west of the country, it's an extremely manageable place to walk around. The center of Cork amounts to a spearblade-shaped island between the North and South Channels of the River Lee. Everything that makes for an enjoyable city walk is contained within this island and on the river banks just north and south of it.

Cork's walkable city center lies between the North and South Channels of the River Lee.

NOT TO BE MISSED:

English Market • St. Fin Barre's Cathedral • Huguenot Quarter • Crawford Art Gallery • Quays along the River Lee

Start your walk in the **English Market** ❶ (see p. 131) at Cork's center. Set off from the Prince's Street entrance. Turn right on Prince's Street and again on South Mall. At the foot of Grand Parade, turn left over the South Channel of the River Lee. Bear right along the south bank for 500 yards (450 m) to reach **St. Fin Barre's Cathedral** ❷ (see p. 132), on the left side of Bishop Street.

After looking around the cathedral, retrace your steps along Bishop Street. Turn left at South Gate Bridge and walk up South Main Street. On your right is the great music pub of **An Spailpín Fánai** ❸ (see p. 131).

Halfway up South Main Street, turn right along Tuckey Street then left up Grand Parade. At the top of Grand Parade, turn right and make your way along St. Patrick's Street, crossing the road in 200 yards (180 m) to turn left along French Church Street into the quieter pedestrian lanes of the **Huguenot Quarter** ❹ (see pp. 132–133).

After soaking up the atmosphere of the brick-paved lanes around **Rory Gallagher Square** ❺ (see p. 133), continue north along French Church Street or Carey's Lane to reach Paul Street, where you turn right.

At the end of Paul Street, bear right for a

Cork City Tours

Compact and full of character, Cork is a great city for walking. **Cork Historic Walking Tours** (tel 085 100 7300, www.walkcork.ie) offers 90-minute guided walks to the sites of Viking and Norman Cork—from the 7th century to the 17th—and tours of the modern city. For open-top bus tours of Cork, try **Bus Éireann** (tel 021 450 8188, www.buseireann.ie) or **Cronin's Coaches** (tel 021 430 9090, www.croninscoaches.com).

0 200 meters
0 200 yards

GLEN RYAN ROAD
CHURCH STREET
ROMAN ST.
JOHN STREET
LEITRIM STREET
RICHMOND HILL
ST. PATRICK'S HILL
DOMINICK ST.
⑨ Church of St. Anne
⑧ Butter Exchange
JOHN REDMAN ST.
DEVONSHIRE STREET
PINE STREET
N8 McCURTAIN STREET
BLARNEY STREET
SHANDON STREET
POPE'S
St. Mary's Church
River Lee (North) QUAY
LAVITT'S
CAMDEN QUAY
ST. PATRICK'S QUAY
GRIFFITH BRIDGE
NORTH MALL
BACHELOR'S QUAY
NORTH MAIN STREET
Cork Opera House ⑦
Crawford Art Gallery ⑥
RORY GALLAGHER SQUARE ⑤
EMMET PL.
ST. PATRICK'S BRIDGE
MERCHANT'S QUAY
GRENVILLE PL.
GRATTAN STREET
KYLE ST.
CORNMARKET STREET
PAUL ST.
CAREY'S LA.
FRENCH CH. ST.
HUGUENOT QUARTER ④
ST. PATRICK'S ST.
MAYLOR STREET
DYKE PARADE
N22
SHEARES ST.
LIBERTY STREET
CASTLE ST.
GRAND PARADE
START ①
PRINCES STREET
OLIVER PLUNKETT STREET
Court House
SOUTH MAIN STREET
STREET
English Market
WASHINGTON STREET
WANDESFORD STREET
BISHOP LUCEY PARK
TUCKEY ST.
SOUTH MALL
N22
CLARK'S BRIDGE
City Library
③ An Spailpin Fánai
River Lee (South)
PARLIAMENT BR.
Holy Trinity Church
SHARMAN CRAWFORD STREET
R610
SOUTH GATE BRIDGE
SULLIVAN'S QUAY
COVE STREET
St. Nicholas' Church
BISHOP STREET
Elizabeth Fort
BARRACK STREET
EVERGREEN STREET
FRIAR ST.
St. Fin Barre's Cathedral ②
DEAN STREET

- See area map p. 129 E2
- English Market
- 2 miles (3 km)
- Half a day
- Church of St. Anne

---

few yards, then turn left along Emmet Place. Soon you will see on your left the **Crawford Art Gallery ⑥** (see p. 133). This is the place to stop if you are feeling hungry or thirsty.

Just beyond the gallery, you pass **Cork Opera House ⑦** (www.corkoperahouse.ie). Cross the North Channel of the river, taking in the great views from the bridge along Lavitt's and Camden Quays. At the far bank, continue up Pine Street. Turn left along Devonshire Street and continue west on Dominick Street.

Take a right to climb Exchange Street and you will find yourself outside the handsome Georgian **Butter Exchange ⑧** (see p. 133). Inside, enjoy the Shandon Craft Centre before climbing on for another few yards to reach the tall tower of the **Church of St. Anne ⑨**. Announce your arrival by striking a tune on the famous **Bells of Shandon** (see p. 133).

From Shandon you could return the way you came. Or, walk west along Church Street opposite St. Anne's, turning left down Shandon Street to regain the North Channel of the River Lee at Griffith Bridge. Cross the bridge, then bear left along the quays to reach the Opera House and Emmet Place, from where you retrace your steps to the English Market.

County Cork

The largest county in Ireland, Cork is also one of the country's most diverse, with farms and forests, bays, inlets and a wide variety of wildlife to suit everyone's tastes. Here you can relax along sunny beaches, delve into medieval Irish history, and relive the painful story of the Great Famine and Ireland's hopeful emigrants.

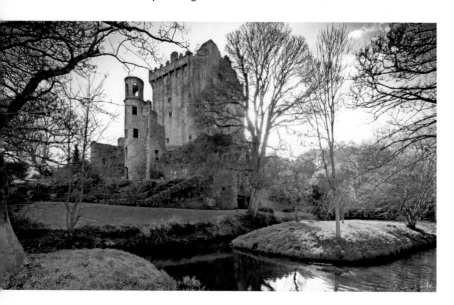

Bloody history and feisty legend cling to the 15th-century stronghold of Blarney Castle.

Blarney Castle

- 129 E2
- Blarney, Co. Cork
- 021 438 5252
- $$$

www.blarneycastle.ie

Blarney Castle

Everyone knows that those who kiss the Blarney Stone at Blarney Castle are magically endowed with the gift of the gab. In fact, the castle and its grounds are imbued with legends—so much so that a stroll about will introduce you to the Rock Close and its "druidical foundations," the Fairy Glade with its "sacrificial altar," and the Wishing Steps that will grant you your heart's desire if you can negotiate them backwards with your eyes closed.

Blarney Castle itself is a battlemented keep standing on a rock outcrop overlooking the River Martin, 6 miles (10 km) northwest of Cork city. Dermot Laidhir (Strongman) McCarthy built it in 1446 on the site of a 13th-century fortified tower. Other towers rise as outposts, giving the whole ensemble a formidable look.

"Blarney" as a synonym for charming claptrap originated with an evasive McCarthy, Lord of Blarney, who was quizzed by the Earl of Leicester, Queen Elizabeth I's emissary. Either the queen had demanded the handing over of the castle or there was some dispute about land ownership, but whatever the disagreement, the loquacious McCarthy never got to the point. When Leicester reported the stalemate to Queen Elizabeth, she burst out: "But this is just more Blarney!"

The Queen's forces never did take Blarney Castle; it fell to Oliver Cromwell's commander Lord Broghill in 1646, but the garrison escaped during the siege by underground passage. There were reputed to be three of these, one running to the nearby lake, one to Cork, and one—not very feasibly—to County Kerry, 50 miles (80 km) to the west.

Blarney Stone: To find the Blarney Stone, climb to the top of the old keep, past the Great Hall with its enormous fireplace, the Earl's bedroom lit by big windows, and the Young Ladies' Room. Once out on the open top of the castle, you'll spot the stone's location easily enough— it's where the line ends amid much giggling and gasping. Kissing the Blarney Stone is one of Ireland's prime visitor activities. Come early in the morning to

INSIDER TIP:

Buses are a great way to travel around Ireland, but carry small change with you. There are no bathrooms on board and the stations often require coins to access the facilities.

—KAREN MARTINEZ
National Geographic Books

avoid lines that can stretch down the castle stairs.

The stone is set into the outer face of a gap in the battlements. You'll have to lie on your back and wriggle your upper body outward and downward to kiss it. It's quite safe, as you perform the feat while gripping two safety bars, supported by a sturdy guard and shielded by a metal grille from the 83-foot (29 m) drop to the ground. Two words to the wise— take all your coins out of your pockets, or they'll shower through the grille, and don't wear a mini-skirt if you value your modesty.
(continued on p. 140)

Legends of the Stone

Legends surround the Blarney Stone. One says that it was brought to Ireland by the prophet Jeremiah and claims it as the stone pillow on which Jacob slept in the desert when he had his dream of angels on a ladder—although that is also said of the Lialh Fail or Stone of Destiny at Tara (see pp. 266–267). Other tales tell of the stone being given to Cormac McCarthy, King of Munster, either by an old witch whom he had saved from drowning or by Robert the Bruce of Scotland, as a thank-you present for sending 4,000 men to help Bruce defeat the English at the Battle of Bannockburn in 1314.

A (marginally) more credible account is that the stone was brought to Ireland by some crusader who had acquired it in the Holy Land as a curiosity, probably already the focus for legends—hence, perhaps, the Jacob's dream connection.

Cobh & the Queenstown Story

East of the city of Cork, Great Island all but fills the northernmost portion of Cork Harbour, one of the world's finest natural sheltered havens. The port known as Queenstown, which developed during the 19th century along the seaward-facing side of Great Island, became Ireland's premier hub for commerce and communications with Britain's colonies and former colonies.

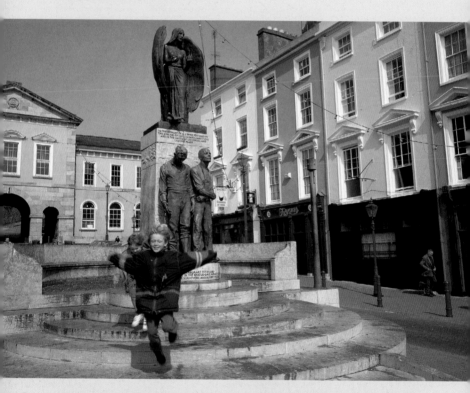

A monument in Casement Square remembers the passengers of the *Lusitania*, torpedoed in 1915.

Queenstown—or Cobh (Cove), as it was called before the visit of Queen Victoria in 1849—meant many things to many people. To sailors at the Admiralty station established here during the Napoleonic Wars, it was a strategic communications post in the North Atlantic. To the troops embarking for the Crimean War in the 1850s or the Boer War 40 years later, it was their last sight of home territory and the launch point to death or

glory. For most of those who boarded the *Titanic* here in 1912, it was their last contact with earth. For prisoners, such as the rebel United Irishmen banished to a penal colony in Australia for their part in the 1798 Rising, it meant the start of six months chained in the lightless, airless hold of a leaky convict ship. Above all, it was the point of embarkation for many millions of poor Irish emigrants seeking a new life in Canada, the

United States, England, or Australia, away from the poverty or oppression that had dogged them in their native land.

In the beautifully refurbished former railway station at the old port—now once more named Cobh—the **Queenstown Story exhibition** (Cobh Heritage Centre, Cobh, Co. Cork, tel 021 4813591, www.cobhheritage.com, $$) tells the tale of those who left Ireland over the course of two centuries through this thronging gateway. Here are ship models of every shape and size, tableaux, photographs, letters, and the poignant personal effects of emigrants—locks of loved ones' hair, rosaries, pocket watches. It is the stories of the men, women, and children, leaving Ireland because there was no other option, that strike home the hardest.

We see these mostly reluctant travelers, bold or frightened, optimistic or downcast, holding "American wakes" on the waterside before parting from relatives and lovers as they board the emigrant ships. These ranged from well-appointed vessels to the rotten old coffin ships, apt to founder in bad weather, that those fleeing the Great Famine of 1845–1849 were only too glad to scramble on board.

We learn of the bad water and food, the vomiting and cursing, the dances and *ceilidhs* in the steerage-class holds, and the daunting strangeness of the arrival on a foreign shore weeks or months later, weak and filthy from the voyage, with only the name of a relative or the vague promise of work to sustain them.

INSIDER TIP:

If you're of Irish descent, chances are some of your relatives left Ireland from Cobh, making the Queentown Story exhibition a must-see.

—CHRISTOPHER KLEIN
National Geographic Traveler
magazine writer

Between 1815 and 1970, some three million emigrants—roughly the population of Ireland today—left Cobh in search of a better life. This vast anonymous army, which enriched so many other countries while it drained the lifeblood of Ireland, is the real Queenstown story.

EXPERIENCE: Exploring *Titanic* & Irish Emigration

After visiting the Queenstown Story exhibition (see above) in Cobh, the last port of call for *Titanic*, walk the **Titanic Trail** (www.titanic-trail.com), a tour along the city's streets and piers. You can learn more about the history of that fateful ship and its Irish emigrants at the **Ulster Folk & Transport Museum** (Holywood, tel 028 9042 8428, www.titanic inbelfast.com, $) near Belfast, where *Titanic* was built. Then delve further into the history of Irish emigration at the **Ulster American Folk Park** (2 Mellon Rd., Castletown, Omagh, Co. Tyrone, www.nmni.com/uafp, $; see pp. 311–313).

Follow in the footsteps of actual Irish emigrants on board the **Dunbrody Famine Ship** (New Ross, Co. Wexford, www.dunbrody.com, $), a reproduction sailing vessel, and at the **Culkins Emigration Museum** (Cannaghanally, Dromore West, Co. Sligo, tel 096 47152), which stands on the site of an emigration office that operated from the 19th century into the 1930s.

Poignant reminders of the cause of the early Irish emigration can be found at the **Famine Museum** (Strokestown Park, Strokestown, Co. Roscommon, www.strokestown park.ie/museum.html, $; see p. 237), which includes devastating written pleas from the estate's starving tenants, while **Gáirdín an Ghorta** (Garden of Remembrance; Newmarket, Co. Kilkenny, www.faminegarden. com) offers a meditative view of Ireland's troubled past and promising future.

Kinsale

⚠ 129 E2

Visitor Information

✉ Pier Rd., Kinsale, Co. Cork

☎ 021 477 2234

Kinsale Regional Museum

✉ Market Sq., Kinsale, Co. Cork

☎ 021 477 7930

🕐 Closed Nov.–March

Kinsale

The town of Kinsale, spread around a tight waterfront of green hills at a bend in the River Bandon's estuary, 15 miles (25 km) south of Cork city, is the perfect jumping-off point for the beautiful, unspoiled coastline of west Cork.

Reckoned the gourmet capital of the southwest, if not of all Ireland, Kinsale is made for wandering, its waterfront and snaking Main Street full of color-washed buildings. Lanes and narrow streets climb the hills behind the harbor, and the houses spread attractively above the water. The only eyesore is a development of close-packed green-and-pink apartments on the east bank of the estuary, brutally out of keeping with everything else in view.

EXPERIENCE:
Sailing & Watersports

The strands and bays of west Cork offer some of the best watersports in Ireland. Sign up for lessons at **West Cork Surf School** (Inchydoney Beach, Clonakilty, Co. Cork , tel 086 869 5396, www.westcork surfing.com) or **Vertigo Kitesurfing** (The Old Farmhouse, Ballinaclashet, Co. Cork, tel 087 957 5668, www.vertigokitesurf ing.com). Learn to sail with the **Kinsale Outdoor Education Centre** (St. John's Hill, Kinsale, Co. Cork, tel 021 477 2896, www .kinsaleoutdoors.com), or explore the coast with **Atlantic Sea Kayaking** (The Abbey, Skibbereen, Co. Cork, tel 028 21058, www .atlanticseakayaking.com). **Baltimore Diving Centre** (Harbour Drive, Baltimore, Co. Cork, tel 028 20300, www.baltimore diving.com) offers scuba diving packages.

St. Multose's Church: St. Multose's Church (tel 021 477 2220) stands in from the harbor, where Higher O'Connell Street meets Cork Street—a squat church dating from the 12th century, whose sturdy Irish Romanesque tower has a curious top, smaller than the lower stories, awkwardly fitted on.

Desmond Castle: Desmond Castle (tel 021 477 4855), half-way up hilly Cork Street, is a fine late medieval fortified tower with craggy crenellations and stone mullioned windows. It has served as a customs house and a jail for French prisoners-of-war.

The castle was also used as a powder magazine during the Siege of Kinsale in 1601, when 4,000 Spanish troops under Don Juan del Aguida landed at Kinsale to support a rebellion by Hugh O'Neill, Earl of Tyrone. The rebels held the town for three months, but when the Spanish failed to back the Irish during the decisive battle, the rebellion quickly crumbled. It was the last roll of the dice for the Gaelic chiefs of Ireland: In 1607, O'Neill and his fellow rebel the Earl of Tyrconnell fled to the Continent—the famous "Flight of the Earls"—and the English Crown took full control of Ireland.

Kinsale Regional Museum: Much Kinsale history is expounded in endearingly ramshackle style at the Kinsale Regional Museum in the old Court House on Market Square. Here are ice picks and fish

Enjoy the magnificent panorama from Charles Fort over the town of Kinsale.

boxing hammers, boatbuilder's tools and Easter Rising rifles, ships' guns and Kinsale lace, all packed into the museum's few rooms. Most affecting are the mementoes of the British passenger liner *Lusitania,* torpedoed by the German submarine *U-20* on May 7, 1915, off the Old Head of Kinsale promontory. Of 1,951 passengers, 1,198 died, many of them women and children. A striped mail bag, a German commemorative medal, a cane deckchair, and a facsimile of the log of the *U-20*, translated into English, bring the tragedy up close.

For light relief there are the vast kneeboot and the unnecessarily massive knife and fork of Patrick Cotter O'Brien (1760–1806), the celebrated "Kinsale Giant." At 8 feet 7 inches (262 cm), O'Brien was certainly phenomenally tall. He was also a

sad figure, unable to walk properly or even rise from his chair without pain, obliged to exhibit himself as a freak to earn a living.

West Cork Coast

Explore this area when you have adjusted to the slow tempo of the southwest. It's no good hurrying over the 100-mile (160 km), in-and-out coast of west Cork because the twisty roads won't let you speed along, and the seaside villages and windy headlands will do their darndest to detain you. It is good to take two days rather than one—better still to take three, or a week.

Charles Fort: Any exploration of the west Cork coast from Kinsale ought to start with the short trip along the east side of the estuary to Charles Fort, an eerie and striking star-shaped

Charles Fort
- 129 E2
- Summer Cove, Kinsale, Co. Cork
- 021 477 2263
- $

fort built in the 1670s to be impregnable from the sea. Designed on the principles of French military engineer Vauban, the fort fell in three days when actually put to the test by King William III's army in 1690—they attacked it from the land.

The extensive interior of Charles Fort is filled with ruined barracks, magazines, officers' quarters, an armory, and a cooperage—all massively constructed, but all now roofless and blank-eyed. Strolling around these lifeless monuments to defense is a surreal, gripping experience. The view from the headland over Kinsale, the boats on the river, and the estuary mouth is sensational.

The Coast Road: From Kinsale, the scenic Coast Road wriggles and snakes for about 80 miles (128 km) westward to Skibbereen, making use of byways and lanes in which you are almost bound to lose yourself. Don't worry: There's always someone to ask when the signposts give out. In any case, this is one of the most beautiful corners of Ireland, a gentle coastal landscape that simply begs you to put the car in low gear and wander aimlessly.

Don't bother going down to the Old Head of Kinsale; an exclusive golf club has taken over the historic headland, and public access is no longer possible. Instead, high-banked lanes colorful

Sea-bitten cliffs at the Old Head of Kinsale, south of Cork, typify the region's dramatic coastline.

with poppies, ragwort, fuchsia, and bindweed will take you on to **Timoleague,** one of several attractive color-washed villages sited around the estuaries whose shining mudflats are haunted by seabirds and crossed by narrow causeways. Timoleague's 14th-century **Franciscan friary** is astonishingly complete—Cromwell despoiled it in 1642, but the shell stands almost perfect in lichen-green stone. Lancet windows, tomb niches, a tall arched nave, and fragments of cloister echo to the cooing of nesting pigeons.

It is worth sidetracking through pretty Courtmacsherry and around the lanes that crisscross the **Seven Heads Peninsula.** The moondaisies, roses, and silver sand beaches around Dunworley are a delight. You can swim here, or pass through the lively town of **Clonakilty** and cross the causeway to Inchydoney Island with its broad strands. At Ballinascarthy near Clonakilty, a silver Model T honors Henry Ford, whose father was born here.

Three miles (5 km) west of Clonakilty, the **Four Alls pub** and Sam's Cross are signposted off the N71. The dark and cozy Four Alls is where the commander-in-chief of the Free State Army, Michael Collins, stopped on August 22, 1922, for his last drink before an IRA bullet felled him in an ambush. The pub walls are covered in photographs, drawings, and newspaper clippings relating to the hero. The **Birthplace of Michael Collins** stands nearby at Woodfield (ask at the pub for directions) and is the object of

many a pilgrimage. A bronze bust of Collins generally has a posy of fresh flowers on its plinth.

Across another estuary stands **Rosscarbery.** The cathedral here has a splendid heavy Victorian chancel roof and some excellent 19th- and 20th-century stained glass, notably the pre-Raphaelite young knight in the south transept who commemorates a dead soldier of World War I.

INSIDER TIP:

In rural Ireland, don't overplan the entertainment. Find a local pub that encourages local musicians, then get yourself a pint and enjoy the free show.

—ROBIN CURRIE
National Geographic author

The **Drombeg Stone Circle** (ca 150 B.C.) is well signposted along the Glandore road. Seventeen slim, man-size stones stand in a tight circle, and nearby you'll find an ancient cooking pit with a primitive boiling oven. Before reaching Skibbereen, seek out the erratically signposted **Ceim Hill Museum** (see sidebar p. 144) and its remarkable curator.

Islands of Southwest Cork

Roaringwater Bay, poetically and aptly named, forms the underbelly of the Mizen Peninsula. There are said to be 127 islands scattered in the bay, and the two

Birthplace of Michael Collins
- 129 D2
- Woodfield, Clonakilty, Co. Cork

Islands of Southwest Cork

⚑ 129 C1

Visitor Information

✉ Áras Fáilte, Grand Parade, Cork, Co. Cork

☎ 021 425 5100

Bantry Visitor Information

✉ Old Courthouse, Co. Cork

☎ 027 50229

🕐 Seasonal

largest—Sherkin Island and Clear Island—are accessible by ferry.

Sherkin Island: Sherkin Island *(10-minute ferry ride from Baltimore or Schull, tel 087 911 7377)* is some 3 miles (5 km) long, a great island for swimming with safe, sandy beaches. The 70 inhabitants run a couple of pubs: the Jolly Roger and Murphy's beside the ruins of an O'Driscoll castle. There's also the ruin of a 1460 **Franciscan friary** to explore, along with the enjoyable little island museum in the volunteer-run **Marine Station,** which monitors the marine environment around the island.

Clear Island: Irish-speaking Clear Island, or Cape Clear as some call it *(ferry from Baltimore, tel 087 282 4008),* lies 6 miles (10 km) out from land at the mouth of Roaringwater Bay. It is roughly the same size as Sherkin but more mountainous and bulky. The island, which has

a bird observatory with a worldwide reputation, is a landfall for millions of migrating birds and sees spectacular flypasts in summer of gannets, kittiwakes, shearwaters, guillemots, cormorants, and storm petrels.

North Harbour, where the boat docks, has a couple of pubs, and there's a third one on the potholed road to sheltered **South Harbour.** On the south side of the island—Ireland's southernmost point—are splendid cliffs from which to gaze out at the rugged hump of the Fastnet Rock, 4 miles (6 km) out into the Atlantic.

Islands of Bantry Bay: In Bantry Bay, northward beyond the Mizen and Sheep's Head Peninsulas, lie four islands. **Whiddy Island** *(ferry from Bantry, tel 086 862 6734)* is little visited, mostly because it holds the ugly remains of an oil storage depot abandoned in 1979, when the tanker *Betelgeuse* blew up with a roar heard 15 miles (24 km) off, killing 51 people.

Ceim Hill Museum

The cottage that houses Ceim Hill Museum *(Union Hall, Skibbereen, Co. Cork, tel 028 36280, $),* crooked and cracked and sunk in a leafy dell, looks as if it has sprouted out of the earth.

Inside, everything is set out higgledy-piggledy on tables, shelves, floor, and walls. Miss Therese O'Mahony, owner and curator, collected everything herself from the land around her cottage: fragments of boar tusk incised with pictures by Stone Age man, ancient stone tools, segments of bone sharpened and rubbed long ago,

and more. The War of Independence room has displays of old photos and newspaper cuttings about Michael Collins (O'Mahony's father was an Irish Volunteer), a bathtub full of shipwreck remains, some gorgeous examples of handmade lace, old caps and kettles, and lanterns galore.

O'Mahony is an herbalist, a healer, and a west Cork countrywoman to her fingertips, and her museum is an absolute gem. The guided tour of the museum is de rigueur.

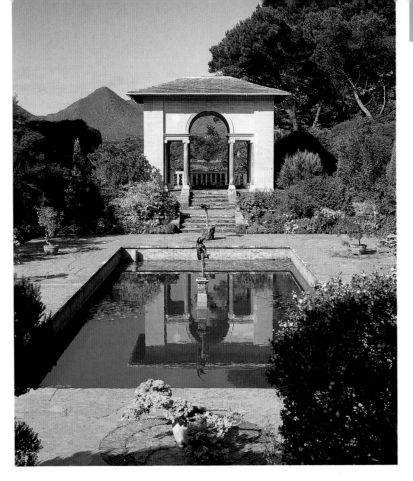

A touch of Romanesque elegance in the Italian garden on Garinish Island in Bantry Bay

Garinish Island, also known as **Garnish** or **Ilnacullin** *(ferry from Glengarriff, tel 027 63116 or 027 63333),* is, at 37 acres (15 ha), a scrap of an island that was bare rock until transformed by the English landscape gardener Harold Peto for the owner Arran Bryce. Between 1910 and 1913, Peto planted on imported topsoil a garden of plants and shrubs from all over the world. Among the lush growth is a formal Italian garden.

Farther down the bay lies **Bere** or **Bear Island** *(ferry from Castletownbere, tel 027 75014),* a former British naval base that has a sailing school and some fine hilly walking and scrambling based on a 13-mile (21 km) stretch of the circumpeninsular Bear (Beara) Way.

Out at the tip of the Bear (Beara) Peninsula, you can sway in a cable car over a furious tidal race to lonely **Dursey Island,** a rugged finger of land where some 50 people live without shop, pub, or other mainland amenities.

Follow a 7-mile (11 km) loop of the **Bear Way** around the island, pausing at the seaward end to look out over the three sea islets of the Bull, the Cow, and the Calf—a wild and glorious prospect.

Three Peninsulas

County Cork boasts three of the five great peninsulas of southwest Ireland—south to north: Mizen, Sheep's Head, and Bear (Beara). Each has a quite distinctive character and individual magic. Try to take a day, at least, of mainland Ireland, with impressive vertical cliffs. You can walk beyond the visitor center and cross a bridge over a rocky sea chasm to see a display of charts, photographs, and signal flags in the old fog station. There's a fine view, too, and maybe a sight of

Whorls and windings of the sea around the shores of the Bear Peninsula

Mizen Peninsula
⬛ 128 B1–129 C1

Skibbereen Visitor Information

✉ Town Hall, Skibbereen, Co. Cork

☎ 028 21766

Mizen Head Visitor Information

✉ Mizen Head, Co. Cork

☎ 028 35115

🕐 Closed weekdays Nov.–March

Sheep's Head Peninsula
⬛ 128 B1–129 C2

on each peninsula; they tend to hide their secrets from those who rush through.

Mizen: Traveling the Mizen Peninsula clockwise from pretty Ballydehob, you enter a sparse world of gorse-covered bog, rock outcrops, and high hills. Roses, purple flowering heather, and brilliant orange monbretia grow in the roadside hedges.

Schull and Goleen are sleepy villages on coastal bays, while charming Crookhaven sits on an isolated mini-peninsula. Barleycove, just beyond, is a huge, fabulous beach system backed by enormous grassy dunes and spreads of *machair* (shell-sand turf). Out at the end, **Mizen Head** is the southernmost point

dolphins, whales, and any number of seabirds.

Sheep's Head: The village of Durrus is where you turn left for the Sheep's Head Peninsula, another clockwise circuit. There are no tourist attractions, which only adds to the magic of this slim and low-rolling promontory, with its scatter of tiny villages and well-ordered farmland that turns wild as you approach the lighthouse at the tip. The scenic drive back to Bantry along the north side is called the Goats Path, with good reason.

Bear: The Bear Peninsula is another matter altogether, a great ragged leg of land, 30 miles (50 km) long, divided

INSIDER TIP:

The Bear Peninsula is a hidden gem. It has all the spectacular scenery as the Ring of Kerry to the north, but without the endless caravans of tour buses.

—CHRISTOPHER KLEIN
National Geographic Traveler
magazine writer

between Cork and Kerry—though Cork has the lion's share. The purple slabs of the Caha Mountains march along the spine of the peninsula, rising to 2,251 feet (685 m), and the Slieve Miskish Mountains are in the west—lower, but no less impressive—rising above inhospitable bog and stony fields. The shoreline is heavily indented. Southward it looks to Bantry Bay and its islands (see p. 144–145); on the north is the Kenmare River, with more, smaller islands and the tremendous backdrop of Kerry's mountainous Iveragh Peninsula (see pp. 150–153).

Tour the Bear in an open-ended figure eight route, starting at the pretty Victorian health resort of **Glengarriff.** In a beautiful location, backed by wooded mountains, the town is full of hydrangeas and palm trees, with 19th-century villas peeping out. Going west along the southern coast road, you soon reach the right turn for the Healy Pass. Try to pick a clear day for the ascent of the narrow mountain road to the pass, at just under 1,100 feet

(334 m), because the view from the Crucifixion shrine at the top is stupendous.

At the northern foot of the pass, you'll find beautiful **Derreen Garden,** with walks to the shore through flowering shrubs and giant feathery tree ferns from Australia. Continue west along a narrow, winding road over the end of Slieve Miskish to **Allihies,** on the black cliffs of west-facing Ballydonegan Bay. Allihies was a copper-mining center in the 19th century, and above the village you can explore the remains of mine buildings.

At the end of Bear is the swaying cable car ride to **Dursey Island** (see p. 145). Back along the south coast, have a look at the extraordinary ruin of **Dunboy Castle,** west of Castletownbere. The IRA torched this mansion in 1921, leaving a Gothic horror of vaults, huge blank windows, and grand rooms open to the sky. ■

Bear Peninsula
🅰 128 B2–129 C2
Glengarriff Visitor Information
✉ Eccles Hotel parking lot, Glengarriff, Co. Cork
☎ 027 63084
🕐 Seasonal

Derreen Garden
✉ Lauragh, Co. Cork
☎ 064 6683103
🕐 Closed Nov.–March & Mon.–Thurs. in Aug.
💲 $$

Gougane Barra Forest Park

Coillte, the Irish state forestry service, owns and administers many forest parks across Ireland, and County Cork's Gougane Barra (*www.coillteoutdoors.ie*) is one of the finest. Here, in a deep rocky bowl of cliffs surrounding peaceful and lovely Gougane Barra lake in the headwaters of the River Lee, Coillte has laid out hiking trails of varying degrees of difficulty—a waterfall trail, an oakwood trail, the trail of the Red Hollow, and more. They introduce you to a beautiful wilderness of coniferous and broad-leaved trees, of rushing streams and falls, and of mountainside lookouts that will take your breath away.

County Kerry

County Kerry is home to the mountains, craggy coasts, and charming small towns and villages depicted in chocolate-box photographs, only close-up and for real. Best known perhaps for the Ring of Kerry, the spectacular coast road around the Iveragh Peninsula, Kerry also boasts the relaxed charm of the Dingle Peninsula, as well as the stark beauty of the Blasket Islands.

The grand beauty of the Lakes of Killarney has attracted visitors for more than 200 years.

Killarney National Park

 129 C3 & 151

Killarney National Park

Some of Ireland's most beautiful lake and mountain scenery falls within the boundary of Killarney National Park. The heart of the park is the 10,000 acres (4,000 ha) of the Muckross Estate, given to the Irish nation in 1932. Careful purchases by the Irish state and donations of land in subsequent decades have safeguarded a total of 25,000 acres (10,000 ha) of wonderful country from development.

Victorian and Edwardian holidaymakers eulogized the Killarney landscape as the "Mecca of every pilgrim in search of the sublime and beautiful in Nature—the mountain paradise of the west." Yet all were agreed that Killarney town itself was far too touristy. Located at the northeast corner of the park, it is still an all-out tourist town where the sales of leprechauns, shamrocks, and shillelaghs keep the gift shops ticking over nicely.

Muckross Estate: While Killarney is just the place to rent a horse-drawn jaunting car complete with a silver-tongued *jarvey*, or driver, to trot you out to the lakes, the town has no views of the lakes themselves. The best thing to do is to refuel and head straight for the Muckross Estate on the shores of Lough Leane.

Muckross is extremely popular and perhaps best avoided on public holidays in summer. At other times of the year, this carefree estate is a great place to stroll by the lake or through the beautifully kept rhododendron and azalea **gardens.**

Muckross House is a Victorian mock-Elizabethan mansion with an appealingly cranky **museum** of folklore and rural life. To the north of the house, you'll find the largely 15th-century cloisters and ruined church of **Muckross Abbey.** Jarveys and their jaunting cars are thick on the ground here, too, if you feel like a horse-drawn tour.

Ross Castle: Head northward along the lakeshore to reach the restored 15th-century fortified *bawn,* or walled tower, of Ross Castle *(tel 064 66 35851).* Hire a rowboat here and pull out across the lake to **Inisfallen,** a lovely little island whose thick woods conceal a church and monastic ruins.

From Ross Castle, head south again along the N71 to reach the Middle and Upper Lakes, where willing boatmen will row you about.

Lakes of Killarney: The star attraction of Middle Lake (also known as Muckross Lake) is the **Meeting of the Waters,** set in a flowery and shrubby dell. Climb past the beautiful Upper Lake to reach **Ladies' View,** a famous viewpoint looking north over the spectacularly narrow Gap of Dunloe and the Killarney Lakes.

INSIDER TIP:

If you're thinking of proposing to that special someone while in Killarney National Park, Torc Waterfall is the local time-honored place to do it.

—WENDY YASCUR
National Geographic contributor

Torc Waterfall, another classic Killarney sight, is signed off the N71 beside Middle Lake. Getting to the fall, a fine 60-foot (18 m) cascade down a staircase of rock overhung with sycamore and mountain ash, involves a short climb up a stepped path. If you feel like a moderate stretch of the legs, you can leave the crowds behind in a twinkling if you carry on up the path beyond the waterfall. Turn around when you've had enough. This is the old road over the mountains to Kenmare (12 miles/19 km away) by way of Esknamucky Glen and Windy Gap, now part of the long-distance **Kerry Way.** It will lead you up through mossy woods of dwarf
(continued on p. 154)

Muckross Estate

✉ Muckross, near Killarney, Co. Kerry
☎ 064 66 70144
🕐 Farms closed Nov.–Feb., & weekdays, March–Apr. & Oct.; house & gardens open year-round
💲 House & farms: $$

www.muckross-house.ie

Drive: Ring of Kerry

This looping route around the coast of the Iveragh Peninsula, known as the Ring of Kerry, is Ireland's best known scenic drive. Although you have to start early, especially in the summer, to avoid becoming stuck behind a crawling line of vehicles, this is one treat you must not miss. A few diversions along even narrower roads are suggested here to give you the chance to explore and to escape any traffic jams on the main road.

Start your full day's drive by leaving **Killarney** for Killorglin along the N72, with great views to your left on the outskirts of town down the wide, mountain-framed expanse of **Lough Leane.** In 12 miles (19 km), you will reach **Killorglin ❶,** a characterful small town where each year in August a wild goat is enthroned as master of an extremely enjoyable three-day revel called Puck Fair.

Leave the main N70 Ring of Kerry route here and enter the town across its bridge, driving up the hill and taking the second street on the right (signed "Caragh Lake"), which soon becomes a bumpy road across forested boglands. At O'Shea's shop in **Caragh** village, fork left (signed "Hotel Ard Na Sidhe"), and in 1 mile (1.6 km), bear left up a forest track (wooden sign: "Loch Cárthaí; Caragh Lake") for

NOT TO BE MISSED:

Cahergeal & Leacanabuaile stone forts • Valentia Island • Views over the Skelligs and Kenmare River • Derrynane House

half a mile (0.75 km) to a **viewpoint ②.** The view here sweeps over Lough Caragh to the mountains—making it a great place for a picnic.

Return to Caragh and turn left to reach the N70, bearing left through Glenbeigh village. A right turn just before you reach the end of the village leads to **Rossbehy (Rossbeigh) Strand ③,** with a wonderful view of a giant

spit of shaggy dunes stretching 3 miles (5 km) north across Dingle Bay toward the mountainous spine of the Dingle Peninsula. The narrow road continues in a loop back to the N70.

Continue on the N70 down the northern coast of the Iveragh Peninsula through glorious hilly scenery. Just before crossing the bridge into the village of **Cahersiveen ④,** glance to your left to see the ruins of the birthplace of Daniel O'Connell (1775–1847), champion of Ireland's poor and the first Irish Catholic to be elected to Parliament in London.

INSIDER TIP:

If you're in Kerry August 10–12, don't miss Puck Fair, one of the oldest traditional fairs in Ireland. Mass revelry ensues when a wild mountain goat is crowned "King Puck" and placed on a platform in the middle of Killorglin town for three days.

—TOM JACKSON
National Geographic Society

Turn right in the village to pass the **Barracks Heritage Centre** (*tel 066 947 2777*), with exhibitions and displays of local interest, then cross a bridge and go left, following brown "Stone Houses" signs, to find **Cahergeal** and **Leacanabuaile stone forts.** Leacanabuaile—certainly inhabited during the Bronze Age, and maybe dating back more than 4,000 years—is especially impressive. Perched on a

Map labels:
Killorglin • R563 • N22 • N72 • START • Killarney • Lough Leane • Macgillycuddy's Reeks • 1039m Carrauntoohil • Gap of Dunloe • Muckross Lake • Upper Lake • Torc Waterfall • KILLARNEY NATIONAL PARK • N71 • R568 • R569 • RING OF KERRY • Kenmare • N71 • R571

See area map pp. 128 A2–129 C1
► Killarney
⊕ 1 day
⟷ 150 miles (240 km)
► Killarney

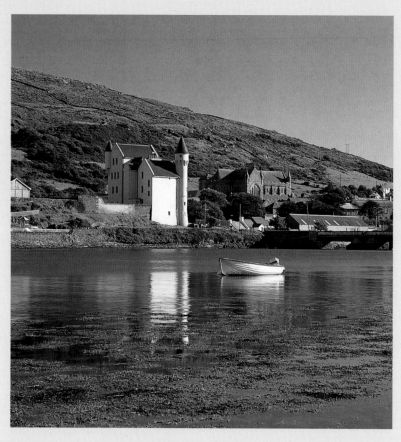

Cahersiveen's old police barracks resembles a Bavarian castle.

rock outcrop, it is a great stone-built enclosure, 80 feet (25 m) across, with a square building in the center and the remains of three beehive huts, all inside a circular 6-foot (2 m) wall.

Three miles (5 km) beyond Cahersiveen, a side road (R565) leaves the N70 and makes for Portmagee, where you cross the causeway onto **Valentia Island** ⑤. This is a most delightful island of tiny patchwork fields, with fine high cliffs on the west and north, and the small but beautiful **Glanleam subtropical gardens** (tel 066 947 6176, $). From the western tip of the island the view looks down to the remote, needle-towered rocks of **Great Skellig** and **Little Skellig.** These towering rocks in the

Atlantic are seabird sanctuaries, but until the 12th century, hardy monks inhabited Great Skellig. Inquiry about boats in Portmagee or Ballinskelligs may yield a fisherman willing to run you out to Great Skellig, where you climb thousand-year-old steps to the sixth-century beehive huts and tiny oratory chapels of the monks, 700 feet (215 m) above the waves. If you can't get hold of a boatman to land you, or sea conditions are too rough, you can always visit the **Skellig Experience Centre** (tel 066 947 6306, $) near the Valentia causeway. Or join one of the regular nonlanding cruises around the islands from Knights Town, the "capital" village of Valentia Island.

Return from Valentia Island to the N70, where you turn right to continue your Ring of Kerry circuit. The seaside resort of **Waterville** stands on the beautiful sandy Ballinskelligs Bay, from where the road climbs (more very fine views of the Skelligs from here) to the classic **viewpoint from Coomakesta Pass** ⑥—back to the Skelligs, then forward to Scariff and Deenish Islands, with the prospect improving all the time as you come in sight of the mighty, islet-fringed Kenmare River, far more like a great bay than an estuary as it opens in front

INSIDER TIP:

On Kerry's Valentia Island, visit Telegraph Field, the site of the first permanent communications link between Europe and North America, established in 1857.

—JUSTIN KAVANAGH
National Geographic International Editions

of you. Turn right at **Caherdaniel**, signposted "Derrynane House," stopping if you wish at the Blind Piper or Freddie's Bar, two excellent pubs.

Derrynane House ⑦ *(tel 066 947 5113, closed Nov.–March, Mon.–Tues. in April & Oct., $)* was the home of Daniel O'Connell from 1825 onward and is now a museum to Swaggering Dan, or "The Liberator," as his fans preferred to call him. O'Connell was a great Irishman, passionate and persevering, and inside the slate-hung house you get a good idea of the Kerry lawyer who inspired such devotion and raised such expectations among the poorest of the poor.

In the dining room a table is set with silverware presented to O'Connell by grateful supporters; upstairs in a display case is a silver cup voted to him in December 1813 by the "Catholics of Ireland." Also here are portraits,

contemporary cartoons, the dueling pistols with which he killed an opponent named D'Esterre, in 1815, and, most poignantly, the bowl he was baptized in and the bed he died in.

Outside, the wooded grounds of Derrynane House are threaded by walking trails that will lead you to a ring fort and to a Mass Rock. It was here, during the 18th century when practicing the Roman Catholic religion was outlawed, that local faithful would gather clandestinely to hear Mass.

Return to the N70 and in 4 miles (6 km) bear left in Castlecove to find the magnificent **Staigue Fort** ⑧. Set in a beautiful lonely valley, this wonderfully preserved ring fort of 1500 B.C. is well over 100 feet (30 m) in diameter, with great thick walls in which steps lead to some fine sea and mountain views.

Back at the N70, turn left and continue as far as **Sneem** village, where you fork left on the R568 for a wild and lonely 30-mile (50 km) mountain run, later passing the lakes of Killarney National Park (see pp. 148–149) and back to Killarney.

Off the Beaten Path

If you find yourself stuck behind a caravan or just fancy taking things slow, there are several worthwhile diversions to make the most of the Ring of Kerry. For example, you could go for a stroll or swim along Rossbeigh Strand, working up an appetite for the fabulous fish at **Jack's Bar and Seafood Restaurant** *(Cromane Lower, Kilorglin, tel 066 97 69102, www.jackscoastguardstation.ie)*. Or enjoy a picnic lunch at Bray Head, on the southern tip of Valentia Island, in full view of the Skelligs. If you want to walk part of the Kerry Way, detour to the left from the N70, between Aghatubrid and Waterville, and follow one of the twisty roads through the Iveragh Peninsula to find where the trail crosses the road.

The atmospheric Dingle Peninsula

Dingle Peninsula

128 A3–B3

www.dingle-peninsula.ie

Dingle Visitor Information

✉ The Quay, Dingle, Co. Kerry

☎ 066 915 1188

Tralee Visitor Information

✉ Ashe Memorial Hall, Denny St., Dingle, Co. Kerry

☎ 066 712 1288

oaks and ancient holly trees to an exciting fording of a mountain torrent by way of stepping-stones.

Dingle Peninsula

The Dingle Peninsula is the connoisseur's choice among the five peninsulas of southwest Ireland. Here are beautiful sandspits, beaches, and mountains, and Ireland's greatest concentration of early Christian sites—not to mention the laid-back charm of Dingle town and the extraordinary literary hothouse of the remote and rugged Blasket Islands. The 105-mile (168 km) Kerry Way footpath circumnavigates the peninsula.

Tralee to Inch: The gateway to the Dingle Peninsula is Tralee, a sizable country town with a bloody history, having been sacked and destroyed in 1583, and again in the 1640s and '50s during the Cromwellian

repressions. These dark deeds are recalled in the excellent **Kerry County Museum** on Denny Street, a fine street of handsome Georgian buildings that leads to Tralee's trademark rose gardens. The annual **Rose of Tralee International Festival** (tel 066 712 1322, www.roseof tralee.ie), held in August, to the delight of the media, pits lovely girls from all over the world (they are supposed to be of Irish extraction) against each other in what is essentially an old-fashioned beauty contest. Tralee is a town of narrow streets, usually crowded, with good traditional music sessions in several pubs—try Paddy Mac's or Bailey's.

Until 1953, the Dingle Peninsula had its own eccentrically delightful railway, which connected Tralee with Dingle town (see sidebar p. 157). A short section of track has been reopened (Tralee to Blennerville Steam Train, tel 066 712

1064), and you can rattle behind a steam locomotive as far as the restored **Blennerville Windmill,** 60 feet (20 m) tall, a grand landmark visible for miles around.

From Tralee, the N86 follows the northern flank of the Slieve Mish Mountains. The western end of this ridge is dominated by the stone-walled promontory fort of **Caherconree,** perhaps built around 500 B.C. You can scramble up to the fort from a minor road, signed to the left off the R559 at the eastern edge of Camp village.

According to legend, Caherconree was the stronghold of King Cu Roi MacDaire, a warrior who made the fatal misjudgment of stealing and "marrying" beautiful Blathnaid, girlfriend of the Ulster hero Cúchullain. Shut up in Caherconree, Blathnaid waited until an auspicious moment arrived for her lover to attack the fort, then summoned him by pouring milk into the springs of the Finglas River. Cúchullain saw the sign, stormed

the fort, slew the king, and was reunited with his beloved.

From the south coast of the peninsula, the superb 4-mile (6 km) sand-dune spit of **Inch** curves out into Dingle Bay—a wonderful sight at low tide with the whorls and channels of sand and water backed by the spectacular Macgillycuddy's Reeks across the bay. West of here is Dingle.

Dingle Town: Dingle has a reputation as a hippyish sort of place. However, this is still a working fishing town and a shopping and socializing center for the wide Gaeltacht area toward the end of the peninsula. It's also a tourist town, often crowded in summer—especially around August, with the Dingle Races, Dingle Show, and Dingle Regatta hard on each other's heels. Each St. Stephen's Day, December 26, the town is given over to the Dingle Wren (see sidebar), when "Wrenboys" dress up and play tricks on each

Dingle Town

🅰 128 A3

Kerry County Museum

✉ Ashe Memorial Hall, Denny St., Dingle, Co. Kerry

☎ 066 712 7777

💲 $$$

www.kerry museum.ie

Blennerville Windmill

✉ West edge of Tralee

☎ 066 712 1064

🕐 Closed Nov.–March

EXPERIENCE: The Dingle Wren

If it is true, as legend tells, that the wren betrayed St. Stephen, then the folk of the Dingle Peninsula in west Kerry have certainly done their best to punish the little bird over the years. In years past, they hunted wrens and nailed them to a pole before parading them through the streets every year on December 26, St. Stephen's Day.

These days, wrens go unharmed come St. Stephen's Day. Instead, "Wrenboys," men dressed in suits and hats of straw, celebrate with music, dancing, and the wild gyrations of the hobby horse—half

steed, half devil—through the streets of Dingle town.

Approach this festival with caution! The **Dingle Wren** (www.dingle-peninsula .ie/wren.html) can get a bit wild, and as a stranger on this day of misrule, you may find yourself the target of some . . . well, let's call it "teasing," especially in the pubs during the later stages of the festivities. It's best to take a backseat and enjoy the craziness from a discrete distance. If you do get involved, don't forget to keep close at hand that most effective of all weapons—a sense of humor.

Dunquin
🅰 128 A3

**Blasket Islands
Interpretive
Center**

✉ Dunquin,
Co. Kerry

☎ 066 915 6444 or
066 915 6371

🕐 Closed
Nov.–May

💲 $

other, with plenty of alcohol
thrown in.

Boat rides run around the
sheltered harbor, enlivened if you
are lucky by a sighting of Dingle's
fabled resident dolphin, Fungie.
Try the Small Bridge pub for
traditional music and don't forget
to sample a Dingle pie, a delicious
mutton pie served with a jug of
mutton broth to pour over it.

Farther west on the R599,
into Irish-speaking territory, you'll
come to **Ventry** on its glorious
curve of sand, and then to the
rich archaeological treasury of
the hillsides under **Mount Eagle.**
Here, a few steps off the road to
either side, are standing stones
and cross-inscribed slabs, beehive
huts, and *souterrains* (underground

storehouses) built on these slopes
by early Christian hermits.

Blasket Islands: As you near
Slea Head at the peninsula's end,
the four Blasket Islands swim
into view—Inishvickillaun, Inishn-
abro, the big green hump of
Great Blasket, and Inishtooskert,
with its sleeping-man shape. Life
was simple for the hundred or
so islanders who once lived on
Great Blasket; yet in the 1930s
they produced three of Ireland's
most respected writers: Tomás
O'Crohan, Maurice O'Sullivan,
and Peig Sayers. The island was
evacuated in 1953 because the
disparity between island poverty
and mainland prosperity had
become too stark.

In Dunquin village on the
mainland, you can learn something
of what Blasket life was like at
the modern **interpretive center.**
Better yet, cross the sometimes
lively Blasket Sound on one of the
regular boats from Dunquin and
wander over the island for yourself.

Dunquin to Brandon Bay:
From Dunquin, the R559 takes
you northeast to the **Gallarus
Oratory,** a boat-shaped chapel
some 1,500 years old. Nearby
is **Kilmalkedar Church.** They
say that if you can squeeze
yourself through the narrow east
window, you'll never suffer from
a bad back (see sidebar).

Soon you come to a signpost
pointing right for **Brandon
Creek,** 5 miles (8 km) north. This
is a wonderfully peaceful spot,
under the slope of the 3,127-foot
(953 m) **Mount Brandon,** second

EXPERIENCE:
Traditional Cures

Early Christian missionaries may have
appropriated the springs, rocks, and trees
sacred to the ancient Celts, but a strong
belief in the efficacy of cures beyond medical or scientific proof has survived. Take, for
example, **Kilmalkedar Church.** According
to tradition, if you can squeeze through
the church's tiny east window, not more
than nine inches (23 cm) wide, you will
never suffer from a bad back. Other similar
cures abound: For homesickness, lie on the
Flagstone of Loneliness by Gartan Lough
(Co. Donegal; see p. 223); for baldness, rinse
your head at **St. Kevin's Well** *(Glendalough,
Co. Wicklow);* for headaches, put your neck
through the stone arch at **St. Colman's Well**
(Kilmoon, Co. Clare); for bad eyes, bathe them
in the **Eye Well at Fairy Hill** *(Dromore, Co.
Tyrone);* and for lameness, bathe and drink at
Doon Well *(Kilmacrennan, Co. Donegal).*

Tralee & Dingle Light Railway

The Tralee & Dingle Light Railway (T&DLR), opened in 1891, was one of the world's great eccentric railways, fulfilling every stereotype of an Irish—and more specifically a Kerry—backcountry branch line. The T&DLR was seldom on time, never worked to capacity or made a profit, and operated with increasingly antiquated locomotives and carriages. It was a friendly, informal line, whose engineers were known to emerge from Fitzgerald's Bar at Castlegregory Junction wiping porter froth from their moustaches as they prepared to drive their trains—a railway whose firemen were valued just as much for the accuracy with which they could throw lumps of coal from the footplate at sheep grazing on the tracks as for their skill in firing the locomotives. The 20-odd-mile (30 km) line incorporated steep gradients and sharp curves, which added to the delays, as did the grass that often smothered the rails. When the T&DLR closed in 1953, it was widely mourned by steam lovers and connoisseurs of curiosities.

highest mountain in Ireland after Carrantuohill (3,414 feet/1,039 m) in Killarney National Park. A ruined oratory at the summit (reachable from nearby Ballyhack via a stiff 3.5-mile/5 km climb up the waymarked Saint's Road—but only in clear weather) is said to be the one St. Brendan prayed in before his epic sixth-century transatlantic voyage in a leather *curragh.* It was from Brandon Creek that the adventurer Tim Severin set sail for Newfoundland in 1976 in his replica boat, following the wake of Brendan (see p. 167).

There are wonderful views from the steep road over the Conor Pass and a warm welcome to be had in O'Connor's pub in Cloghane on the north side of the peninsula before you set course eastward for Tralee. First, though, stretch your legs around the tip of the beautiful **Magharees sand-spit** (see pp. 158–159). ∎

Dog meets dolphin, an everyday Dingle Bay delight

Walk: The Magharees

This is an easy stroll, all on the level, in the flat but remarkable landscape of the Magharees sandspit that divides Tralee Bay from Brandon Bay on the north side of the Dingle Peninsula.

Early Christian hermits lived and prayed in the wildflower fields of the Dingle Peninsula.

Start your walk in the tiny village of **Fahamore,** and follow the road north to **Scraggane Bay ❶** at the tip of the scimitar-shaped spit. Local men paid by the Congested Districts Board, a body set up to aid poverty-stricken and overpopulated rural Ireland, built **Scraggane pier** in 1887. At that time, the United States was taking as many barrels of salted mackerel as Ireland could supply.

In the bay, you'll see moored the black fishing canoes, tough and responsive in lively seas, that are so characteristic of the west

NOT TO BE MISSED:

Scraggane Bay with its namhogs & pier • View of the Magharee Islands • St. Senach's Church, Kilshannig • Brandon Bay

of Ireland; they are built here at Fahamore. Elsewhere this kind of craft is known as a *curragh,* but hereabouts it is called a *namhog* (pronounced na-VOGUE).

Clustered offshore you will see the **Magharee Islands,** also called the **Seven Hogs.** On the largest, **Illauntannig,** a wall encloses two tiny oratories and three *clochans,* or stone huts, the remnants of an early Christian monastery. You may be able to persuade a local boatman to take you out there at a price. Farther out is **Inishtooskert,** off which the German vessel *Aud* idled for a day and a night during Easter Week of 1916. She was waiting for an all's-well signal from accomplices on Inishtooskert, when they were to bring ashore weapons to support the planned Easter Rising, but the signal never came. At last *Aud* departed, and a day later the crew scuttled her off Cobh Haven in County Cork (see pp. 138–139) when they were accosted by the Royal Navy.

Follow the shore to your left around the curve of Scraggane Bay for 1 mile (1.6 km). Halfway around the bay, turn briefly inland where the road makes a right angle to see a fine, tall **standing stone** ❷, a pagan monument carved with a rough cross by some early hermit in an attempt to appropriate its power.

Continue along the shore, then turn inland through the hamlet of **Kilshannig** to reach the ruin of **St. Senach's Church** ❸. Look inside the 16th-century building to see an incised slab marked with a chi-rho crucifix symbol, dating from the seventh century.

Aftrer exploring the church ruins in Kilshannig, head east. Turn

right for 1.5 miles (2.5 km) along the beach until you come opposite **Lough Naparka** ❹. Cross the spit here (looking out for sea holly and pyramidal orchids in the splendid dunes), and return to Fahamore up the glorious wide **beach** ❺.

If you wish to double the length of the walk, continue for another 1.5 miles (2.5 km) from Lough Naparka to the outflow from **Lough Gill** ❻, and follow it inland to reach the lough—a famous place for bird-watching, especially when black swans come from Siberia to overwinter.

From Lough Gill, continue to the west side of the spit for a 2-mile (3 km) beach walk back to Fahamore.

See area map p. 128 B4
► Fahamore
🕐 2 hours (4 hours with extension to Lough Gill)
↔ 6 miles/10 km (11 miles/18 km)
► Fahamore

Lough Gur

Scattered in a loose ring around the small, C-shaped Lough Gur is a multitude of stone structures, evidence of occupation of this site for the past 5,000 years. An interpretive center helps pull the known facts together around the sites. Of these, the Grange Stone Circle is truly breathtaking.

The Grange Stone Circle at Lough Gur is the largest prehistoric stone circle in Ireland.

Lough Gur
🅰 129 E4

**Lough Gur
Interpretive
Centre**
✉ Bruff Rd.,
Holycross,
Co. Limerick
☎ 061 360788
🕐 Closed
Oct.–April
💲 $

Interpretive Center

Since many of the ancient sites are on private land and thus inaccessible, the short video in the interpretive center is necessary viewing. It describes how the shores of the lake hold hut circles, field systems, circles of standing stones, wedge tombs, *crannogs* (artificial fortified islands), stone and earth forts, and a couple medieval castles—a tremendous archaeological record, going back to 3000 B.C.

The importance of Lough Gur was first noticed in the 19th century, when the lake level was lowered and thousands of artifacts came to light. They included the Lough Gur shield, a beautiful bronze ceremonial shield dating from about 700 B.C.. The original is now in the National Museum in Dublin (see pp. 56–59), and many other Lough Gur finds can be seen in the Hunt Museum in Limerick's Custom House (see p. 162). The interpretive center has copies and genuine items—axes, tools, weapons, pottery, arrowheads, and a metalworker's furnace.

The Spectacles

Once outside, you are within a 100 yards (100 m) or so of the spectacles, the foundations of a farmstead of about 900, its tiny fields separated by stone walls. Bones of cattle, sheep, pigs, and dogs have been found on site, along with knives, bone combs, and bronze pins, together with neolithic or late Stone Age pottery and flint scrapers.

Bolin Island Crannog

Down on the lake shore, it's a five-minute clockwise walk to the reed bed where you can stare across at Bolin Island crannog, now dense with trees. Just 100 feet (30 m) in diameter, the crannog can only have held one family at a time during its occupation between A.D. 500 and 1000. It was made by encircling a mound of small stones with larger boulders, then constructing a platform of earth and brushwood layers that held a house and sheds.

Medieval Castles

Two castles stand nearby— the 15th-century **Bourchier's Castle,** with slit windows and four boxy corner turrets (there are plans to open it to the public and site a restaurant in its basement), and the foliage-entangled **Black Castle,** which the Earls of Desmond used periodically from the 13th century onward.

Giant's Grave

The two remaining attractions are a short car ride away. The first is the huge Giant's Grave megalithic wedge tomb, on the left, 1 mile (1.6 km) toward the Limerick–Bruff road from Lough Gur Cross. The bones of eight adults and four children were found in the tomb during excavations in 1938. The tomb was constructed about 2500 B.C. with a curb of upright stones around a central grave of massive boulders, topped by four huge side-by-side capstones. In the 19th century, still covered by its original mound of stones, it was the home of an old woman.

INSIDER TIP:

Lough Gur hosts the Storytelling Festival [www.loughgur.com] every October. In addition to storytelling, events include drama, dancing, and child-friendly workshops.

—STEPHANIE ROBICHAUX
National Geographic contributor

Grange Stone Circle

The 4,000-year-old Grange Stone Circle, a mile (1.6 km) up the Limerick road, is a place of grandeur and mystery, the largest and most impressive stone circle in Ireland. Some hundred stones guard a sunken circle under ancient trees, undoubtedly the scene of Bronze Age spiritual rituals. ∎

More Places to Visit in Southwest Ireland

Adare

Limerick's prettiest village exudes charm from every thatched cottage and flowery garden. The Earl of Dunraven laid it out in Victorian times as an estate village. www.adare.org 🔺 129 D4 ✉ On the N21, 10 miles (16 km) SW of Limerick, Co. Limerick ☎ 061 396255 🕐 Closed Jan.

Ardfert Cathedral &
Banna Strand

Beautiful lancet windows grace the 13th-century cathedral at Ardfert. Next door are the shells of two chapels, one with lovely south window carvings, the other with two intertwined wyverns (heraldic winged dragons) on the northeast window. Nearby, Banna Strand offers a 5-mile (8 km) stretch of glorious beach that looks out over Tralee Bay toward the Magharee Islands. 🔺 128 B4 ✉ On the R551, Ballyheige Rd., 4 miles (6 km) NW of Tralee, Co. Kerry ☎ 066 713 4711 🕐 Closed Oct.–April 💲 $

Béal na Bláth
(The Hollow of the Flowers)

A Celtic cross marks the spot where the commander of the Irish Free State Army, Michael Collins—still a hero to many in Ireland—was ambushed and shot dead by anti-Treaty gunmen on August 22, 1922, during the Irish Civil War. 🔺 129 D2 ✉ On the R585, 3 miles (5 km) SW of Crookstown, Co. Cork ☎ 026 43280

Carrigafoyle Castle

This 15th-century stronghold has a wonderful location on the banks of the Shannon. Climb the 95-foot (29 m) tower for memorable views along the estuary. 🔺 129 C4 ✉ On the Shannon Estuary; signed (2.5 miles/4 km) off the R551 at Ballylongford, 8 miles (13 km) N of Listowel by the R552, Co. Kerry

Fota Wildlife Park &
Fota House Arboretum

Fota Wildlife Park has free-running zebras, giraffes, antelopes, kangaroos, and oryx, as well as caged cheetahs, its breeding specialty. The arboretum possesses rare and beautiful trees from South America, Australasia, the Himalaya, China, and Japan. www.fotawildlife.ie, www.fotahouse.com 🔺 129 E2 ✉ Carrigtwohill, Co. Cork, signed on the R624 Cobh Rd., off the N25, 7 miles (11 km) E of Cork city ☎ 021 481 2678 💲 $$$

Jameson's Old Midleton Distillery

See the world's biggest copper still and a huge old waterwheel—then sample Jameson's golden, nectarous whiskey. www.irish-whiskey-trail.com 🔺 129 E2 ✉ Midleton, off the N25, 10 miles (16 km) E of Cork, Co. Cork ☎ 021 461 3594 🕐 1-hour guided tours 9 a.m.–6 p.m., last tour 4:30 p.m. 💲 $$

Limerick City

Stroll the quays of Limerick to admire **King John's Castle** (Kings Island, tel 061 360788, $$), a massive 13th-century fortification on the River Shannon, juxtaposed with the ultramodern City Hall. **St. Mary's Cathedral,** just south of these, has extraordinary 15th-century misericord carvings of demonic beasts. South again is the old Custom House, now the home of the **Hunt Museum** (Rutland St., tel 061 312833, $$), a wonderful collection of medieval processional crosses, bishops' crosiers, and other artifacts.

Opinions differ as to why the five-line type of verse is called after the city. But there was a popular drinking song, "Will you come up to Limerick," which followed the five-line form and was all the rage in the 19th century around the time limericks became popular. www.limerick.com 🔺 129 E5 ✉ Arthur's Quay, Limerick, Co. Limerick ☎ 061 317522

From the Connemara Mountains and the flowery Burren hills
to the ancient mystery of Mayo—a region that breathes romance

West Ireland

Malachy Kearns, Connemara's master
maker of traditional bodhráns (goatskin drums)

West Ireland

Of those visitors to Ireland who intend to get any farther than Dublin, the majority head out west. Anyone who has heard anything about the character of the different regions of Ireland will have been told that west is best, whether you want wild traditional music, spectacular coast and small island scenery, vast open tracts of ruggedly beautiful landscape, or the most laid-back approach to life in this admirably relaxed country.

The west presents an Atlantic-facing seaboard, but its peninsulas and bays are not as elongated or clearly defined as those of Kerry and Cork. Here the coast is fractured and battered by the sea into ragged lumps and gashes, all dotted with fragments ranging from well-populated islands to tiny scraps of offshore rock.

Three great inlets shape the coastline: the mouth of the Shannon running in under the avocet's bill of southwest Clare, the squarish indentation of Galway Bay with the three Aran Islands at the entrance, and the islet-spattered

NOT TO BE MISSED:

Reveling in the music and craic of
Willie Clancy Week **167**

The flowery limestone of the Burren
region in late spring **168–173**

The view from the magnificent
Cliffs of Moher, part of Burren
National Park **171–172**

Enjoying a memorable session of
traditional music at Hoban's or
McHale's in Westport **175**

Spending a night on Inishmaan,
the most traditional of the three
Aran islands **179**

Venturing through the weird rocky
landscape of Gorumna Island,
Galway Bay **181**

Climbing Croagh Patrick, Ireland's
holy mountain **194–195**

A day out on Achill Island **196–198**

Clew Bay in southern Mayo. With the domed hills of Clare, the all-but-uninhabited mountains, and the lakes and boglands of Galway and Mayo, it adds up to a memorably untamed mingling of land and sea.

County Clare is the greenest, mildest, and gentlest of the West's three counties. Down in the southwest are old seaside towns such as Kilrush and Kilkee, while farther north you come into the strange, haunting landscape of the Burren region—naked gray limestone hills where an incredibly rich flora flourishes.

Galway has a lively county capital in Galway city. It also boasts the rugged beauty of the mountains and boglands of Connemara, the westernmost part of the county, as well as the great fishing lakes based around mighty Lough Corrib and a cluster of Irish-speaking islands.

As for County Mayo, discerning explorers are beginning to wake up to the wild beauty of this boggy and mountainous northern corner of the west, with its holy mountain of Croagh Patrick, its buzzing music town of Westport, and its empty, glorious beaches.

Benwee Head
Erris Head
Doonamo Point
Inishglora
Duvillaun Islands
Inishkea
Achill Head
Keem

Portacloy
Porturlin
Termoncarragh Lake
Pollatomish
Belmullet
Mullet Peninsula
Bangor
Carrowmore Lake
R314
Céide Fields

Downpatrick Head
Bally-castle
Killala Bay
Killala

NORTHWEST IRELAND p. 203

Nephin Beg Range
Lough Conn
Ballina
Moy
N59
N59
N26
Foxford
Swinford

M A Y O
Slievemore
Achill Island
Dooagh Keel
Cliffs of Minaun
R319
Mallaranny
Rockfleet Castle
Burrishoole Abbey
Newport
N5
Castlebar
N58
N5
N84
N17

Clare Island
Knockmore
Clew Bay
Kildaunet Castle
Westport House
Westport
R330
Ballintober Abbey
Ballyhaunis
N60
N60
N83

Inishturk
Louisburgh
R335
Murrisk
Aghagower
Croagh Patrick
Partry Mts.
Partry
Claremorris
Lough Carra

St. Colman's Abbey
Inishbofin
Doo Lough Pass
Sheeffry Hills
Doo Lough
Killary Harbour
Leenane
Lough Mask
Ballinrobe
Clare
N17
N83

Inishshark
Kylemore Abbey
Cleggan
Maumturk Mountains
R345
Cong
N84
Tuam
Mountbellew Bridge

addaghduff
CONNEMARA N.P.
Pollacappul L.
The Twelve Pins
Recess
Maam Cross
Lough Corrib
Knockmoyle Abbey
N63

Mannin Bay
Clifden
N59
Connemara
Oughterard
CENTRAL IRELAND p. 233

Derrygimlagh Bog
Ballyconneely
Pearse's Cottage
Roundstone
Bertraghboy Bay
300m
Errisbeg
Iar-Connacht
Costelloe
G A L W A Y
Athenry
R348
Ballinasloe
N6

Lettermore
Lettermullan
Gorumna
R336
Spiddle
Galway
N6
Turoe Stone
Loughrea
Clontuskert Abbey
N65
Clonfert Cathedral

Galway Bay
Dunguaire Castle
St. Brendan's Cathedral
Lough Rea
Portumna
Shannon

Inishmore
Dunaengus
Dún Dúchathair
Kilronan
ARAN ISLANDS
Inishmaan
Inisheer
Fanore
Ballyvaghan
Newtown Castle
Rathborney Church
Cahermacnaghten
Lisdoonvarna
Doolin
Corcomroe Abbey
Aillwee Cave
Gleninsheen
Poulnabrone
Kilfenora
BURREN N.P.
Thoor Ballylee
R353
COOLE PARK
Gort
Kilmacduagh
Lough Derg

Cliffs of Moher
Caherbally-kinvarga
Leamaneh Castle
Dysert O'Dea
Holy Island
E

Lehinch
C L A R E
R352
Milltown Malbay
N85
Doo Lough
Ennis
Craggaunowen Project
Killaloe

Doughmore Bay
N67
N68
Bunratty Castle & Folk Park
N18
Shannon
Bunratty
R463
Shannon

Kilkee
Kilrush
Scattery Island Centre
Kilrush
Scattery Is.
SOUTHWEST IRELAND p. 127

Loop Head

6
5
4
3
2
1

A   B   C   D

0   30 kilometers
0   15 miles

Southern Clare

The southwest corner of County Clare is gentle, easygoing, and essentially rural—a long green peninsula where countryside or seaside are yours for the asking. Hereabouts, you'll grow accustomed to the slow tempo of daily life, livened with a splash of nighttime gaiety.

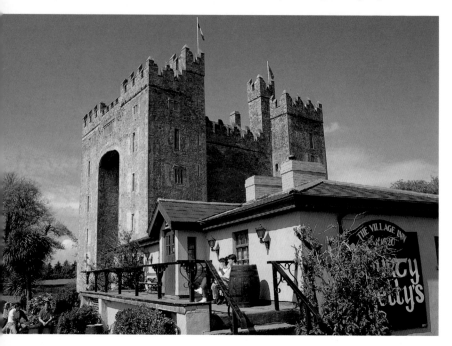

The great arches of Bunratty Castle lead to medieval feasts of meat and mead.

Southern Clare
🗺 165 B1–D2

Visitor Information
✉ The Square, Kilrush, Co. Clare
☎ 065 905 1577
🕐 Closed mid-Sept.–late May

Bunratty Castle & Folk Park

Bunratty Castle & Folk Park, off the N18 Ennis–Limerick road, is worthwhile if you don't mind sharing your enjoyment with a few thousand others.

The well-restored castle, built around 1460, has a splendid keep where nightly "medieval banquets" are held. You can quaff mead and eat with your fingers, while minstrels serenade you and serving wenches bustle around with platters and jugs.

To those who have already traveled among and appreciated real, living Irish villages, the folk park—a reconstructed 19th-century village set on 25 acres (10 ha)—can seem a theme park travesty; however, if you come out of season to enjoy the cottages, shops, small businesses, and pub without the holiday crowds, you can catch an appealing atmosphere enhanced by the blacksmith, weavers, spinners, and butter makers who bring a touch of life to the place.

Craggaunowen Project

Ten miles (16 km) north, off the road from Kilmurry to Moymore, you'll find the Craggaunowen Project. Centered around a fortified tower house of 1550, Craggaunowen tells the story, via costumed guides, of the Irish Celts, their domestic lives, their warfare and religious practices, and the way they hunted and farmed. Specially constructed features include a walled ring fort enclosing typical fifth- or sixth-century huts under conical thatched roofs; a causeway to a lake-bound *crannog*, or artificial fortified island, sheltering a wattle-and-daub house; burial sites; and a *fulacht fiadh* (hunter's cooking pit).

Also on display is the leather-hulled *curragh, Brendan,* in which explorer Tim Severin sailed to Newfoundland in 1976–1977.

Other Attractions

County Clare sweeps away southwest in a narrowing spike of a peninsula. The south coast of this 40-mile (65 km) promontory forms the northern shore of the widening Shannon Estuary, while the cliff-bound north coast, far more indented and battered, faces out into the Atlantic. The hinterland is gentle and green, while the coast is lined with long, sandy swimming beaches. There are a handful of old-style seaside resorts and some nice quiet country towns.

North coast resorts with plenty of accommodations and sandy beaches are **Lehinch** (Lahinch) and **Kilkee,** the former with a beautiful golf course, the latter with some exciting natural rock-pool swimming in the Duggerna Rocks at the western end of the beach. Between them is **Milltown Malbay,** normally a quiet town, where Willie Clancy Week *(information: tel 065 708 4148),* an annual music festival in July, celebrates the life and skill of local piper Willie Clancy.

Loop Head, at the southwestern point of the peninsula, has fine cliff walks, while farther around into the mouth of the Shannon is the handsome riverside town of **Kilrush.** Ask at the **Scattery Island Centre** *(tel 065 682 9100)* on Merchant's Quay about boats to **Scattery Island,** a mile (1.6 km) offshore. Here you'll find several ruined medieval churches and a 110-foot-high (33 m) round tower. ∎

Bunratty Castle & Folk Park

- 165 D1
- Bunratty, Co. Clare
- 061 360788
- $$$

Craggaunowen Project

- 165 D2
- 4 miles (6 km) SE of Quin
- 061 360788
- Closed mid-Oct.–mid-April
- $$$

EXPERIENCE:
Going to the Horse Fair

Held in late June every year for the past 300 years, the **Spancilhill Fair** *(just outside Ennis, Co. Clare, www.spancilhillfair.com)* is one of Ireland's most characterful horse fairs, a genuine slice of old Ireland. Crowds are big and loud, with a tremendous amount of knowledgeable horse talk flung about. And, of course, there is a multitude of horses of every kind; you can even buy one if you have the money—and the cheek. Fiercely contested prizes include best cob, best pony, best donkey, and more.

Other Irish horse fairs include the well-known **Ballinasloe Horse Fair** *(Co. Galway, www.ballinasloeoctoberfair.com),* a week of fun and frolics in October, only some of it horse related; and the lively **Cahirmee Horse Fair** *(at Buttevant, Co. Cork, in July and Borris, Co. Carlow, in Aug.).*

Burren National Park

Mysterious and concealing, yet lying wholly open to view, the Burren region of north County Clare is a remarkable and haunting place. Among its bare gray hills lie hidden ancient tombs, churches, dwellings, and ring forts in a bleak setting jeweled with Ireland's richest flora. At the outer edge of the hills are villages that seem to run entirely on wonderful music. And the flanks of the hills themselves, solid though they look, conceal a heart of rock riddled with caves, passages, and seldom-seen underground rivers.

Mighty dolmens, burial places of pre-Christian chieftains, stand on the limestone of the Burren.

The Burren forms the whole of northwest Clare, some 200 square miles (500 sq km) bounded on the north and west by the sea and on the south and east by typical Clare grazing country, mild and green. But there is nothing green, mild, or typical about the Burren. *Boireann,* its Gaelic name, means "rocky land." The region rises from a sharp-cut sea coast through a collar of meadows into a cluster of dome-shaped hills with their rounded tops and stepped flanks, their pale gray limestone seemingly naked of vegetation. It looks like a dry, harsh landscape, drained of life—one in which nothing can have flourished for a very long time. It is not until you get into the heart of the Burren, abandon your car, and walk out into this barren-looking world that you begin to appreciate just how much life and interest there is. And the fascination is not all above ground: The **Aillwee Cave,** south of Ballyvaghan, offer a glimpse of the stalactites and stalagmites, cavernous spaces, waterfalls, and passages at the heart of the hills.

Limestone & Flowers

The Burren region is formed of rough, cracked limestone known as karst. The surface of the limestone is fractured into deep, narrow channels (*grykes*) a few inches wide but several feet long, with oblongs of rock (known as clints) of varying sizes islanded among them. To the untuned eye, it looks like rubbly, useless land. Gen. Edmund Ludlow reported to Oliver Cromwell in 1651 that the Burren region "had not any tree to hang a man, nor enough water to drown him, nor enough earth to bury him"—a telling remark, considering the Puritan leader's intentions for the Irish at that time. But Ludlow was observant enough to add: "Their cattle are very fat, for the grass growing in tufts of earth of two or three foot square that lie between the rocks, which are of limestone, is very nourishing."

It is the space "between the rocks," and the soil and rainwater trapped in the grykes, that allow such an extraordinarily varied range of plants to flourish in the Burren. These limestone crevices are sheltered from the salt wind, watered by the frequent rainfall of the area, and warmed by the Gulf Stream that moves just off the Clare coast and by sunlight reflected into their depths off the pale limestone. Plants that would not normally be found on the same continent, let alone on the same hillside, find the Burren conditions right for them. Some botanists think that certain Arctic alpine plants are descendants of those that arrived in the Burren as seeds moving south in melting Ice Age glaciers 10,000 years ago.

INSIDER TIP:

Standing on the cliffs of the Burren gives you the sense that you're on a precipice overlooking the entire Atlantic—that you're on the bow of a mighty ship that is Europe, heading west.

—ALEX DI SUVERO
National Geographic photographer

Here you'll see plants of the north, such as the large creamy cups of mountain avens, coexisting with plants of the south like the yellow hoary rock-rose. In certain places, streams bring acid bog peat to lodge in hollows of the alkaline limestone so that acid-loving plants such as heather and saxifrage thrive side by side with lime-loving plants like milkwort and tormentil.

What this means in practical terms is a glorious flood of color

Burren National Park

🗺 165 C2

Visitor Information

✉ Cliffs of Moher tourist information office, Liscannor, Co. Clare

☎ 065 708 1171

Aillwee Cave

🗺 165 C3

✉ Ballyvaughan

☎ 065 707 7036

💲 $$$

www.aillweecave.ie

EXPERIENCE: Wildflowers of the Burren

The violet throats of selfheal open along the grassy verges of the Caher River, overlooked by the parrot beak–shaped seedheads of the yellow rattle. Sulfur-colored lady's bedstraw peeps out from a gryke, a shadowed slit in the limestone pavement, while acid-loving Irish saxifrage—rarer than hens' teeth—thrives in the hollow of a clint, or natural cobble, of pure limestone. Everywhere you look are the diminutive white peepers of eyebright. Where else could you be but the Burren? This unique region of northwest County Clare, with its pale gray domes of limestone hills, is home to the richest plant life in Ireland (see pp. 172–173).

You could rummage around on your own in such a botanical jewel case for the simple pleasure of bedazzlement by color, shape, and scent—especially with one of Tim Robinson's (see sidebar p. 179) incomparable *Folding Landscapes* maps in hand. But those who walk with Mary Howard's **Burren Guided Walks and Hikes** (*tel 065 707 6100 or 087 244 6807, www.burrenguided walks.com*) enjoy an experience they will never forget. Mary is a Burren resident and a passionate devotee of the Burren landscape. She also really knows her plants and has a knack for bringing the apparently dry and barren terrain to life.

Newtown Castle

 165 C3

 SW of Ballyvaghan

☎ 065 707 7200

🕐 Closed Nov.–March

across the gray hills and coastal shelves, and endless fascination hopping across the rocks with a flower book. You don't have to be an expert to appreciate the delicately marked orchids, the brilliant blue trumpets of spring gentians, or the extraordinary flush of magenta that stains the hills overnight to announce proudly the dramatic June flowering of the bloody cranesbill.

Past Inhabitants

The Burren interior is completely devoid of settlements today, thanks to its shortage of water—the thirsty karst draws the rivers underground—and to what amounted to an ethnic cleansing policy by Cromwell, but there is plenty of evidence of a vigorous population in times gone past. The splendid portal dolmen of **Poulnabrone** and the nearby **Gleninsheen** wedge tomb show with what

pomp and ceremony the prehistoric Burren-dwellers buried their chiefs. Stone-walled Celtic ring forts abound—**Cahermacnaghten** and **Caherballykinvarga** lie close to roads and can be explored. The law school run in medieval times by the O'Davorens at Cahermacnaghten was so well regarded that pupils came from all over Ireland to learn the tenets of ancient Brehon law (see p. 24). Nowadays it stands empty, a magnificent circular enclosure where cattle shelter.

Graveyards, crosses, and ruined medieval churches dot the Burren. **Rathborney Church** was built inside a pre-Christian circular earthen rampart that must have been an object of superstitious awe, while the ruins of **Corcomroe Abbey** (fine stonework) in the northeast and of the church at **Dysert O'Dea** (magnificent high cross and a bizarre doorway of sculpted heads) in the south are notable examples.

Life in medieval Ireland being the risky business it was, there are also some fine fortified towers and houses in the Burren—**Newtown Castle,** southwest of Ballyvaghan (Ballyvaughan), and **Leamaneh Castle** *(closed),* east of Kilfenora, are worth a look.

Hundreds of such sites lie tucked away across the Burren, and to help find them you can't do better than to buy Tim Robinson's hand-drawn *Folding Landscapes* map of the Burren (ISBN 0-9504002-1-1)—by far

INSIDER TIP:

Watch for Tina Mulrooney singing and playing her harp on the steps by the dramatic Cliffs of Moher. Her CDs make wonderful souvenirs.

—ROZ HOAGLAND
Private guide, Hoagland Art Travel

the most informative guide you could wish for and widely available locally. It also features the many holy wells and "old faith" cures for headaches, sore backs, tooth trouble, and weak eyes to which Burren people still resort.

Cliffs of Moher

The rocky coastline of the Burren is relieved by caravan-ridden dunes at **Fanore,** then trends southwest for another 15 miles

(25 km) to culminate in the mighty **Cliffs of Moher,** at 665 feet (200 m) a magnificent piece of natural sculpture in layers of flagstone and shale. O'Brien's Tower, a Victorian viewpoint, tops them off. A new "Visitor Experience," completed in 2007, offers cliff-edge

Cliffs of Moher
- 🅰 165 C2
- ✉ SW of Doolin
- ☎ 065 708 6141
- 💲 $
- **www.cliffsofmoher.ie**

O'Brien's Tower, built in 1835, looms at the summit of the Cliffs of Moher, which face out to the Atlantic Ocean.

walkways and seating, viewing platforms and a subterranean visitor center. Seabirds abound, and the view on a good day from the top of O'Brien's Tower takes in a circle of more than 100 miles (160 km), from the Kerry hills to the Aran Islands and the Twelve Bens of Connemara—even to a far glimpse of Croaghaun on Achill Island up in County Mayo.

Villages of the Burren

Looped around the skirts of the uninhabited Burren hills is a string of villages that rely mainly on farming and tourism—all of them great places for conversation and music.

Ballyvaghan (Ballyvaughan) is the northernmost settlement, looking out to Galway Bay. Monk's Bar is the place for music here. **Doolin,** however,

The Flora of the Burren

Burnet rose

Waltrue
Asplenium Ruta-murania

Maidenhair fern

Fly orchid
Ophrys insectifera

Bee orchid
Ophrys apifera

Rusty-backed fern
Ceterach officinarum

Wood sage

Hazel

Geranium
sanguineum

Spring
gentian

Hoary rockrose

Pearl-bordered
fritillary

Dark red helleborine
(orchid) Epipactis atrorubens

Mountain avens
Dryas octopetala

is the music-lover's mecca (see pp. 174–175).

Sleepy **Lisdoonvarna** comes alive each September for its Matchmaking Festival *(tel 065 707 4005, www.matchmakerireland.com, held Sept.–early Oct.),* when unmarried men and women of the west converge on the village for a week of taking the spa waters, dancing, and making acquaintance. Part media circus, part revival of an old tradition, this is a good-time week that anyone can enjoy.

At **Kilfenora,** there's a 12th-century cathedral without a roof and four carved high crosses of the same date; the **Burren Centre** *(tel 065 708 8030, www.theburren centre.ie, $$),* with excellent displays on the wildlife, geology, and archaeology of the Burren; and two great music pubs in Vaughan's and Linnane's. ∎

Ajuga pyramidalis

Hart's tongue fern
Phyllitis
scolopodendrium

Twayblade (orchid)
Listera orata

Pyramid orchid
Anacamptis
pyramidalis

Cat's foot mountain everlasting
Antneria dioica

Spiranthes spiralis
(orchid)

Dense-flowered orchid
Neotina maculata

Harebell

Irish hare

Shrubby
cinquefoil

Bearberry

Irish saxifrage

Fragrant orchid
Gymnadenia conopsea

Pubs & Music of West Ireland

Pub-going in the west of Ireland is an activity as natural as breathing. You'll find yourself gravitating naturally to the pub because it's there that you'll meet local people and other visitors, join in the *craic* (pronounced "crack"), and hear the best music in Ireland. Note that information about sessions is given over the bar on the day—don't be afraid to ask.

Get out of the rain, into the bar, and up with the mood at an exhilarating traditional music session.

Whatever it is about the west of Ireland—the lifestyle or the land, the peculiarly magical atmosphere woven by mountains, boglands, and coasts, or something in the water—it's a well-attested fact that the traditional music here is something special.

Some connoisseurs claim to detect a correlation between the character of the music and the shape and nature of the landscape it springs from—a smooth gentleness to the compositions and performances of Clare, for

instance, or a melancholy wildness to those of Mayo. You can judge for yourself, as either a participant or an onlooker, in the numberless great music pubs of the west.

In southwest Clare, try **O'Mara's** on O'Curry Street, Kilkee, where you'll get music of all sorts and great atmosphere, and **Clancy's** and **Queeley's** in Milltown Malbay for wonderful traditional sessions.

Around the Burren—famous music territory— you'll enjoy **Linnane's** in Kilfenora and the

Roadside Tavern on the edge of Lisdoonvarna (great music here), while in the music-to-its-fingertips village of Doolin it's McGann's by the bridge for evening tune sessions, and O'Connor's nearer the sea for rollicking ballads and showmanship, day and night. Ennistymon, too, is a famous town for music, in the Archway—beautifully placed by the River Cullenagh—and a dozen other pubs.

Galway city offers good impromptu music in Taaffe's bar, on Shop Street, and more of the same in the wonderful old-fashioned Ti Neachtain on Cross Street, all cozy snugs and odd corners—there's a first-class restaurant here as well.

Out in Connemara, there's a great pub around every corner, but for real character you could try the Irish-speaking Ost na nOilean down at the foot of Gorumna Island or the even more remote and Gaelic pub on Inishmaan, the middle one of the three Aran Islands. The Strand Bar, out at Claddaghduff in the far west (always known as Sweeney's), does a great hot whiskey when the weather is biting back.

As for Mayo—head for Westport if you want music. Matt Molloy, flute player with celebrated traditional music band the Chieftains, owns a bar on Bridge Street named Matt

INSIDER TIP:

Taaffe's bar has the best live music in Galway. They stop serving food after lunchtime, though, so have an early dinner at one of the many nearby restaurants before choosing your spot for the free show.

—KAREN MARTINEZ
National Geographic Books

Molloy's, where the back bar sessions are regularly infiltrated by the great names of Irish music (including Molloy himself when he's around). Hoban's and McHale's are two other marvelous pubs for music, where quiet-mannered whistle player and tour leader Olcan Masterson (see p. 190) leads blinding sessions with modesty and good humor.

In the country, westward, Owen Campbell's enormously friendly bar in Murrisk, the port of call for outward or incoming pilgrims walking up the holy mountain of Croagh Patrick (see pp. 192–195), is often still humming at midnight.

The *Craic*

Even if you would never normally set foot in a bar, you should do so—regularly—in Ireland. The Irish pub is far more than a boozing den, and it has become even more enjoyable since the smoking ban took hold in 2004. In the city, the pub is where that great Irish art, conversation, is practiced away from the roar and bright lights, while in small country towns and villages, it is the focus of community activity. You get advice, make friends, and hear charming nonsense; the pub is where you pick up local news, get a bite and a sip, and enjoy that wonderful tide of live music—traditional tunes, ballads, country, and rock music.

All this mixture of talk, fun, music, leg-pulling, and drink goes under the generic name of the *craic* (pronounced "crack"). You'll hear the craic talked of wherever you go—"You should have been in McGing's, the craic was mighty"; "We'll call in on Joe and have a bit of craic"; "Marie? Ah, she's great craic." You might run across the craic in a pub, a back kitchen, a corner shop, or a country lane—you never know your luck. But you'll know it when you find it.

Galway City

Galway is a lively city, one of the liveliest in Ireland thanks to its university and colleges and to a great revival in its economy and optimism over the past 20 years or so. At any time of year, but particularly in the summer, Galway's an exciting place to be. The *Tourist Trail of Old Galway* guidebook, available from the visitor information center, is excellent for sightseeing on foot.

You'll find plenty of Irish dancers in Galway, from formal performances to just a few people enjoying the moment.

Galway City
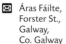 165 C3

Visitor information

✉ Áras Fáilte,
Forster St.,
Galway,
Co. Galway

☎ 091 537700

The Anglo-Normans built Galway into an important castle town and port in the mid-13th century, and for 400 years it was an Anglicized enclave amid the Irish people and culture of Connemara. The "Fourteen Tribes of Galway" were the Anglo-Norman families who prospered on trade with Europe, notably with Spain. Oliver Cromwell put an end to this golden age when he sacked Galway in 1652, and King William III completed the job in 1691. It took 300 years, but Galway rose again, thanks to high-tech industries and the economic boom of the 1990s (see p. 14).

City Attractions

As it runs south from the tree-shaded gardens of **Eyre Square,** Galway's main street changes name, from Williamsgate to William Street, then Shop Street, High Street, and finally Quay Street as it reaches the River Corrib. Curious carved stones sit high on the walls of shops and houses—heraldic shields, beasts, foliage, and human faces, mostly dated to show when eminent persons married or took possession of the premises. After a while you develop quite a talent for spotting them.

At the Four Corners, where William Street becomes Shop Street, stands **Lynch's Castle,** a very fine late 15th-century fortified stronghold tower with a bank on its ground level. On the walls are coats of arms, elaborate roundels, several lions with human faces, and a row of gargoyles supporting the top of the tower.

A sidestep up Church Lane leads to **St. Nicholas' Collegiate Church** (*www.stnicholas.ie*), rich in this vigorous, expressive Galway carving. A seductive mermaid clings to the west window. Inside are some fine tombs and more examples of the mason's art—they include graveslabs carved with the symbols of their incumbents' trades. Another stone carving has a low-slung cur chasing a hare, bug-eyed with terror, over the arch of the bell-tower door.

North of the church stands the rebuilt Lynch memorial window. On this spot in 1493 the chief magistrate of Galway, James Lynch Fitzstephen, hanged his own son Walter for murder. "Stern and unbending justice" is how a plaque describes the father's action. Across the way, at 8 Bowling Green, lived Nora Barnacle before she ran off with James Joyce in 1904. It is now the **Nora Barnacle House Museum.**

A very pleasant walk follows the River Corrib to the whitewater sluices beyond Salmon Weir Bridge and a randomly arranged, but neatly labeled, jumble of exhibits in the enjoyable **Galway City Museum.** Here you'll find everything from fish spears and a sack-sewing contraption to badger traps, photos, and pikes from the 1867 Fenian Rising.

Summer Festivals

A great time to be in Galway is around the end of July, when the **Galway Arts Festival** *(tel 091 509700, www.galwayartsfestival.ie)* is immediately followed by the weeklong jamboree of the **Galway Races** *(tel 091 753870, www.galwayraces.com)* at Ballybrit Racecourse, just northeast of the city. It's a hectically crowded but very enjoyable three weeks, during which normal life is suspended as activities from classical music and literary lectures to street theater and music keep the place buzzing day and night.

No sooner have the final Arts Festival fireworks fizzled out than attention switches to the track. There's a full card of racing each day—enthusiastically supported by locals and visitors alike—and the city puts on dances, pub music, and exhibitions for gamblers both lucky and unlucky. ∎

Nora Barnacle House Museum

- ✉ 8 Bowling Green, Galway, Co. Galway
- ☎ 091 564743
- 🕐 Closed mid-Sept.–mid-May
- 💲 $

Galway City Museum

- ✉ Spanish Arch, Galway, Co. Galway
- ☎ 091 532460
- 💲 $

www.galwaycitymuseum.ie

EXPERIENCE: Learn Irish Dancing

Compared to lavish productions like Riverdance, traditional Irish dancing can seem pretty staid. Dancers clip their arms to their sides, their expressions immobile as only their twinkling feet seem to convey any emotion. However, you don't need to be a real connoisseur to enjoy Irish dancing, and as with traditional music, it's best to have a go yourself.

Classes in Irish dancing of all kinds are available in Galway City. **Conradh na Gaeilghe** (tel 091 567824, www.cnag.ie) runs popular bilingual classes in Sean-Nos, a solo style of dancing that is perfect for complete beginners. Instructors are expert dancers and very patient.

Spontaneous dancing often occurs in pubs, drawing an enthusiastic audience and exciting good-natured competition. In Galway, you are most likely to find dancing at the **Crane Bar** (Sea Road, tel 091 567419, www.thecranebar.com), on the west bank of the River Corrib, and **Quays Bar** (Quay St., tel 091 568347).

Around Dublin, try the **Merry Ploughboy** (Edmonstown Rd., Rathfarnham, Dublin, tel 01 493 1495, www.mpbpub.com), where you can watch an Irish dancing show, or take a class at the **Glenside** pub (Landscape Rd., Churchtown, Dublin, tel 01 298 5932). Consult www.setdancing.com and www.ceili.ie for more listings.

Aran Islands

The Aran Islands are a byword for harsh, unforgiving landscape, and their Irish-speaking people have always epitomized hardy self-reliance. Things are changing fast under the influence of tourism and modern amenities, yet there's a strong thread of a way of life long passed into history elsewhere in Ireland.

The 2,000-year-old sea forts of Inishmore stand dramatically at the very brink of the cliffs.

Aran Islands

🅜 165 B3–C2

Visitor Information

✉ Kilronan tourist information, Inishmore, Aran Islands, Co. Galway

☎ 099 61263

The three islands (not to be confused with County Donegal's Aran Island) resemble a family of sea beasts swimming northwest out of Galway Bay. Inishmore, the largest island at 8.5 miles long (14.4 km), is followed by Inishmaan, which is 3 miles (5 km) long. Round-bodied Inisheer—the smallest island, at less than 2 miles (3 km) across—brings up the rear.

Wind-scoured, sea-bitten limestone gives the Aran Islands their extraordinary atmosphere, more out-of-this-world than any other landscape in Ireland. The dark gray limestone is scored with thousands of north–south fractures, giving each of the three islands the appearance of having been raked by a giant comb.

These are virtually treeless islands, where soil has been built up laboriously by hand out of sand, seaweed, compost, and manure, and shielded from blowing away in stone-walled fields. The stone walls—the islands' best-known feature—are built of thousands of loosely stacked blades of unmortared limestone through which pours the light, so that on a sunny day they form a lacy mosaic of gray stone and blue sky. The walls are repositories for unwanted stone cleared off the fields as much as they are wind-breaks or property boundaries.

Inishmore

As the capital island, Inishmore has a defined port village, Kilronan, and gets almost all the visitors, many of whom leave with one of the trademark fishermen's sweaters still made on the islands. Minibuses offer whistlestop tours of the island; pony traps do the same thing at a more leisurely pace. It's best to rent a bicycle or set out on foot, however, if you want to catch the spirit of the place.

The chief attraction is undoubt-edly **Dunaengus** (tel 099 61008, $), the Fort of King Aengus, which stands two-thirds of the way up the south coast—a mighty semicir-cular stronghold some 2,000 years old, breathtakingly sited on the brink of a 300-foot (91 m) cliff. A cunning chevaux-de-frise (belt of upright stone blades) was set up to guard it from onrushing enemies.

Dún Dúchathair, the Black Fort, located a couple of miles (3 km) down the cliffs from Dunaen-gus, is less well preserved than its better known neighbor. But here you are more likely to have elbow room in which to admire the crumbling stairs and walkways in its 20-foot (6 m) walls of dark stone and the enigmatic little labyrinth at its heart.

Other Inishmore sites well worth seeking out with the help of your *Folding Landscapes* map (see sidebar), available in Kilronan, Ros-saveal, and Galway, are the ruined but beautiful churches that are scattered across the island.

EXPERIENCE:
Walking the Aran Islands

When Englishman Tim Robinson moved to the Aran Islands in 1972, he became captivated by the extraordinary landscape of stark flat limestone and its history. The more he walked the stone-walled lanes and talked to the islanders, the greater grew his ambition to record what he found. Many superbly written books resulted, as well as an admirable and unique series of *Folding Landscapes* maps, treasured by legions of walkers and amateur explorers.

To get the most out of your walks in the Arans, be sure to pick up your own *Folding Landscapes* maps. You will be amazed at what they bring to light, including standing stones, ancient churches, forgotten tombs, and a whole tumble of holy wells. You can buy the maps, and Robinson's books, from **Folding Landscapes** (Roundstone, Co. Galway, tel 095 35886, www.foldingland scapes.com).

Emigration of youngsters and the influence of incomers and holi-daymakers have brought Inishmore further into line with mainland thinking and attitudes than the two smaller Aran Islands.

Inisheer & Inishmaan

Inisheer, cheerful and relaxed in atmosphere, makes a memo-rable day trip from Doolin on the Clare coast. But it is on the middle island, Inishmaan, that you are most likely to hear Irish spoken and see old folk still wearing homespun clothes. The south end of Inishmaan, with its spouting blowholes and stony coast, is as wildly bleak and beautiful a spot as any you'll find in Ireland. ■

Connemara

Few place-names in Ireland are more evocative than Connemara, and no region is more steeped in the romance of harshly beautiful, remote, and alluring country. Irish city-dwellers in search of their roots find inspiration and a confirmation of their Irishness in this wild western half of County Galway, and you can expect the same magic as you wander among Connemara's mountains, bogs, and lakes and along its ragged coasts.

A line of craggy mountains forms the horizon between wide waters and vast cloudscape skies.

Connemara

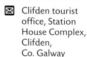 165 B4

Visitor Information

✉ Clifden tourist office, Station House Complex, Clifden, Co. Galway

☎ 095 21163

🕐 Closed Nov.–Feb.

Lay of the Land

Connemara is the region of west Galway bounded on the north by the narrow fjord of Killary Harbour, on the east by Lough Corrib, on the south by Galway Bay, and on the west by the Atlantic. In the center rise the mountain ranges of the Twelve Bens and the Maumturks. From the feet of the mountains, untamed boglands riddled with lakes and spattered with granite boulders stretch to a coast cut by the sea into rags and tatters

of inlets, coves, headlands, and hundreds of islands.

This uncompromising landscape has always demanded backbreaking labor from its small-time farmers and fishermen in return for a meager living. Sour land of rock and bog, geographical isolation, and poor communications spelled hardship and poverty for Connemara inhabitants until very recently. Even today plenty still eke out a thin livelihood from the soil and sea.

INSIDER TIP:

A horseback beach trek should be on everyone's itinerary in Connemara. The area is famed for both its horses and its fabulous stretches of sand.

—ALLY THOMPSON
National Geographic contributor

"You can't eat scenery" is an oft-heard local reaction to a compliment on Connemara's untamed landscape. But tourism, the bread-and-butter of the region these days, is turning the truism on its head—not packaged, bus-borne tourism for the most part, but a stream of independent visitors enjoying the lonely white-sand beaches, tiny towns with their musical pubs, offshore islands, and mountain paths.

The long upper coast of Galway Bay, the southern edge of Connemara, runs due west from Galway city past the resort of Spiddal. After some 20 miles (30 km), this straight westward line shatters into an explosion of islands linked by causeways— Lettermore, Lettermullan, Gorumna, Furnace, Dinish, and their offshoot islets and rocks. If you enjoy strange, hard-edged country, windswept and weath-erbeaten, turn south at Casla. Hungry locals built the causeways that link these Irish-speaking islands at a time late in the 19th century when this area was the poorest and most overpopulated in Ireland. Life is still hard here.

The stone walls separating the tiny fields carry on over granite boulders and through rushy bogs to mark out exactly which morsel of poor land belongs to whom. Rainstorms off Galway Bay are fierce and frequent here, double rainbows commonplace, sunsets magnificent, visitors few and far between. If you hit Ost na nOilean, the Hotel of the Isles at the toe-tip of Gorumna, on the right Saturday night, you may be lucky enough to take part in a ceilidh that you'll never forget.

Inland of the islands, there is a vast apron of granite-studded bogland, terraced and crenel-lated with turf beds cut by hand for domestic fuel, that stretches north to the southern skirts of the Maumturk Mountains.

Connemara Exposé

In 1905 the British *Manchester Guardian* newspaper sent a writer and an artist to report on the state of southern Connemara. The stories and pen-and-ink drawings that recorded the poverty, exploitation, misery, and neglect of the locals shocked the nation with their power—and no wonder, for the reporters were Jack Yeats, artist brother of Irish national poet W. B. Yeats, and leading author John Millington Synge. Many of Jack Yeats's drawings are in Sligo's Model Arts and Niland Gallery (see p. 206).

Padraic Pearse's Cottage

Padraic Pearse's Cottage

⚐ 165 B3

✉ Rosmuc, near
   Gortmore,
   Co. Galway

☎ 091 574292

⏱ Closed mid-
   Sept.–late May

$ $

On the shores of Lough Oiriúlach near Gortmore stands Padraic Pearse's Cottage, whitewashed under a thatched roof and plainly furnished with hard beds and simple furniture. It was to this peasant house and landscape that Padraic Pearse brought groups of students in the early 20th century to learn their native language and culture. The cottage and its Connemara backdrop were a source of refreshment and inspiration for the dreamy Dublin schoolmaster and poet who would become the symbol of Ireland's struggle for independence, proclaimer of the fledgling republic from the steps of Dublin's General Post Office on Easter Monday 1916, and patriotic martyr a few days later when he was shot for treason in the yard of Kilmainham Gaol (see pp. 30–32 and 74–79).

Roundstone

The coast road twists on from Costelloe (Casla in this Irish-speaking area) and the islands to skirt the wildly indented shores of Bertraghboy Bay. At Roundstone on the west side—a beautifully placed village with the easily climbable 1,000-foot (300 m) mountain of Errisbeg at its back—lives and works Malachy Kearns of

Traditional ways are still widespread in the Gaeltacht (Irish-speaking) areas of Connemara.

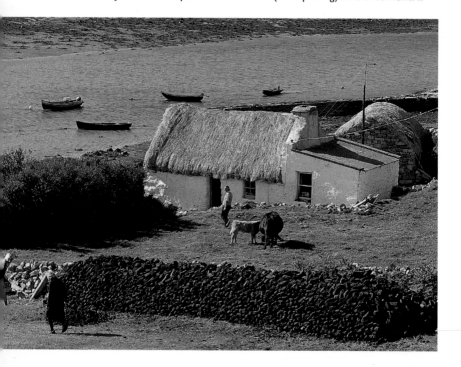

Roundstone Musical Instruments *(tel 095 35808, www .bodhran.com)*. He has gained his nickname, Malachy Bodhrán, through nearly 30 years of hard labor over his handcrafted *bodhráns*. These goatskin drums provide the *rum-a-dum, rum-a-dum* beat behind Irish jigs and reels, and the great names of Irish traditional music trust Malachy to choose the right skin to stretch and pin over an oiled circle of beech or birch wood.

Continue by the white shell sands of Gorteen Bay and Dog's Bay and the strands of Ballyconneely and Mannin Bay with their "coral" made of the calcareous seaweed lithothamnion. You will pass the hillside memorial to Sir John Alcock and Sir Arthur Whitten Brown, who completed the first nonstop transatlantic flight in June 1919 by landing their Vickers Vimy bomber plane nose-down in Derrygimlagh bog.

Clifden

And so to Clifden, Connemara's one and only town, a handsome and lively bayside resort planned in the early 19th century in the classic layout: oval in shape, with three main streets, a market square, and a jail, courthouse, and harbor. Its two 19th-century churches are worth visiting: **St. Joseph's RC Church,** built in 1879 with emigrant money in post-famine times; and **Christ Church,** built in 1853 and offering superior views over town.

Nowadays, Clifden is mostly known for its summertime

EXPERIENCE:
Archaeological Walks

Visible archaeology is a fact of life in Ireland. Everywhere you look, standing stones, ring forts, ruined churches, stone crosses, and castles dot the landscape. Michael Gibbons, who runs the **Connemara Walking Centre** *(tel 095 21379)* in Clifden, can help you make sense of what you see. Gibbons—an expert practical archaeologist, local historian, and dry humorist—conducts expeditions of discovery and enlightenment through the wilds of Connemara, drawing participants into the region's great 8,000-year saga. Walk in his company and soon you, too, will begin to see the tombs, holy wells, hut circles, and lazybed strips shaping themselves as if by magic out of the grass and heather.

Other organizations that cater to visitors in search of Ireland's archaeological riches include **Setanta Tours** *(tel 0871 335159, www.setantatours.com),* which specializes in the history of northwest Ireland. Tours explore the Cooley Peninsula of County Louth, the Mourne Mountains of County Down, and County Armagh's Ring of Gullion hills. **Tour the Ages** *(www .tourtheages.com)* takes you around Dublin, the Boyne Valley, and County Louth.

Connemara Pony Show. Sturdy little Connemara ponies, bred for hard work in the boglands, are gathered for judging and sale in an atmosphere of fun and celebration. This mid-August show brings together many of the best attributes of Connemara—west Galway people in festive mood in a beautiful setting backed by the Twelve Bens, with a touch of sharp reality in the deals struck and judgments delivered.

Kylemore Abbey

🅰 165 B4

✉ Kylemore, Connemara, Co. Galway

☎ 095 41146

💲 Abbey: $$, garden: $$; joint ticket available

www.kylemore abbey.com

Claddaghduff & Omey Island

In Clifden, the scenic Sky Road forks off to encircle the Kingstown Peninsula, while another narrow road continues along the north shore of Streamstown Bay to Claddaghduff at the western tip of Connemara. At low tide, cross the sand causeway to visit the ancient **graveyard** and **St. Fechin's Well** on Omey Island. If you get caught on the island by an incoming tide, you'll have an enforced stay of six hours before the causeway is dry again, but this will give you plenty of time to explore. The low cliffs of Omey Island hold remnants of medieval cooking sites (look for the burned red stones), and locals in search of a cure or help from St. Fechin still leave offerings all around the holy well on the reverse slope of the island.

Kylemore Abbey

From Claddaghduff, it's only a few miles to the harbor of Cleggan for the ferry to Inishbofin

INSIDER TIP:

For perfect photos of Clifden, walk west out of town. Watch for the gate that leads into a cow pasture and up to an amazing overlook.

—KATE RENNER
National Geographic Television

(see sidebar). Head east on the N59 through Letterfrack to the mock-Tudor Kylemore Abbey on Pollacapul Lough, deservedly one of Ireland's most photographed buildings. A mile (1.6 km) or so farther east, the view across Kylemore Lough to the Twelve Bens mountain group is stunning.

Through the Mountains

The N59 is the main highway through Connemara, the choice of those who want to avoid the tortuous coast road. Travel west from Galway city to Clifden via Maam Cross and Recess, with superb views

Inishbofin

One of the most enjoyable of Connemara expeditions is the short ferry cruise from Cleggan out to Inishbofin. The island, 4 by 3 miles (6 by 5 km), has a small and friendly population and a landscape that is low-lying, boggy, and wildly beautiful. You can find the ruins of the 13th-century St. Colman's Abbey on the site of the seventh-century monastery founded by Colman (there are two very early Christian slabs inscribed with crosses, too), a star-shaped fort built by

Cromwellian soldiers who imprisoned and killed Catholic priests on the island, and the outlines of Stone Age and Bronze Age field systems, huts, and cooking pits. A paperback guide, *Inis Bó Finne: A Guide to the Natural History and Archaeology* by David Hogan and Michael Gibbons (available at Michael Gibbons' Walking Ireland, *www.walkingireland.com*), is the companion to take—along with your binoculars, and your singing boots if you intend to spend the night.

A glorious view: The great pile of Kylemore Abbey, dwarfed by the wooded mountain slope behind

en route of the mountains at the heart of Connemara—the **Twelve Bens** (often marked on maps as the Twelve Pins) and the **Maumturks.**

Just west of Recess, the R344 leaves the N59 to follow the spectacular Inagh Valley northward as it squeezes between the two ranges. These are real mountains, although the Twelve Bens rise to only 2,395 feet (730 m) and the Maumturks to 2,300 feet (701 m). The Twelve Bens cluster close around their summit peak of Benbaun, while across the Inagh Valley, the Maumturks swing southeast in a long curved ridge. Capped with quartzite that glitters white in sunlight, they look majestic.

The **Western Way** offers a low-level walk along the flanks of the Maumturks to the east of the Inagh Valley. If you're after something tougher, seek advice at Ben Lettery hostel on the N59, 5 miles (8 km) west of Recess.

A great but demanding circuit of six of the Twelve Bens can be made from the north end of the side road that leaves the N59, a mile (1.6 km) back toward Recess. But you don't have to hike—the road also offers stunning, close-up views of the rugged mountains. ■

Drive: Shores of Lough Corrib

Sprawling for some 27 miles (44 km) northwest of Galway city, Lough Corrib is a vast sheet of water that hides itself cunningly in a low-lying landscape. This drive seeks out its hidden delights.

Cong Abbey is a picturesque ruin amid wooded hillsides on the north shore of Lough Corrib.

Start out of Galway on the N59 Clifden road. In Moycullen, turn right ("Tullokyne, Knockferry" sign) between stone-walled fields and thick hedges for a few miles to **Carrowmoreknock ❶** (or is it Collina-muck, or even Callownamuck? The signs seem unsure!), where there is a peaceful jetty with boats and a view over Lough Corrib to the mountains.

At the next T-junction, turn left to the N59, then right to resume your drive. In 2 miles (3 km), a sign on the right leads to **Aughnanure Castle ❷** (Oughterard, tel 091 552214, closed Nov.–late March, $), a fine six-story O'Flaherty castle bristling with murder holes, secret rooms, and bartizan side turrets, enclosed in a walled ward with its own

NOT TO BE MISSED:

Aughnanure Castle • Lakeshore detour in Oughterard • Cong Abbey • Annaghdown Priory

picturesque lookout tower. The floral carvings on the window of the old banqueting hall are best seen from the external walkway.

Back on the N59, continue to the little town of Oughterard. Keep an eye out for the sign on the right that points to the **Lakeshore Road ❸**, a beautiful, meandering 5-mile (8 km) drive through intensely green and lush backcountry of rhododendrons and woodland to the shores of the lake at Currain with fine hilly scenery all around.

Return to Oughterard by the same route and follow the N59 northwest to **Maam Cross ❹,** which lies bleak and exposed in the bogland. Here a signed turning on the right leads over wild moors to Maam (aka Maum), where you turn right on the R345 for Cong. Soon **Lough Corrib ❺** appears on your right, offering superb lake views and opportunities for bird-watching.

Continue on the R345 to **Cong ❻** (visitor information, tel 094 954 6542, seasonal), a beautifully kept village. At the far end, you'll come to **Cong Abbey,** a handsome gray-stone monastery founded in 1128. Carved flowers, leaves, and tendrils decorate the pillar capitals, and tiny staring heads peep out among the leaves.

From Cong, follow the R346 to Cross, then the R334 southeast to Headford, where you'll see signs to the glorious monastic ensemble of **Ross Errilly ❼** out in the fields by the sullen Black River. Under the slim church tower, the 14th- and 15th-century buildings stand simple and perfect—the best-preserved Franciscan friary in Ireland. Elaborate tombs abound, such as that of Hugh O'Flaherty under the east window; there are huge fireplaces, spouts, chutes, and bread ovens, giving an eerie feeling of monkish presence.

Five miles (8 km) south of Headford, another detour from the N84 brings you to Annaghdown. Turn right immediately past the graveyard ("Annaghdown Pier" sign) to find the blunt and undecorated ruins of **Annaghdown Priory ❽,** a complete contrast to the elegance of Ross Errilly. St. Brendan died here in 577, nursed by his sister Brigid, in the nunnery he had founded.

Return to the N84 and turn right for your journey back to Galway.

East Galway

Most visitors traveling west ignore the eastern region of County Galway, intent as they are on immersing themselves in the dramatic beauty of Connemara as quickly as possible. But the quiet, low-lying landscape of east Galway—an area larger than Connemara—holds some enjoyable places, too.

St. Brendan's Cathedral at Loughrea houses a unique collection of Celtic Revival art treasures.

Tuam
🗺 165 D4
Visitor information
✉ Tuam Mill
Museum,
Co. Galway
☎ 093 25486
or 093 24463
🕐 Seasonal

Tuam

The city of Tuam, 20 miles (30 km) northeast of Galway city, has two cathedrals. The Protestant **Cathedral of St. Mary,** with a 200-foot (61 m) spire, is mostly Victorian neo-Gothic work, but the red sandstone chancel is a relic of the 12th-century cathedral founded here and has a splendid Romanesque arch. The Roman

Catholic **Cathedral of the Assumption** has some notable windows by one of Ireland's best known exponents of stained-glass work, the symbolist artist Harry Clarke (1889–1931).

More memorable church art is on show at 12th-century **Knock-moyle Abbey,** 8 miles (13 km) southeast of Tuam on the River Abbert. A rare early 15th-century fresco shows three kings out hawking, while three other dead kings admonish them: "We have been as you are; you will be as we are." Knockmoyle is a beautiful building with some fine carving in the chancel. It was founded by Cathal "Red Hand" O'Connor in 1189 to celebrate a great victory over the invading Normans and takes its ominous name from the battlefield—Cnoc Muaidhe, the Hill of the Slaughter.

Athenry & Loughrea

Athenry (pronounced a-then-RYE), 14 miles (22 km) east of Galway city, preserves its Norman castle keep, the ruins of a 13th-century Dominican friary, and the North Gate and other sections of the defensive walls built around the town in 1211.

From here, the R348/R349 will take you 12 miles (19 km) southeast to Loughrea, where **St. Brendan's Cathedral,** built between 1897 and 1903, is a treasure-house of Celtic Revival craftsmanship—textiles, wood, stone carving, metalwork, and wonderful windows by Michael Healy, Sarah Purser, and Evie Hone, leading lights of the hugely influential 20th-century collective of stained-glass artists An Túr Gloine, the Glass Tower.

Monastic Sites

Near the eastern border where the counties of Galway, Offaly, and Longford meet, two notable monastic sites lie not far apart. The diminutive **Clonfert Cathedral,** built around 1160 on the site of a monastery founded in 563, possesses a masterpiece

Turoe Stone

Take the R350 north from Loughrea for a couple of miles (3 km) to Bullaun. Just outside the village, off the left turn signed Kiltullagh, you'll find the extraordinary Turoe Stone standing 3 feet (1 m) tall in a field. This granite pillar—heavily carved with swirling and zigzag patterns, the outline of a bird's head, and a four-pointed St. Brigid's Cross—dates from the late Iron Age period, 300 B.C.– A.D. 100, and was brought here from a nearby earth-banked hill fort known as the Rath of Fearmore, the Big Man's Fort.

of Irish Romanesque art in its wonderful west doorway of red sandstone. Six recessed orders of round arches frame the door, each carved with animal heads and flowers, while above rises a tall triangular tympanum filled with alternating triangular darts and human heads, some grinning, others simply gazing.

Off the R355 Portumna– Ballinasloe road, 10 miles (16 km) northwest of Clonfert, stand the ruins of the Augustinian **Clontuskert Abbey,** founded during the 12th century in the flat meadows by the River Suck. Most of what you see is 15th-century work. Saints Michael, Katherine, and John—along with a pelican, a curly-haired mermaid, and others— flank the west doorway of 1471. ■

Athenry
 165 D3

Visitor Information

✉ Athenry Arts and Heritage Centre, The Square, Athenry, Co. Galway

☎ 091 844661

$ $

Westport & Clew Bay

Westport is the most agreeable town in County Mayo, a lively place full of music and talk. To the west of the town opens one of the most beautiful bays in Ireland, Clew Bay, spattered with a reputed 365 islands and dominated on the south by the cone of Croagh Patrick (see pp. 192–195).

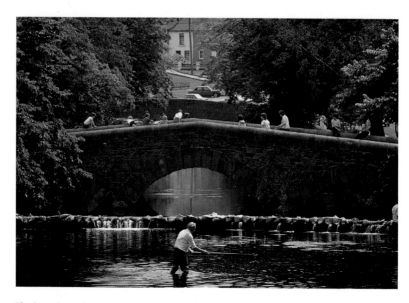

The River Carrowbeg tumbles under a series of old stone bridges through the heart of Westport.

Westport

🅰 165 C5

Visitor Information

✉ James St.,
   Westport,
   Co. Mayo

☎ 098 25711

www.mayo-ireland.ie

Westport

Laid out in 1780 by English architect James Wyatt (1746–1813), Westport has an air of elegance, especially strong along the tree-shaded mall that flanks the River Carrowbeg that flows through the middle of town. From here, Westport's two parallel main streets run uphill—Bridge Street to the **Clock Tower** and James Street to the **Octagon,** its tall column crowned by a statue of St. Patrick.

Shops in Westport are friendly, chatty places—so are the pubs, many of which boast fine traditional music in the evenings (see p. 175). A prime mover on the scene is whistle player Olcan Masterson (*tel 098 27034, e-mail olcanshari@eircom.net*), one of the guiding hands behind the fabulous sessions of traditional music in Hoban's, McHale's, and other bars in town. Masterson is also a knowledgeable and sensitive guide to the area.

Settlers from all over the world have come to this trim town for its agreeable atmosphere, its glorious scenery, and the energetic friendliness of its locals. Their presence has given the town an arty, liberal-minded flavor, best seen during the **Westport Arts Festival** (www .westportartsfestival.com) in October.

On **Westport Quay,** west of town, stand handsome 18th-century stone warehouses. From here you look out across Westport Bay, itself only a corner of the great seaward opening of Clew Bay.

Clew Bay

Eight miles (13 km) across from north to south, 13 miles (21 km) from its inner eastern shore to its mouth in the west, Clew Bay is a mighty chunk carved out of the Mayo coast. Scattered across the eastern half of the bay are 365 or so green humpbacked islands; they originated as drumlins or hillocks of glacial rubble. Their seaward sides have been eaten by the prevailing western winds into low cliffs of pebbly clay so that they resemble a shoal of green sea creatures baring their yellow teeth as they set off into the Atlantic.

Spectacularly beautiful when the setting sun lays their black shadows on silvered water, the islands once supported a population of thousands. These days, just a few hardy folk live and work on the islands—fishermen on **Inishlyre,** a sailing school on **Collan More,** a couple tending an organic garden on **Island More** at the western edge of the archipelago.

John Lennon bought **Dorinish,** one of the Clew Bay islands, on a whim. Lennon hardly set foot on the island, but for a few years Dorinish was a miserably uncomfortable hippie hangout, to the bemusement of locals.

You'll find wonderful sandy beaches between **Louisburgh** and **Murrisk,** on the south shore of Clew Bay, and at **Mallaranny** on the north side.

Sporty souls can sail (Mayo Sailing Club, Rosmoney Quay; contact Westport visitor information) or fish (Sea Angling Centre, Westport) in Clew Bay, while lovers of wild local history should seek out Burrishoole Abbey and Rockfleet Castle near Newport, on the north shore of the bay. The 15th-century tower and arches of **Burrishoole Abbey,**

Westport House & Country Park

Westport House & Country Park, on the western edge of town, is a Georgian country house whose construction started about 1730; celebrated architect James Wyatt completed the job half a century later. Inside you can admire family portraits (and a beautiful "Holy Family" by Rubens), Georgian silver and glassware, and fine mahogany furniture. The wood was brought to Westport from the Jamaican sugar plantations owned by the wife of the second Marquess of Sligo, who lived here during the early 19th century. Dungeons from an earlier castle that stood on the site, horse-drawn caravan rides, a zoo, and slot machines cheer and cheapen the tone.

founded by sea raider Grace O'Malley's second husband, "Iron Dick," stand at the edge of the bay. **Rockfleet Castle,** just along the coast, is also right on the water, a wonderfully grim late medieval tower house, where Grace got the better of "Iron Dick" in 1567 (see sidebar p. 202). ■

Westport House & Country Park

✉ Westport Estate, Westport, Co. Mayo
☎ 098 27766 or 098 25430
⊙ Closed Sat. & Dec.–Feb.; open Sun. only Oct.–Nov. Attractions open summer only, call for times
$ $$
www.westport house.ie

Croagh Patrick

Tall, graceful, and impressive, Croagh Patrick ("the Reek" to locals) rises on the southern shore of Clew Bay. Around its cone-shaped head, legends have gathered over millennia. An object of reverence to all manner of religious believers, it is the destination of one of the world's great Christian pilgrimages—and a stunningly beautiful mountain in its own right.

Croagh Patrick
🗺 165 B4
www.croagh-
patrick.com

The Legend of St. Patrick

Traveling through Ireland on his great missionary expedition, St. Patrick reached County Mayo in 441. There he climbed the 2,510-foot (764 m) peak of Cruachan Aigil, a mountain feared and venerated by the pagan Irish of the region. A canny operator with an excellent understanding of his fellow man, Patrick was not about to turn his back on a place with such spiritual resonance for thousands of potential

converts. Instead, he fasted 40 days and 40 nights at the summit, a feat that must have seemed tremendously brave to minds that had peopled the peak with demons, and made them more receptive to his message of baptism and salvation.

What happened at the peak quickly became the stuff of stories. Patrick secured assurances from God that the Irish would never lose their faith and that they would be saved on Judgment Day—in fact, that Patrick himself would be their judge. Patrick also cleared Ireland of all its poisonous and offensive beasts by repeatedly ringing his Cloigin Dubh or Black Bell and then hurling it over the precipice of Lugnanarrib, sweeping masses of snakes, toads, and other nasties to their doom with every throw. Helpful angels retrieved the bell and returned it to the saint after each consignment. The Cloigin Dubh also came in handy for dealing with a cloud of evil spirits in the form of black birds, which dispersed when Patrick slung his bell through their ranks.

The Holy Mountain

Within a short time, the mountain peak had become a holy site for Christian pilgrims that neither storms, lightning strikes, nor legal prohibitions could halt.

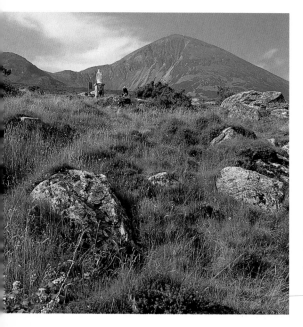

Croagh Patrick, Ireland's holy mountain

EXPERIENCE: Join a Pilgrimage

Few group activities are more friendly and sociable than an Irish pilgrimage, and there is no better way of understanding the unique mix of Christian and "older" faith that underpins so much of Ireland's social fabric than to take part in one. You are not expected to share the faith of your fellow pilgrims, merely to respect it. These communal expeditions, with an earthy spirituality and sense of groundedness, are a wonderful way to get to know the "real" Ireland.

The famous annual pilgrimage up Croagh Patrick (see pp. 194–195) is only one of hundreds of pilgrimages in Ireland waiting to be discovered. A tougher prospect is the **Lough Derg** pilgrimage *(Station Island, Lough Derg, Co. Donegal, www.loughderg.ie)*, a spiritual journey centered around a 24-hour vigil during which the penitent stays awake, walking barefoot and repeating a prayer cycle.

Pilgrimage participants are restricted to one meal a day, and the whole experience acts as a serious unburdening of body and spirit and serves as a tremendous bonding exercise between those who take part. The three-day pilgrimage takes place from late May to mid-August; one-day retreats are also held from early May to late September.

The monastic site of **Clonmacnoise** in County Offaly (see pp. 252–255) marks St. Ciarán's Day (Sept. 9) with a pilgrimage, while the town of **Máméan** in County Galway holds one-day pilgrimages on St. Patrick's Day (March 17), Good Friday, and the first Sunday in August. At **Glendalough** in Co. Wicklow (see pp. 102–103), you can navigate your own pilgrimage around St. Kevin's holy valley and monastic site with Fr. Michael Rodgers's superb guidebook, *Glendalough: A Celtic Pilgrimage* (Columba Press).

A 23-mile (37 km) pilgrim path, **Tóchar Phádraig** (see p. 195), was established from Ballintober Abbey along an ancient pagan route to the sacred mountain. Garland Sunday, the last Sunday in July, became the "official" day to climb Croagh Patrick—maybe because of its proximity to August 1, the date of a wild festival of fire and dancing that celebrated the Celtic harvest feast of Lughnasa.

In the late 20th century, a spate of accidents put a stop to the traditional night climb—an unforgettable spectacle as thousands of torches wrapped a glowing chain of light around the mountain. But the pilgrimage itself remains as popular as ever,

with up to 50,000 people climbing the mountain on Garland Sunday, many of them barefoot, to attend Mass on the summit. Nonbelievers can climb, too—it is one of the world's classic "anyone-can-do-it" ascents (see pp. 194–195).

In 1988, gold was discovered on Croagh Patrick and a license applied for. But so numerous and passionate were the protests—from all over the world—that the scheme to mine the mountain was rejected, no matter how much County Mayo might need the jobs and money. The Reek still carries the scar of the road cut by the mining company, a slowly fading mirror image of the pilgrim path kept fresh by countless feet each year. ∎

Walk: To the Top of Croagh Patrick

A hike up the holy mountain of Croagh Patrick is one of the classic activities in the west of Ireland. It's demanding and tiring, but good for body and spirit, and when you finally reach the summit, you will be rewarded with a stunning view. Whether you opt for the short but challenging route from Murrisk or the 23-mile (37 km) pilgrimage route from Ballintober Abbey, go prepared and do not attempt the trip in thick mist or heavy rain.

St. Patrick stands in statue form at the foot of the Pilgrim Path, overlooking Clew Bay.

To tackle Croagh Patrick you will need a good pair of walking boots, a stick, and plenty of determination. The route is clear and you need little skill, but you will find it impossible to get all the way to the top if you are out of condition. Don't be put off if you see the summit wrapped in clouds; they may just part when you reach the top.

Short Climb

Set off west from **Murrisk,** ❶ beside **Owen Campbell's pub**—where you can admire the collection of pilgrimage photographs and memorabilia—and then head due south along the signposted lane. In about 200 yards (200 m), you will pass the **statue of St. Patrick,** blessing your start.

NOT TO BE MISSED:

Owen Campbell's pub • Statue of St. Patrick • Leacht Mionnain cairn or "station" at the foot of the summit cone • St. Patrick's Church at summit

Follow the path southward, ascending to a **saddle of ground** ❷ at 1,650 feet (500 m). At this point, the pilgrimage route from Ballintober Abbey (see p. 195) joins the path. You might want to take a rest here because your next task is arduous. The summit awaits at the end of a very steep and boulder-strewn ascent of 860 feet (265 m).

At the top, you'll spot **St. Patrick's Church ❸**. The magnificent view from here, at 2,510 feet (764 m), encompasses the Connemara Mountains, the Nephin Beg range, the whole of Clew Bay and its islands, Achill Island, and Clare Island. You can even glimpse the Slieve League cliffs some 80 miles (128 km) to the northeast on the coast of County Donegal.

From the summit, return back down to the pub the way you came.

Pilgrimage Route

Following the pilgrimage route to the summit is a long and tiring journey, and unless you are very fit and determined, you will need two days to complete it. Anyone who intends to take this walk must register with Ballintober (Ballintubber) Abbey *(tel 094 903 0934)* before setting out.

To follow the ancient pilgrim route, start at **Ballintober Abbey** and take the route westward, guided by marker stones incised with crosses and numbered stiles. An enormously useful guidebook, *Tóchar Phádraig, A Pilgrim's Progress,* is available at the abbey. It points out the holy wells, standing stones, inscribed rocks, enchanted woods, and fairy hillocks that you

will pass along the way. It also contains detailed information on flora and fauna, the history of each field you go through, and plenty of stories both credible and incredible.

Break your two-day journey at the village of **Aghagower,** where there is an ancient church and a round tower. From here you can order a cab to Westport (a ten-minute ride away) to get a good meal and a bed for the night.

On day two, return to Aghagower and continue your journey west, following the track up the south flank of Croagh Patrick to the saddle (see ❷ opposite), where the path from Murrisk merges. Follow the directions for the Short Climb to reach the summit.

🅼 See area map p. 165 B4

▶ Owen Campbell's pub, Murrisk. Pilgrimage route: Ballintober Abbey, signed off the N84 Castlebar–Ballinrobe road, 7 miles (11 km) S of Castlebar

🕐 Depending on fitness, allow 4–5 hours. For the pilgrimage route, allow 2 days

↔ 5 miles (8 km) up and down. Pilgrimage route: 23 miles (37 km)

▶ Owen Campbell's pub

Northwest Mayo

One of the least visited parts of Ireland, northwest Mayo is about as rugged, lonely, and beautiful as you can get. Islands, peninsulas, cliffs, and bays indent the coastline, while the interior is mountain and bog . . . interspersed with bog and mountain. If you love wild places, this is the region for you.

The dark, dramatic ramparts of the Minaun Cliffs loom beyond Keel Bay on Achill Island.

Northwest Mayo
🗺 165 A5–B6

Visitor Information
✉ James St.,
Westport,
Co. Mayo
☎ 098 25711

Achill Island
🗺 165 A5–B5

Visitor Information (seasonal)
✉ On the road between Achill Sound and Keel, Co. Mayo
☎ 098 45384

Achill Island

From Westport, it's a leisurely hour's drive via Mallaranny (aka Mulrany) to Achill Sound, with the mountainous profile of **Achill Island** growing ever more prominent ahead. At roughly 14 by 12 miles (22 by 19 km), Achill is Ireland's largest offshore island. **Knockmore** (1,119 feet/340 m) and **Minaun** (1,320 feet/403 m) command the view as you cross the bridge over Achill Sound. Their loftier sister mountains, **Croaghaun** (2,195 feet/668 m) and **Slievemore** (2,204 feet/672 m), rise in the north of the island. Achill is very rarely crowded, though tourism has begun to

infiltrate—welcomed by most of the islanders, who until only a few years ago were generally eking out hard lives.

Drop into Sweeney's supermarket at the island end of the bridge to catch the current buzz of the island before heading south on the narrow and winding coastal road labeled "Atlantic Drive."

Atlantic Drive: Many islanders still farm in traditional ways, and in season you'll see ricks of cut turf and hay weatherproofed with vividly colored canvas "headscarves." Monbretia and fuchsia brighten the roadsides; silver sand and orange seaweed fill the rocky bays.

At the southern tip of the island, the tall, grim 15th-century **Kildaunet Castle**—once a base for the famed Mayo "pirate queen" Grace O'Malley (see sidebar p. 202)—stands near the ruined **Kildaunet church.** There are many poignant graves in the cemetery here and a brackish holy well on the shore.

The character of Achill changes as soon as you swing north up the west side of the island, with a tremendous coastline of wave-battered rocks and cliffs. There's a beautiful view down over **Ashleam Bay.**

At **Keel** you will find a fine Blue Flag beach (conforming to EU standards of cleanliness and safety; there are others at Keem and Doogort) and a spectacular prospect of the **Minaun Cliffs.**

Dooagh has attractive whitewashed cottages under thatch or tiles, and the Pub, where you can look through a book of photographs recording the arrival of Don Allum. He reached the shore here on September 4, 1987, after 77 days at sea—having just completed the first there-and-back rowing of the Atlantic.

Keem Strand, a couple of miles (3 km) beyond Dooagh, is a perfect beach in a pincer-shaped bay under the slopes of Croaghaun. Amethysts are found on this southern part of the mountain.

Back in Keel, continue straight at Minaun View, and in a mile (1.6 km) steer straight ahead again where Atlantic Drive bends to the right. Just in front, on the slope of **Slievemore,** you'll see an abandoned village of roofless

houses—"booley houses," or summer pasture dwellings, depopulated when famine struck Achill in the mid-19th century. You can walk the streets, peer at cold fireplaces and empty stone cupboards, and ponder on the harshness and simplicity of island life back then. Then it's back across the bridge to the Mayo mainland.

The country between Achill Island and the Mullet Peninsula is harsh, rolling brown bogland patched with somber green forests. Just inland rise the **Nephin Beg Mountains,** Ireland's loneliest and most remote range. One footpath threads them: the **Bangor Trail,** a demanding and boggy but extremely rewarding

EXPERIENCE:
Horse Races on the Beach

Because it's on the beach, **Lacken Strand** (betw. Killala & Ballycastle, Co. Mayo) spends part of its life underwater. But come late May, this 5-furlong racetrack is the annual home to exciting horse races that draw passionate crowds and mighty *craic*. In days gone by, the family-friendly Lacken Strand Races were a far more rustic affair, with anyone who fancied his chances turning up to have a go aboard every kind of steed, from racehorses and prime Connemara ponies to knock-kneed old nags from the local stables and farms. The modern event is a lot more professional, and you have the chance of seeing some excellent racing by top jockeys and horses. Whatever you do, don't pass up this chance to enjoy a very Irish bit of fun. The **Laytown Races** (Laytown Strand, Co. Meath, Sept., www .goracing.ie) is another well-known beach racing event in Ireland.

Children of Lir

Inishglora, a scrap of an island off Cross Strand just west of Binghamstown, is the setting for the poignant conclusion of one of Ireland's best known legends, the story of the Children of Lir.

Turned into swans (but retaining their beautiful voices) at the hand of their jealous stepmother's magical powers, the four children of the powerful chief Lir are condemned to spend 900 years in exile from their home. The final 300 years are spent on Inishglora, and it is here that the coming of Christianity finally releases them from their enchantment. But the shapes they resume are those of 900-year-old human beings.

A holy man (could it have been St. Brendan? He built a church on Inishglora in the sixth century) baptizes the Children of Lir before they crumble into death and buries them on the island as they have directed—standing upright, with their arms supportively around each other in death as in life.

22-mile (35 km) hike—for the fit and determined only! A guidebook, *The Bangor Trail* by Joe MacDermott, is widely available locally.

The Mullet Peninsula

Bangor is a village isolated in the bog, and **Belmullet,** 12 miles (19 km) to the northwest, is equally easy-paced. Belmullet is the gateway to the **Mullet Peninsula,** a little-visited but beautiful finger of land that runs south for some 20 miles (32 km). Deeply indented, the peninsula shelters Blacksod Bay on its east and looks out west from a treeless and weathered coast to a scatter of Atlantic islands offshore. Like Achill Island, the Mullet is a Gaeltacht or Irish-speaking area, where locals receive grants to preserve traditional speech, culture, and ways of life.

Belmullet stands on an isthmus connecting the peninsula to the mainland. North and northwest of the isthmus, the Mullet Peninsula coast fractures into innumerable rocky headlands—**Doonamo (Doonamore) Point,** segregated beyond an ancient wall, contains house foundations and fortifications of pre-Christian date.

Reedy, shallow **Termoncarragh Lake** supports rare red-necked phalarope and other bird species. Houses are widely scattered down the peninsula, with only Binghamstown calling itself a village. Of the superb beaches, the west-facing ones such as Belderra, Portacarn, and Carricklahan are wilder and more weed-strewn. Cattle walk the strands and feed on the flowery shell-sand meadows or *machair.*

INSIDER TIP:

A self-guided bike tour of western Ireland is a wonderful experience. Don't be afraid to strike out on your own: The locals are especially welcoming and friendly to the single biker.

—KATE RENNER
National Geographic Television

The offshore **Inishkea** and **Duvillaun islands,** and little **Inishglora** (see sidebar opposite), are uninhabited these days. Their low green curves enhance already sublime Atlantic views.

The country and coast northeast of Belmullet is as wild as can be. This is quintessential Mayo bogland, across which switchback roads lead to pretty little **Pollatomish,** tiny **Portacloy** on its slip of sandy beach, and the equally small fishing harbor of **Porturlin.**

A little farther east, you will find the astonishing archaeological site of **Céide Fields.** In the

At the modern visitor center, learn how blanket bog crept in to smother the Stone Age farmers' green fields with up to 15 feet (5 m) of turf. The climate certainly became wetter around 3000 B.C., and the early farmers probably contributed to the growth of the wet bog by felling trees so that rain soaked the ground instead of evaporating off the forest leaves. This smothering of the fields and settlements by the creeping bog kept the ancient landscape intact; almost all other such sites were destroyed by the later generations who took over the land. Guided

Céide Fields Visitor Center

🅰 165 C6
✉ Ballycastle, Co. Mayo
☎ 096 43325
🕐 Closed Nov.–mid-March, except by appointment
💲 $

Hand-raked haycocks stand in the village fields at Dooagh, Achill Island.

1930s, local schoolteacher Patrick Caulfield began to investigate the ancient stone walls being unearthed by turf-cutters in the boglands between Belderrig and Ballycastle. In the 1970s, his son, Dr. Séamus Caulfield, put archaeological students to work, and they traced the patterns of a 5,000-year-old farming landscape hidden in the bog.

tours show you what there is to be seen on the ground—mostly lengths of crude stone walling, which don't look too exciting to the nonexpert.

Just east of Céide Fields, the promontory of **Downpatrick Head** makes a stimulating walk. There's a giant rock stack just off the head and a couple of blow holes that can drench you. ■

More Places to Visit in West Ireland

Clare Island

Out beyond the mouth of Clew Bay lies Clare Island (population 150), accessible by ferry from **Roonah Quay** (tel 098 28288 or 098 25045). This beautiful green island, its harbor guarded by a castle, was the home of Grace O'Malley (see sidebar p. 202). It has a sandy beach near the harbor, fantastic music in the pub (island work rhythms of fishing and farming mean it can open at midnight and close the following noon, if then), and the shapely and steep hill of Knockmore (1,529 feet/461 m) for a literally breathtaking climb and view. *www.clare-island.org* ⓐ 165 B5 ✉ Mouth of Clew Bay, Co. Mayo

Coole Park

The home of Lady Augusta Gregory, friend and patron of W. B. Yeats, no longer stands, but its beautiful grounds continue as a national park. You can view the **Autograph Tree,** where literary luminaries such as J. M. Synge, George Bernard Shaw (flamboyant initials), Sean O'Casey, English poet laureate John Masefield, and many others carved their names, and follow a waymarked walk leading through woods to Coole Lake. *www .coolepark.ie.ie* ⓐ 165 D2 ✉ Signed off the N18 Galway–Ennis road, 2 miles (3 km) N of Gort, Co. Galway ☎ 091 631804 🕒 Closed Oct.–Easter 🈂 $

Dunguaire Castle

Occupying a beautiful spot on Kinvarra Bay, Dunguaire is a four-story tower house complete with *bawn* (defensive wall). It was built by the O'Hynes around 1520 and restored during the 20th century by the poet-surgeon Oliver St. John Gogarty. "Medieval" banquets are held here daily.

The calm surface of Killary Harbour conceals Ireland's deepest sea inlet.

165 D3 ✉ Kinvarra, on the N67
Ballyvaughan–Galway road, Co. Galway
☎ 061 360788 ⏰ Closed Oct.–mid-April
$ $ **Medieval Banquet** ☎ 061 360 788
⏰ Daily 5:45 p.m. & 8:45 p.m. $ $$

Ennis

The county town of Clare, Ennis is a characterful place of long, narrow streets packed
with little pubs. There's a tall column with
a statue of "Swaggering" Dan O'Connell,
elected in 1828 to represent Ennis in the
British Parliament as the first Catholic MP.
Carvings on the tombs in the 13th-century
Franciscan friary are particularly fine.
www.visitennis.ie 165 C2 ✉ Arthur's Row,
Ennis, Co. Clare ☎ 065 682 8366

Iar-Connacht

The loneliest, wildest, most extensive
bogland in County Galway, crossed by a
single winding road, is sheer bliss for solitude
seekers and lovers of bleak landscapes.
165 C3 ✉ Bounded by the road triangle
of the R336 Galway–Ballynahown–Maam
Cross and the N59 Maam Cross–Galway, Co.
Galway ☎ 091 537700

Killary Harbour

The splendid fjord of Killary Harbour forms
the western Galway/Mayo border. It runs
in from the west for 10 miles (16 km) in
an upward-curving saber shape and in
places is more than 150 feet (45 m) deep.
Tremendous mountains sweep up from its
shores—the **Maumturks** on the south, the
massive **Mweelrea** (2,699 feet/819 m)
near the western entrance, and **Ben Gorm**
(2,303 feet/750 m) toward the eastern head
of the inlet. Their flanks are scarred with
the corduroy stripes of lazybeds, the potato
ridges tended by peasants of not so long ago.
From **Leenane,** the impossibly photogenic
one-street village at the inland end of Killary
Harbour, the R335 passes north through the
narrow, dramatic defile of Doolough. **Doo**

EXPERIENCE:
Learn to Speak Irish

If you spend any time in the west of
Ireland, particularly in the Gaeltacht or
Irish-speaking areas, you'll long to know
more of the complex, beautiful Irish
language—even if it's only to say "Good
morning–*Dia duit ar maidin,*" "Thank
you–*Go raibh maith agat,*" and "Cheers!–
Sláinte!" Opportunity beckons at the
Ennis Trad Festival (*Ennis, Co. Clare,
early Nov., www.ennistradfesti val.com*),
where amid the music there's a chance
to learn a little beginner's Irish.

There are also many Irish-learning
resources online. Find toasts, jokes, stories, songs, sayings, greetings, and more
at *www.irishpage.com* and a spoken Irish
course at *www.gaeltalk.net.* Courses,
contacts, and teachers can also be
found through *www.irishlanguage.net.*

Lough itself, the Black Lake, is a moody stretch
of water 2 miles (3 km) long, hugged by the
road that weaves through **Doolough Pass**
between Mweelrea and the 2,500 feet (750 m)
bulk of the Sheeffry Hills. This pass, like the
Pass of Glencoe in Scotland, seems darkened
as much by its own history as by the crowding
mountain slopes, for it was along here that
600 men, women, and children struggled to
Delphi Lodge to beg for food during the Great
Famine of 1845–49. Having been turned away
empty-handed, 400 died on the return journey
through the pass. 165 B4 ✉ 20 miles (30
km) SW of Westport (N59), Co. Mayo

Kilmacduagh Monastic Site

Backed by the layered gray hills of the
Burren, here are the ruins of four churches
(some tenth-century or earlier), a beautiful
roofless cathedral, a medieval tower house,
and a 115-foot (34 m) round tower leaning
out of perpendicular.

Dunguaire Castle on Kinvarra Bay was built by 16th-century descendants of a seventh-century king of Connaught.

⚠ 165 D2   ✉ On the R460 Gort–Corofin road, 3 miles (5 km) SW of Gort (N18 Galway–Ennis road), Co. Galway **Galway visitor information** ☎ 091 537700

Lough Derg

This long, ragged-edged lake, a great favorite with boaters and fishermen, is handsomely backed by mountains and dotted with pretty villages. **Killaloe,** the main town at the south end, has the 12th-century **St. Flannan's Cathedral and Oratory.** From Mountshannon, a boat *(tel 086 2601173 or 086 8749710, closed Oct.–May, $$$)* will land you on **Holy Island** to explore the remains of four churches (including a 16th-century cathedral), an 80-foot (24 m) round tower, elaborately carved medieval tomb slabs, and the holed Bargaining Stone of the monks. *www.loughderg.org* ⚠ 165 D2–E2   ✉ From Killaloe, Co. Clare, NE for 20 miles (30 km) to Portumna, Co. Clare **Killaloe visitor information** ☎ 061 376866 (seasonal)

Thoor Ballylee

W. B. Yeats bought the neglected 14th-century tower house of Ballylee Castle in 1916. Simply but stylishly restored, it became his much-loved country retreat and inspired his 1928 collection, *The Tower and the Winding Stair.* Recordings of the poet reading his own verse accompany your trip round the exhibition of Yeats memorabilia and first editions. ⚠ 165 D3   ✉ Signed off the N66 Gort–Loughrea road, 3 miles (5 km) NE of Gort, Co. Galway ☎ 091 631436 (April–Sept.), 091 537700 (Oct.–March) ⏲ Closed Oct.–May ⑤ $

Grace O'Malley

With dashing skill, Grace O'Malley (ca 1530–1603), the daughter of a Connacht chief, ran her own army and fleet of privateers from Clare Island (see p. 200) and strongholds along the coast. Stories say that she had the mooring ropes of her fleet run through her bedroom in the castle on the island and tied to her big toe so that she would wake if anyone tried to steal her ships while she slept. She and her privateers exacted pilotage charges and cargo levies from passing shipping until she controlled the entire sea trade from the west of Ireland to the Continent.

Grace was 16 when she married her first husband, Donal O'Flaherty. In 1566, two years after he was murdered, she married Anglo-Irish lord "Iron Dick" Burke on the understanding that, after a year, either could divorce the other. This she duly did, slamming the door of Rockfleet Castle (see p. 191) against him—having first secured all of Iron Dick's castles by putting her own people in charge.

The mountains and coasts immortalized by the Yeats brothers,
and the wild hills and peninsulas of Donegal

Northwest Ireland

A Carrowmore dolmen in northwest
Ireland, stronghold of the Stone Age

Northwest Ireland

The three counties that make up northwest Ireland differ greatly. Sligo, to the southwest, has a sandy coastline based around the inlets of Sligo Bay and a lake-filled southern border, while Donegal, to the north, bursts out westward into a vast number of peninsulas and islets. Little Leitrim, squeezed in between, has a coastline only 3 miles (5 km) long and a wooded, hilly interior with Lough Allen as its main water feature.

The landscape around Gortahork is typical of the wide wilderness that forms so much of County Donegal.

William's poetry, while the settings for many of Jack's paintings can easily be identified.

Some of Ireland's most impressive prehistoric monuments lie in County Sligo—examples range from dozens of megalithic tombs in the cemeteries of Carrowmore and Carrowkeel to great prehistoric tombs such as the Labby Rock portal dolmen near Lough Arrow and the court tomb at Creevykeel.

Leitrim, sandwiched between the literary and artistic resonance of Sligo and the grand wildness of Donegal, lacks the glamour of these neighboring counties. For spectacles, Leitrim claims the Glencar Waterfall and Parke's Castle on Lough Gill, but this is mostly

Sligo is forever associated with the Yeats brothers, poet William and painter Jack, who spent much of their childhood around Sligo town. The town itself is one of Ireland's most enjoyable, a lively but relaxed place of narrow streets and musical pubs. Weathering and glacial scraping on the limestone of the surrounding hills has produced striking table mountains with flat tops and shiplike prows. This is Yeats Country—there is a signposted drive around many sites connected with

NOT TO BE MISSED:

a county for watery pleasures: boating on the Shannon–Erne Waterway around Carrick-on-Shannon or fishing in Lough Allen and dozens of smaller lakes.

"It's different up here" is the Donegal tourism slogan—a fair summing-up. Donegal feels remote; the county is all but detached from the Irish Republic, with only a 5-mile (8 km) border connecting it to Leitrim. Much of the west of the county is Gaeltacht (Irish-speaking); in the south rise the spectacular cliffs of the Slieve League, while up in the diamond-shaped Inishowen Peninsula, at the top of Donegal, you reach the wild, northernmost tip of Ireland. ■

Sligo Town

Although it can seem a staid and sleepy place, laid-back Sligo is the social and commercial center of northwest Ireland. At night, there's great music in the pubs; by day, shoppers pack its narrow Georgian and Victorian streets, appealingly lined with old-fashioned shop fronts. There is a May arts festival, the town's main jamboree in August, and autumn music festivals.

Warm sunny days attract many a diner to a riverside restaurant in Sligo town.

Sligo Town

🅰 205 C2

Visitor Information

✉ Áras Reddan, Temple St., Sligo, Co. Sligo

☎ 071 916 1201

Model Arts and Niland Gallery

✉ The Mall, Sligo, Co. Sligo

☎ 071 914 1405

www.modelart.ie

The Yeats Brothers

Sligo owes its place on the tourist map to the Yeats brothers (see pp. 208–209)—poet William Butler (1865–1939), widely known as W. B., and painter Jack (1871–1957)—who spent their childhood holidays here. The town has several Yeats sites. At the **Model Arts and Niland Gallery,** the Niland Collection contains some 50 of Jack Yeats's paintings. There are a number of W. B. Yeats's manuscripts—including several first drafts of poems—in the **County Library**

(tel 071 911 1850) on Bridge Street. The **Sligo County Museum** on Stephen Street has some W. B. Yeats memorabilia, but the majority of it is in the **Yeats Memorial Museum** *(tel 071 914 2693)* on Hyde Bridge, crammed full of manuscripts, letters, and photographs of W. B. and his 1923 Nobel Prize.

On Stephen Street is Rowan Gillespie's impressionistic statue of the poet (erected in 1989), all spindly legs and billowing cloak overprinted with lines from Yeats's poetry. Just across Hyde

Bridge is the **Yeats Memorial Building** *(Hyde Bridge, Sligo, tel 071 914 2693)*, headquarters of the Yeats summer school (see sidebar p. 208) and home to the Sligo Art Gallery *(www.sligoartgallery.com)*.

History of Sligo

Sligo is not all Yeats, by any means. A poignant sculpture on Quay Street of a ragged, skinny man, woman, and child is a reminder of how badly the town suffered during the Great Famine of 1845–49, when about a third of Sligo's population died or emigrated. Bad times had hit the town before: Vikings raided it in the ninth century, local clans fought over possession of Sligo Castle (later completely destroyed) in medieval times, and in 1641, Sir Frederick Hamilton took and burned the 13th-century Dominican Friary, killing many of the monks. The roof-less ruins of the friary church on Abbey Street—Sligo's only surviving medieval building—contain some beautifully carved tombs and stonework and a fine set of cloisters.

Exploring the Town

Follow the broad, shallow Garravogue River through town, passing colorwashed houses old and new. Fishermen brave the slippery rocks in hopes of a catch. Or wander along Abbey Street, turning left up Teeling Street to find the engraved window of (now defunct) solicitors Argue and Phibbs.

Return to Abbey Street and continue along Castle Street and Grattan Street (Cosgrove's Delicatessen, where Market Street cuts in, is the place to buy the makings of a picnic lunch), before turning right along O'Connell Street to find **Hargadon's pub.**

Hargadon's is a Sligo institution, one of the rare, genuine "talking pubs," where music is not allowed to interfere with the pleasures of rambling conversation. The front part of the pub remains unchanged, a dark den of partitioned snugs with sagging apothecary's drawers and shelves of old jars. Back rooms ramify into recently constructed bar and

INSIDER TIP:

For many visitors, the name Yeats immediately draws to mind the poet W. B.—but his painter brother Jack's output is equally impressive. See his work at Sligo's Niland Collection.

—LARRY PORGES
Editor, National Geographic Books

eating areas, but with Hargadon's general ease of atmosphere.

If you are after an evening of superb traditional music, head for **Furey's pub** on Bridge Street. It's owned by Sligo band Dervish, who have made their name playing breakneck traditional music on the concert stages of the world. Band members take part in the fast and furious sessions here whenever they are in town. ■

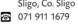

Sligo County Museum

✉ Heritage Centre, Stephen St., Sligo, Co. Sligo

☎ 071 911 1679

Sligo & the Yeats Brothers

In spite of the worldwide experience and fame they gained as, respectively, Nobel Laureate poet and celebrated Postimpressionist painter, William Butler Yeats and his younger brother, Jack, looked on this small corner of Ireland as the primary source of their inspiration.

Their mother, Susan Pollexfen, was a Sligo woman; their father, John Butler Yeats, was a lawyer turned not-too-successful artist. When money got tight, as it frequently did, Susan would take the boys and their sisters from their home in Dublin to stay for weeks and months at a time with her parents in Sligo. Both William and Jack responded passionately to the dramatic mountains and coasts, the swirling Atlantic skies, and the life of the harbor town and its countryside—horse races, market days, and country fairs; sailors, jockeys, and ballad singers.

A 1907 etching of W. B. Yeats by Augustus John

W. B. Yeats

The tales, legends, and other yarns that William heard in and around Sligo stirred his imagination. His beloved uncle George Pollexfen had a servant, Mary Battle, who would regale Willliam with tales of fairies, goblins, and wee folk. Mary had the "second sight," a door of spiritual imagination that opened at times, fascinating the young boy. He learned tales of Queen Maeve, or Medb, whose "tomb" he could see from his grandparent's house in profile on top of the hill of Knocknaree (see pp. 210–211), and the story of Fionn MacCumhaill's final reckoning

---

EXPERIENCE: Learn About Yeats First-Hand

William Butler Yeats—Ireland's master poet and playwright of the 19th and early 20th centuries, winner of the 1923 Nobel Prize in Literature, and author of such iconic poems as "The Lake Isle of Inisfree," "Byzantium," "Easter 1916," and "When You Are Old"—is without doubt the most famous figure in Sligo history. Born and bred in Dublin, Yeats himself frequently acknowledged that it was the time he spent in Sligo that made him a poet and shaped all his writing.

That's why every year, from late July to early August, hundreds of Yeats scholars and enthusiasts from all over the world gather in Sligo for the two-week Yeats

International Summer School *(www .yeats-sligo.com)*, run by the Yeats Society Sligo. Events include lectures and short seminars, dramatic readings and musical presentations by some of Ireland's renowned performers, and workshops with leading poets, actors, and theater directors. Performances and readings are held at the **Hawk's Well Theatre** *(Temple Street, Sligo, tel 071 916 1526, www.hawks well.com)*. Check online for application and scholarship information.

For other events in Sligo related to W. B. Yeats, and Irish poetry and drama in general, check with the **Sligo Arts Service** *(tel 071 911 1826, www.sligoarts.ie)*.

Information on all things Yeats can be found at the redbrick Yeats Society (left) in Sligo town.

with his cuckolder Diarmuid on the slopes of Benbulben mountain (see pp. 214–215).

These stories from Ireland's deep mythical past were generally regarded in the 1870s and '80s as superstitious nonsense fit only for peasant nursemaids and children. But the Yeats brothers continued to holiday regularly around Sligo later in life, steeping themselves in this highly distinctive and seductive landscape and culture. It was at the root of William's passionate championing of a specifically Irish literature enriched by tradition—what would become the Gaelic Revival, from the 1890s onward, intertwining with republican politics in the years leading up to the Easter Rising and the War of Independence. And Sligo drew the poet back at the end of his life to lie under a self-penned epitaph, "under bare Ben Bulben's head," in the graveyard at Drumcliff, where his great-grandfather had been rector.

Jack Yeats

Susan Pollexfen's father, William, was a grim, solid businessman, disapproving of his feckless son-in-law and silently stern with his Yeats grandchildren. Grandmother Elizabeth was warm and loving to the Yeats children, but grandfather William was forbidding with all—except young Jack, with whom he struck up a very close relationship. Between the ages of 8 and 16, Jack lived with his grand-parents, an immersion in the Sligo scene that influenced him all his life. In adulthood, he continued to visit whenever possible, staying in his uncle George's seaside house out at Rosses Point (see pp. 211–212) and sketching local scenes. "Sligo was my school, and the sky above it," he wrote later. From 1910 on, Jack was painting in oils, increasingly blurry and mystical in style and subject matter.

Sligo town has finally paid its adoptive artist son the honor he deserves with a gallery dedicated to his work (see p. 206). Donating his painting of Uncle George, himself, and his wife, "Leaving the Far Point," to the Sligo Corporation in 1954, Jack wrote, "From the beginning of my painting life every painting which I have made has somewhere in it a thought of Sligo." ■

Yeats Country

The lonely, sandy coasts of Sligo Bay, Drumcliff Bay, and Ballysadare Bay, the flat-topped mountains of the Benbulben range north and east of Sligo town, and the deeply indented shores of Lough Gill to the southeast—these contain the haunts of William and Jack Yeats and the landscape that influenced them from childhood onward. An established Yeats Country Drive, marked with brown-and-white quill-and-inkstand signs, runs a meandering course for about 100 miles (160 km) around the area.

The mighty wrinkled table of Benbulben, W. B. Yeats's favorite among the Sligo mountains

Yeats Country

🗺 205 B2–C3

Visitor Information

✉ Aras Reddan, Temple St., Sligo, Co. Sligo

☎ 071 9161201

Queen Medb's Cairn

A good place to start the Yeats circular route (*details from Sligo visitor information*) is at the 1,074-foot (328 m) summit of **Knocknaree** (Knocknarea). Shaped like an upturned dish with a round button on top, it towers over the landscape west of Sligo town. You can reach it by leaving the town along Castle Street—passing en route the

house of Thornhill, where the Yeats boys often visited their uncle, George Pollexfen (see pp. 208–209).

In 3 miles (5 km), a turn on the left (*signed "Meascán Meadhbha"*) leads to a parking lot. From there, it's a 45-minute hike to the summit. The "button" is in fact the huge Stone Age monument of Queen Medb's Cairn, a mini-hill of boulders (estimated

INSIDER TIP:

Climb Benbulben for fantastic views of Sligo. The south face is the easier side to scale, as winds from the Atlantic make the north slope dangerous.

—STEPHANIE ROBICHAUX
National Geographic contributor

at 40,000 tons/36,000 tonnes of stone) that covers a passage grave. It was Queen Medb ("Maeve" to W. B. Yeats), the mythical (probably) first-century warrior queen of Connacht, who initiated the famous Cattle Raid of Cooley (see p. 334). Her tomb reflects the size of her reputation: It stands 80 feet (24 m) high and measures 630 feet (192 m) around the base.

The extensive view from the summit is foregrounded by the tidal channels and sandbanks of Sligo Bay and Ballysadare Bay. Due west of the mountain lies the stony shore at **Strandhill**, backed by huge sand dunes. Ulster hero Cúchulainn fought the sea here.

Coney Island

Farther around the blunt-headed Strandhill Peninsula you reach the tidal causeway to Coney Island, much beloved of Jack Yeats in his day. He set his late painting "The Sea and the Lighthouse" (1947) here, with a wind-torn figure staring out into a dark blue sky lit by a piercing beam from the Oyster Island lighthouse. You can see

the painting in the Model Art and Niland Gallery in Sligo (see p. 206). The great swath of sand enclosed in the bay is Cummeen Strand, often whipped by storm winds out of the west.

Rosses Point

Across the bay is the shark-tooth peninsula of Rosses Point, scene of so much childhood freedom for the Yeatses, as children and well into adulthood. Rosses Point is a neat, compact little place with fine sandy beach walks. A metal effigy of a sailor stands in midtide pointing to the safest shipping channel, and on foggy days the bell buoy tolls dolefully. William loved the muted, often melancholic attractions of Rosses Point, from

EXPERIENCE:
Take a Seaweed Bath

If you are in need of some downtime or are just up for a new and strange experience, you shouldn't leave Sligo without paying a call on **Kilcullen's Seaweed Baths** *(Enniscrone, Co. Sligo, tel 096 36238, www.kilcullenseaweedbaths.com, $$).* Here, in a rather grand Edwardian bathhouse—complete with huge period porcelain tubs and brass taps—you lie back in a bath full of hot, pure Atlantic seawater. The highly concentrated iodine released from the seaweed gives the water an amber tint and has natural therapeutic properties. As you soak, your aches and pains, worries and tensions, fade away. You leave (after a needle-sharp cold shower) with silky smooth skin and a fantastic sense of well-being. Kilcullen's also offers steam baths and massages.

Picnicking in Yeats Country

If you have any of the poet or painter in you, don't rush through Yeats Country. Get out of the car, spread a blanket, and do some daydreaming. As Maurteen metaphorically tells Shawn as he opens a bottle in *The Land of Heart's Desire*, "It's precious wine, so take your time about it." For stunning views, try **Queen Medb's Cairn** (see pp. 210–211) on Knocknaree.

For a shore picnic with connections to Jack Yeats, walk out from Rosses Point (see pp. 211–212) to the **Far Point** of the Low Rosses ("Leaving the Far Point"). Other tranquil, W. B. Yeats–inflected picnic spots are **Glencar Lough** (see p. 215) and the shore of **Lough Gill** (see p. 215), opposite Innisfree *(turn off the R287 between Slish Wood and Dromahair).*

Lissadell House and Gardens

- 205 B2
- Ballinfull, signposted from the N15 at Drumcliff
- 071 9163150
- Closed Oct.– mid-March
- $

www.lissadell house.com

where he could see Knocknaree and Benbulben.

Rosses Point came to stand at the heart of Jack's art, and many of his best paintings were set here: "Shruna Meala, Rosses Point" of 1923, an early watercolor "The Metal Man," and "The Old Pilot House, Rosses Point," in which two capped figures stare seaward out of one of the pilot house's round windows.

Other pictures, such as "White Shower" (1928) and "The Grave-yard Wall" (1945), are clearly set on a seabound landscape such as this. Most ethereal and suffused with spirituality is "Leaving the Far Point." Jack in a dark hat and his wife Cottie—a young woman in the painting, with one hand steadying her hat against the sea wind—are walking the wet gray strand at Rosses Point under a wild, cloud-streaked sky. With them is the otherworldly figure of Uncle George Pollexfen, faint to the point of transparency. He had died in 1910, so this painting is a study on past happiness and the presence of loved ones long gone. Cottie Yeats died soon after the painting was finished, adding poignancy to its effect.

Lissadell House

From the northerly tip of the Rosses Point sandspit, one looks across Drumcliff Bay to the estate of Lissadell, 2 miles (3 km) away. It was a clear view in Yeats's day, but now conifers and tangled woodland make it hard to see the Gore-Booth family mansion of Lissadell.

Lissadell House, having fallen into decay, is now restored and open to the public. W. B. Yeats first visited it in 1894 as a sensitive poet of nearly 30, fully into his "Celtic Twilight" phase of romantic nostalgia and soft-focus nationalism. He became friends with the two Gore-Booth girls, Constance and Eva, who provided plenty of hard-edged realism as a counterbalance—especially Constance, who was to gain notoriety as Countess Markiewicz at the Easter Rising and during the run-up to the 1919–1922 War of Independence. A fervent Irish nationalist and an active participant in the fighting, she was given a death sentence (immediately commuted) for her part in the Dublin fighting on Easter 1916. She was soon imprisoned again for making speeches in support of the outlawed Sinn Féin. W. B. Yeats wrote of her at that time, in "On a Political Prisoner," as "Blind and leader of the blind / Drinking the foul ditch where they lie."

William himself had gone through an intensely nationalistic phase. After the Easter Rising he became more conservative, but both he and Jack still supported nationalism—Jack expressing this sentiment in his 1924 painting "Communicating with Prisoners." In 1927, in "In Memory of Eva Gore-Booth and Con Markie-wicz," William remembered: "The light of evening, Lissadell / Great windows open to the south / Two girls in silk kimonos both / Beautiful, one a gazelle."

In the house you can see photographs and portraits of the Gore-Booth sisters, along with elongated caricatures of male family members, the butler, the gamekeeper, the woodman, and the dog, painted on the walls of the dining room by Constance's husband, Count Markiewicz.

Drumcliff & Benbulben

Back on the N15 Sligo–Bundoran road, at **Drumcliff** is the austere gray **Church of St. Columba,** the stump of a round tower, and an ancient cross carved with biblical scenes, including Cain axing Abel in the head and Adam and Eve shielding their private parts under the branches of the Tree of Knowledge. The church incorporates a visitor center with poetry readings, guided tours, and an interactive Yeats-related computer suite.

Next to the northwest angle of the church tower is the grave of W. B. Yeats and his wife, Georgie

Drumcliff
🅜 205 B2

Drumcliff Church & Visitor Center
✉ Drumcliff, Co. Sligo
☎ 071 9144956
💲 $

W. B. Yeats lies buried in the churchyard of Drumcliff Church.

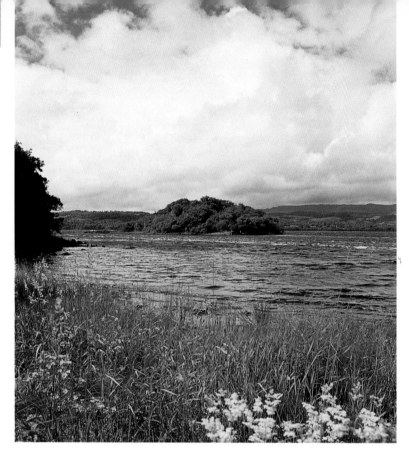

The romantic islet of Innisfree in Lough Gill inspired Yeats's best-loved poems.

Benbulben
🏔 205 C3

Hyde-Lees (1892–1968). The view from the graveside, through a thin screen of churchyard trees to the great bareheaded bulk of Benbulben, is as simple as it is majestic.

Noble-looking **Benbulben** (Benbulbin) dominates the landscape for 50 miles (80 km). It is table-topped, with sheer, deeply furrowed cliffs dropping from the summit to the upper rim of a great skirt of green that slants down to the agricultural lands below. The Yeats boys roamed all over the mountain, fishing for trout in the pools and streams. In "The Tower" (1926), W. B. looked back nostalgically to "boyhood, when with rod and fly / Or the humbler worm, I / climbed Ben Bulben's back / And had the livelong summer day to spend."

Jack slipped the distinctive dreadnought-prow shape of the mountain into his 1946 painting "The Mountain Window," as a silhouette seen in a cottage window, crowned with a cloud through which a gold sun is bursting.

Legends abound on Benbulben, the best known being the saga of Diarmuid and Gráinne, with the final face-off between the elderly Fionn MacCumhaill and Diarmuid, who had run off with Fionn's betrothed, the beautiful Gráinne. It was on the slopes of Benbulben that Fionn's warriors, the Fianna, drove a savage boar toward Diarmuid. In the act of killing it Diarmuid was gored. Twice Fionn went to the sacred spring for healing water, remembered Diarmuid's treachery, and let the water trickle through his fingers. The third time he relented and brought the water, but it was too late—Diarmuid was dead. The bed where Diarmuid and Gráinne made love is suitably heroic in size, a huge rock arch 40 feet (12 m) high and 60 feet (18 m) wide, standing above the inner end of Gleniff, 3 miles (5 km) east of Benbulben summit. You can admire it during a circuit of the spectacular **Gleniff Horseshoe,** signposted from Ballintrillick Bridge *(reached via Cliffony on the N15).*

The road at the foot of Benbulben curves southeast around the mountain's flank to reach beautiful **Glencar Lough** and its waterfall. Diarmuid built a **crannog** in the lake to hide Gráinne from the Fianna. The waterfall is signposted from the road—a paved path leads up through mossy trees to where the stream plunges over a sill into a pool. In "Towards Break of Day," W. B. Yeats described it as "a waterfall / Upon Ben Bulben side / That all my childhood counted dear."

Lough Gill

One of the Yeats brothers' favorite Sligo places was the large, beautiful Lough Gill, east of Sligo town, with a 24-mile (38 km) scenic drive around much of its deeply indented shoreline. The southern shore road (R287 Sligo–Dromahair) passes a parking place at

Dooney Rock, where marked paths lead up to the top of the rock—a well-known beauty spot and lookout point. W. B. had his "Fiddler of Dooney" rejoicing: "When I play on my fiddle at Dooney, / Folk dance like a wave of the sea."

Farther on around the lake, the road skirts **Slish Wood** ("Sleuth Wood" to Yeats), where the young poet once trespassed and spent a sleepless night in fear of the wood ranger—the subject of much saucy teasing by the servants. Close to the shore here lies **Innisfree,** the tiny wooded islet that W. B. made the subject of his best known poem.

INSIDER TIP:

There's no finer picnic spot in all Ireland than on the shores of Lough Gill on a sunny day. The views across the lough from the top of Dooney Rock are spectacular.

—ALLY THOMPSON
National Geographic contributor

You can reach the "Lake Isle of Innisfree" by boat from Parke's Castle (see p. 230) on the north shore and wander where Yeats longed to live in dreamy seclusion: "I will arise and go now, and go to Innisfree, / And a small cabin build there, of clay and wattles made: / Nine bean-rows will I have there, a hive for the honey-bee, / And live alone in the bee-loud glade." ∎

Lough Gill
205 C2

Dooney Rock
205 C2

Slish Wood
205 C2

Innisfree
205 C2

Prehistoric Sligo

Sligo is a county rich in prehistoric monuments, and its various ancient burial sites—from cairns and portal dolmens to court tombs and whole cemeteries—are atmospheric places to visit. Most have far-ranging views. Wandering the hilltops and field slopes puts one's imagination to work on the nature and motivation of the people who labored so hard to build these monuments to the dead.

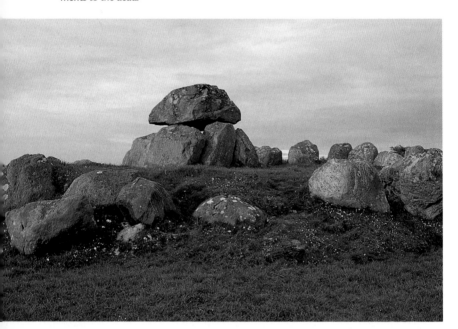

Stone Age mourners constructed the remarkable tombs at Carrowmore, just outside Sligo town.

Carrowmore
 205 B2

West of Sligo Town

In the north Sligo country around Sligo town, several sites are well worth exploring. To the west of the town *(brown sign)* lies **Carrowmore megalithic cemetery** *(tel 071 916 1534),* the largest and oldest such site in Ireland. About 30 monuments remain, some mere scatters of stones, others complete with lintels and interior walling. Cremated bones, stone and bone ornaments, and flint arrowheads have been found here, the artifacts of burials covering some two or even three thousand years. The oldest passage tombs may date as far back as 5000 B.C.

A couple of miles (3 km) away is **Meascán Meadhbha** or **Queen Medb's Cairn,** the giant mound of stones on the top of Knocknaree (see pp. 210–211). The cairn is still unexcavated (it is bad luck to remove any stone), but it probably covers a 5,000-year-old passage tomb.

Deerpark & Creevykeel

East of the N15 Sligo–Bundoran road lie two remarkable court tombs, each built between 4000 and 3000 B.C. There are many examples in Ireland of this style of tomb, in which a ceremonial open-air court (presumably for rituals) gives access to a number of burial chambers arranged in galleries inside the covered part of the tomb. But Deerpark and Creevykeel are two of the finest.

Deerpark court tomb is reached by turning right *("Giant's Grave" sign)* off the road to the north of Colgagh Lough *(via the R287 Sligo–Dromahair road),* then walking uphill for 30 minutes from the parking lot. The whole structure, on an open ridge-top above woods, is about 100 feet (30 m) long, with a central court, twin galleries on the east, and a simple gallery on the west.

Creevykeel court tomb *(signed off the N15 just north of Cliffony)* is trapezoidal, with a pincer-shaped court, its rectangular chambers placed centrally and let into the sides of the huge pebbly monument. Massive jambs still support one of the lintels.

South Sligo

A cluster of three monuments lies around Lough Arrow in south Sligo. Among the hilltops of the Bricklieve Mountains, to the west of the lake, are the scattered passage tombs of **Carrowkeel Neolithic cemetery,** signposted from Castlebaldwin on the N4 Collooney–Boyle road. Superbly sited to catch all the best views (and to be

seen from far off), they vary in type—some have corbeled roofs like beehives and three central chambers, others fall between court and passage tombs. All date from circa 3800–3300 B.C.

Just north of Lough Arrow stands **Heapstown Cairn** *(follow "Cromlech Lodge" signs from Castlebaldwin to the Bow and Arrow pub at the crossroads—the entrance is some 100 yards/90 m north of the pub),* a huge, unexcavated 5,000-year-old

INSIDER TIP:

Survey the grand panorama from Carrowkeel Neolithic cemetery with binoculars and you'll be able to spot many more cairns on the neighboring hilltops.

—CHRISTOPHER SOMERVILLE
National Geographic author

cairn. Two miles (3 km) southeast *("Cromlech Lodge" signs from Castlebaldwin—park at the lodge and follow the marked path)* is the magnificent **Labby Rock** portal dolmen. Built between 4000 and 2500 B.C., both burial chambers have a capstone and entrance jambs, The Labby Rock's capstone, a single block of limestone 14.5 feet (4 m) long and up to 6 feet (2 m) thick, weighs an estimated 70 tons (64 tonnes).

To find out more about the archaeology of Sligo, contact the Sligo visitor information office *(tel 071 916 1201).* ∎

Deerpark court tomb
🅼 205 C2

Creevykeel court tomb
🅼 205 C3

Carrowkeel Neolithic cemetery
🅼 205 C1

Heapstone cairn
🅼 205 C2

Labby Rock
🅼 205 C2

Southwest Donegal

County Donegal, northernmost and remotest of the Irish Republic's counties, throws dozens of peninsulas west and north into the Atlantic. The southwest corner of this ragged coastline bulges out the farthest, leading at its tip to Europe's highest sea cliffs and the beautifully enfolded sacred site of Glencolumbkille.

Tiny Station Island, otherwise known as St. Patrick's Purgatory, Lough Derg

Donegal Town

🅰 205 C4

Visitor Information

✉ The Quay,
Donegal,
Co. Donegal

☎ 074 972 1148

Donegal Town & Points South

Donegal makes its tenuous connection with the rest of the Republic south of Donegal town, a 5-mile (8 km) border shared with County Leitrim. **Bundoran,** a first-class little seaside resort, has a Blue Flag beach (conforming to EU standards of cleanliness and safety) and all the holiday trimmings.

A little farther north comes **Ballyshannon,** where myth sites the first invasion of Ireland—a landing by Parthelanus, a descendant of Noah. Parthelanus built a house on a rock in the mouth of Ballyshannon Harbour and named the islet Inis Sainer after a favorite dog belonging to his wife, Dealgnait. It was a remorseful naming—Parthelanus had killed Sainer the hound with his own hands, believing that it had treacherously allowed Dealgnait to carry on an affair with a servant. You can look out on Inis Sainer, and the winding sandbanks and grassy dunes of the River Erne's estuary, from Ballyshannon Harbour, where a beautiful memorial commemorates three drowned fishermen, showing the men transformed into gamboling dolphins.

On the way north to Donegal town, it is worth turning east to **Lough Derg,** where **Station Island,** long a place of retreat to restore the soul, is smothered in early 20th-century buildings of functional design. They cater to the many thousands of Roman Catholics who make a pilgrimage to the island each May *(tel 071 986 1518, www.loughderg.org),* enduring three days and nights of barefoot perambulation and prayer while fasting.

Donegal town is an enjoyable place to idle for a day. The central square is known as the Diamond, as are the squares of plantation towns all across the ancient province of Ulster. County Donegal was one of the disputed "three counties" where Catholics were in the majority—the others were Cavan and Monaghan—arbitrarily separated from Ulster by the 1920 act that created Northern Ireland.

The accents you'll hear in County Donegal seem harder and more rapid than those in the rest of the Republic—closer, in fact, to the speech of Northern Ireland. The celebrated Donegal style of playing traditional music is noticeably quick and staccato,

too. Catch the brisk style for yourself in one of the many excellent music pubs in Donegal town.

It is worth taking a whole day over the 75-mile (120 km) clockwise drive from Donegal town around the roundlung bulge of County Donegal's most southwesterly peninsula. There are so many places to stop, stare, and explore, and the roads are twisty and humpbacked. Glencolumbkille (see pp. 220–221) in particular is not a place to hurry through.

West of Donegal Town

A few miles west of Donegal town, a thin 8-mile (13 km) peninsula runs southwest from the village of Dunkineely to **St. John's Point.** Out toward the tip of the peninsula, you pass through a wild landscape

INSIDER TIP:

If you're traveling by car, don't hesitate to venture down any of the numerous tiny side roads, especially if you see a sign with "trá" on it—it's Irish for "beach."

—ALEXANDRA BURGUIERES
National Geographic contributor

of limestone pavement rich in flowers, with fine views from the lighthouse at the tip that extend—with the help of binoculars—on a clear day from the north Mayo coast through Sligo and Leitrim to the cliffs just east of Slieve League.

Bundoran
205 C3

Visitor Information
- The Bridge, Bundoran, Co. Donegal
- 071 984 1350
- Closed Nov.–March

Ardara
🅰 205 C4

Cliffs of Slieve League
🅰 205 B3

One Man's Path
🅰 205 B3

Glencolumbkille
🅰 205 B4

Glencolumbkille Folk Village Museum
☎ 074 973 0017
🕐 Closed Oct.– Easter Sunday
💲 $
www.glenfolkvillage .com

The Glencolumbkille Peninsula

Northwest of Donegal town, on the Glencolumbkille Peninsula, the mountains begin to rise around **Killybegs,** Donegal's premier fishing town. The harbor is lined with tough-looking, salt-rusted trawlers painted red and blue, and a fishy aroma wafts from the big fish-processing factory. West of Killybegs the coastal landscape becomes wild, a broken region of heathery headlands and small green fields sloping up to the feet of the mountains. The Coast Road detour *(marked with brown signs off the R263)* shows you the best of this wild landscape, where trees are wind-

Ardara

Ardara (pronounced ar-da-RA) is a friendly little town east of Port on the Glencolumb-kille Peninsula that grew prosperous in times past through the tweed-weaving industry. Visitors can see demonstrations of handloom-weaving at the **Ardara Heritage Centre,** located beside the bridge in the town center, and half of the shops in town seem to sell Aran sweaters and Donegal tweed garments. **Nancy's,** half-way up the hill, and **Peter Oliver's,** around the corner, are great pubs for music.

blown and farmhouses are built of rough stone under slate roofs. You are into the Gaeltacht now, Irish-speaking country.

At Carrick, a left turn (marked "Teelin Pier") leads off the main road. Soon, signs to **Bunglass: The Cliffs** point up a steeply winding road that climbs through

gates and around rocky shoulders to a windy parking place and view-point above a ruined Napoleonic watchtower in a most precarious position. A few steps from the car bring you to a stunning view of the **cliffs of Slieve League,** reput-edly the tallest in Europe, towering some 2,000 feet (600 m) out of the sea in a wall of black, yellow, orange, and brown. Brave scram-blers with a head for heights can attempt the **One Man's Path** (or Pass), a flywalk 2 feet (0.6 m) wide in places that teeters between the sheer cliff top and the sloping rock above to reach the summit. Do not attempt this path in wet or gusty weather.

An expanse of wild bogland, ramparted by the workings of many generations of turf-cutters, leads from Slieve League to the beautiful green valley of **Glen-columbkille** (Glencolmcille), one of Ireland's "special places" whose magical atmosphere far transcends the merely picturesque. Glen-columbkille runs due west, a long, sheltered valley that reaches the sea between rugged headlands.

There is a smallish amount of tourist traffic based around the **Folk Village Museum.** The museum manages to escape the tweeness that so often attends such heritage centers partly because it was set up in the 1960s as a cooperative self-help scheme by the villagers of Glencolumbkille themselves, rather than being imposed from outside on a wave of EU grant money. If you fancy a bottle of seaweed or fuchsia wine, the Shebeen shop is the place to buy one.

Trawlers lie up in the fishing harbor at Killybegs, a Donegal town with a friendly, fishy atmosphere.

But the real magic of Glen-columbkille has most to do with its connections with St. Columba, the Donegal-born saint from whom the valley takes its name. Born in 521 at Gartan Lough, Columba established monasteries and places of retreat in several Donegal locations and was drawn by the loneliness of Glencolumb-kille as well as by its reputation among pagan locals as a center of spirituality—witness the many standing stones and pre-Christian burial sites in the valley.

An Turas Cholmcille, Columba's Journey, is a 3-mile (5 km) circuit of 15 stations or sacred sites, followed barefoot at midnight by pilgrims every year on Columba's feast day, June 9. You can seek out these sites and follow the Turas at your own pace from station 1, a court tomb in the churchyard, via standing stones and slabs incised with crosses, and a cluster of stations around **St. Columba's Chapel, Bed, and Well** on the north slope of the glen. The chapel is a sturdy box of chest-high walls on a knoll among incised cross slabs, and his highly uncomfortable bed in one corner of the chapel is a low-lying arrangement of two stone slabs boxed in by flanking stones.

From Glencolumbkille, the road ribbons on eastward across stark bogland toward Ardara (see sidebar opposite). A detour that's worth taking leaves the main route at a turning on the left in 2 miles (3 km). The narrow road becomes progressively bumpier after 5 miles (8 km) as it forks left and runs down to the abandoned fishing village of **Port,** a wonderful spot for lazing on the hillside above the ruins of old houses, looking out over a white pebbly beach to blue sea and sky. Only occasionally do any fishermen come down to Port, so it is a perfect place for seekers of solitude. ■

Port
🗺 205 B4

West & Northwest Donegal

Dozens of granite-scabbed, lake-strewn peninsulas, great and small, make up the spectacular coastline of west and northwest Donegal. Together with the mountainous interior, they form a landscape wild, harsh, and extraordinarily compelling. Hereabouts, you'll find spoken Irish, tall tales, and breakneck music.

**West &
Northwest
Donegal**
🗺 205 B4–D5
Visitor Information
✉ Blaney Rd.,
Letterkenny,
Co. Donegal
☎ 074 912 1160

Dawros Peninsula

The Dawros Peninsula sticks out across the bay of Loughros More, with views across to the mountains around Glencolumbkille. Low hills hide numerous lakes. In **Lough Doon,** between Kilclooney and Rossbeg, you'll find a fine island ring fort perhaps 2,000 years old, with walls standing up to 15 feet (5 m) tall. Row yourself to the island in a rented boat *(signposted)*.

The peninsula has flat coasts of sand dunes and sandy beaches—especially around sheltered **Narin,** looking north into Gweebarra Bay. Sandbanks and shining mudflats in the tidal creeks attract large numbers of overwintering geese.

Dooey Point & Crohy Head

North of Dawros juts **Dooey Point Peninsula,** with more fine beaches and dunes. The **Crohy Head Peninsula,** north again, is rougher country with a meandering coast road good for walking or driving on the seaward slopes of a more mountainous interior. Try the 40-mile (64 km) drive from Lettermacaward northeast up the Owenwee Valley into the skirts of the Derryveagh Mountains, then down the Owenbeg and back by Fintown and Lough Finn.

The Rosses

Donegal has more Irish speakers than any other county in Ireland, and the indigenous Irish language and culture are maintained most strongly in the Rosses, north of Crohy. The population is growing

The majestic simplicity of the Donegal coast near Gweedore

and new houses are being built, but the landscape here is harsh—pieces of granite pushing through bog, uncountable loughs and lakelets, and a deeply cut and broken coastline.

Donegal's little airport (tel 074 954 8284 or 074 954 8232) is at **Carrickfinn,** on the flat grassy coast north of Annagry.

Burtonport has trawlers in its harbor and some salty fishermen's pubs, though the fishing the town

IINSIDER TIP:

Tune your radio to Raidió na Gaeltachta (RnaG; 92–94 FM) to hear the beauty of spoken Irish and the wonderful traditional Irish music and song.

—CHRISTOPHER SOMERVILLE
National Geographic author

relies on is going through hard times. You can get a sea angling trip from here (tel 074 954 8403), or catch the ferry to Aran (Arranmore) Island (see p. 228).

A more visitor-oriented village is **Dungloe,** on the south side of the Rosses, with its annual "Mary from Dungloe" charm and beauty contest (tel 074 952 1254)—an excuse for a few weeks of money-making and drinking in late July/ early August.

Two further enjoyable Rosses venues are **Cruit Island,** a spit of land a couple of miles (3 km) north of Burtonport with fine beaches and bird-haunted reed

beds, and far-famed **Leo's Tavern,** at Meenaleck near Crolly in the north of the region. The owners' children are fine musicians—most perform under the name of Clannad. Their famous sister, Enya, is queen of ambient Celtic lullabies.

North again from the Rosses is **Gweedore,** where sandy coasts harden to the red cliffs of **Bloody Foreland.** Inland stands bulky **Tievealehid,** 1,413 feet (430 m) tall. This is lonely country of twisty lanes on hillsides yellow with gorse (purple with heather in season), with marvelous sea views from Bloody Foreland—notably the low block of **Tory Island** (see p. 229), some 7 miles (11 km) to the north. **Meenlaragh,** 5 miles (8 km) east of the Foreland, is the port of embarkation for the island.

Derryveagh Mountains

Southeast of these peninsulas rise the Derryveagh Mountains, whose highest peak, **Errigal** (see pp. 224–225), is the highest mountain in Donegal, at 2,466 feet (751 m). A series of glens runs through the mountains, some with beautiful long lakes such as **Lough Beagh** and **Gartan Lough.** Overlooking the west shore of Gartan Lough, a cross marks the place of St. Columba's birth in 521 (signposted from the road).

A collapsed Bronze Age tomb lies nearby, its capstone covered in copper coins slipped into the cupmarks gouged into the stone. This is the **Flagstone of Loneliness,** where emigrants would come to lie in penance before setting out for America. ∎

Dungloe
🗺 205 C5
Visitor Information
✉ The Quay, Dungloe, Co. Donegal
☎ 074 952 1297
🕐 Closed Oct.–May

Flagstone of Loneliness
🗺 205 D5

Walk: To the Top of Errigal Mountain

At 2,466 feet (751 m), Errigal is the highest mountain in Donegal. It may look formidable from down below, but the hike presents no technical difficulty and the 150-mile (240 km) view from the top is reward enough for the long, upward slog.

The reward for your effort is the breathtaking view toward Lough Altan.

As you approach from the northwest, along the R251 (the Bunbeg direction), Errigal Mountain appears at its most formidable, its sharp-peaked cone apparently covered in snow. As you get closer, you see that its dazzling whiteness is not snow but quartzite. Corries (circular hollows) scoop shadowed chasms in its southern flanks, and whitened curtains of scree cover its shoulders. By the time you reach Dunlewy on the shore of Dunlewy Lough, directly under the mountain, you may be thinking that it all looks a bit much for an ordinary walker to tackle.

But take courage! You can get information

NOT TO BE MISSED:

Views of Errigal from the north-west • Dunlewy Lakeside Centre • Summit path • Glorious views from the "far" summit

and reassurance at **Dunlewy Lakeside Centre** (tel 074 953 1699, closed Nov.–mid-March, $–$$$). The staff there will direct you the 3 miles (5 km) along the road to the start of the climb and tell you, "Sure, there's nothing to it."

You will find, however, that there is quite a lot of upward effort to it. This is not a hike to attempt if you are unfit, nor when low cloud, mist, or rain is obscuring the peak. Yet, in normal conditions, it's a climb that anyone who is reasonably fit and wearing a good pair of ankle-supporting boots can manage.

From the **pull-off and "walking man" sign** on the R251, the track is obvious, rising steadily up the long southeast shoulder of the mountain. In clear weather you cannot mistake the way.

At first you climb among grass and heather; then, as you get higher up the mountain, rough scree of slippery stone shards and boulders take over. Now you are into the quartzite zone—in sunshine you may see these upper slopes of the mountain sparkle with a million diamond winks of light. Near the top, the stones become more fractured and slablike, and the path weaves around and over shelves and outcrops of bare quartzite as it steepens and zigzags.

The ridge curves around to the right above and ahead of you, with antlike figures moving slowly along it. The first **summit** is reached, and then the trick of Errigal becomes clear— there is a second, narrower peak beyond,

connected to the first peak by a short ridge only 2 feet (0.6 m) wide in places. Vertigo sufferers could have difficulty here, since the slopes descend sharply on the right side.

It's worth attaining at least the second (lower) peak, though, for the 360-degree view. This is a stunning prospect, with a foreground of scree dropping 2,000 feet (608 m) to lakes (Altan to the right, Dunlewy and Nacung to the left) and a magnificent far-flung backdrop of mountains and coasts. These generally extend to about 50 miles (80 km) and, in exceptionally clear, weather might be three times that—150 miles (240 km) from the Connemara Mountains in the southwest to Antrim and even across to Scotland in the northwest.

Return to the pull-off by the same path.

- See area map p. 205 C5
- ► "Walking man" sign in a pull-off on the R251, 3 miles (5 km) east of Dunlewy
- ⏱ Allow 2.5–3 hours round-trip, depending on fitness
- ↔ 1.5 miles (2.5 km) each way and about 1,750 feet (530 m) of ascent
- ► "Walking man" sign

Inishowen & the Northeast Peninsulas

The northeast of Donegal is a wonderfully wild region of bog, heather, and rocky slopes, cut into tatters by the sea. It's worth taking the time to skirt these coasts at leisure, savoring the loneliness, the seabirds, and the untamed scenery.

The Northeast Peninsulas

Three peninsulas of very different character lead east to Donegal's largest and least visited peninsula, Inishowen. The most westerly of these smaller three is the **Horn Head Peninsula.** At **Dunfanaghy,** a smart plantation

Rugged pinnacles of rock mark the northernmost point of Ireland—Malin Head—at the top of the Inishowen Peninsula.

village, the former workhouse, built in 1845 at the start of the famine, has been reopened as a museum. Called the Workhouse, it tells the story of the famine and demonstrates the grimness of workhouse life. North of Dunfanaghy, the peninsula bulges out to a mountainous tip where the 600-foot (180 m) cliffs of Horn Head plunge to the sea, their ledges lined with guillemots and puffins.

Eastward is **Rosguill,** less dramatic but even more beautiful, with an 8-mile (13 km) Atlantic Drive that corkscrews up steep lanes to superb coast views.

East again lies **Fanad,** a fractured mass of land split almost in two by the narrow and tortuous inlet of Mulroy Bay. This is a flatter peninsula of lovely beaches—the best at **Ballymacstocker Bay,** on the east or Lough Swilly side.

Rathmullan, farther south, has a Blue Flag beach. On September 14, 1607, this was the embarkation point for the Flight of the Earls, when Hugh O'Neill, Rory O'Donnell, and Cuchonnacht Maguire, Ulster chiefs who could not accept British crown rule, sailed into exile on the Continent.

Inishowen

Most easterly of all Donegal's peninsulas, and also the largest

Carrickabraghy Castle

The story of Carrickabraghy Castle could stand for so many of the ruined castles a visitor sees all over Ireland, strongholds built in the turbulent 15th and 16th centuries when local lordlings fought and feared each other and the invading English with almost equal intensity.

Such fortresses quickly became superfluous once the rule of English law had become established. When Phelemy Brasleigh O'Doherty built Carrickabraghy

in Tudor times it boasted seven towers, a hugely strong *bawn* or fortified courtyard, and a sturdy keep. O'Doherty was pro-English and needed the stout castle to preserve himself and his followers. But once the dust had settled and the English and Scots settlers had the upper hand, the castle on the Inishowen headland became redundant. Within half a century it stood empty and abandoned, never to be reoccupied.

and most northerly, is the great diamond-shaped mass of **Inishowen.** From a southern neck near Londonderry city only 8 miles (13 km) wide, the head of Inishowen broadens to three times that width before narrowing again toward its tip at Malin Head.

Inland, Inishowen features barren uplands above fertile valleys and long seacoasts—especially to the southeast, where a string of resorts faces Lough Foyle. Few visitors trouble to explore the beautiful, if bleak, northern and western parts, but the peninsula is worth a day of back-road motoring.

Up at **Malin Head** there's not much to see except an old signaling tower and a fine vista. Most visitors come here to stand on Ireland's most northerly point and, strangely, look south into Northern Ireland.

Both coasts of Inishowen make enjoyable drives, detouring often onto the little country lanes that bring you near the sea. The western or Lough Swilly coast is the more dramatic, with three wonderful beaches in its northern section:

White Strand Bay, near Malin Head; **Pollan Bay** on the dune-covered Doagh Isle Peninsula; and the estuary of **Trawbreaga Bay** near Malin village. Doagh Isle also offers the multicolored stonework of 16th-century **Carrickabraghy Castle** (see sidebar), a dolefully beautiful ruin, on its northwest tip. A mountainous coast runs south down to **Inch Island** and its bird-haunted mudflats.

The greatest archaeological treasure of Inishowen is undoubtedly the cashel or circular stone fort of **Grianan of Aileach,** set commandingly on an 800-foot (245 m) hill northwest of Londonderry. Dr. Walter Bernard reconstructed it in the 1870s, restoring it to how it must have looked when built around 1700 B.C.—a mighty ring fortress, rising in three tiers to a narrow rampart 18 feet (5 m) tall. The O'Neill chiefs of Ulster made it their stronghold from the 5th to the 12th centuries, and St. Patrick preached here in 450. From the wall-top rampart, the views extend across Londonderry city and over Lough Foyle and Lough Swilly. ■

Inishowen & the Northeast Peninsulas

🗺 205 C5–E6

Visitor Information

✉ Blaney Rd., Letterkenny, Co. Donegal
☎ 074 912 1160

The Workhouse

✉ Dunfanaghy, Co. Donegal
☎ 074 913 6540
🕒 Closed Nov.–Feb.
💲 $$

www.dunfanaghy workhouse.ie

Aran Island & Tory Island

Donegal's two main inhabited islands, Aran and Tory, differ tremendously. Each has accommodations, or you can visit on day trips—although in the case of the more remote Tory, be prepared for an overnight stay due to a sudden worsening in the weather. You should not leave Donegal without experiencing one or other of these idiosyncratic outposts.

Windswept Tory Island has inspired its own school of naïve painting that reflects island scenes.

Aran Island

 205 B5

 20 minutes from Burtonport by Arranmore Island Ferry Service

 074 952 0532

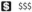 $$$

www.arranmore
ferry.com

Aran Island

Aran (locally called Arranmore to avoid confusion with the Aran Islands in County Galway; see pp. 178–179) lies a couple of miles (3 km) west of Burtonport in the Rosses area (see pp. 222–223). Close to 1,000 people live on this hilly island that rises to 750 feet (228 m) in the center and measures about 3 miles (5 km) wide by 4 miles (6 km) long. August is a good time to visit—the island's festival sees everyone letting their hair down. But with half a dozen pubs, you are able to find music and conversation anytime in the island's village of **Leabgarrow.**

A long morning or afternoon would suffice for a walk around the rugged coast. Roads and boreens (narrow lanes) climb from the low-lying eastern shore into the wild, boggy interior, but with a good pair of boots you can strike across the heather, rock, and rough grass. There's tremendous bird activity around **Green Island,** off the southwest tip of the island.

Tory Island

Aran is conveniently close to the mainland and sees a fair number of visitors, but you have to be more adventurous—and a better sailor—for **Tory Island,** 7 miles (11 km) off the northern coast of Bloody Foreland. In contrast to Aran, Tory lies low, a slim bar measuring about 2.5 (4 km) miles long and less than a mile (1.6 km) wide. Wind is a constant factor, whipping up the intervening seas, often driving salt-laden spray across the island. Anything that is grown here has to be protected in little stone-walled fields. Fishing is good enough, but hazardous. For the tiny Irish-speaking community, times have always been tough—they were nearly evacuated during a particularly bad winter in the 1970s. It took a tremendous publicity campaign by the priest of Tory to gain a sheltered harbor and regular ferry service for the island, along with proper sanitation and electricity.

Tourism has supplied a lifeline for Tory Island, which has archaeological treasures such as the ancient **Tau Cross** (now displayed at the pier in West Town, Tory's main village), and visitors enjoy the strong flavor of the life of this proudly independent island that has been (and still is) ruled by its own king since St. Columba first appointed a Tory islander in the sixth century.

Craic can be mighty in the pubs, especially during the festival in July, but the islanders do not put on an act for the visitors—they are as frank and outspoken about the difficulties of island life as they are willing to pass on Tory Island legends and beliefs. The island was the lair of the ferocious Fomorian brigands, who attacked the mainland in the mythical era under their chief Balor of the Evil Eye, whose single eye was in the back of his head.

Painting for pleasure was almost unknown on Tory Island until 1968, when local fisherman James Dixon chanced upon English artist Derek Hill painting a Tory landscape and suggested that he could do a better job. He proved his point, and other islanders became interested, until a Tory Island school of naïve art was flourishing. Examples are on view (and for sale) in the **James Dixon Gallery,** in the late fisherman-painter's former home. ■

Tory Island

🅰 205 C6

⛴ 1–2 hours from Bunbeg, depending on weather

☎ 074 913 5502

⛴ 45 minutes– 1 hour from Magheroarty by Turasmara Teo

☎ 074 953 1320 or 953 1340

💲 $$$

www.toryisland ferry.com

James Dixon Gallery

✉ Near the school

🕐 Closed mid-Sept.–May

Tory Islanders

Two factors allow the population of Tory Island to stay put in such a tough, windy, salt-sprayed, and bare environment: The commitment of successive Irish governments, and hence Irish taxpayers, to underwrite the island economy, and the grit and determination of the islanders themselves. Rather than their ways of livelihood or dress, it is their warmth and hospitality in the face of adverse circumstances that make the Tory Islanders an iconic example of a traditional, Irish-speaking community.

County Leitrim

Leitrim is certainly the most overlooked and undervisited county in the west of Ireland. It has no glamour, but an understated charm well repays a day or two, especially if you are fond of fishing, boating, or hill walking.

County Leitrim

⬛ Map p. 205

Visitor Information

✉ Old Barrel Store, Carrick-on-Shannon, Co. Leitrim

☎ 071 962 0170

🕐 Seasonal

Leitrim lies squeezed by Donegal and Fermanagh on the northeast, Cavan on the east, Longford to the south, and Roscommon and Sligo to the west. Its coastline is a strip only 3 miles (5 km) wide, which explains why it is not more popular with visitors. But only a few miles inland rise the beautiful heartlands of the **Dartry Mountains,** bookended by beautiful lakes. **Lough Melvin,** on the Fermanagh border, has a spatter of islands and some

fine hill slopes on the south.

County Sligo to the southwest has the lion's share of **Lough Gill,** but Leitrim's eastern quarter of the lake boasts **Parke's Castle,** a handsome fortified house with a turreted *bawn* (tower) built in 1609 for Capt. Robert Parke on a lakeside knoll. The castle was abandoned by the Parkes in 1691 and stood in ruins until the mid-20th century. Now it has been restored using Irish oak for the roofs—held together with wooden dowels in the traditional manner.

Dromahair

Just to the south of the lake head is the village of Dromahair, scene of an abduction (or perhaps seduction and elopement) that dramatically changed Irish history. The 17th-century **Old Hall** stands on the site of Breffni Castle, a 12th-century stronghold of Tiernan O'Rourke, whose wife, Dervorgilla, made off with O'Rourke's bitter rival, Dermot MacMurrough, King of Leinster. In 1166, O'Rourke and his ally, King Rory O'Connor, drove MacMurrough out of Ireland. But it was a Pyrrhic victory. MacMurrough rallied support from Richard "Strongbow" de Clare, Earl of Pembroke, with

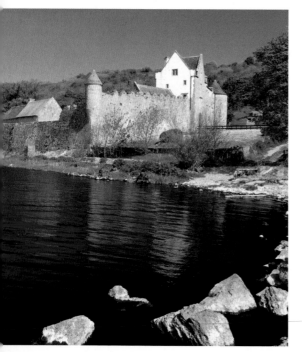

Parke's Castle stands sentinel on the shores of Lough Gill.

INSIDER TIP:

For a unique Lough Allen experience, Lough Allen Adventure *(www .loughallenadventure .com)* offers kayaking, windsurfing, and more.

—STEPHANIE ROBICHAUX
National Geographic contributor

the backing of King Henry II of England. Strongbow landed in Ireland in 1169, obtaining a foothold for the Anglo-Normans that eventually became an islandwide conquest.

The Leitrim Way

Northeast of Dromahair is **Manorhamilton.** A well-marked long-distance footpath, the **Leitrim Way,** reaches Manorhamilton at the end of a 30-mile (48 km) northward course from Drumshanbo. Walking the path *(Irish Ordnance Survey 1:50,000 sheet No. 26)* is the best way to get a feeling for this rolling countryside, especially as the first section runs up the east bank of **Lough Allen.**

On emerging at the foot of the lough some 8 miles (13 km) south, the Leitrim Way winds past the neat village of **Drumshanbo** to reach modest **Leitrim town** at the start of the **Shannon-Erne Waterway.** Reopened in 1994 after 125 years of dereliction, this meandering 40-mile (65 km) waterway provides the final link in a chain of lakes and rivers that can be navigated from Belleek (see pp. 318–319), on Lough Erne

in County Fermanagh, all the way south to Limerick and the Shannon Estuary, a total distance of 239 miles (382 km).

The canal began life as the Ballyconnell and Ballinamore Canal in 1860, but it soon fell victim to competition by the Sligo, Leitrim, & Northern Counties Railway (known locally as the Slow, Late, and Never Completely Reliable). It winds eastward to Upper Lough Erne through attractive green countryside of rounded drumlin hills, lakes, and small farms—the

EXPERIENCE:
Onto Leitrim's Waters

Leitrim's pride is its waterways—lakes, rivers, and the mighty Shannon-Erne Waterway. For cruising, **Ballinamore** is a good center—it's a sizable place with all the facilities you'll need *(www.locaboat.com, www.cruiseireland .com)*. The same goes for **Carrick-on-Shannon,** the acknowledged Shannon-Erne cruising center *(www.world-wide-river-cruise .com)*. Information on fishing can be found at *www.shannon-fishery-board.ie* or at *www .leisureangling.co.uk*—here you'll find details of locations from rivers to lakes, which species you can expect, fishing-friendly accommodations, charts, contacts, permits, and more.

setting for many of the novels and short stories of Leitrim's master storyteller, John McGahern.

This is prime fishing country, with plenty of well-stocked rivers and lakes. It's boating country, too, especially downriver at **Carrick-on-Shannon.** Here you can hire boats for cruising or angling, or sit back and enjoy a river cruise with humorous local commentary. ∎

Parke's Castle

✉ Dromahair, Lough Gill, near Sligo, Co. Leitrim
☎ 071 9164149
🕐 Closed Nov.–mid-April
💲 $

More Places to Visit in Northwest Ireland

Ballysadare

At Ballysadare (Baile Easa Daire, the "town of the waterfall of the oak tree"), the Ballysadare River runs through town over a series of weirs, with the remains of mills standing along its banks. A jungly graveyard surrounds the shell of a medieval church on the site of a seventh-century monastery. W. B. Yeats rode and rambled in the fields around here during his boyhood holidays: his Pollexfen relations owned the Ballysadare mills.

🅰 205 B2 ✉ Junction of the N59 (Ballina) & N4 (Boyle) roads, 3 miles (5 km) S of Sligo town, Co. Sligo **Sligo Visitor Information** ☎ 071 916 1201

Doon Well & Rock of Doon

Bushes at the approach to Doon Well are laden with rags, pairs of spectacles, and tiny holy statues, a clear message that the purported healing water of this famous well still draws large numbers of pilgrims. Steps lead from the parking lot to Carraig a' Duin, the Rock of Doon, its summit imprinted with the shape of a human foot. From the 13th century to the Flight of the Earls in 1607, each O'Donnell King of Tyrconnell was crowned here. 🅰 205 D5 ✉ Signposted off the N56 betw. Kilmacrenan & Termon, 9 miles (14 km) N of Letterkenny, Co. Donegal **Letterkenny Visitor Information** ☎ 074 912 1160

Glebe House

Built as a rectory in 1828 and bought by English artist Derek Hill in 1953, Glebe House has an Arts and Crafts feel, decorated with William Morris wallpaper and the colorful naïve paintings of Tory Islanders, including James Dixon (see p. 229). The **Derek Hill Gallery,** opened in 1982, displays work by Picasso and Augustus John, as well as Irish artists such as Jack Yeats (see pp. 208–209). *www.heritageireland.ie*

🅰 205 D5 ✉ Churchhill, Gartan Lough, on the R251, 10 miles (16 km) NW of Letterkenny (R250), Co. Donegal ☎ 074 913 7071 🕐 Closed Oct.–late May & Fri. 💲 $

Glenveagh National Park

Based around Lough Beagh, Glenveagh National Park covers 23,887 acres (9,650 ha) of hilly country. At the heart of the park is **Glenveagh Castle,** built of granite in Scottish baronial style by John George Adair, who notoriously evicted 244 tenants in the harsh winter of 1861 so that he could incorporate their land. His wife, Cornelia, laid out the rhododendron gardens and introduced the red deer that have become Ireland's largest herd. *www.glenveaghnationalpark.ie*

🅰 205 C5–D5 ✉ Entrance on the R251, 10 miles (16 km) E of Dunlewy & Errigal Mountain, Co. Donegal **Glenveagh visitor information** ☎ 074 37090 🕐 Closed Nov.–mid-March

Sligo Folk Park

You can explore many aspects of life in Sligo at this splendid folk park in southern County Sligo. In the 19th-century **Millview House,** visitors can experience how a well-off family would have lived a century years ago. **Mrs. Buckley's Cottage,** surrounded by a lovely garden, was transported to New York in the mid-1980s for a special exhibition and then returned to its site here. An exhibition hall, built in the style of a traditional residence, features an excellent display of rural history and agricultural heritage, along with special events and temporary exhibitions. The park also has a craft center carrying quality items, many made locally. A coffee shop serves homemade food and snacks. *www.sligofolkpark.com* ✉ Millview House, Riverstown, Co. Sligo ☎ 071 916 5001, 🕐 Open mid-May–Sept.; Oct.–mid-May by appointment only 💲 $$

The least well known part of Ireland, with farms, lakes and bogs, and medieval abbeys—a secret waiting to be discovered

Central Ireland

Faith and art at Monasterboice

Central Ireland

The midlands inspire little of the heightened expectation that travelers feel when they see the grand mountains and coasts of the west. But given the chance, the round drumlin hills, secretive lakes, and great sullen boglands of the Irish heartland—where the pace of life is easy and unruffled—will work their magic on you.

From the air, central Ireland appears a vast green flatland, patched brown with bogs and winking with lakes. On the ground, it gives the impression of endless miles of farm country, its lakes well hidden, its bogs sterile and barren. This uncrowded land, owing as much to water as to earth, is just the place for country pursuits—canoeing along the River Shannon, angling for pike in the Cavan lakes, tramping the Slieve Bloom Mountains, riding a horse along byways and green lanes, cruising up the Grand Canal in a narrowboat.

The nine counties of the central region fall loosely into three groups. Monaghan and Cavan are neighbors on the borders with Northern Ireland. Like Donegal, they were part of ancient Ulster and still have a plantation feel to their neat, well-laid-out towns. They are drumlin counties, pimpled with small hills and trenched with hundreds of valleys.

The five most central counties—Roscommon, Longford, Westmeath, Offaly, and Laois—are dairying regions with old-fashioned market towns and hedged, gently rolling landscapes. The River Shannon flows on the borders of all but Laois, draining immense boglands that have recently begun to be conserved after decades of exploitation. Clonmacnoise, Fore and Boyle Abbeys, Strokestown Park House, and Birr Castle are prime attractions.

Meath and Louth, coastal counties north of Dublin, are rich in historical sites, from the remarkable Stone Age necropolis at Brú na Bóinne to Monasterboice and the abbeys at Bective and Mellifont. ∎

0   30 kilometers
0   15 miles

NORTHERN IRELAND
p. 275

◁6

NORTHERN IRELAND
p. 275

Cuilcagh Mountains

N2

Monaghan

Clones

N54

M O N A G H A N

Ballybay

Castleblayney

Ballyconnell

N87

Belturbet

Shannon-Erne Waterway

◇ **Redhills Equestrian Centre**

Butlers Bridge

N3

Lough Oughter

KILLYKEEN FOREST PARK

Cavan

Crossdoney

R180

Inishkeen

Carrickmacross

N2

Slieve Foye Carlingford ☆

R173 Cooley

R53 Cooley Peninsula

Dundalk

◁5

Dundalk Bay

Irish Sea

C A V A N

R165

Kingscourt

L O U T H

Ardee

R166

Dunleer

M1

N52

Monasterboice ◇

Mellifont Abbey ◇

Dowth ☆

Knowth ◇

Drogheda

Brú na Bóinne Visitor Centre

Newgrange

Erne

R198

N55

Lough Sheelin

Virginia

Lough Ramor

R154

N3

Granard

N4

Oldcastle

◇ **Loughcrew Passage Graves**

Kells

Blackwater

Seven Wonders of Fore ◇

Fore

Lough Lene

Fore Abbey

Longford

N63

G F O R D

Inny

N4

Lough Derravaragh

N57

M3

Navan

M E A T H

N2

Royal Canal

R392

Lough Owel

N52

Boyne

Bective Abbey ◇

Hill of Tara ◇

DUBLIN
p. 47

N55

R390

Lough Ennell

Mullingar

Trim

R125

N3

◁3

W E S T M E A T H

N6

N6

N4

M4

△E   △F

Kilbeggan

R400

Edenderry

R402

Grand Canal

N80

Brosna

Tullamore

O F F A L Y

R420

EAST IRELAND
p. 87

◁2

N52

Rosenallis

R422

Barrow

Mountmellick

N7

Birr Castle ☆

Slieve Bloom Mountains

R423

N80

Emo Court

R421

R462

Nore

Portlaoise

M7

Rock of Dunamase

L A O I S

N7

Abbeyleix

R78

N80

◁1

N8

△C   △D

Area of map detail

Belfast ☆

Dublin ☆

Strokestown Park House & the Irish National Famine Museum

Unlike almost every other Ascendancy house in Ireland, Strokestown Park House retains the effects accumulated by one family over 300 years. The Irish National Famine Museum explores the disaster that befell rural Ireland in the 1840s. After seeing the style in which a Big House family lived, the high-handed attitudes of so many landlords in the time of the Great Famine fall into perspective.

When they extended Strokestown Park House in the 1730s, the Mahon family chose severely classical architecture.

Strokestown Park House & the National Famine Museum

🅰 234 B4

✉ Strokestown, Co. Roscommon

☎ 071 963 3013

🕐 Closed Nov.– mid-March

💲 House: $$ Garden: $$ Museum: $$

www.strokestown park.ie

Strokestown Park House

The last of the Pakenham-Mahon family to live at Strokestown was Olive, born here in 1894—she sold it in 1978 to local garage owner Jim Callery, whose company still owns and runs the estate. Looking to buy 5 acres (2 ha) of land to park his fleet of trucks, Callery actually purchased the entire estate!

The **drawing room** where Olive and her husband ended up living, eating, and sleeping in the 1970s, selling pictures off the walls in order to keep solvent, contains family photos that include one of

Olive's mother, her waist corseted to an incredible 16 inches (40 cm).

The **library** has more photos, including a poignant one of Olive's first husband, Edward Stafford-King-Harman—he was killed during World War I only four months after their marriage, while Olive was carrying their child. To lighten the mood, the guide sets the wind-up gramophone to play a 78-rpm record of Margaret Burke-Sheridan singing "Galway Bay" in the fruitiest of operatic voices.

Upstairs you view the **Lady's and Gentleman's bedrooms,** with their four-poster beds; the children's **schoolroom,** where 1930s copybooks lie on their desks; and a wonderful **playroom** full of evocative old toys, dress-up clothes, and a dolls' tea party.

The **kitchen** downstairs lay forgotten behind false walls until Callery rediscovered it after he had bought the house, complete with a huge black range and an 18th-century gallery from which the lady of the house could inspect the domestics at work without having to come into contact with them.

INSIDER TIP:

Set aside time to explore Strokestown's beautiful gardens, complete with a lily pond, rose garden, croquet lawn, and amazing perennial border.

—LARRY PORGES

Editor, National Geographic Books

Irish National Famine Museum

How the families of the domestic servants suffered during the Great Famine of 1845–1849 (see pp. 28–29) is vividly, though even-handedly, told in the Irish National Famine Museum, housed in the old stable block. Original Strokestown documents and well-mounted reproductions of contemporary cartoons and lithographs lead you through the story of what happened after a fungus reduced the Irish potato crop to black slime.

The English government—and the English in general—thought of the Irish poor as "indolent, idle, inclined to do evil, and beyond the pale of civilization." Relief was ineffective, insufficient, and callously withdrawn when it was most needed. Dependent entirely on the potato, the peasants starved. Responsibility for helping the destitute people was thrown on landlords and rent-payers who were unwilling or unable to play their part. Evictions for nonpayment of rent were widespread, enforced emigration commonplace.

At Strokestown, Maj. Denis Mahon, in the process of evicting two-thirds of his tenants (about 5,000 people), was shot dead in 1847, one of seven landlords or agents murdered that year. Anguish and resentment followed the poor and rode with them on the disease-ridden emigration ships.

Blaming the landlords alone is too simplistic. Major Mahon received little government help, had no resources to help those dependent on him, and had to either watch them starve or pay for them to emigrate. More culpable were English politicians, who made such statements as: "The great evil with which we have to contend is not the physical evil of famine, but the moral evil of the selfish, perverse and turbulent character of the people." ■

Potato Fungus

Phytophthora infestans is a fungus that attacks both leaves and tubers of the potato. White growths seen around infected leaves are the tubes that carry the fungus spores, which spread most readily in typically Irish conditions of gentle wind and warm misty rain. In such conditions, one diseased plant can produce several million spores, attacking neighboring plants. The leaves wither; the potatoes blacken and rot. The fungus can be controlled with copper sulfate, but this fact was unknown in the 1840s.

Boyle Abbey

Boyle Abbey, near County Roscommon's border with County Sligo, is a rare survival in Ireland—a remarkably complete, very early Cistercian monastery. Equally remarkable is the fact that Boyle owes its survival to the military. Instead of following its usual pattern of destroying what it found, the military took over the buildings in the seventeenth century and converted them into a barracks.

Few monastic sites survived Ireland's bloody wars and repressions as unscathed as Boyle Abbey.

Boyle Abbey

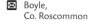 234 B5

✉ Boyle,
Co. Roscommon

☎ 071 966 2604

🕐 Closed mid-
Sept.–Easter

💲 $

History of Boyle Abbey

Monks from Mellifont Abbey (see p. 274) came to Boyle in 1148 looking for a place to build a new abbey and fired with enthusiasm for a Spartan but charitable way of life. Six years earlier, a group of them had returned to Ireland fresh from a visit to France, where they had been inspired by the discipline and self-denial of the monks at St. Bernard's monastery. After founding the Cistercian abbey of Mellifont, the monks were keen to spread their influence.

The MacDermot clan, sensing an opportunity to gain prestige, gave the monks 1,000 acres (400 ha) of land on which to build their abbey and community at Boyle.

At its height of its prosperity, from the 13th to 15th centuries, Boyle Abbey ruled vast tracts of land and supported a community of more than 400, but, by the time of its dissolution in the mid-16th century, there was only a handful of monks in a range of decayed buildings. Queen Elizabeth I granted the monastic lands to the Cusack family, and they allowed the monks to linger on in the abbey. Then, in 1603, the new Stuart king of England, James I, gave the estate to a Staffordshire adventurer, John King. He turned the abbey into a garrisoned fortress known as Boyle Castle, and it remained in use as a military barracks for a century and a half. In 1788, the Connaught Rangers—a rough lot—moved on, and the old buildings began a period of decay that was not arrested until the 20th century.

Touring the Abbey

Imagination and a sense of history are kindled from the outset as you walk into the site through the arch of the **gatehouse,** notched by the sword cuts of the idle soldiery. The inner gate jambs are incised with graffiti cut by bored guards. In the gatehouse, an exhibit sets the scene around a scale model of the abbey in its heyday. In monastic times, the gatehouse would have contained a 24-hour guard and quarters for unexpected guests.

Cloister Garth: Stepping through the archway, you come into the wide, grassy cloister garth, or garden, with low walls. Around these rises the outer wall of the abbey complex, patched roughly where it was broken through to create military gateways.

Daily Life in the Abbey: You will find **kitchens** with enormous fireplaces to the south. The cooking, cleaning, and general spadework of the abbey was done by a large community of laypersons—St. Benedict's original decree that monks attend eight services of prayer a day while remaining self-sufficient through their own hard work

proved impossible to obey.

In the big **refectory** to the southeast, the monks ate in silence (a custom common to most Cistercian abbeys) while edified by readings of scripture from a wall lectern. Between mid-September and Easter, they ate only once a day—and since they rose at 2:30 a.m., those days must have seemed long indeed.

INSIDER TIP:

Taking a guided tour around the extensive ruins of Boyle Abbey is an atmospheric experience that shouldn't be missed.

—CHRISTOPHER SOMERVILLE
National Geographic author

Farther along the east wall were **reading rooms, dormitories** with a calefactory (hot room) to warm them, a **parlor** for occasional conversation, the **chapter house,** and the **abbot's house.**

Abbey Church: A low arch leads into the splendid abbey church—austere Romanesque at the eastern end, more decorative Gothic toward the west. Capitals become floral and the pillars more elaborate. The westernmost capital of the north wall (which slopes alarmingly outward) has 14 little grimacing men peeping out of foliage—the master mason's team, suggests the guide, caricatured by him as a signing-off gesture on completion of the church's construction. ■

County Cavan

If you like lakes, you'll love County Cavan. The little border country is spattered with them so thickly that a Cavan view without a slip of water in it soon feels strange. Bring your fishing rods, and you could do worse than to pack your walking boots, too. Out to the west sticks a long thin panhandle separating Leitrim from Fermanagh, where the Iron Mountains meld into the Cuilcagh range and the land rises and becomes beautifully wild, ideal for hill tramping.

Retreating glaciers formed the hillocks and lakebeds so characteristic of County Cavan.

Cavan Town

🅼 235 D5

Visitor information

✉ 1 Farnham St., Cavan, Co. Cavan

☎ 049 433 1942

🕐 Seasonal

The trim little county town of **Cavan** is not particularly visitor-oriented but is pleasant enough as a base for exploring the lakes. Or you could try the villages of **Butlers Bridge** and **Belturbet,** a little nearer to the lakes.

Upper Lough Erne wriggles down from Fermanagh and breaks up into hundreds of thin, winding watercourses. These lakes, lakelets, and threads of river make islands and peninsulas of the green, well-wooded land between Belturbet, near the border, and the point near Crossdoney where the River Erne emerges to flow on south.

Killykeen Forest Park

Driving and walking here is puzzling at first, with innumerable signs pointing to different lakes. Look for brown signs to **Lough Oughter**—leading to a meandering circuit through brackeny back lanes with Killykeen Forest Park *(tel 049 433 2541)* at its hub. The Cavan tourist office will give you information about the park, including directions to the **Killykeen Equestrian Centre** *(7 miles/12 km NW of Cavan town, tel 049 436 1707)* or **Redhills Equestrian Centre** *(tel 047 55042)* and to the best fishing locations. Or you can follow one of the marked trails through the woods of the park.

Most of the country lanes hereabouts are *boreens*—grass-green tracks that make for fine strolling. But beware: The roads twist and bend, and it's easy to get lost! Fishing is excellent at Belturbet and Butlers Bridge, and plenty of local experts can tell you where to try for fat lake trout.

Ballyconnell

Farther west, at Ballyconnell, you reach the Ballyconnell and Ballinamore Canal, better known as the **Shannon-Erne Waterway.** It starts at Leitrim town and is navigable all the way to the south shore of Upper Lough Erne at Foalies Bridge. The 1994 reopening of this 36-mile (60 km) link between the Erne and Shannon river and lake systems turned the formerly sleepy village of Ballyconnell into a lively boating center. Rent a boat in Ballyconnell to cruise the waterway to Ballinamore in County Leitrim or up the canal to Fermanagh.

The Cuilcagh Mountains

West of Ballyconnell, the Cuilcagh Mountains dominate the bleak, wild landscape. They climb in a series of flattish peaks to the summit of the range on Cuilcagh itself at 2,180 feet (663 m). The summit is best climbed along the Ulster Way from Florence Court Forest Park in Fermanagh—about 10 miles (16 km) round-trip with a climb of about 1,350 feet (410 m).

The Cavan Way

The well-marked Cavan Way runs from Blacklion on the Fermanagh border for 16 miles (26 km) south to Dowra. The path hops over the outlying northwest toe of the Cuilcagh range and runs by the Shannon Pot, where the 230-mile (368 km) river—the longest in the British Isles—has its birth; from here the path follows the infant Shannon to Dowra. ∎

FISHING PERMITS: Licenses are available from local visitor information offices and fishing shops. For more information contact the North West Tourism *(tel 071 916 1201)* or the Northern Regional Fisheries Board *(tel 071 985 1435).*

EXPERIENCE: Attending a Gaelic Athletic Match

Founded in 1884, the Gaelic Athletic Association (GAA; www.gaa.ie) ensures that traditional Irish sports survive and thrive. Two sports have always dominated its calendar—Gaelic football and hurling.

Gaelic football is a super-fast, thrilling, and passionately supported game in which the 15 players of each team run and score with the ball in hand or at foot. In hurling, the oldest team game in Europe, the *sliothar* or ball travels at ferocious speed, propelled by a thwack of the *camán* or hurley (stick). Players must be extremely brave, determined, and quick to make headway. Crowds are noisy, knowledgeable, and ready with invective.

Croke Park *(Jones Rd., Dublin 3, tel 01 819 2300, www.crokepark.ie)* in Dublin is the national home of the GAA and site of many exciting matches. But it's even more fun to turn up at some small-town ground, where the crowd knows all the players and the bantering is richly personal. **County Cavan** *(http://cavan.gaa.ie)* is home to several hurling and Gaelic football teams worth seeking out.

Monaghan Town & Around

County Monaghan and County Cavan complement each other topographically. Cavan (see pp. 240–241) is full of lakes and Monaghan is full of hills—little ones, roundish drumlins of rubble and clay dumped by retreating glaciers 10,000 years ago. The hills give the sprawling border country of Monaghan an intimate, enclosed character very different from the open landscapes of the southern midlands or the west.

Monaghan Town

🅰 235 D6

Visitor Information

✉ Castle Meadow Court, Tirkeenan, Monaghan, Co. Monaghan

☎ 047 81122

www.monaghan tourism.com

Monaghan Town

The county town of Monaghan, stone-built and solid, epitomizes the virtues of hard work and respectability. Though County Monaghan has lain in the Republic since 1921, it formed part of the ancient kingdom of Ulster and was planted or colonized by non-Catholic Scottish settlers in the early 17th century. Monaghan shared Ulster's rise to prosperity through the linen trade, reflected in the substantial architecture of the county town with its three squares, great Victorian drinking fountain, and huge **St. Macartan's Cathedral** (constructed 1861–1891), whose 250-foot (76 m) spire dominates the town.

The **Monaghan County Museum** is one of the best of its kind, with an archaeological overview covering 5,000 years. Chief prize is the 14th-century **Cross of Clogher,** a beautifully worked altar crucifix of bronze from the ancient bishopric of Clogher a few miles northwest.

Carrickmacross & Clones

South of Monaghan, the two lacemaking towns of Carrickmacross and Clones still ply their trade, though for the specialist collector market these days. You can see occasional demonstrations of the art in the **Carrickmacross Lace Gallery** on Market Square.

In Clones, it's also worth looking for the weathered but still striking tenth-century **high cross,** relocated on the Diamond from the ruins of St. Tiernach's Monastery on Abbey Street.

Monaghan lacemakers need keen eyes and quick fingers.

EXPERIENCE: Join In the Festival Fun

Hilton Park (http://hiltonpark.ie) is a grand country house turned splendid hotel. It's also the site of the **Flat Lake Literary & Arts Festival** (Hilton Park, Clones, Co. Monaghan, www.theflatlakefestival.com), a tremendously fun three-day event that draws tens of thousands of people each year.

Dreamed up by local author Patrick McCabe and Welsh filmmaker Kevin Allen, the relatively new festival mixes poetry readings and music performances with competitions, crazy games such as Catch the Hen and Toss the Sheaf, and art auctions. You'll also find stand-up comedians, poets celebrated and obscure, one-woman shows, history talks, films, and plenty for the kids. As for the music, you can expect everything from the tried and true to romantic lounge lizards and the latest young firebrands. If this is country-house culture, it's been a long strange road here from cucumber sandwiches in the Blue Drawing Room.

Panels on the south side show Old Testament scenes, while on the north, New Testament miracles are depicted.

Inishkeen

So to the eastern border of the county and the countryside around Inishkeen—poor farming land, where small farms make the best of the steep drumlin sides and reedy valley bottoms. Ireland's greatest poet of the mid-20th century, Patrick Kavanagh (1904–1967), celebrated, excoriated, and revealed this hedged-in landscape in his wonderful poems, colorful or black according to mood. Kavanagh was a small-time farmer around Inishkeen until he left in his early thirties to live as a writer in London and Dublin. Drink and cancer took charge of him before he died.

Inishkeen was always the spur to his talent, from lyrical works, such as the autobiographical *The Green Fool* (1938), to bitterly realistic poems such as "Stony Grey Soil" (1940), in which he writes of how peasant life and work sapped his joy and restricted his range.

In Inishkeen, **Kavanagh's birthplace** (not open to the public) is signed off the road—a dour gray house on a ridge. The old church in the village contains the excellent **Patrick Kavanagh Centre and Inishkeen Folk Museum,** which features a fascinating exhibition about the poet and his work. Kavanagh's grave lies outside, marked with a simple wooden cross and the words: "And pray for him who walked apart on the hills, loving life's miracles."

Just past the modern church, on the road to Carrickmacross from Inishkeen, a brown sign marked "My Black Shanco" indicates a track that winds for a mile (1.6 km) toward Kavanagh's farm of **Shancoduff,** mentioned in many of his poems. "The sleety winds fondle the rushy beards of Shancoduff," he wrote in "Shancoduff," and here you can walk the lane and the rushy fields that the poet loathed and loved. ∎

Monaghan County Museum
- Hill St., Monaghan
- 047 82928
- Closed Sun.

Carrickmacross
- 235 E5

Lace Gallery
- Market Sq., Carrickmacross
- 042 966 2506
- Closed Nov.–March
- www.carrickmacrosslace.ie

Inishkeen
- 235 E5

Patrick Kavanagh Centre and Inishkeen Folk Museum
- Inishkeen
- 042 937 8560
- Summer: Closed Mon. & Sat; Winter: Closed Sat.–Mon.
- www.patrickkavanaghcountry.com

Cruise: River Shannon & Lough Ree from Athlone

The bustling if not exactly beautiful town of Athlone sits in the center of Ireland, more or less at the midpoint of the Shannon, Ireland's longest river. It makes a great base for exploring the Shannon—southward to the monastic site of Clonmacnoise or northward among the wooded islands of Lough Ree. You can rent your own cruiser or travel onboard one of the excursion boats.

In the old town of Athlone, plenty of relaxing pubs offer good stout and music.

When you set off south from **Athlone ❶** *(visitor information, Athlone Castle, St. Peter's Sq., Athlone, tel 090 649 4630)* for Clonmacnoise, you'll need to take account of Athlone's lock, through which you have to pass before reaching the Shannon. It's best to be first in line, early in the day—otherwise you may have to wait an hour or so for the lock to fill and empty several times. But it's a pleasant place, where freshwater admirals exchange yarns and boats bump companionably together. Once through, just remember to keep the black markers on your left and the red ones on your right.

NOT TO BE MISSED:

Athlone lock & waterfront
• **Clonmacnoise** • **Inchcleraun**
• **Fishing—bring a rod!**

The broad Shannon curves gently through grazing meadows; several of these are left uncut until late in the summer to give shelter to the now very rare corncrake. You probably won't see this unassuming brown bird, but if lucky, you may hear the male's loudly

Lanesborough

N63

Roscommon

Lough Ree

Inchenagh

Ballymurray

Hind

Clogás Oratory

Churches

④

Inchcleraun

L O N G F O R D

Lecarrow

⑤ *Saint's Island*

R O S C O M M O N

Tang

Tang

⑥

Inchturk

Nun's Island

Lough Funshinagh

N61

⑦

Inchmore

N55

Lough Ree

Hare Island

R362

R390

Cross

Ballykeeran

③

Lough Ree Yacht Club

ATHLONE

①

START

N6

🅼 See area map p. 234 B3

▶ Jolly Mariner Marina, Coosan
(tel 090 647 2892, $$–$$$)

🕐 Half a day, either trip

↔ Clonmacnoise and back,
19 miles (30 km); Lough Ree,
22 miles (36 km)

▶ Athlone

Shannon

② Clonmacnoise

Limerick

O F F A L Y

6 kilometers

3 miles

grating repetition of his Latin name, *crex crex,* before the towers of **Clonmacnoise** ❷ (see pp. 250–251) come in sight. A convenient jetty lies below the monastic site. Allow up to half an hour longer for the return journey to Athlone as you'll be sailing against the current.

Cruising upriver from Athlone, it's only a mile or so (1.6 km) before you pass the **Lough Ree Yacht Club** ❸, founded as far back as 1770, on your right. Don't forget that for upriver travelers, the black markers are now on your right and the red on your left.

If you wish to land on any of the islands, make sure that your boat has an anchor and a dinghy—complete with oars and rowlocks—attached. Ree is a great fishing lake, and you can take full advantage if you are in a rented craft.

Of the many islands and islets in Lough Ree, the most interesting in terms of its archaeological remains is **Inchcleraun** ❹, sometimes known as the **Quaker's Island,** in the northern part of the lake. If you want to explore, you'll need to anchor near the red lake-navigation marker No. 7 and row to the bouldery island

One of the most enjoyable pastimes in central Ireland is to explore the many islands of Lough Ree.

Beyond the yacht club, the waterway broadens out into the great expanse of **Lough Ree** at the heart of the Shannon. It is wise to heed the navigation advice given you at the Jolly Mariner Marina, Coosan, as the lake is shallow and has plenty of rocks and barely submerged reefs. The lough is 16 miles (26 km) long, shaped like a pointy-headed leprechaun with one ragged sleeve extended to the east. Its shore lies flat and is mostly smothered with trees; low hills rise beyond, made to look taller by the flatness of the landscape.

waterline to scramble ashore. On haphazardly grazed grass in a smother of trees you'll find the tiny, ancient **Teampull Diarmuid Church,** the 13th-century **Teampull Mor** (Big Church), with its big gable and low door with a rugged lintel, and the little 12th-century **Chancel Church** and **Church of the Dead** near the shore. Toward the higher center of the island stands the dignified 12th-century **Clogás Oratory,** with its square bell tower.

Harder to find is the ruin of **Fairbrother's House**—Fairbrother was the Quaker who lived on Inchcleraun early in the 19th century. While he was building the cottage, so stories say, he took the cornerstones from the Clogás Oratory to use in his work. St. Diarmuid, sixth-century founder of the island's monastery, saw what was going on from his seat in heaven and was not amused. The saint "smote the Quaker's horse with the bolt of his holy revenge, which caused it to run furiously, untamedly, terribly, outrageously, irresistibly mad." Then all the beasts on the island ran crazy and were only restored to sanity when the Quaker vowed to touch no more of the holy stones.

It was only natural for reclusive early Christian hermits to choose the islands of Lough Ree as their prayerful refuges. There are remains of churches on **Saint's Island** ❺ (in fact the tip of a peninsula) and on **Nun's Island,** both now used as pasture.

Early in the 20th century, most of the islands supported resident families of eel-fishermen, who would hitch their boats to the back of passing Guinness barges for a free ride down to Athlone. Now many of the islands have become holiday retreats.

Some incumbents have found the realities of island life at odds with their fantasies, like the Dublin bookmaker who painstakingly built

a beautiful retreat for his family on **Inchturk Island** ❻ with wood interior, thatched roof, and local stone. The wife and son came over, spent one night, and pronounced it too quiet: The place was abandoned forthwith.

On **Inchmore Island** ❼, the largest in the lake *(private property),* St. Liobán's Monastery shows a few remains.

Queen of Connacht

Lough Ree is not only full of fish—it's also full of legends. One of the best concerns the mythical Queen of Connacht, the warlike and lecherous Medb (see p. 335). Forbaid, Prince of Ulster, from whose father Medb had stolen the Brown Bull of Cooley, hid out on the shores of Lough Ree and planned to avenge his father's loss. He discovered the place where Medb loved to bathe, measured the distance from there to the shore, and practiced his slingshot skills at that exact range. When Medb came down to bathe, Prince Forbaid stove her head in with a well-aimed shot. Just why he chose to use a hard piece of cheese as the missile, though, has never been explained.

EXPERIENCE: Sailing & Cruising Central Ireland

Boating is the best way to explore the fascinating Irish midlands. You can take to the water in a slick cruiser or choose a barge instead, a wider version of the traditional narrowboat.

To rent a cruiser, try **Locaboat** *(The Marina, Ballinamore, Co. Leitrim, tel 071 964 5300, www.locaboat.com),* **Carrick-craft** *(The Marina, Carrick-on-Shannon, Co. Leitrim, tel 01 278 1666, www.cruise-ireland .com),* **Waveline Cruisers** *(Killinure Point, Glasson, Athlone, Co. Westmeath, tel 090 648 5711, www.waveline.ie),* or **Silver Line Cruisers** *(The Marina, Banagher, Co. Offaly, tel 057 915 1112, www.silverlinecruisers.com).*

For barges, contact **Riversdale Barge Holidays** *(Riversdale, Ballinamore, Co. Leitrim, tel 071 964 4122, www .riversdalebargeholidays.com),* **Royal Canal Cruisers** *(along the Royal Canal; 12th Lock, Castleknock, Dublin 15, tel 01 820 5263, www.royalcanalcruisers.com),* or **Canalways Ireland Barge Holidays** (Grand Canal, Barrow River Navigation; *Spencer Bridge, Rathangan, Co. Kildare, tel 045 524646, www.canalways.ie).*

The **Inland Waterways Association of Ireland** *(tel 1890 924991, www.iwai.ie)* maintains a database of other boat rental services, charts, and day-trip listings.

Seven Wonders of Fore

In a quiet Westmeath valley, 15 miles (24 km) northeast of Mullingar, a remarkable group of monuments—some man-made, some works of nature—lies on the outskirts of the tiny village of Fore. On a fine day, you will have an experience to savor as you explore these curiosities, known as the Seven Wonders of Fore.

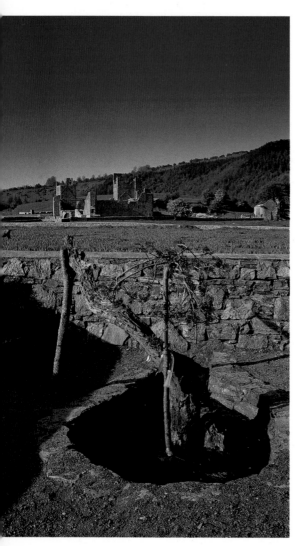

Looking from the Tree That Won't Burn and the Water That Won't Boil toward the Monastery in the Quaking Scraw

Monastery in the Quaking Scraw

A Quaking Scraw is a bog, on which nothing can normally be built. The Monastery in the Quaking Scraw, also known as Fore Abbey—a group of largely 15th-century Benedictine monastic ruins a couple fields away from the road and—seems to be surrounded by bog but is in fact founded on an islet of solid ground within the marsh. The most extensive Benedictine ruins in Ireland, they have a full range of monastic buildings with huge fireplaces and solid walls abutting a plain but lovely church. Restored cloister arches have discreet carvings of long-stemmed flowers. East stands the gatehouse, in use as a farm building; northeast are the circular remains of a dovecote.

St. Fechin's Bath

Walking back down the path toward the minor road, you'll find an ash tree standing over a tumble of mossy stones beside the wall on your right. This is St. Fechin's Bath (not in fact one of the seven wonders, but curious all the same); St. Fechin founded the first monastery at Fore in 630. The tree is usually hung with rags and the bark of its trunk crammed with coins—the traditional offerings to leave at holy wells. The mossy stones are the remnants of the basin where the saint kneeled praying in cold water all night. Ailing children were bathed here in expectation of a cure.

Other Wonders

The **Mill Without a Race**—a jumble of broken walls—and the **Water That Flows Uphill** are on your left as you reach the road. St. Fechin commissioned the original mill despite an absence of water, which he supplied by striking a hill at Lough Lene (south of Fore) with his staff. The water still flows.

Copper poisoning and the depredations of souvenir-hunters have reduced the **Tree That Won't Burn** to a stub. It stands

INSIDER TIP:

The coffee shop at Fore Abbey hosts readings every September of the works of the renowned Irish poet, Fore-born Michael Walsh (1897–1938).

—STEPHANIE ROBICHAUX
National Geographic contributor

near the road beside St. Fechin's Well, which contains the **Water That Won't Boil**—a muddy puddle these days. Bad luck attends anyone rash enough to make the experiment.

Across the road you'll find the **Stone Raised by St. Fechin's Prayers.** It forms the massive lintel of a church that mostly dates to the 12th century. Look for the little seated monk carved on the chancel arch. The stone may be much older. On it is carved a Greek cross in a circle, a more Eastern than Western religious symbol.

Up the bank from the church dwelt the hermit Patrick Begley, the **Anchorite in a Stone,** in the early 17th century. His humble cell was later incorporated into the grand mausoleum of the Greville Nugent family. The cell is marked with a Latin inscription translated as: "I, Patrick Begley, hermit of the sacred retreat, hidden and buried in this hollow heap of stones." The key to the mausoleum is kept at the Seven Wonders pub in Fore, a friendly place for a drink. ■

Mullingar
- 235 D3

Visitor Information
- Market House, Mullingar, Co. Westmeath
- 044 964 8650

Fore
- 235 D4

Visitor Information
- Fore Abbey Coffee Shop, Fore, Castlepollard, Co. Westmeath
- 044 966 1780
- Closed Mon.–Sat., Oct.–May

The Seven Wonders
- 235 D4
- Head N from Mullingar on the R394 to Castlepollard, then NE on the R395 to Fore. The Stone Raised by St. Fechin's Prayers and the Anchorite in a Stone lie to the south of the minor road through the Fore Valley, the other five wonders to the north.

Clonmacnoise

Beautifully situated among isolated meadows on a bend of the River Shannon, Clonmacnoise is the most complete and evocative monastic site in the central region. With its exquisitely carved high crosses, multitude of ancient churches, and splendid round tower, Clonmacnoise is claimed by many as the best such site in all Ireland.

Clonmacnoise is well sign-posted from Ballynahown on the N62, 7 miles (11 km) south of Athlone, and you can reach the site equally easily 5 miles (8 km) north of Shannonbridge, on the R357, 8 miles (13 km)

Don't whisper your secrets too close to the west doorway at MacDermot's Church—someone might hear them.

southeast of Ballinasloe. But the most memorable way to arrive is by water from Athlone (see pp. 244–247), with the tower and churches of the site outlined against the sky above their own reflections in the Shannon.

The grandeur of the site lies partly in its superb rural and river location, partly in the variety and splendor of its buildings. St. Ciarán founded the first monastery here circa 548, building it on Esker Riada, the Kings' Highway—a glacial ridge that ran west as a high road through the kingdoms of Leinster and Connacht. Between its foundation and the coming of the Normans in the 12th century, Clonmacnoise was Ireland's most important center of Christian faith, literature, and art.

The kings of Connacht and the High Kings of Tara were buried here. In spite of scores of assaults by Danes and ill-disposed Irish—it was attacked 27 times and burned 12 times by the native Irish between 720 and 1205—the influence of Clonmacnoise grew to extend over northern Europe. But after the Normans landed in Ireland, the monastery's power waned. In 1179, there were reported to be at least 100 houses and 13 churches in the monastery precincts; 300 years later, the place had declined in status to the seat of a minor bishop. In 1552, an English regiment marched down from Athlone, wrecked the building, and stole every treasure they could carry—even the books, stained glass, and church bells.

Castle & High Crosses

The ruins of a 13th-century Anglo-Norman **castle** totter on a hillock overlooking the Shannon. Entering the site, you pass through a visitor center with a must-see exhibit—it contains the monastery's three high crosses (replicas brave wind and rain in their original positions outside).

The tenth-century **Cross of the Scriptures** is richly covered with carved panels. Scenes include a flute player summoning the righteous to judgment; the devil lying on his back, his upraised feet providing a seat for St. Anthony; and a bird administering the kiss of life to Christ, who wears a beaded halo and lies in the tomb guarded by two Viking-looking warriors. Also exhibited is a collection of inscribed graveslabs.

Inside the Walls

The walled site itself is roughly circular. A landmark for miles around, **O'Rourke's Tower,** some 65 feet (20 m) high, is named after Fergal O'Rourke (died 964), King of Connacht. The top was shattered by a lightning strike in 1135 and never properly reconstructed.

Scattered around the site are several smaller churches: **Teampull Doolin, Teampull Hurpan,** and **Teampull Finghin,** with a dogtooth chancel arch and round tower belfry. Some call Teampull

Finghin McCarthy's Church; built around 1160, this beautiful chapel contains fine Romanesque carvings. The door of the attached tower is at ground level; by the time the church was built, the Viking threat had faded, so the tower was probably constructed as a belfry rather than for defense.

The Lepers' Confessional

East of O'Rourke's Tower lies the cathedral, or **MacDermot's Church,** built in 904 and rebuilt during the 12th century. There is a side chapel full of carved stone fragments and a Gothic west door of many recessed courses, decorated with dragons and foliage, overseen by Sts. Francis, Dominic, and Patrick in statue form. This doorway was erected, says the 15th-century Latin inscription, for the eternal glory of God. Press your ear to one side of the doorway and you can hear someone quietly whispering at the other side—priests used this to hear lepers' confessions in safety.

Around Clonmacnoise

Just up the slope stands tiny **St. Ciarán's Chapel,** burial place of the saint. The floor of the chapel lies below ground level—generations of local farmers have scooped up handfuls of soil mixed with saintly dust to scatter in their fields, thereby ensuring a good crop.

Most beautifully carved of all is the **Nun's Church,** 500 yards (450 m) east of the walled site, with heavy dogtooth arches, tiny faces, and, in the outer doorway, 11 beaked heads with bulging eyes. A penitent Dervorgilla, the Irish Helen of Troy (see sidebar p. 257), built the chapel in 1167. ∎

Clonmacnoise
- 234 B3
- Shannonbridge, Co. Offaly
- 090 967 4195
- $$

Birr Town & Castle

The fortunes of Birr have been bound up since 1620 with one talented and out-of-the-ordinary family—the Parsons clan, who became Earls of Rosse. They built a fine Georgian town in the farmlands of County Offaly, and at Birr Castle successive generations were at the cutting edge of scientific inquiry all through the 19th century, the great age of the amateur gentleman scientist.

The Earl and Countess of Rosse welcome the public to the beautiful grounds of their home.

Birr Town

⛰ 234 B2

Visitor information

✉ Brendan St., Birr, Co. Offaly

 057 912 0110

 Closed mid-Sept.–April

Birr Town Trail

The way to get the best out of Birr is to follow the Birr Town Trail *(leaflet guide available from the visitor information office)*. You start in **John's Mall,** one of the fine strolling streets laid out by the Parsons family. Another, farther along the trail, is **Oxmantown Mall.** John's Mall is shaded by well-grown Jerusalem plane trees, its small Georgian houses with their wide front door fanlights looking out on flowerbeds and neat white chain railings.

The trail takes you past the **Mercy Convent** behind its high wall (English architect Augustus

Pugin, 1812–1852, designed it), and along **O'Connell Street** and **Main Street** with their handsome old shop fronts. Many of these have carved wood surrounds. Keep an eye out for the druidic mistletoe-gatherers outside Mulholland's Pharmacy and more examples at Guinan's Footwear, Owen's Fruit and Veg, and Barber the Watchmaker.

Birr Castle & Estate

Closed to the public, Birr Castle is still the residence of the Earl and Countess of Rosse. But the estate (gardens and parkland) is open to all. These are some of the finest grounds in Ireland, continually being refurbished and improved. Paths crisscross the entire demesne, giving access to parkland and river and lake walks.

Particular features are the immense box hedges, which are more than 200 years old and up to 60 feet (18 m) tall. Walking between the hedges is a creepy but enjoyable experience. So, too, is searching for **"Sweeney,"** the wickerwork figure of the legendary Irish half-king, half-bird. With knees drawn up to a pointed beard, he sits in the fork of a holly tree near Lovers' Walk. Other delights are the roses, magnolias, and intricate formal gardens.

INSIDER TIP:

Is it true that Guinness tastes better in Ireland than at home? A fine spot to conduct some research is The Thatch [see p. 372], a beautiful 200-year-old pub in Crinkill 2 miles (3 km) outside Birr town.

—KAREN MARTINEZ
National Geographic Books

Ireland's Historic Science Centre

To appreciate the extent of the achievements of the Parsons family in the fields of science, it is worth spending an hour looking around Ireland's Historic Science Centre, established in the castle stables. The absorbing exhibition has plenty of original material—plans, letters, photographs, models, and instruments. Charles Parsons (1859–1931) invented the steam turbine, spent $22,000 and 25 years trying to make diamonds, and got a steam-powered helicopter off the ground in 1897—six years before the Wright brothers' official first powered flight.

William Parsons (1800–1867), the 3rd Earl of Rosse and president of the British Association for the Advancement of Science, planned and built the **"Leviathan,"** a monstrous telescope with the largest cast-metal mirror ever made. It took four months to cool after casting and four years (1841–1844) to grind and polish it to a perfect parabolic curve.

By the mid-19th century, the sky had been mapped into 7,000 areas of light, and the great puzzle was what exactly they were. When William Parsons first looked through his telescope in April 1845, he saw what he named a "whirlpool nebula"—another galaxy 40 million light years away.

Thanks to William's wife, Mary, a pioneer of photography, we have remarkable images of the great telescope in action. Even better, the instrument itself—beautifully restored and still in its original position in the demesne—is housed between two mock castle walls, a giant black barrel almost 70 feet (21 m) long. On rare demonstrations, chains and weights raise the telescope along its immense curved rails. You don't have to be a scientist to appreciate this extraordinary feat. ∎

Birr Castle
- 235 C2
- ☎ 057 912 0336
- 🕐 Grounds only open (daily year-round)
- 💲 $$$

www.birrcastle.com

The Thatch Bar and Restaurant
- ✉ Military Rd, Crinkill, Birr, Co. Offaly
- ☎ 057 912 0682

Bogs Beautiful

Fifty years ago, anyone who found beauty in the bogs would have been dismissed as a fool. But eco-awareness has brought a new understanding and appreciation of these magnificent, if moody, landscapes.

Cutting turf from a bog in the Maumturk Mountains near Cong and the Connemara, County Galway

About one-seventh of Ireland is bog—three million acres (1,200,000 ha) of the stuff, either in the form of blanket bog or raised bog. Blanket bog tends to occur in the west, generally above 1,000 feet (300 m). It is undulating grass, heather, and other plants, and can smother archaeological sites to a depth of 6 to 10 feet (2–3 m).

Ireland is an ideal location for the growth of bog. The retreating Ice Age glaciers scraped hollows in the rock and plastered them with impermeable clay. In the rainy climate that followed, lakes developed and filled with vegetation that died but did not rot because of the underlying acidity. Peat formed, piling up into thick mattresses of bog fed by plentiful water supplies—peat that can perfectly preserve bodies for thousands of years, as in the case of the Iron Age men, ritually murdered, who were excavated from bogs at Croghan Hill, in County Offaly, and Clonycavan, in County Meath, in 2003.

Decades of Exploitation

Peat—"turf" in Ireland—burns hot and slow when dried, and for thousands of years it was cut by hand for domestic use. But the exploitation increased in a quantum leap in 1946, when Bord na Móna, the Peat Board, was set up to remove as much turf as possible for use in electricity-generating stations, as peat moss for gardeners, and as turf briquettes for domestic fireplaces. Bord na Móna owned more than 200,000 acres (80,000 ha) of land perceived as otherwise valueless, which could yield several million tons of milled peat every year. For half a century, the turf-cutting machines ripped up and devastated the bogs, with only the occasional pioneering conservationist voice raised to oppose them.

Changing Awareness

But opinion changed. The bogs came to resemble World War I battlefields, sodden black wastelands so ugly that people began to mourn the destruction. Awareness has grown of their unique interdependent wildlife—the plants that thrive in these inhospitable places, the insects that are attracted by the plants, and the birds that live off the insects.

Today, Bord na Móna (*www.bnm.ie*) no longer purchases bog, and it is committed to cease exploitation by 2030. There are grand plans to turn the ruined bogs into wildlife reserves and outdoor recreation areas with lakes, fens, and forests.

A soon-to-be-bygone practice? Peat is harvested at a bog near Drumlish, County Longford.

Visiting the Bogs

If you want an absorbing experience of the bogs, either walking out across the quaking turf on a duckboard trail or actually rolling up your sleeves and helping with hands-on planting and conservation work, visit the **Bog of Allen Nature Centre** (see sidebar p. 93), 30 miles (50 km) west of Dublin. Also worth a visit are **An Creagan** in County Tyrone (see pp. 316–317) and the **Céide Fields** of County Mayo (see p. 199).

EXPERIENCE: Walking the Girley Bog

Inaugurated by the Meath County Council in 2009, the **Kells Girley Bog Eco Walk** follows a 3.5-mile (6 km) route around ley bog and through the surrounding forest.

The trail begins and ends at the Drewstown car park, accessed on the N52, 3 miles (5 km) from Kells (see p. 260) toward Mullingar. The walk is not strenuous, but walking or hiking boots are essential due to the uneven terrain.

You will pass through woodlands (stunning in autumn when the foliage is multicolored), along trails flanked by conifers, and down an old bog road that circles Girley Bog. Girley is one of Ireland's raised bogs, so named because

they are dome-shaped and receive their nutrients only from rainwater, not groundwater. Raised bogs are a rare and threatened habitat.

Girley Bog is home to an abundance of flora and fauna, as well as a variety of birdlife, including the willow warbler, whose sounds walkers often hear along the trail. Interpretive panels along the self-guided walk tell the history of Irish bogs, provide information on wildlife in the area, and display photos of the carnivorous great sundew and other plants.

The trail takes most walkers approximately two hours to complete. For a trail map and a detailed description of the walk, visit *www.discoverireland.ie*.

Rock of Dunamase

Broken walls, arches, and runs of masonry, outlined against the sky, rise from flowery grass banks on the Rock of Dunamase in County Laois. Two and a half thousand years of history can be read in these high and poignant remnants of fortifications.

The middle ward, the ruin of the main gate, and the hilly landscape of County Laois

Portlaoise

🅰 235 D2

Visitor Information

✉ Portlaoise,
    Co. Laois

☎ 057 862 1178

The landscape in the eastern half of County Laois, which borders County Kildare to the east and Counties Kilkenny and Carlow to the south, is generally either flat plain or rolling valleys. As a result, the abrupt limestone crag of the Rock of Dunamase, 3 miles (5 km) east of Portlaoise, draws the eye. The jagged ruins of the fortifications that cover the crag look doubly intriguing because of their elevation and the way they stand out of jungly banks of bracken and scrub. Towers and walls appear as natural extensions of the broken rock on which they stand.

The Egyptian astrologer Ptolemy was probably referring to Dunamase when he reported on an Irish stronghold he called Dunum. If the rock was fortified as long ago as 500 B.C., it was a natural choice, given its eagle-eye command of 50 miles (80 km) of country. Iron Age men walled the summit with stone. By 845, the fortification was significant enough for the Vikings to plunder it. In the 12th century, Dermot MacMurrough (see sidebar opposite), King of Leinster, built a castle on the rock, which was strengthened by the formidable Anglo-Norman warlord Richard de Clare. In 1650, Cromwell's forces destroyed it.

What you see, looking up from the little parking lot, seems like a jumble beyond interpretation, but a quick glance at the explanatory board by the entrance gate will soon give you your bearings. Essentially the rock is divided by walls into **three wards** or defended enclosures through which you climb to reach the summit.

Outer Ward: You climb across ditches and up banks shaggy with feathery grasses and bracken and spattered with wildflowers to reach the **outer gate** that pierces the first wall. Walk through the gate's tall arch and continue your climb up the steep, uneven slope of the outer

INSIDER TIP:

Visit the dramatic ruins of the 12th-century castle on the Rock of Dunamase for a sweeping panorama across the rolling farmland of the central plain.

—TOM JACKSON
National Geographic Society

ward or barbican, defended from above and below by stronghold gates. Soon you reach the curtain wall that encloses the top of the rock; its tremendously strong main gate has slit spyholes in each of its flanking towers so that the garrison could keep a watch on all incomers.

Middle Ward: Once through the main gate, you are in the wide middle ward. To your right are the square foundations of an excavated gate; to the left, a path curves up to a corner of the middle ward's upper wall, with the arched and offset remains of a sally port, from where defenders could rush out and surprise attackers.

Fatal Attraction

It was Dermot MacMurrough, King of Leinster and builder of the castle on the Rock of Dunamase, who was responsible for bringing the English—or at any rate the Anglo-Normans—over to Ireland in 1169.

MacMurrough's affair with Dervorgilla, wife of Tiernan O'Rourke, had resulted in exile at the decree of O'Rourke's patron Rory O'Connor, High King of Ireland. England's King Henry II had obtained a Papal Bull in 1155 that authorized him to conquer and subjugate Ireland, and when the exiled MacMurrough approached him for help in his quarrel, Henry had exactly the excuse he needed.

Inner Ward: If you prefer the direct approach, climb up through nettles and scrub into the inner ward on the top of the rock. The separating wall has all but vanished; but three angles of Strongbow's Norman **keep** stand firm, with round-arched windows in plain, massive walls. The view is wonderful, from the Slieve Bloom Mountains in the west, 15 miles (24 km) away, to the peaks of the Wicklow Mountains 35 miles (56 km) off in the east. ∎

Walks: Slieve Bloom Mountains

The Slieve Bloom Mountains rise from the level grassy plains of County Laois, a range of heathery hills with tremendous views from their windswept tops. Tucked into their flanks are secret valleys with waterfalls, woodlands, and plenty of sheltered paths. Here are two walks to introduce you to these splendid hills—one in a hidden valley, the other up on the crest.

The Slieve Bloom Mountains provide wonderful walks for strong and determined hikers.

Walk 1—Clamphole Falls

From the **Glenbarrow parking lot,** walk down a track marked "Tinnahinch 3 km." In about 200 yards (200 m), bear left at a yellow arrow through the trees for 1 mile (1.6 km). This forest plantation of mainly spruce and pine is a beautiful shady walk. Watch for red squirrels, which sadly have become extremely rare in Britain but are still quite widespread in Ireland.

After about 0.5 mile (1 km), you will reach an area of bare rock along the riverbed, an **old quarry ❶** where the sandstone floor has been shaped into square flags. Shortly, you will reach **Clamphole Falls ❷,** a lovely stretch of water

NOT TO BE MISSED:

Red squirrels in the plantations • "Wave" lines in the rock of the riverbed • A paddle in the pools at Clamphole

tumbling over sandstone boulders where locals come to picnic. In the sandstone of the riverbed, you'll be able to distinguish some rippling lines—marks hewn by the constant action of waves when the Slieve Bloom Mountains were a flat flood plain in ancient times.

From the falls, simply retrace your steps to the parking lot.

Walk 2—Ridge of Capard

From the **Ridge of Capard parking lot,** pass the waymark for the **Slieve Bloom Way** ❶. This fine long-distance footpath makes a 31-mile (50 km) circuit of the peaks and ridges of Slieve Bloom. It's a tough but enjoyable hike.

Follow the Slieve Bloom Way, a moorland track labeled "Monicknew 8 km," through the heather for about 500 yards (450 m). Turn right along a graveled road for 100 yards (100 m) before bearing left across the heather, following pole markers southwest for 1.5 miles

(2 km) to the **Stoney Man cairn** ❷, seen ahead as you approach.

The Slieve Blooms swell out of a wild area of low-lying midlands country, and views from the Ridge of Capard are superb, extending over scores of miles out across the flat landscape of hayfields and woodland some 1,000 feet (300 m) below. Don't spurn the wildlife of the heather: there are beautiful mosses and lichens of different types. The tall cairn called the Stoney Man is a great place to picnic.

From the cairn, either retrace your steps to the parking lot or bear right and descend over thick heather and through trees to the forest road in the valley bottom. Turn right, and where the road divides, take the left fork to return to the parking lot.

WALK 1
- See area map p. 235 C2
- Glenbarrow parking lot (N7 to New Inn, 13 miles/21 km W of Kildare; R422 to Rosenallis; follow signs to Glenbarrow parking lot)
- 2 miles (3 km)
- 1–2 hours
- Glenbarrow parking lot

START
Glenbarrow parking lot

Quarry ❶

SLIEVE BLOOM WAY

SLIEVE BLOOM WAY

Clamphole Falls ❷

350m

Ridge of Capard parking lot

START

0 — 1 kilometer
0 — 1/2 mile

•••••• walk route 1
•••••• walk route 2

Barrow

Slieve Bloom Mountains

SLIEVE BLOOM WAY

❶

❷ Stoney Man cairn

483m
Clarnahinch

Ridge of Capard

WALK 2
- See area map p. 235 C2
- Ridge of Capard parking lot (from Rosenallis—see above—take the Mountrath road and follow "Ridge of Capard" signs)
- 3.5 miles (5.5 km)
- 2 hours
- Ridge of Capard parking lot

Kells & Trim

The modest country town of Kells in the northwest of County Meath is famous for just one thing: the Book of Kells, created in the monastery here about A.D. 807. Kells people are proud of the connection, so don't raise the possibility that the "world's most beautiful book" might actually have been made in St. Columba's monastery on the Scottish island of Iona! Although the glorious book is kept in Trinity College, Dublin (see pp. 54–55), Kells is worth exploring for its magnificent high crosses and tiny oratory known as St. Columba's House.

Giant Trim Castle stands above the River Boyne, an enduring expression of Norman power.

Kells

🄼 235 D4

Kells Heritage Centre & Visitor Information

✉ Headfort Pl., Kells, Co. Meath

☎ 046 924 7840

🕐 Call ahead; days vary year to year

💲 $$

Kells

St. Columba founded Kells Monastery in 559. A tenth-century **round tower** stands in a churchyard on the site now, a fine but capless cylinder 100 feet (30 m) high.

Just up from the churchyard is **St. Columba's House,** a little oratory with a steep corbeled roof and a ladder to a tiny room under the roof space. It probably dates to the tenth century, but it might be contemporary with the arrival of the Iona monks at the turn of the ninth century.

The four ninth-century **high crosses** in the churchyard are worth close inspection. The **South Cross,** or **"Cross of St. Patrick and St. Columba,"** is the finest, carved with scenes typical of high-cross art, including the Burning Fiery Furnace, Doomsday, and the Crucifixion. The **North Cross** is only a stump. The **West Cross** is a shaft with Noah's ark and the Judgment of Solomon, while the **East Cross** displays a Crucifixion.

The tenth-century **Market Cross** stands outside the **Heritage Centre,** home to monastic finds and replicas of the Market Cross and Book of Kells. Stories say that United Irish rebels were hanged from the cross in 1798.

INSIDER TIP:

Several scenes from the 1995 Mel Gibson movie *Braveheart* were filmed at Trim Castle. A tour of the keep with one of the castle guides is a must.

—STEPHANIE ROBICHAUX
National Geographic contributor

Trim

Set on the River Boyne some 15 miles (24 km) south of Kells, the historic town of Trim has two castles, two cathedrals, and enough monastic remains to keep you interested for a day. The main sights are grouped north and south of the Boyne, with another group a mile (1.6 km) to the east around the cemetery and St. Peter's Bridge.

Trim Castle, the largest fortress in Ireland, looms over the south side of the river. It was built mostly in the early 13th century on the site of an earlier castle burned by Rory O'Connor, King of Connacht, in 1174.

By the mid-13th century, the new castle had a curtain wall almost 500 yards (450 m) long that enclosed 3 acres (1.2 ha) of ground, a huge square keep 70 feet (20 m) tall with walls 11 feet (3 m) thick, several sally ports, and ten D-shaped towers.

Opposite the castle on the north bank of the Boyne stands **Talbot's Castle,** a fine fortified manor built in 1415 by Sir John Talbot, battlefield opponent of St. Joan of Arc. Behind it the 14th-century **Yellow Steeple** is all that remains of St. Mary's Abbey.

Along the Boyne east of town is **St. Peter's Bridge,** a handsome Norman span. South of the river here is the **Crutched Friary**—a fine 13th-century chapel and keep that belonged to the Crutched or Crossed Friars.

North of the river and a little west is the ruined early 13th-century **Cathedral of St. Peter and St. Paul.** In the cemetery alongside lie the effigies of Sir Lucas Dillon (died 1593) and his wife, Jane. The sword separating them symbolizes the rift caused when Jane had a fling with her brother-in-law. If you suffer from warts, prick them with a pin dipped in the pool of rainwater between the husband and wife—a certain cure, so locals say. ∎

Trim

235 E3

Visitor Information

Town Hall, Castle St., Trim, Co. Meath

046 943 7227

seasonal

EXPERIENCE:
Attending a Rural Mass

The priest intones a blessing, and the congregation stretches and sighs. They get to their feet and straggle out into the sun and wind to exchange greetings and wisecracks by the church gate. For the past hour you have sat, stood, and knelt among tiny tots and elderly folk, fidgety teenagers and staid farmers, nuns and hangover victims, all bonded by ritual movements and responses. The clothes, hairstyles, and liturgical language have changed over the past few years, and nowadays the country priest has to earn the respect that was once his by right, but the Catholic Church's central act of worship remains an integral part of many, if not most, small communities in rural Ireland. Attending Mass, you'll see it alive, well, and in action.

Hill of Tara

The Hill of Tara rises from the Meath plains and commands 100 miles (160 km) of view. For a thousand years, all through the first millennium, the High Kings of Ireland based themselves at Tara, and it became the symbol and seat of Irish government. It is a powerfully moving place, soaked in history and heroic myth.

In the Royal Enclosure, Cormac's House stands to the right of the Royal Seat, with the Stone of Destiny at the hub. Beyond lies the smaller Mound of the Hostages.

History & Legend

It was here that beautiful Gráinne persuaded Diarmuid of the Fianna to elope with her on the eve of her wedding to Fionn MacCumhaill. Tara was also the venue for the great war council of Nuada the Silver-handed, king of the magical De Danaan, when defeat by the fierce Fomorians looked inevitable. The god Lugh the Long-handed turned up providentially and proved his right to act as the De Danaan's champion by slinging heavy flag-stones over the palace wall and beating all comers at *fidchell,* a kind of mythic chess. When the time came for single combat, Lugh felled the Fomorian cham-pion, Balor of the Evil Eye—his own grandfather—with a well-aimed *tathlun,* or magic stone.

Another tale tells of Conn of the Hundred Battles standing on the Lialh Fáil, the Stone of Destiny on the Royal Seat, and causing it to let out a great scream—the sign by which the rightful High Kings of Ireland could be identified.

In 435, St. Patrick lit an Easter fire on the nearby Hill of Slane to challenge the pagan fires on Tara. Then he came across to negotiate with Laoghaire, the High King, for the right to preach Christianity— not in a spirit of confrontation but with a suggestion of partnership.

Tara Fictions

• In the 1890s a group of British Israelites became convinced that the Ark of the Covenant lay hidden in a graveyard abutting the Rath of the Synods. The mounds caused by their excavations in search of the Ark can still be seen.
• Some believe that the Lialh Fáil, or Stone of Destiny, was Jacob's pillow when he had his dream of angels on a ladder.
• Others feel the Stone was brought to Tara by the immortal De Dannan from Falias, one of the four cities of Tir na nÓg, the Land of the Young, where they had previously lived and learned their craft of poetry and magic.

Exploring the Site

Archaeologically speaking, the Hill of Tara was occupied for at least 3,000 years before its abandonment in 1022. Entering the site from the **visitor center** (a former church), you are aware of multiple lumps and bumps, and with the center's booklet in hand, your imagination will quickly clothe them with both fact and fancy.

The northern part of the hill contains the huge trenches of a sunken entrance to Tara, 750 feet (230 m) long, known as the **Banquet Hall**—a thousand men could feast in it together, say the legends. Nearby is **Gráinne's Fort,** a ditched mound, and the circular **Sloping Trenches** where

Dúnlaing, King of Ulster, massacred 30 princesses of Tara in 222.

Going south along the hill, opposite the visitor center you pass the three-ringed Iron Age hill fort called the **Rath of the Synods,** where two superb gold collars or torques were found in 1810 (now in Dublin's National Museum of Archaeology and History; see pp. 56–59). The largest embanked area, the **Royal Enclosure,** comes next and encloses three sites. **Dumha na nGiall,** the Mound of the Hostages, a grassy hummock with a low doorway, is a Stone Age passage grave where High King Cormac MacArt (A.D. 227–266) imprisoned captives from Connacht until they died.

INSIDER TIP:

Get in touch with your inner Gael at the Hill of Tara, ancient seat of the High Kings of Ireland and the center of power for the island's pre-Celtic dwellers.

—JUSTIN KAVANAGH
National Geographic International Editions

Side by side to the south are **Cormac's House,** a Bronze Age burial mound, and the ring fort called the **Royal Seat,** where the **Lialh Fáil** or Stone of Destiny—a fine pillar stone—stands alone. Farther south from the Royal Enclosure you reach another ring fort, **Rath Laoghaire,** where King Laoghaire is said to be buried upright in full battle gear. ■

Hill of Tara
🅰 235 E3
Visitor Information
✉ Off the N3, 7.5 miles (12 km) S of Navan, Co. Meath
☎ 046 902 5903
🕐 Closed mid-Sept.–mid-May; hill accessible at all times
💲 $

Brú na Bóinne

In a long bend of the River Boyne lies Brú na Bóinne, the Palace by the Boyne—more than 50 ancient monuments that record the beliefs and religious practices of pre-Christian ancestors, in Europe's most concentrated site. Though most of that record is indecipherable, the sheer power of these tombs, henges, forts, and standing stones—especially the giant passage grave of Newgrange—is overwhelming.

On the winter solstice, the rising sun pierces into the heart of the burial mound of Newgrange.

Brú na Bóinne
- 235 E4
- Boyne Valley Archaeological Park, 7 miles (11 km) SW of Drogheda, Co. Meath
- 041 988 0300
- $

Visiting the Site

Most of the monuments of Brú na Bóinne stand on private land and are inaccessible to the public, and it is the three great passage graves of Newgrange, Knowth, and Dowth that attract all the attention. Of these, **Dowth** is open only to archaeological excavators for the foreseeable future, while **Knowth**—its stones richly carved with circles, arcs, snake patterns, and one extraordinary "sundial" motif—can be visited only on an external tour.

So the kernel of a visit to Brú na Bóinne consists of the exhibition in the **visitor center,** followed by a tour to the heart of the Newgrange tomb. This tour is

immensely popular, so arrive early in the day to secure a place.

Newgrange

Across Europe, the period between 4000 and 3000 B.C. saw the building of passage graves—tombs of stone, with a passage leading from the entrance to a burial chamber or complex of chambers at the heart of the structure. They varied from small tombs only a few feet long to vast mounds that took decades to complete.

Newgrange is one of the biggest, a man-made hill 280 feet (85 m) in diameter and 35 feet (11 m) high. The core of the mound consists of stones, at least 200,000 tons (182,000 tonnes), layered with clay and shells from the Boyne, while a row of 97 massive stone blocks secures the circular external wall of the tomb. The small Stone Age farming community living around this curve of the Boyne Valley 5,000 years ago—average life expectancy 30 years—would probably have taken between 40 and 80 years to erect the tomb.

But this was no haphazard mounding of material. The huge hill of stone is a covering for the internal structure of the tomb—a stone-lined and stone-roofed passage 62 feet (19 m) long that leads from the doorway, with its threshold stone elaborately carved in spirals, to a corbeled **chamber** deep inside. Off this chamber lie three recesses, holding two big shallow sandstone bowls or dishes. Passage and recesses are heavily carved with whorls, spirals, and wavy lines.

More remarkable still is the slit-shaped aperture above the door, known as the **roof-box.** The mound's doorway is precisely aligned with the position of the sun at dawn on December 21, the winter solstice, in such a way that

INSIDER TIP:

Entrance into Brú na Bóinne and many other key sites in Ireland is covered by the Irish Heritage Card. Good for a year, you can buy the card at any of the participating sites—visit *www.heritageireland.ie* **for a complete list.**

—LISA MCCLOUGHRY
National Geographic Society

on that day, and a couple of days on either side of it, a ray of the rising sun penetrates the roof-box and pierces into the very heart of the tomb. For about a quarter of an hour, the central chamber is flushed with golden light; then the finger of light withdraws along the passage. It is an intensely moving experience for the lucky few who are admitted each winter solstice. So keen is the competition to witness the phenomenon that a a lottery system has been set up to handle the many requests (see sidebar below).

EXPERIENCE: Winter Solstice Sunrise

Tens of thousands of people want to witness the winter solstice illumination from inside the Newgrange tomb, but the central chamber holds only 20. So places are allocated by lottery. Each September local children draw 50 names, ten for each of the 5 days around December 21 that the phenomenon occurs. Each winner can bring a guest. A reserve list of 50 is also drawn, in case winners can't attend or can't be contacted. To apply for tickets, either fill in a form at the visitor center or, if you can't show up there in person, e-mail your address and a contact telephone number to *brunaboinne@opw.ie,* and the staff will complete an application form on your behalf. Remember, there's no guarantee—if it's cloudy, you'll see nothing!

The white stones that face the walls of the monument are of Wicklow quartz and must have been brought by sea raft or coracle. **Standing stones** guard the tomb in a loose ring.

What the tomb-builders intended is open to speculation,

A pattern of whorls decorates the Threshhold Stone that guards the entrance to the Newgrange tomb.

Mound of stones and earthwork

Newgrange in its restored condition today

Front retaining wall of white quartzite stones

Remains of stone circle surrounding mound

but clearly something irresistible drove them to take on the huge task of planning and building. A clue may lie in the ashes found in the central recesses' shallow dishes. They formed the remains of only half a dozen people, and it is surmised that the tomb may have been periodically cleared of remains to make way for the next few months' cremations. Perhaps the people believed that, on the shortest day of the year, the spirits of their dead rode the shaft of light out of the tomb to help ensure the return of spring. ■

Cruciform central chamber with recesses

Corbeled roof

Orthostats lining entrance passage

Roof-box

Decorated entrance curbstone

Drive: Drogheda to Dundalk Along the Coast

You could zip from Drogheda to Dundalk in half an hour by way of the M1 highway, but the aim of following this meandering route northward up the coast of County Louth is to take your time, dipping in and out of the coastline and the little villages en route with neither time nor other visitors on your heels.

Boats at port along the shore of the Irish Sea in County Louth

Built of gray stone beside the River Boyne, historic **Drogheda** ❶ *(visitor information, tel 041 983 7070 or 041 984 5684)* offers plenty to see and do. From **Millmount,** the ancient mound south of the river, you get a good panorama over Drogheda. Millmount is topped by a **Martello tower** built in 1808 as a defense against a possible invasion by the French under Napoleon Bonaparte. Below the tower, the fine **Millmount Museum** *(tel 041 983 3097)* displays the splendid 19th-century painted canvas banners of the Drogheda trade guilds.

In the town itself, **St. Peter's Church** on West Street is notable for displaying the prison letters, cell door, and leathery brown severed

NOT TO BE MISSED:

Millmount Museum • Relics of St. Oliver Plunkett, St. Peter's Church • Termonfeckin high cross

head of St. Oliver Plunkett (1629–1681), Archbishop of Armagh, who was hanged, drawn, and quartered for treason. He was canonized three centuries later.

From Drogheda, take the N1 Belfast road and turn off to **Termonfeckin** ❷ *(signed on the right just uphill from the bridge in Drogheda).* In the churchyard of St. Fechin's

Coastal Strolls & Picnics

Far from the rush and roar of the M1, you can stroll along the strands and cliffs of Ireland's unfrequented northeast coast. A beautiful sandy beach runs south from Clogherhead toward Termonfeckin; anywhere along here is great for a leg stretch or a picnic. North of Clogherhead, the R166 cuts across the hinterland behind Dunany Point; several side roads and lanes lead to the lonely coast beyond the villages of Dunany and Salterstown, great for strolling and eating, with superb views north across Dundalk Bay to the hills of the Cooley Peninsula.

Church in Termonfeckin (entrance on the right some 150 yards/135 m past the bridge) stands a tenth-century **high cross,** blotched with lichens, with Christ in Glory on the west face and fine interlacing on the east. In front of the cross is set another ancient piece of sculpture—a much-weathered **Crucifixion** featuring a soldier piercing Christ with his spear.

Beyond the church (signed) stands the rugged three-storied **Termonfeckin Castle** (key from the bungalow opposite), whose corbeled roofs still hold up. Previous owners, including the Archbishop of Armagh, had the right to first choice of the local fishermen's catch.

From Termonfeckin, continue along the R166 to the small town of **Clogherhead ❸;** bear right in the village to reach the sandy **beach,** great for exploring rock pools and walking. Back on the road, a right turn (blue "Port Oriel" sign) leads in a mile (1.6 km) to the little **harbor** with its rusty trawlers. Here stands a roadside shrine to Mary, Queen of the Sea, built

in memory of locals who lost their lives at sea.

Back on the R166, in 1.5 miles (2.5 km) a right turn (blue "scenic route" sign) leads to a beautiful lonely **scenic drive** by sandy beaches and through forgotten farmland where long straight tracks lead to houses hidden among trees.

Turn left on the R166 ("Annagassan 4" sign), with superb views of the Mourne Mountains ahead, to **Annagassan ❹,** with its friendly **Glyde Inn** next to **O'Neill's Bakery.** The little **harbor**—with creel boats, an old ivy-covered kiln, and huge iron anchor—is signed off the village street. Continue to the N1 at Castlebellingham, then head north to Dundalk.

- ⓜ See area map p. 235 E4
- ► Drogheda
- ↔ 27 miles (43 km)
- ⏱ 2–3 hours
- ► Dundalk

Monasterboice

In this compact site in County Louth northwest of Drogheda, many superb early Christian monuments rub shoulders. Muiredach's Cross, in particular, is the finest high cross in Ireland, a tenth-century masterpiece of the stonecarver's art.

The tower at Monasterboice was built in the tenth century as a stronghold against the Vikings.

Monasterboice

 235 E4

✉ Collon,
Co. Louth,
6 miles
(10 km) NW
of Drogheda.
Turn left off
the N1 from
Drogheda near
Monasterboice
Inn

☎ 041 983 7070

Monasterboice stands in a beautiful rural location among rolling green fields, although trees mask the full glory of the site until you are right up close. Then you see the round tower, the high crosses, and the shells of the churches and realize that this is one of Ireland's most striking collective monuments.

A disciple of St. Patrick, a hermit named Buite (or Buithe, Boethius, or Boyce—even Boyne: It's claimed that the river was named after him) founded the monastery late in the fifth century. Buite died in 521; the angels lowered a ladder from the sky to enable him to climb straight into heaven. His monastery became a famous center of learning.

Round Tower: Monasterboice survived a Viking occupation in 968, during which the marauders were driven out by a force from Tara led by the High King himself, Donal. After that, the 110-foot (33 m) round tower was constructed, a tremendously tall structure tapering toward the top, built with curved stones. The windows are no more than impenetrable defensive slits, and the door is 6 feet (2 m) off the ground.

The monks entered via a ladder, which could be pulled up in times of attack. The interior of the tower burned in 1097, along with many of Monasterboice's valuables, and shortly afterward, the monastery declined as the newly built Mellifont Abbey (see p. 274) prospered.

Churches & Crosses:

Ancient graveslabs, some perhaps from monastic times, surround the round tower and the two ruined churches—**An Teampall Theas,** the South Church, and **An Teampall Thuaidh,** the North Church.

In pride of place, though, are the three tenth-century high crosses. The **North Cross,** standing beside the graveyard wall, has a weatherbeaten, whorly pattern to its head. The **West Cross,** beside An Teampall Thuaidh, is 21 feet (6 m) tall and composed of separate shaft, wheelcross, and cap. Many of the carved panels have eroded, but the Crucifixion in the center of the west-facing wheel is clear, and on the east face are scenes of Christ walking on the Sea of Galilee, the giant Goliath, and the children of Israel worshiping the golden calf.

Muiredach's Cross: The
South Cross near the site entrance—otherwise known as Muiredach's Cross—stands 18 feet (5 m) tall. Wheel and shaft were carved from the same piece of sandstone, with a cap shaped like a gabled house and a base inscribed "*Or do Muiredach Lasndernad Chros*"

(A prayer for Muiredach, for whom this cross was made). Muiredach (died 923) was abbot of Monasterboice, and the high cross was erected shortly after his death as a memorial and symbol of the wealth of Monasterboice.

The cross is heavily carved with biblical scenes. On the east face, Christ sits in judgment in the central boss of the wheel. Beneath his feet, St. Michael weighs souls, while the devil yanks down the scales. On the shaft below, the

St. Buite & Monasterboice

St. Buite owed much of his fame and certainly his monastery to his supposed powers of healing. After he was said to have cured the mortally sick daughter of the King of Dalriada, the grateful father paid for Buite to found the monastery at Monasterboice late in the fifth century. When the saint died on December 7, 521, he foretold on his deathbed the imminent birth of "a child illustrious before God and men"—and St. Columba was born that very day.

four Wise Men worship the Infant Jesus; Moses knocks water out of a desert rock while ranks of Israelites look on; David readies a slingshot for Goliath; and Eve offers Adam the fateful apple, while Cain smacks Abel with a cudgel. On the west side is a central Crucifixion; Christ presenting St. Peter with the keys of heaven; Doubting Thomas having his misgivings disproved by a rank of tablet-wielding apostles; and Judas delivering a betrayer's kiss in the Garden of Gethsemane. ∎

Walk: The Cooley Peninsula & Táin Trail

This is a straightforward there-and-back walk with the most spectacular coastal and mountain views as reward for a little effort. The Cooley Peninsula in County Louth is a largely unfrequented corner of Ireland so you are more than likely to have all this beauty to yourself.

Carlingford village ❶ *(visitor information, tel 042 937 3033, closed Oct.–May)* looks out on Carlingford Lough, a superb wide inlet that separates County Louth in the Republic of Ireland from the Mourne Mountains in County Down, Northern Ireland.

Carlingford stands on the northern shore of the Cooley Peninsula, a glorious humpbacked piece of country with a mountainous spine and fertile green skirts. The village's neat, white-washed streets stand under 1,930-foot (588 m) Slieve Foye, highest point of the knobbly ridge of Carlingford Mountain.

By the water's edge is the 12th-century **King John's Castle,** clinging romantically to its rock overlooking the fishing harbor. On the waterfront street stands **Taaffe's Castle,** a 16th-century tower house of grim aspect.

Begin your walk at the **Village Hotel** on the square in Carlingford. Walk up the road that rises from the top of the square, and in

---

NOT TO BE MISSED:

Carlingford village and its castles
• View of Carlingford Lough and the Mourne Mountains from the Táin Trail
• View to the southwest from the pass

The wild moorland hills of the Cooley Peninsula offer superb, uncrowded walks.

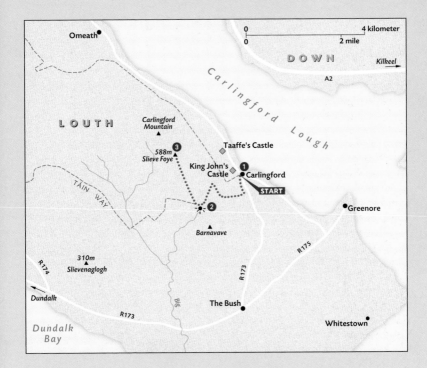

about 300 yards (250 m), turn left for 0.5 mile (0.75 km). At a T-junction, you'll see a "Táin Trail" marker post with its "walking man" logo. Turn right and follow the Táin Trail posts up onto a grassy path that bends back to the right above the village as it climbs the mountainside. This is a zigzag trail, steady but not steep!

Be sure to stop and look around frequently because the views get better all the time. Across Carlingford Lough, you will see the **Mourne Mountains** rise in ruggedly beautiful shapes, 1,600-foot (485 m) Slievemartin toward the left above the northern lough shore, the bulks of Eagle Mountain (2,090 feet/635 m) and Slieve Muck (2,210 feet/672 m) miles back in center frame, and over to the right the 2,450-foot (745 m) peak of Slieve Binnian. Up the lough, the twin villages of Rostrevor and Warrenpoint lie by the water.

The view is at its best from the **saddle of the pass ❷** at the top of the path, and another spectacular southwesterly view opens

🏔	See area map p. 235 F5
➤	Village Hotel, Carlingford, Cooley Peninsula
↔	5 miles/8 km (7 miles/11 km with ascent of Slieve Foye)
🕐	2 hours (3 hours)
➤	Carlingford

from this vantage point as well. The slopes of Carlingford Mountain rise away to your right, the lower shoulder of Barnavave to your left. In front, the broad green valley of the Big River falls away toward Dundalk Bay, with a great sweep of coastline running away south for 15 miles (24 km) to Dunany Point.

You can retrace the Táin Trail down to Carlingford from here, but if you have the energy it is worth bearing northeast for the steep but not difficult climb to the **summit of Slieve Foye ❸** (around another 950 feet/300 m), where the views are even better.

From here, return the way you came.

More Places to Visit in Central Ireland

Abbeyleix

Viscount de Vesci, 18th-century lord of Abbeyleix House, had a model village laid out at his gates—wide streets lined with trees, handsome buildings, and a Georgian sense of order and calm. The **Abbeyleix Heritage House** in the former school gives a good run-through of the place's history. Walk around the village, then take it easy over a pint in the self-consciously charming **Morrissey's** pub on Main Street, an old-fashioned bar dating from 1735. 🗺 235 D1 ✉ On the N8 Portlaoise–Kilkenny road, 9 miles (14 km) S of Portlaoise, Co. Laois **Abbeyleix Heritage House** *www.heritage housemuseum.com* ☎ 057 873 1653 💲 $

Bective Abbey

In a glorious setting on the Knightsbrook River, the ruins of Bective Abbey, a Cistercian monastery, do full justice to their setting. The cruciform church and the rib-vaulted chapter house are 13th-century work, while the cloisters date from the 15th century. After the abbey was suppressed in the 16th century, an added tower—incongruous but impressive-looking—turned the complex into a fortified house. Hugh de Lacy, Anglo-Norman lord of Meath, was buried here in 1195. 🗺 235 E3 ✉ Signed off the R161, 4 miles (6 km) NE of Trim, Co. Meath **Trim Visitor Information** ☎ 046 903 7111 or 046 903 7227

Emo Court

James Gandon, designer of Dublin's fabulous Custom House, designed Emo House in 1792 for Lord Portarlington, creating a superb neoclassical house under a big dome. The main rooms, beautifully restored, form the focus of a tour around the house. In the immaculate gardens, classical statues stand among azaleas and rhododendrons; paths lead down to a gorgeous lakeside walk. *www.emocourt.net* ☎ 235 D2 ✉ Off the N7 Kildare–Portlaoise road, at New Inn, 6 miles (10 km) NE of Portlaoise, Co. Laois ☎ 05 786 26573 🕑 House closed mid-Sept.–mid-June; gardens remain open 💲 $

Loughcrew Passage Graves

Up on the peaks of Sliabh na Caillighe, the Hill of the Witch, 32 passage cairns (3000–2500 B.C.) wait to be explored. Many have their stones incised with markings—mazy circles and zigzags, snaky lines, and what seem to be flowers. Take a flashlight, and be prepared for a 15-minute uphill climb. *www.loughcrew.com* 🗺 235 D4 ✉ On Sliabh na Caillighe hill (parking lot), signed from the R154 5 miles (8 km) SE of Oldcastle (13 miles/21 km NW of Kells by the R163/R154), Co. Meath ☎ 049 854 1240 or 087 052 4975 🕑 Closed Oct.–May 💲 Deposit required for key

Mellifont Abbey

At the height of its power, Mellifont Abbey supported a community of 400 and commanded more than 20 lesser houses. It was the nerve center of the Cistercian order in Ireland, having been the order's pioneer house when established in 1142 by St. Malachy, Archbishop of Armagh. By the 1550s, the abbey had been turned into a fortified house. In 1727, it was abandoned, and by the 19th century, it was being used as a pigsty. These days you can admire the big gatehouse, a gorgeous 14th-century vaulted chapter house, and something unique among Irish monastic remains: an octagonal 12th-century lavabo, or monks' washing place. Four of the eight sides remain, with beautifully carved Romanesque archways. 🗺 235 E4 ✉ 5 miles (8 km) NW of Drogheda, signed off the R168 and N2, Co. Louth ☎ 041 982 6459 🕑 Closed Oct.–May 💲 $ ■

The mordant wit of Belfast and Londonderry, the easy pace of conversations in the country towns, and humor wherever you go

Northern Ireland

Liquid gold at the Bushmills Distillery

Northern Ireland

A troubled province in the past, Northern Ireland is still very little visited today. Even its capital, Belfast—one of the most interesting and enjoyable cities in either the Republic of Ireland or Northern Ireland—is undervisited and misunderstood. Yet the people here are extraordinarily welcoming and justly proud of a landscape that boasts huge lakes, several fine hill ranges, and a coastline that runs to the spectacular in places.

NOT TO BE MISSED:

Having a drink in Belfast's beautiful Crown Liquor Saloon 282–283

Wandering through the galleries of the Ulster Museum in Belfast 285

A Black Taxi tour of Belfast's history and gable-end art 285–292

Visiting the Giant's Causeway, a storm of dramatic spray 302–303

The ancient Beaghmore stone circles near An Creagan 317

Cruising Lower Lough Erne 323

Enjoying spectacular views from the top of Slieve Gullion 327

The six counties of Northern Ireland fan out like segments of a wheel from the central hub of Lough Neagh, the biggest lake in the British Isles. County Antrim is the best known because of its glorious coastline stretching north from Belfast—a succession of east-running glens ending in superb cliffs, with the 37,000 hexagonal basaltic columns of the Giant's Causeway as the icing on the cake.

County Londonderry (or Derry), west of Antrim, possesses Northern Ireland's second city, Londonderry (Derry), a lively and forward-looking town whose heart is enclosed within the best-preserved set of city walls anywhere in Ireland. On the cliffs of the north-facing Londonderry coast you'll find the 18th-century country estate of Downhill, while inland are forests and the northern range of the Sperrin Mountains.

County Tyrone is the setting for the bulk of the Sperrins, glorious hills for striding over or for exploring by car. At the waist of Tyrone, a wide belt of bogland holds a rich collection of archaeological sites.

Out to the west, County Fermanagh

boasts Upper and Lower Lough Erne, which offer superb cruising, fishing, and island-hopping.

County Armagh has the Lough Neagh Discovery Centre, the historic city of Armagh, drumlin hills, and volcanic Slieve Gullion.

Northward toward Belfast is County Down, last of the six, with the beautiful Mourne Mountains in the south, St. Patrick's Country in the center, and the wildfowl paradise of Strangford Lough in the north.

Belfast

No capital city in Western Europe had a higher news profile in recent times than Belfast. Yet ordinary visitors are less likely to experience trouble in Belfast than in most other comparable European cities. Uncertain and halting as the peace process may be, Belfast people—like the people of every corner of Northern Ireland—are only too keen to show how greatly they appreciate visitors as symbols of the better times that are opening for the whole province.

Belfast's "Beacon of Hope" was erected in 2007 as a symbol of the country's renewed optimism amid reconciliation.

Belfast

⚠ 277 F3 & 279

Visitor Information

✉ Belfast Welcome
Centre,
47 Donegall Pl.,
Belfast

☎ 028 9024 6609

**www.gotobelfast
.com**

Belfast sits handsomely at the inner end of Belfast Lough, with a fine ridge of hills on the west—Black Hill, Black Mountain, Divis, Squire's Hill, and Cave Hill. The city is divided by the River Lagan, which winds its way north into Belfast Lough. East of the river, there's very little to see; the city center and almost all the other attractions are to the Lagan's west.

If you are expecting a gleaming modern city, you will be disappointed. Belfast was made

prosperous by the textile and shipbuilding trades, and it has the appearance of a Victorian manufacturing city, one that could have been transplanted whole from the industrial north of England. There are grandiose 19th-century public buildings and churches, canyonlike shopping streets, acres of redbrick terraced workers' housing, and tree-lined avenues.

Since 1998, marking the end of the 30-year Troubles, "peace money" has seen a certain amount of rebuilding and redesigning. The once stinking River Lagan in particular has been cleaned up, and the riverfront now has a visitor center plus an array of new and refurbished buildings. Yet Belfast retains its old essential character—solid, busy, and rather shabby. The grandest buildings—the Town Hall, the Opera House, and St. Anne's Cathedral in particular—stand in the heart of the city, with the Botanic Gardens, that splendid symbol of Victorian philanthropic provision, to the south.

The best way to see all this is slowly. Be sure to talk to as many people as possible. Chat to the driver as you ride in a Black Taxi to see the sectarian murals, have a drink and a plate of champ (mashed potato and spring onions) in the ornate Crown Liquor Saloon, or stroll up on

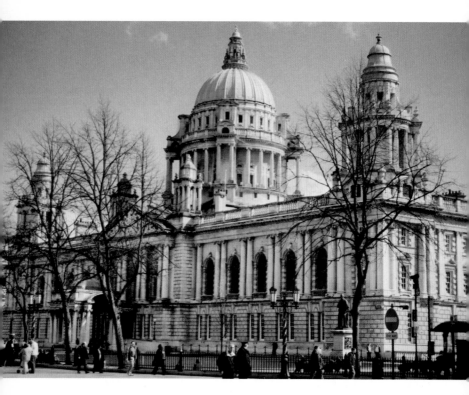

Impressive City Hall, downtown Belfast's Victorian masterpiece

City Hall

Map p. 279

✉ Donegall Sq., Belfast

☎ 028 9027 0456

🕐 Public tours: Mon.–Sat.

**www.belfastcity
.gov.uk**

Cave Hill or out along the Lagan towpath. Belfast generosity and black humor make a potent tonic.

Donegall Square

Belfast city center has two distinct characters: the solemn grandeur of great Victorian public buildings and the quickfire humor and friendliness of the locals. Any stroll should start in Donegall Square, in the very heart of the city. This fine wide plaza, with its central lawns and gardens, contains many of Belfast's best civic buildings.

City Hall: Pride of place goes to the giant City Hall, a great white wedding cake of a building in pale Portland stone. Begun in 1898 and opened in 1906, its sheer size—a mighty portico in a facade 300 feet (90 m) long, a verdigris-green central dome of copper that rises 173 feet (53 m)—and the elaborate confection of its four corner turrets still breathe Edwardian confidence. Queen Victoria stares stolidly from her plinth in front of the entrance.

Other fine monuments encircle City Hall, notably the **memorial to the crew of the Belfast-built** *Titanic* and the splendid **statue of Frederick Temple,** Lord Dufferin, and Ava

(1826–1902). Anyone who needs a reminder of the intertwined histories of Britain and Ireland should look at Lord Dufferin's effigy. Imperious but humorous-looking in his breeches and waxed moustache, he personifies the Empire-ruling Briton of the Victorian era. He was viceroy of India from 1884 to 1888 (a turbaned Sikh flanks him with shield and saber), governor-general of Canada (a woolly-hatted and fur-coated Canadian guards his other side, toting a rifle and a caribou head), and ambassador to Moscow, as well as the catalyst for bringing Burma into the British Empire.

Walk below the huge **pediment** (where Hibernia presides over figures emblematic of Belfast's success in industry and the arts) and enter the **great hall,** highly decorated with three different kinds of Italian marble. Ornate plasterwork of swags and medallions decorates the walls and the interior of the **great dome—**this is viewed from below, crowning a cylinder of circular galleries and murals depicting the city's history.

The **Council Chamber** is the highlight of the daily tours of the City Hall. It is a sumptuous room, paneled in hand-carved Austrian oak, with red **benches** for the city councilors and a heavily carved **throne** for the Lord Mayor under **stained-glass windows** and a splendid crimson-and-white **dome.** Here you can also see the plain round wooden **table** at which Sir Edward Carson signed the Solemn League and Covenant against Home Rule on September 28, 1912, a document

subsequently signed by thousands of Orangemen (see pp. 306–307), some in their own blood. The table was knocked together quickly out of rough wood especially for the signing ceremony.

In a nearby corridor hangs a vigorous and moving **painting** of Ulstermen in a conflict that united Irishmen across the political and religious divides. Thousands of Northern Irish Catholics and Protestants, unionists and nationalists, joined up to fight with British

EXPERIENCE:
Quiet Reading

If you're looking for a quiet place to settle in with the newspaper or a good book, a place where conversations, cell phones, and iPods are not tolerated, head to Belfast's wonderful **Linen Hall Library** (see p. 282). The strict no-noise policy here means you can read in peace. Of course, if you want a bit of chatter, make for the library's fabulous coffeehouse or the children's area. For something similar in Dublin, try the solemn **Old Library** in the Long Room at Trinity College (see p. 55).

Crown forces during World War I. The picture shows 17-year-old 2nd Lieutenant Thornley and his men of the Ulster Division on July 1, 1916, the opening day of the Battle of the Somme, rushing forward from a captured trench, fresh blood on their bayonets.

Around Donegall Square:
Notable commercial and civic buildings flank Donegall Square. The ornate, sculpture-encrusted

Linen Hall Library
- Map p. 279
- 17 Donegall Sq. North, Belfast
- 028 9032 1707
- Closed Sun.

www.linenhall.com

Royal Belfast Academical Institution
- Map p. 279
- College Sq. East, Belfast
- 028 9024 0461

www.rbai.org.uk

Grand Opera House
- Map p. 279
- Great Victoria St., Belfast
- 028 9024 1919

www.goh.co.uk

Crown Liquor Saloon
- Map p. 279
- 46 Great Victoria St., Belfast
- 028 9027 9901

www.crownbar.com

Scottish Provident building, on the west side, shows dolphins, queens, and lions, while the red sandstone **Marks & Spencer** building, on the north, looks fabulously Italianate.

At the northwest corner of the square stands the **Linen Hall Library,** housed in what was a Victorian linen warehouse—stone swaths of the stuff are bunched over the doorway. This is a real old-fashioned library, where hushed voices are in order and books stand on wooden shelves by the tens of thousands.

INSIDER TIP:

The Crown Liquor Saloon is a must. Go before 3:00 p.m. and eat in the pub downstairs—it's the same great food as the upstairs restaurant but with better ambience.

—KAREN MARTINEZ
National Geographic Books

In the **Members' Room,** elderly Belfast folk quietly read the daily papers (see sidebar p. 281), and you can get an excellent cup of tea in the popular **Tea Room.** A fine curved wooden staircase leads to the upper floor and more labyrinthine shelving. You will find crusty old books, both rare and curious, in the **Governor's Room,** and there are bound copies of the *Belfast Newsletter*—the oldest newspaper in the country—dating back to 1738.

Any visitor is welcome to trawl through the library's collections. The **Political Collection,** on the second floor, documents the course of the contemporary Troubles through newspaper clippings, posters, tracts, and other material.

Beyond Donegall Square

A counterclockwise stroll from Donegall Square around the city center sights could start with a westward walk along Wellington Place to College Square, where the handsome brick-built **Royal Belfast Academical Institution** stands in a green setting. It was built in 1814 to a design by Sir John Soane, who also designed the Bank of England and many other London buildings.

Going south from the "Inst" (as its pupils, and most of the rest of Belfast, call it), College Square East leads to Great Victoria Street and the wonderfully overblown **Grand Opera House** of 1894–95. "Smiley (comedy) and frowny (tragedy)" symbolic theatrical masks adorn the outside, while inside it is all crimson plush and huge gilt plasterwork elephants, cherubs, and thespians. The Opera House was restored in 1980, partially wrecked by bombs in 1991 and 1993, and restored to glory once more.

Opposite the Opera House is a Belfast drinking institution, the **Crown Liquor Saloon,** such a remarkable example of extravagant late Victorian pub design that the National Trust now looks after it. Note the crown mosaic at the entrance. The story goes that during an 1895 refurbishment of what was then the Railway

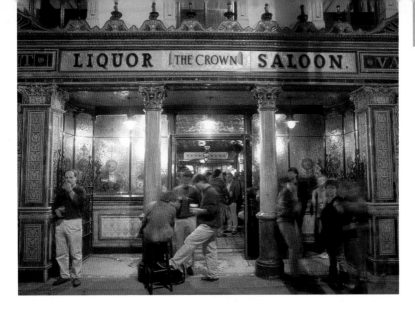

For imbibing amid high Victorian decor, head to the Crown Liquor Saloon.

Tavern by the owners, Mr. and Mrs. Patrick Flanagan, the lady—a keen loyalist—demanded that the pub be renamed the "Crown" and that a crown image be created and installed. Patrick Flanagan, a dedicated nationalist as well as a wise husband, agreed to carry out his wife's wishes but had the crown put on the floor so that everyone would wipe their feet on it. You can order a drink at the curved, tiled bar under the plaster foliage and scrollwork of the brown ceiling and sip it in one of the carved wooden snugs with their frosted glass and handy metal match-strikers. Try the Crown's famous "champ," a delicious mess of mashed potato and scallions (spring onions), maybe with a couple of pork and leek sausages.

On Ormeau Avenue (due south of Donegall Square by way of Linenhall Street), you'll find the **Ormeau Baths Gallery,** an imaginative conversion of an old swimming bathhouse into a gallery of contemporary art, strong on

Irish artists. Just northeast of the gallery, on Alfred Street, is an early Victorian gem, Catholic **St. Malachy's Church.** An unpromising exterior of dark brick and pink paint hides an exuberant interior with fan-vaulting, plasterwork, and art nouveau stained-glass windows with tall purple lilies.

Northeast again, where Oxford Street meets May Street, stands the redbrick **St. George's Market,** a handsome late Victorian market hall where Belfast comes on Tuesdays and Fridays to shop for fresh flowers, fish, fruit, and vegetables under the glass-and-cast-iron roof. Arts events, exhibitions, and craft fairs take place here, too (*tel 028 9043 5704 for details*).

North and east of Donegall Square is another clutch of delights. **The Entries** is a tangled area of alleyways just south of High Street, the heart of old Belfast and full of characterful pubs .

At the top of High Street stands an unmistakable Belfast landmark, the 113-foot (35 m)

Ormeau Baths Gallery

Map p. 279

18a Ormeau Ave., Belfast

www.ormeaubaths .co.uk

Albert Memorial Clock Tower, built in 1865. The tower inclines 4 feet (1.25 m) out of perpendicular; it had to be founded on wooden piles because of the marshy ground, and these foundations have shifted over the years. "Albert has the time and the inclination!" say locals.

Graduation Day at Queen's University

Cathedral Church of St. Anne

🅰 Map p. 279

✉ Donegall St., Belfast

☎ 028 9032 8332

🕐 Closed Sat.; open Mon.–Fri. & Sun. before & after services

www.belfast cathedral.org

The same stretch of boggy ground is responsible for the bumpy nave floor in the Protestant **Cathedral Church of St. Anne** on Donegall Street, west of the Albert Tower. Consecrated in 1904, it is founded on 80 feet (25 m) of log piling, which has shifted. The nave floor is beautiful, though, with Canadian maple and Irish marble, its shapeliness enhanced by the upward sweep of pillars that rise

to capitals carved with scenes of the "Occupations of Mankind"– spinning flax, weaving, shipbuilding, seed-sowing. Stone from each of Ireland's 32 counties was used in the construction of St. Anne's. There are three beautiful modern east windows full of Christian symbols. Against the north wall, you'll find a modest bronze memorial above the grave of Lord Carson (1854–1935), fierce opponent of Home Rule and the leader of Ulster from 1911 to 1921.

South of the City Center

If the center of Belfast is where the heart and soul of the city reside, then its stomach and liver have probably got lost somewhere a mile or so south of the city center. The long University Road and its tributary streets, running south from Shaftesbury Square and Bradbury Place to meet the Malone Road just past **Queen's University,** is where most of the serious and fashionable eating, drinking, and late-night street partying takes place. Queen's University, another fine Lanyon building (1845–49) in the Tudor style, caters to nearly 10,000 students, which can make its colonnaded quad and the quietly elegant squares around the university pretty lively from time to time.

Beyond Queen's, on Stranmillis Road, you reach the splendid **Botanic Gardens,** beautiful to stroll in, and irresistible with their high Victorian iron-and-glass monsters of glasshouses. The hot and steamy **Palm House** of 1839–1840, with its rounded prow and long wings, is superb, as is the glass-roofed **Tropical Ravine,** established in 1887 by curator Charles McKimm in an attempt to reproduce the sultry heat and fecundity of a rain-forest gully. A raised balcony lets you wander at canopy level, or farther down, among ferns, orchids, dombeya, Dutchman's pipe, and guava, banana, and cinnamon trees.

Ulster Museum: Near the Tropical Ravine stands the absorbing Ulster Museum, one of Ireland's best city museums. The art collection is wonderful, ranging from Pissarro and Sickert through Stanley Spencer to Henry Moore, with a superb collection of watercolors and drawings. Turner, Gainsborough, Reynolds, Stubbs, and Wilson are old-guard members, and there are plenty of examples of the work of Belfast-born artist Sir John Lavery (1856–1941).

Ancient artifacts include bronze crosses, brooches, and holy relic shrines. In the Technology Section, you can wonder at the machines that brought textile prosperity to Belfast during the industrial revolution.

Most intriguing of all are the personal effects and the treasure of jewels, gold, and silver salvaged in 1967–69 from the wreck of the *Girona,* a Spanish warship that went aground near the Giant's Causeway (see pp. 302–303) during the fiasco of the 1588 Spanish Armada.

Black Taxi Tours

A city like Belfast, with its

troubled and ever evolving history, is often best appreciated at the elbow of a native who can put what you are seeing into context. Depending on your mood and the chattiness of your driver, a Black Taxi tour of Belfast can be the best fun you'll have in the city. In fact, given a gabby cabby (and almost all of them are), there's no better way to see Belfast from the insider's perspective. You're bound to catch stories, opinions, and insiders' versions—especially related to the past Troubles in the city—that you would never get hold of by yourself. You needn't necessarily believe everything you are told, however! Furthermore, whatever the political or religious affiliations of the driver, he or she will certainly not intrude them on you unless you ask.

You can of course use one of the regular service black taxis—sometimes known as People's

(continued on p. 290)

Botanic Gardens
- Map p. 279
- Stranmillis Rd., Belfast
- 028 9031 4762

Ulster Museum
- Map p. 279
- Botanic Gardens, Belfast
- 028 9042 8628
- Closed Mon.
- www.nmni.com/um

Black Taxi Tours
- Depart from Belfast city center
- 028 9064 2264; Freephone 0800 052 3914
- Tours at 10 a.m., noon, 2 p.m., 4 p.m., 6 p.m. (8 p.m., summer only)
- 1–2 passengers: $$$$$; 3-6 passengers: $$$ per person
- www.belfasttours.com

Titanic Facts

The "Belfast Symphony" was the name for the pulsating, incessant rhythm of riveters' hammers that rang out from the Belfast shipyard during the building of the *Titanic*. The great ship consumed 3 million rivets, weighing 1,200 tons (1,090 tonnes). Her rudder alone used 101 tons (92 tonnes) of steel. The makers needed 23 tons (21 tonnes) of tallow, soft soap, and railway grease to lubricate the slipway at her launch on May 31, 1911. When fully equipped she carried 29 boilers, 159 furnaces, 8,000 tons (7,250 tonnes) of coal, 40 tons (36 tonnes) of potatoes, and five grand pianos.

Gable-End Art & the Troubles

As "political" murals—the euphemism employed by the tourist trade—many of the famed sectarian murals of Belfast are way over the top. But as folk art expressing raw emotion, they have great power. Murals come and go as buildings are demolished and new developments inspire fresh commentary, but the sites remain roughly the same.

Militaristic loyalist artists credit their paramilitary heroes with the organization of a formal army.

Your first sight of the murals can be a shock. They seem to pump anger and the threat of violence across the city, with their balaclava-clad gunmen and intolerant assertions—"Irish Out," "England's Geno-cide," "No Surrender"—blazoned house-high across gable ends and street walls. At the same time, there is a kind of playground machismo about these paintings that robs them of some of their menace.

Republican & Loyalist Murals

Republican murals are thickest on the ground around the Falls Road and Springfield Road, the streets around the Ballymurphy estate and the Ardoyne farther north, and in the Short Strand district of East Belfast. Loy-alist ones tend to be around the Shankill and Crumlin Roads and in East Belfast around Lower Newtownards Road.

The character of the murals reflects the nature of the 30-year confrontation known as the Troubles. Loyalists with their siege mentality and desire to keep the status quo tend to produce aggressive, die-hard images of bully-boy paramilitaries hefting guns, advertising a bewildering number of outlawed orga-nizations: UDA (Ulster Defence Association), UVF (Ulster Volunteer Force), UFF (Ulster Freedom Fighters), LVF (Loyalist Volunteer Force), and many more. Republican murals are more aspirational, romantic, and imaginative.

Smiling hunger strikers exhort everyone to play a part, figures from Ireland's mythological past imperiously dispatch British soldiers back across the Irish Sea. The standard of execution varies from schoolboy crude to extremely skillful.

History of the Troubles

Discriminated against in housing, work, policing, and social services, and with local political representation fixed in favor of Protestants, Catholic activists began a series of civil rights marches in 1968 that soon turned into confrontations with the police and with loyalists—especially around Londonderry's Bogside, an impoverished Catholic ghetto quickly renamed "Free Derry" in pioneer republican murals. British troops appeared on the streets of Londonderry on August 14, 1969, and in Belfast two days later (see sidebar p. 34). At first, Catholics saw the soldiers as protectors, but they soon had them lumped in with the Royal Ulster Constabulary as oppressors—and foreign ones at that.

The 1980s hunger-striker Bobby Sands remains a hero to many in the Catholic community.

EXPERIENCE:
Viewing the Murals

The Troubles are still too recent for many museum exhibitions to have been organized around them. Exhibits at the **Ulster Museum** in Belfast (see p. 285) and the **Tower Museum** in Londonderry (see pp. 304, 308) are the most complete as yet. As a result, the best way for you to catch the authentic flavor of the Troubles is to view the gable-end murals for yourself. **Belfast City Taxi Tours** (*tel 078 4973 8329, www.belfastcitytours.com*) offers a complete 800-year history of Belfast with particular concentration on the city's gable-end and wall murals. The tour also includes a stop at the city's peace wall.

INSIDER TIP:

Don't miss a personalized Black Taxi tour through Belfast's sectarian neighborhoods, but make sure your driver is allowed through both Catholic and Protestant areas.

—CHRISTOPHER KLEIN
National Geographic Traveler *magazine writer*

Escalating Violence

In 1971, the IRA campaign of shooting and bombing to force a British withdrawal began. A government crackdown saw the imposition of internment without trial and direct rule from Westminster. On January 30, 1972—"Bloody Sunday"—British paratroopers shot 13 people dead in Londonderry. Three years later, the IRA began a bombing campaign on the British mainland, killing 21 youngsters with pub bombs in Birmingham. Loyalists retaliated by activating their own paramilitary groups, and two bitter decades of tit-for-tat killings ensued. Loyalists

Murals along the Falls Road side of the divide

wanted Northern Ireland to stay within the United Kingdom; nationalists wanted civil justice and to be part of a united Ireland. Neither would budge nor listen to the other side. It was as simple, and as complicated, as that.

In 1975, internment without trial was suspended, but republican prisoners had their status as "political" detainees withdrawn. "Blanket protests" (refusal to wear prison clothes) and "dirty protests" (refusal to "slop out" the cell toilets and the consequent smearing of cells with excrement) followed. Prison protests escalated to their awful conclusion in 1981, when ten hunger strikers, led by Bobby Sands MP, starved themselves to death in the Maze prison south of Lisburn in an abortive attempt to force a return to political status. Their faces appear on the Falls Road murals.

Movement Toward Peace

In the 1980s, more extremist splinter groups split off from the main paramilitary organizations. But political moves were

being made. A 1973 attempt to set up a power-sharing executive to govern Northern Ireland had been brought down the following year by a province-wide Protestant worker's strike. In 1982, a power-sharing Northern Ireland Assembly was established on a very limited basis. The year 1985 saw the signing of the Anglo-Irish Agreement, which brought Dublin on board to some extent. The involvement of the Republic's government, for so long negatively anti-British and reiterative of its supposed claim to reasserted the points made in the Downing Street declaration, ended the Republic's claim over the six counties, promised the release of paramilitary prisoners, decommissioning of paramilitary weapons, and an independent commission on policing in Northern Ireland, and proposed a Northern Ireland Assembly elected by proportional representation. All signatories committed themselves to "exclusively democratic and peaceful means" of resolving political differences.

Future of Northern Ireland

Huge problems remain for Northern Ireland. The euphoria generated by the Good Friday Agreement has long abated, and the fledgling Northern Ireland Assembly, which took full powers of devolved government in 1999, has been suspended on four occasions—the latest suspension, from October 14, 2002, is still in force. But moves toward

sovereignty over the North's six counties, was vital to any resolution.

Signs of moderation grew in the 1990s. The 1993 Downing Street declaration saw the British government renounce any "selfish strategic or economic interest" in Northern Ireland, while Dublin accepted that any change in constitutional status would have to be subject of the agreement of a majority of the people. On August 31, 1994, the IRA declared a "complete cessation" of violence. Loyalist paramilitary groups followed suit. The British responded with some troop withdrawals and the demolition of roadblocks and border crossings.

An End to Violence

The seeds of hope were briefly frozen in 1996, when the IRA resumed mainland bombing. Then, in May 1997, a Labour government was elected in the United Kingdom, and the mood changed. The new government's majority was big enough to shrug off Unionist opposition. On April 10, 1998, the Good Friday Agreement was announced, a historic accommodation by all sides. It

A republican artist makes her point along Falls Road in Belfast.

a permanent peace have been made. In July 2005, the IRA declared an end to its armed campaign, followed by a verification in September 2005 of the decommissioning of all its arms—positive steps on the long road to peace in Northern Ireland.

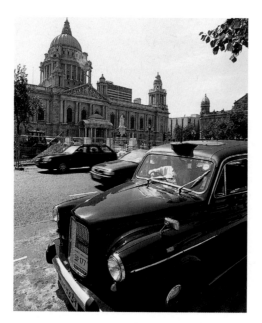

Black Taxi tours are the best way to see the famous murals.

Taxis—that ply routes around West Belfast. These started up in the 1970s, when bus services were withdrawn from West Belfast because so many buses were being hijacked and used as barricades. The taxis undercut bus fares and operated a buslike service along regular routes. They still operate like buses, so you'll find them stopping to drop and pick up passengers frequently. But the presence of other passengers in the cab may inhibit you from asking questions, and you won't be able to stop when you like. It's better to go for the NITB-approved Black Taxi tours run by Michael Johnston.

You can discuss the route with your driver, who will be happy to tailor-make your tour. The standard route tends to take in

some of the waterfront—generally the Lagan Weir, Lagan Lookout, and glimpses of the big Samson & Goliath cranes in Harland & Wolff's shipyard (see p. 293)—as well as city center sights such as the Crown Liquor Saloon, City Hall, and the Grand Opera House (see pp. 280–283). But the main interest of the tour comes when you swing off toward the Shankill and Falls Roads and the "frontline" Troubles enclaves of West Belfast.

Crumlin Road: Protestant West Belfast starts on the Crumlin Road, with its heavily fenced-in **Orange Hall,** where a statue of King William III rides high on the roof beside the inevitable loyalist Union Jack flag. Curbstones are painted red, white, and blue (the colors of the flag) hereabouts. Unemployment is high, and many of the old Victorian side streets are slums—though they are being replaced by better housing.

The **Crumlin Road Courthouse** stands forbiddingly on the road, designed by Belfast's paramount Victorian architect, Sir Charles Lanyon, to personify the Dignity of the Law, with its massive portico and statue of Justice on top.

Facing it is the even more oppressive dark brick **Crumlin Road Gaol;** a tunnel beneath the road connects the two. In the 1970s and '80s, the Diplock Courts held their enclosed trials here; in some circumstances, a prisoner on remand could find himself incarcerated for years before coming to trial. Now thankfully abandoned, the grim pair await refurbishment and a new life—no one seems to know in what capacity.

Shankill Road: A block farther south, the **Shankill Road** runs parallel with the Crumlin Road. The Shankill is the main artery of Protestant West Belfast, essentially an old-fashioned suburban thoroughfare of small family-run shops, pubs, betting shops, and sole-proprietor businesses. You won't fail to notice the barbed wire and reinforced steel around the bookies' premises, though, nor the heavy steel shutters on some shops—telltale signs of a community that feels itself under siege.

The fierce loyalist sense of identity is expressed in the enormous murals that cover gable ends and whole house walls (see pp. 286–289). The Black Taxi driver is well aware that the murals, on both sides of the divide, are the main attraction and is quite happy to stop while you photograph. He'll also tell you about what went on here—in garish detail if you want, but with thoughtful insight if he sees that you are prepared to listen.

If you carry on the whole length of the Shankill Road and continue to the end of Glencairn Road, you'll find **Fernhill House,** a run-through of the social history of the Shankill and also an abridged history of Unionism that will help you better understand the background and the mind-set of these Protestant enclaves.

The area of sectarian violence

in Belfast was astonishingly small. Barely 100 yards (100 m) separates the Shankill Road from the Catholic-dominated Falls Road and Springfield Road to the south. Here the **Peace Line** was built to keep both sides' extremists, and their firebombs, out of the opposing enclave. You can write your own peace message alongside thousands of others on this ugly and depressing, but necessary, 20-foot (6 m) wall of concrete, wire, and corrugated tin.

INSIDER TIP:

A budget-friendly alternative to a Black Taxi tour is buying an all-day public bus pass and riding one of the city's pink double-deckers to Shankill.

—ALEXANDRA BURGUIERES
National Geographic contributor

Falls Road: In much of its appearance and atmosphere, the Falls Road mirrors the Shankill, though here the curbstones and flags are orange and green, the nationalist colors. You'll find the same small shops and businesses, the same kind of pubs, and a tremendous array of murals. Hereabouts, you may see a sight vanished from almost every other industrial city in the British Isles—children playing on a lamppost swing, scooting and swinging round and round on homemade loops.

Insights into Belfast's Catholic

Fernhill House
- Map p. 279
- Glencairn Rd., Belfast
- 028 9071 5599
- Closed Sun. a.m.
- $
www.fernhillhouse.co.uk

**Cultúrlann
MacAdam
O'Fiaich**

✉ 216 Falls Rd.

☎ 028 9096 4180

www.culturlann.co

cultural heritage can be found in Sinn Féin's little center on the Falls Road, or in **Cultúrlann Mac-Adam O'Fiaich** a little farther out, an Irish cultural center where you can get lunch or a cup of tea.

Up on the Springfield Road, which runs northwest off the Falls Road, the **police station**—a regular target for attacks at the height of the Troubles—is still hideously fortified. Your driver can tell you about it and about the many republicans buried in **Milltown Cemetery** a mile (1.6 km) farther along the Falls Road.

It will be strange indeed if you don't finish your tour with more of an understanding of the city and its problems, and an admiration for the stoicism and decency of ordinary Belfast people.

River Lagan Cruise

The River Lagan was a stinking open sewer until the building of the Lagan Weir in 1994. It's hard to believe nowadays, with salmon and sea trout coming upriver and anglers to be seen along the banks. The River Lagan cruise on MV *Joyce* shows you a side of

Belfast Tours

In addition to the famous Black Taxi tours (see. p. 285), Belfast boasts a wealth of tours so varied and numerous that you will certainly find something to suit every interest. If you like the idea of short guided walks around the city, the **Belfast Tourism Development Office** (*tel 028 9024 6609*) lays on an Old Town walk and a Belfast City Centre walk. Check with **Belfast City Guided Walking Tours** (*www.belfast-city-walking-tours.co.uk*) for other insightful guided tours.

Perhaps the most agreeable form of guided city walk is the **Historical Pub Tour of Belfast** (*tel 028 9268 3665*), which leaves from the Crown Dining Rooms upstairs at the Crown Liquor Saloon (see pp. 282–283) on Thursdays at 7 p.m. and Saturdays at 4 p.m., from May to the end of September. Each of these pleasant pub crawls takes in 6 out of 11 carefully chosen premises.

Particularly enjoyable are **White's Tavern** in Winecellar Entry off Lombard Street, Belfast's oldest pub (it dates back to 1630), a black-beamed, stone-floored drinking den with great character; the splendid peninsula wooden bar and railed-

off snugs in the stylish old **Morning Star** in Pottinger's Entry; and **Bittles Bar** on Victoria Square, a sharp triangular building filled with paintings of celebrated literary figures by local artist Joe O'Kane. The best, hanging over the dais at the "sharp end" of the pub, shows W. B. Yeats, James Joyce, Brendan Behan, George Bernard Shaw, and Samuel Beckett drinking at a bar, with Oscar Wilde manning the beer pumps and Flann O'Brien looking on from a picture frame behind the bar.

If you'd rather not walk through the city, there are plenty of bus tours to choose from. **Belfast through the Millennium** (*tel 028 9045 8484*) focuses on the history of the city during the Troubles. Or join the **Belfast City Tour** (*tel 028 9033 7004*), which is given in English, French, German, or Spanish.

For something completely different, **Hard Hat tours** (*tel 028 9024 6609, www .gotobelfast.com*) take you to candy and tea factories, crystal manufacturers, newspaper offices, and a wine warehouse.

For lists of other guided walks and tour operators in the city, check online at *www.schmap.com*.

An evening crowd at Waterfront Hall along the River Lagan

Belfast that you won't discover any other way. From Donegall Quay, there are two options, either up or down river.

Downriver Cruise: The downriver cruise takes you past the big new **Odyssey** entertainment complex, **Abercorn basin,** and the giant cranes and slipways of the once-great **Harland & Wolff shipyard,** where the *Titanic* was built in 1909–1911 (see sidebar p. 285).

Upriver Cruise: On the upriver cruise, the boat goes under the **Queen's Bridge,** Sir Charles Lanyon's first major Belfast project, with its ornate triton lamp standards. Andy Scott's **"Beacon of Hope,"** a great 50-foot (15 m) sculpture of a woman in a silver wire, now stands at the end of the bridge.

Then the boat passes the old **Custom House** (see p. 297) and the west bank developments that include the circular **Waterfront Hall** (1997) and the glassy **Belfast Hilton** (1998). On the opposite bank, you catch a glimpse of the giant shipyard cranes, **Samson & Goliath,** over the long redbrick wall of the old Sirocco works that once made tea-drying machines. Things get more countrified past the big green trees of **Ormeau Park** and the redbrick terraces of the **"Holy Land"**—Damascus Street, Palestine Street, Jerusalem Street—located around the Ormeau Road.

Oystercatcher, sandpiper, and curlew can be seen on the gravelly river beaches, and the river supports eels, gray mullet, and even sea bass and baby plaice. Kingfishers flash electric blue across reedbeds planted by the Laganside Development Corporation. The overall impression is of a river, and a riverside environment, coming back to life. ∎

River Lagan Cruise

✉ Lagan Boat Company, Donegall Quay, Belfast

☎ 028 9033 0844 or 07718 910423

🕐 Cruises daily March–Dec.; call for times

💲 $$

www.laganboat company.com

Walk: Cave Hill

This fine walk, a favorite with Belfast folk, takes you up the mountain behind the city to visit prehistoric caves, to the promontory where United Irishmen pledged their lives in 1795, and to the heritage center in Belfast Castle.

The tremendous view over Belfast Lough is worth every step up Cave Hill.

Start from the parking lot on the south side of Belfast Castle. Follow the **Blue Route footpath** (*blue arrows*) and walk up to a T-junction and turn right. After about 550 yards (500 m), bear left and then turn uphill under the great basalt cliff of **Napoleon's Nose ❶**. In about 300 yards (275 m), at a stone with two blue arrows and "McArt's Fort" sign, bear uphill through trees.

Emerge from the wood, and in another 300 yards (275 m) or so, turn left, aiming for a large **cave ❷** in the cliff face. With care you can scramble up the rock face into the cave. Up here the view is tremendous—Belfast spread out along Belfast Lough, with the dark bulk of the Ards Peninsula hills rising beyond, crowned by the rocket shape of Scrabo Tower.

NOT TO BE MISSED:

Napoleon's Nose • Cave • View from McArt's Fort • Cave Hill Heritage Centre

The cave itself is one of five Neolithic excavations—Stone Age men found flint in the chalk under the basalt hill cap. Iron was mined here, too, opening up the delvings. "The Wages of Sin Is Death," warns a painted message on the cave wall. It may have been here, or at **McArt's Fort ❸** on the summit, that Wolfe Tone, Henry Joy McCracken, Dr. William Drennan, and a small band of friends—mostly

Presbyterians—met in 1795 to swear an oath that Irishmen of every creed should unite for independence. It was the birth of the United Irishmen, a rebel organization whose leaders came to a bloody end in the 1798 rising.

To reach McArt's Fort, bear right as you face the cave on a narrow path along the grass slopes under the cliff. It soon trends uphill. At the top of the slope, cross a cattle grid near a post with blue and yellow waymarks. Bear left uphill. In about 300 yards (275 m), cross a cattle grid and continue uphill with a fence on your right, bearing left to reach the fort at 1,182 feet (360 m). This old earthwork was named after Brian McArt O'Neill, one of the last Irish chieftains to die in the Tudor repressions—he was killed by Lord Mountjoy in 1601.

From the fort, retrace your steps and descend through the woods to the stone with two blue arrows. Bear left downhill here; in about 150 yards (135 m), go straight ahead at a meeting of woodland tracks.

Follow the blue arrow on a stone at the **Volunteers' Well ❹** to meet a road. Bear right along it; at a parking area, bear right to reach **Belfast Castle ❺**, built in 1867–1870 in baronial style for the Marquis of Donegall.

The **Cave Hill Heritage Centre** *(Belfast Castle, tel 028 9077 6925)*, on the second floor, gives fascinating insights into the wildlife, geology, and history of the area.

- 🏔 See area map p. 277 F3
- ➤ Belfast Castle parking lot, Cave Hill Country Park— signed off the A6 Antrim road, 4 miles (6 km) N of city center. City bus 8, 9, 10, 45–51 from Donegall Square
- ⏱ 2 hours. Free trail map and literature available from Cave Hill Heritage Centre
- ↔ 2 miles (3.5 km)
- ➤ Belfast Castle

More Places to Visit Around Belfast

Lagan Towpath

If you want to explore the River Lagan on foot upriver from Belfast, there is an 11-mile (18 km) **Lagan Towpath Walk** through the beautiful, wooded Lagan Valley Regional Park. Pick up one of the brochure guides available from the Belfast Welcome Centre.

The walk starts at the parking lot on Lockview Road. Leaving the gates of the Botanic Gardens, turn left beside the Ulster Museum and continue up Stranmillis Road. Then turn right onto Lockview Road. The old towpath takes you through a 4,000-acre (1,600 ha) mixture of woodland and pasture, wetlands and forest, to its end at Union Locks in Lisburn.

In 3 miles (5 km) from the start of the Lagan towpath, you can reach two of Belfast's most pleasant green oases. **Malone House** *(Barnett Park, Upper Malone Rd., Belfast, tel 028 9068 1246, city bus 70, 71, www.malonehouse.co.uk),* south of the city center, is a fine restored late Georgian house with an excellent restaurant. It stands on 100 acres (40 ha) of grounds ablaze with azaleas and rhododendrons in spring.

A mile (1.6 km) along the Upper Malone Road from Malone House, you'll find **Sir Thomas and Lady Dixon Park** *(Ulsterbus 13d from Europa Bus Station),* a varied mosaic of meadows, woodland, and water with the City of Belfast International Rose Gardens at its heart—11 acres (4 ha) of more than 30,000 shrub roses. These are spectacular beginning in mid-July, and in spring daffodils fill the park. ▲ Map p. 279

The Waterfront

Belfast's waterfront areas have been revitalized since the 1994 building of the Lagan

Sir Edward Carson (1854–1935), vehement Unionist, shakes a defiant fist outside Stormont.

Weir's five steel sluice gates. The weir has stabilized river levels, eliminated offensive smells, and made Laganside a pleasant area to explore.

The **Lagan Lookout Centre** (*Lagan Weir, Donegall Quay, tel 028 9031 5444*) has large windows overlooking the weir. Here there are displays on Belfast shipbuilding and the story of the River Lagan. You can look across to the giant twin cranes of Samson & Goliath in Harland & Wolff's shipyards, their gaunt yellow frames towering more than 300 feet (91 m) high and 450 feet (137 m) long. They symbolize a shipbuilding power that is all but gone from the yards where *Titanic* was built and launched in 1912. At their height, the shipyards employed more than 25,000 men; today, barely a couple hundred work there.

Just behind the Lagan Lookout, you'll see the Sir Charles Lanyon–designed **Custom House** of 1854–57, its pediment crowded with nautical statuary—Neptune, Britannia, dolphins, and anchors.

East of the Lagan: Across the river, playing Impudence to the Custom House's Dignity, stands **Odyssey Arena** (*Queen's Quay, tel 028 9076 6000, www.odysseyarena .com*), a 150-million-dollar sports and culture venue of the most modern kind—evidence the confidence Laganside Development Corporation has engendered.

Walking seaward from the Lagan Lookout along Donegall Quay and under the motorway bridge, you round the corner to find two of Belfast's most interesting buildings side by side. The **Harbour Commissioner's Office** (*Corporation Sq., tel 028 9055 4422, group visits by prior arrangement, www.belfast-harbour.co.uk*), opened in 1854, has an interior rich in stained glass and elaborate plasterwork. Upstairs highlights include fine paintings of sailing ships in heavy seas, superb paintings of old Belfast harbor scenes by well-known turn-of-the-20th-century painter Eyre Macklin, and the Barnet Room, with its painted stucco barrel

roof and stained-glass windows portraying the arms of Belfast's trading partners in days of the Empire—Australia, Canada, Russia, the United States, India, Italy, and the Cape Colony of South Africa.

Just along the street, look for the **Sinclair Seamen's Church** (*Corporation Sq., tel 028 9071 5997, open Wed. 2–5 p.m. & Sun. for services at 11:30 a.m. & 7 p.m., and by appt.*), designed by Sir Charles Lanyon and opened in 1857.

Stormont

A great place for walks is around Stormont, 5 miles (8 km) east of Belfast city center (see map p. 279). The 1928 Portland stone Stormont Castle (tel 028 9076 0556, city bus 16, 17, 20), seat of the Northern Ireland Assembly, is spectacularly sited at the crown of a mile-long (1.6 km) drive. The castle itself is only open to the public by appointment, but you are free to wander the 300 acres (120 ha) of parkland and woods.

Throughout the furnishings of this remarkable L-shaped Presbyterian church, with its separate Italianate tower, a nautical theme predominates, from the semaphore flags that spell out "Welcome" at each door to the ship's binnacle used as a font. Fishing boats and tugs feature in the stained-glass windows, the collection boxes are miniature lifeboats, and the pulpit is shaped like a ship's prow. On the walls hang the mast of a Guinness barge, port and starboard ship lights, and a silver flashlight with which some shipwreck victims summoned help. Fifty seats are kept empty for visiting sailors every Sunday, and the start of the service to which they are welcomed is signaled by six strokes on the brass ship's bell of HMS *Hood,* sunk at the mouth of Portsmouth Harbour, England, in World War I to deny entry to enemy submarines. *www.laganside.com* Map p. 279

County Antrim

The pride and glory of County Antrim resides in its spectacular coast and green hinterland. Stretching 75 miles (120 km) from Carrickfergus to Portrush and forming the northeastern rim of Northern Ireland, this playground of basalt and sandstone is like a giant natural sculpture park. Driving the Antrim coast road is one of the great highlights of any trip to Ireland.

Carnlough displays all the neatness, order, and architectural harmony of a planned village.

Carrickfergus

🅼 277 F3

Visitor Information

✉ 11 Antrim St., Carrickfergus, Co. Antrim

☎ 028 9335 8049

www.carrickfergus .org

Carrickfergus Castle

✉ Marine Hwy., Carrickfergus, Co. Antrim

☎ 028 9335 1273

💲 $

Carrickfergus

The A2 coast road, heading north out of Belfast, passes through the suburb of New-townabbey to reach Carrick-fergus. Big and well-preserved, **Carrickfergus Castle** stands on a rocky promontory by the harbor, a 90-foot (28 m) keep rising from gray battlemented walls. Sir John de Courcy built the castle in 1180 as a deterrent to any attacker advancing up Belfast Lough. It suffered various sieges and captures in its time, by Scots and French forces, as well as the English—all owing to its vital strategic position at the lough entrance.

In the town center, you can explore the 12th-century **Church of St. Nicholas** off the market-place. The church contains notable late medieval glass and the beauti-fully carved 17th-century tomb of Sir Arthur and Lady Chichester, 1st Earl and Countess of Belfast, and their poignantly tiny son.

Just north of Carrickfergus, you'll see the **Andrew Jackson Cottage and U.S. Rangers Centre.** Though this thatched cottage offers a collection of Jackson-related material, fans and family of the former U.S. President (1767–1845) should be aware that his connection to the house is ten-uous. Jackson's parents emigrated from the town two years before Andrew was born, and this house was not their home.

Island Magee Peninsula

Beyond Carrickfergus, you can take a worthwhile detour around the 7-mile-long (11 km) Island Magee Peninsula (reached by the B150, off the A2 just north of Whitehead). The tidal inlet of **Larne Lough,** all but enclosed by the eastward arm of Island Magee, is good for bird-watching and boating, while the peninsula itself has the very fine **cliffs of the Gobbins** looking out east into the Irish Sea. In 1641, a party of soldiers from Carrickfergus garrison hurled locals, alive and dead, off the cliffs in retaliation for the killing of some of their number. Island Magee was known as a witchy kind of place—the last eight witches to be convicted at Carrickfergus court were Island Magee women tried in 1710.

The Coast Road

A ferry connects Ballylumford at the northern end of the peninsula with **Larne,** a coastal ferry port with plenty of bustle but not much charm. But Larne is the gateway to the real delights of the Antrim coast, which you skirt all the way north on the A2. Sir Charles Lanyon, chief architect of 19th-century Belfast, designed the road in 1834 as a project to enable destitute locals to earn some money.

Built by Scottish engineer William Bald, the coast road hugs the cliffs and passes the mouth of each of the nine Antrim Glens. Before the road was built, the inhabitants of the coast villages of Carnlough, Glenariff, Cushendall, and Cushendun had been all but cut off by intervening cliffs from each other and from Ballycastle to the north and Larne to the south. Trade in goods, and very soon in holidaymakers hungry for romantic scenery, quickly improved once the coast road opened.

INSIDER TIP:

The drive from Belfast along the Antrim coast is an essential road trip for any visitor to Northern Ireland. It's one of the most stunning scenic drives in the world.

—ALLY THOMPSON
National Geographic contributor

Antrim Glens

From Ballygalley, the coast rises to some fine limestone cliffs at **Carnlough,** a pretty fishing village around Carnlough Bay. But they are only the prelude to the dramatic Antrim coast. There are many glens or valleys in Antrim; nine in particular are recognized as the Antrim Glens—from south to north they are Glenarm, Glencloy, Glenariff, Glenballyeamon, Glenaan, Glencorp, Glendun, Glenshesk, and Glentaisie.

Carved by rivers and shaped by Ice Age glaciers and meltwaters, frosts, and other weathering processes, the Antrim Glens veer

Church of St. Nicholas

✉ 3 Lancastrian St., Carrickfergus, Co. Antrim

☎ 028 9336 0061

**www.saintnicholas
.org.uk**

Andrew Jackson Cottage and U.S. Rangers Centre

✉ Boneybefore, Larne Rd., 2 miles (3 km) N of Carrickfergus on the A2

☎ 028 9335 8049

Larne

⚠ 277 F4

Visitor Information

✉ Narrow Gauge Rd., Larne, Co. Antrim

☎ 028 2826 0088

www.larne.com

EXPERIENCE: Treats at the Fair

Two delicacies you can't avoid at the **Ould Lammas Fair** (Ballycastle, Co. Antrim, last Mon. & Tues. in Aug., www.northantrim.com/thelammasfair) are yellowman and dulse. Yellowman is basically that brittle fairground toffee known as honeycomb, with a dash of vinegar to give it some bite. In his classic ballad "The Ould Lammas Fair," John Henry MacAuley is overcome with nostalgia as he recalls: "The scene that haunts my memory is kissing Mary Ann / Her pouting lips all sticky from eating Yellow Man," a rather charming image.

Another long tradition in Ireland is savoring the beautiful crimson seaweed Palmaria palmata ("dulse" or "dilisk"

to locals, creathnach or duileasc to Irish speakers)—not in its leathery shoreline state but after it has been thoroughly dried. Apart from its crunchy texture and salty, slightly citrus taste, it has a reputation for expelling parasite worms, guarding against "women's longing," and curing hangovers while giving a relish to the taste of beer—all useful properties at the Ould Lammas Fair.

Other Irish delicacies worth trying are colcannon (potato, onion, and cabbage), boxty (griddled potato cakes), champ (potatoes, chives, spring onion), soda bread, farls (Northern Ireland's fabulous flatbread), porter cake (fruitcake with stout), and barm brack (fruit bread).

Glenariff Forest Park

- 🗺 277 E4
- ✉ On A43 Ballymena–Waterfoot Rd.
- ☎ 028 2955 6000
- 💲 $

northeast as they bend and wriggle through limestone, sandstone, and basalt to the coast. There is something magical in their quiet depths, all well grown with woodlands, and in the moorland and bare rock that rims them.

The glens are a very popular visitor destination, but few visitors leave their cars. If you set out to explore these delectable valleys on foot, you should have the landscape more or less to yourself.

Glenarm & Glencloy: Glenarm and Glencloy reach the sea at **Carnlough Bay,** from where the coast road curls on at the feet of the cliffs around **Garron Point.** Here the limestone hands over to dusky red sandstone as the cave-burrowed cliffs shoot up some 800 feet (250 m).

Glenariff: Around the corner from Garron Point begins the

most striking section of the Antrim coast as the coastal plain flattens into a green apron of land 3 miles (5 km) long. Glenariff, Glenballyeamon, and Glenaan converge here, their mouths separated by the dominant flat-topped 1,153-foot (350 m) prow of Lurigethan.

Turn left inland from the coast village of **Waterfoot** on the aptly named **Red Bay,** its shore stained with the iron ore mined in Glenariff until the turn of the 20th century. Continue up Glenariff, widest and grandest of the glens, under dark granite slabs, over which waterfalls pour after heavy rain.

Glenariff Forest Park is signposted high up the glen. You can enjoy a number of short nature trails, a medium-size scenic trail, and the 3-mile (5 km) **Waterfall Trail** around some of Glenariff's best falls.

Glenballyeamon to
Glendun: Back on Red Bay, the road continues to **Cushendall,** where the B14 leads up Glenbal- lyeamon. From Cushendall, a country road leads past the golf course over the hill of Cross Slieve, a short route to Cushen- dall's sister village of Cushendun at the foot of Glendun.

But if you bear inland with the A2, you can turn off in 1 mile (1.6 km) on a marked road to **Ossian's Grave.** Leave your car at the foot of the steep farm track that climbs to the monument; the reward for 10 or 15 minutes of upward walking is a wonderful view over glens, mountains, and coasts from Ossian's Grave. This is a 4,000-year-old horned cairn, a court grave, with pointed "horns" guarding its sacred enclosure; leg- end names it as the burial place of Fionn MacCumhaill's son, Ossian.

A side road climbs **Glenaan** to a junction of roads in wild moorland; bear right to return seaward down the beautiful wooded **Glendun.** You pass the triple-arched red sandstone viaduct by which Sir Charles Lanyon brought the main coast road over the Glendun River, and then **Craigogh Wood,** where an 18th-century Mass rock carries an incised Crucifixion scene.

Cushendun, just below, is a charming model village (now cared for by the National Trust) created for Lord Cushendun in the early 20th century by the visionary architect Clough Williams-Ellis. Its rugged cottages feature plenty of whitewash and slate as they peep out of the trees.

Ballycastle &
Rathlin Island
The A2 now takes off inland for a 10-mile (16 km) moorland run to Ballycastle. A much more enjoyable alternative, however, is the rough, bumpy coast road *(signed "Scenic Route"),* which snakes and switchbacks through a high, rolling coastland of farms and sloping fields by way of **Torr Head** (a parking area here and wonderful sea views to add spice to a picnic lunch) to rejoin the A2 at Ballyvoy.

From here, it's a short run into **Ballycastle,** a handsome little seaside resort that comes alive at Lammastide, the last Monday and Tuesday of August. This is the date of **Ould Lammas Fair**

Carrick-a-Rede rope bridge

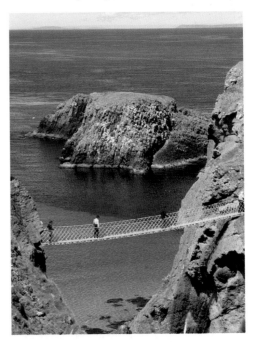

Ballycastle
⛺ 277 E5
Visitor Information
✉ 7 Mary St.,
 Ballycastle,
 Co. Antrim
☎ 028 2076 2024

Boathouse Centre
- 277 E5
- Rathlin Island Harbor
- 028 2076 2024
- Closed Sept.–April

Kebble Cliffs National Nature Reserve
- 277 E5
- W end of Rathin Island
- 028 2076 3948 (call ahead)

(see sidebar p. 300), held here for the last 400 years, when lovers of seaweed, shellfish, and yellowman toffee arrive for an orgy of tasting. The seaweed is dulse, picked off the rocks locally and dried—eaten au naturel or lightly toasted according to taste. Yellowman toffee, available throughout the town, is a bright yellow, very hard toffee that has to be broken up with a hammer.

From Ballycastle, a ferry leaves daily for **Rathlin Island,** a friendly and beautiful place that you certainly shouldn't miss. The L-shaped island, roughly 5 miles (8 km) from east to west and 3 miles (5 km) from north to south, is home to about 70 islanders who rely on tourism, farming, and fishing—in that order—for their survival. Chief attraction is the **Kebble Cliffs National Nature Reserve** out at the west end of the island, where 250,000 seabirds—fulmars, kittiwakes, puffins, razorbills, guillemots—whirl and shriek during the April to July nesting season. At the harbor village, there's a pub, and an excellent island museum in the **Boathouse Centre.**

Carrick-a-Rede Rope Bridge

Located near Ballintoy, the **Carrick-a-Rede rope bridge** is a scary cat's cradle of ropes and planking slung each salmon-fishing season by local fishermen between the mainland cliffs and a huge offshore rock—almost an island. The rock stands right in the path of salmon on their spawning run, forcing them to divert course into the nets cunningly set by the fishermen. The 60-foot (20 m) bridge, administered by the National Trust, is a great visitor attraction. Although it sways, bucks, and lurches as you walk 80 feet (25 m) above the sea, it's quite safe.

Giant's Causeway

Seven miles (11 km) beyond Carrick-a-Rede, and very well signposted, lies Northern Ireland's most celebrated tourist site, the Giant's Causeway,

The hexagonal columns of the Giant's Causeway

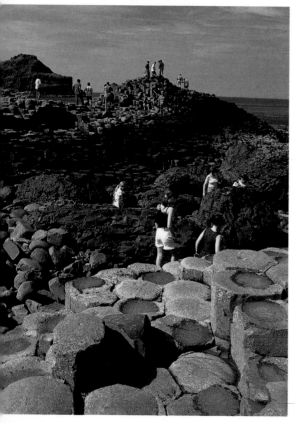

The Old Bushmills Distillery

Just inland of the Giant's Causeway is the village of Bushmills, where Northern Ireland's finest whiskey is made at the Old Bushmills Distillery *(2 Distillery Rd., Bushmills, Co. Antrim, tel 028 2073 1521, www.bushmills.com)*. Bushmills is the world's oldest licensed distillery, first operating in 1608. Take a tour and view the gleaming copper stills and quaking brew in the giant mash tuns. The delightful warehouse is full of the sweet fragrance of the "angels' share"—whiskey vapor evaporating from the seams of the piled wooden butts. You get a sample or two and the chance to buy a bottle of blended or single-malt Bushmills.

37,000 hexagonal columns of cooled basalt, formed from lava after a volcanic eruption some 60 million years ago. The cooled lava flow can be seen in the form of dark columns remarkably like closely stacked pencils, up to 40 feet (12 m) high, in the face of the 300-foot (92 m) cliffs. Victorian guides named the most striking of these formations the Giant's Organ Pipes, a very apt title. The giant was—who else?—the mighty Fionn MacCumhaill, and the best known part of the lava flow, the long shelf of tessellated columns that noses into the sea, is the causeway he laid down to reach his girlfriend on the Hebridean island of Staffa.

The mythology and geology of the Giant's Causeway is explained in the **visitor center** *(tel 028 2073 1855)* on the cliffs above. From here you can take a road train down to the causeway, or you can stroll down in 10 minutes. Walkers can continue from the causeway to the Organ Pipes, then turn back to the visitor center along a cliff path with excellent views down onto the causeway and back along the spectacular basalt cliffs.

Dunluce Castle

Before reaching the resort of Portrush and the border with County Londonderry, turn for one of Ireland's most evocative sights: the extensive ruins of Dunluce Castle perched on the edge of the cliffs in a wonderfully romantic setting. In 1584, its gallant and bloody-handed

INSIDER TIP:

The Giant's Causeway is one of only a handful of geological formations of its kind in the world—another is directly across the sea in Scotland.

—JIM FEENEY
National Geographic contributor

owner, Sorley Boy MacDonnell, recaptured the castle from the English in a fantastically daring attack. MacDonnell later fortified it with cannon from the wreck of the Spanish Armada galleon *Girona* (see p. 285). In 1639, the castle kitchens fell into the sea during a storm. Dunluce was abandoned and left in ruin. ■

Carrick-a-Rede Rope Bridge
- 🅰 277 E5
- ✉ 5 miles (8 km) W of Ballycastle off B15
- ☎ 028 2076 9839
- 🕐 Closed Nov.–Feb.
- 💲 $

Dunluce Castle
- 🅰 277 D5
- ✉ Port Ballintree, on the A2, 3 miles (4.8 km) E of Portrush
- ☎ 028 2073 1938
- 💲 $

County Londonderry

County Londonderry (or Derry) forms the northwestern segment of Northern Ireland. A stretch of coast less dramatic than that of neighboring Antrim, but with its own charm, leads along the east and south shore of Lough Foyle to Londonderry city. Inland, the Sperrin Mountains spill over the border from County Tyrone, and a great stretch of hilly, forested country rises above the farmlands along Londonderry's eastern boundary of the River Bann.

Londonderry's superbly preserved 17th-century city walls offer memorable views over the city.

Londonderry City

🗺 276 C4

Visitor Information

✉ 44 Foyle St.,
Londonderry,
Co. Londonderry

☎ 028 7126 7284

**www.derrycity
.gov.uk**

Londonderry City

Generally, you will hear the city called Londonderry if the speaker is a Protestant or a mainland Briton, Derry if the speaker is a Catholic and/or a nationalist. Londonderry, or Derry, is Northern Ireland's "second city" after Belfast—a vibrant, lively, small city, very conscious of its past as a springboard to its future.

Maybe it's the more rural surroundings that make Londonderry conversation and humor seem lighter and less caustic than their Belfast counterparts. Or maybe it's just

the effect of being a very small city that has moved on a long way from the dark days of the 1960s and early '70s. Whatever the cause, Londonderry breathes a most attractive energy and optimism. This is a great place to spend a day or two, and the locals are only too happy to bend your ear or lend an ear—whichever you choose.

History of the City: Londonderry, meaning the "Place of the Oaks," stands on the River Foyle at the point where the river begins to widen into the sea outlet of Lough Foyle, a prime location for trade and defense. In 1613–18, at the start of the plantation of Ulster with Protestant outsiders (see p. 26), the London trade guilds that had taken over Londonderry built a tight lozenge of defensive walls around the heart of the city. The walls had their most testing trial toward the end of that century when, in April 1689, the deposed Catholic king of Britain, King James II, laid siege to the town. Londonderry had in fact been in a state of siege since the previous December, when 13 apprentice boys had locked the city gates against the Jacobite army. By the time the siege was broken in July 1689, 7,000 of the 30,000 defenders lay dead of disease, wounds, and starvation.

The Great Siege fueled centuries of provocation and bitterness. These flared in the 1960s as the city's Catholic majority, resentful of their lack of civil rights, found no redress from a city council dominated by supremacist Protestants. Bloody Sunday 1972 (see p. 287), when British paratroopers shot dead 13 civil rights marchers, was a Londonderry tragedy. Levels of violence soared, especially in the hard-line extramural Catholic ghetto of the Bogside (see sidebar p. 34). At one point, three-quarters of all buildings outside the walls had been damaged or destroyed by fire, bombs, or neglect.

City Sights: You'll be hard put to recognize any sign of past miseries in today's Londonderry. The bars along **Waterloo**

Street, just outside the walls to the west, are thronged at night. The **Craft Village** (tel 028 7126 0329), inside the northern angle of the walls, is flourishing, with craft workshops, eateries, wine bars, and cafés around little paved squares.

Touring Londonderry

Get to know the city from a new perspective by joining one of the many guided tours available to visitors. If you are interested in learning more about the city's nationalist Bogside neighborhood or its fierce and funny sociological murals, try **Irish Tour Guides** (tel 028 7127 1996, www .irishtourguides.com) or **Michael Cooper** (tel 028 7136 1311, www.derrybluebadgeguide .com), the only Blue Badge tourist guide in Derry. Based in the Bogside, **Free Derry Tours** (tel 028 7126 2812, www.freederry.net) offers political walking tours that include the city's famous walls and St. Columb's Cathedral, while **Tours and Trails** (tel 028 7136 7000, www.toursntrails.co.uk) leads a walk along the walls that includes stories, songs, and even sweets!

There are exhibitions of Irish music and dance every summer weekday lunchtime in the thatched **Bridie's Cottage** (tel 028 7126 9033) here—not quite an authentic *ceilidh* house (see p. 389) but a sign of budding social life in the city.

The town's splendid 1890 **Guildhall,** built in local red sandstone under a monstrous clock tower, has the 1689 Siege of Derry depicted vividly in its stained-glass windows, and more stained glass in its Council Chamber and Main Hall.

The **Tower Museum,** in Union (continued on p. 308)

Guildhall
- Guildhall Sq., Londonderry
- 028 7137 7335
- Closed Sat. & Sun.

The Orange & the Green

Every July 12, the city streets and country lanes of Northern Ireland resound with the thump of Lambeg drums (marching drums with a painted skin) and the squeal of flutes as the Orange Order men go marching. For outsiders, it can be hard to understand the passionate commitment that these sober-faced, bowler-hatted Protestants in their orange sashes feel for this ritual and the bitter resentment it provokes in Catholic onlookers.

Orangemen on the march, the very picture of Unionist pride and defiance

A Source of Conflict

At Drumcree on the outskirts of Portadown, County Armagh, the July 12 marches have caused enormous anger and some bloodshed in recent years—so much so that successive Drumcree marches have been banned by the Parades Commission set up to control such explosive situations. Other venues across the province have been flashpoints for trouble, too.

If you ask an Orangeman, he will tell you that he is marching for two reasons. The first is to commemorate the victory of Protestant King William III over the deposed Roman Catholic King James II at the Battle of the Boyne on July 12, 1690. The second reason is

to uphold Protestant tradition. If a nationalist Catholic gives an opinion, it will be that the Orange marches are a show of triumphalism, a reinforcement of the traditional Protestant upper hand. There is truth in both assertions.

History of the Orange Order

The Orange Order was formed in September 1795 after a Protestant vigilante group, the Peep O'Day Boys, repulsed a raid made by the Defenders, a Catholic group, on Dan Winter's farm at Loughgall in County Armagh. An Orange Order museum has now been established at the house (see sidebar opposite). The July 12 march first took place the following year, 1796, and has continued as a Protestant tradition ever since.

Plenty of salt has been rubbed in Catholic wounds along the way, especially with the making of offensive gestures during the march and the playing of inflammatory sectarian tunes as the marchers pass through predominantly Catholic areas. Yet most Protestants in Northern Ireland deplore such provocation and are greatly distressed at the image the outside world has of them as insensitive supremacists.

The other side of the coin, on St. Patrick's Day

Marches in Londonderry

Other Orange marches have been used to taunt Catholics, too, particularly the parades held around the walls of Londonderry on the Saturday nearest August 12 (the anniversary of the 1689 relief of the Great Siege; see p. 305) and the Saturday nearest December 18 (the date of the locking of the city gates by the 13 apprentice boys in 1688; see p. 305). Overlooking the Catholic enclave of Bogside, these marches symbolized the Orangemen's possession of the political and economic, as well as the physical, high ground. But with the recent hope of better interdenominational relations, the Derry Walls parades have dwindled in size and contentiousness.

Catholic Reaction

The Ancient Order of Hibernians, a Catholic organization, was founded in 1838, although it has its origins way back in Tudor times. The green-sashed members of the order continue to mount two of their own marches each year—on St. Patrick's Day, March 17, and on the Feast of the Assumption, or Lady's Day, August 15. But these marches are lower-key affairs than their Orange Order counterparts, more rural and more church-based, and provoke little or no aggression and bad feeling.

Partisan Museums

Although the violence associated with the Troubles has largely subsided, the historic division between the Orange and the Green has woven itself into the fabric of everyday life in Northern Ireland. Two museums offer interesting, if highly partisan, views of the region's fraught and divisive history.

The site of a raid by a Catholic group in September 1795 (see p. 306), **Dan Winter's Cottage** (*The Diamond, Loughgall, Co. Armagh, tel 028 3885 1344, weekends by arrangement, www.danwinterscottage.co.uk*) opened to the public as a museum in 2000. Here, you can learn about the raid, dubbed the Battle of the Diamond, and the events surrounding the foundation of the Orange Order. You can also experience traditional crafts such as spinning and weaving. The cottage's loom, which is about 200 years old, has been restored and is in full working order.

Imprisoned in Armagh Gaol from 1973 to 1977, Eileen Hickey died before realizing her dream of a museum dedicated to Irish republican history. The **Eileen Hickey Museum** (*Conway Mill Complex, Conway St., Belfast, tel 028 9024 0504, www.eileenhickeymuseum.com*), opened in 2007, houses a collection of artifacts and handicrafts from the time of the Troubles. Objects include republican posters and paintings, a bed from Armagh Gaol, and historic articles and papers

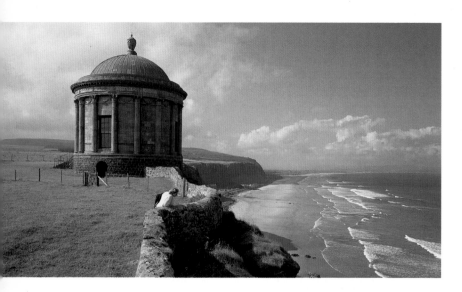

Frederick Hervey, Bishop of Londonderry, built Mussenden Temple on the cliffs at Downhill.

Tower Museum

✉ Union Hall Pl., Londonderry, Co. Londonderry

☎ 028 7137 2411

🕐 Call for opening times

www.derrycity.gov.uk

St. Columb's Cathedral

✉ London St., Londonderry, Co. Londonderry

☎ 028 7126 7313

🕐 Worshipers only on Sun.

www.stcolumbs cathedral.org

Hall Place inside the walls, built in the 1970s, gives a balanced history of Londonderry. The displays start with prehistoric times and continue through a series of brick-lined tunnels, replicas of those built under the city after the seige. You learn of 17th-century prosperity, 18th-century industrialization, and the Home Rule movement of Victorian times. Last comes an exploration of the Troubles.

Walking the Walls: By far the best way to appreciate Londonderry is to walk the **Walls of Derry** *(tel 028 7126 7284),* starting the 1-mile (1.6 km) circuit from the Tower Museum. Looking outward, you'll see the slogan-painted Bogside, poor Protestant estates, new shopping areas, and a gorgeous view of the surrounding hills. Inward are shiny new shops and restaurants and regenerated

housing. Make time to look into **St. Columb's Cathedral** inside Bishop's Gate, a shrine to the Great Siege and to Protestant nostalgia.

Downhill Demesne & Mussenden Temple

Five miles (8 km) west of Coleraine via the A2, on the northern Antrim border, a strange collection of buildings stands on the cliffs above the golfing resort of Castlerock. This is **Downhill Demesne,** an estate that once belonged to Frederick Hervey, 4th Earl of Bristol and Protestant Bishop of Londonderry. Erected on the cliffs in the 1780s, Downhill was built with a vast gallery to accommodate Hervey's art collection.

You can wander the sprawling ruins of the castle and its walled garden complete with icehouse and dovecote. Then stroll to the cliff edge to view the domed **Mussenden Temple** (1783–85), built by Hervey—some say for one of his mistresses.

If you like flat, lonely, wind-swept coastal scenery, carry on west from Downhill to where the shark's-nose peninsula of **Magilligan Point** almost closes Lough Foyle—only a mile (1.6 km) of water separates it from the Inishowen shore in County Donegal. Side roads will give you access to this flat, fertile curve of coast, much of it reclaimed from the sea for agriculture.

Limavady

Inland and due south of Magilligan Point sits **Limavady,** a neat little Georgian town on the River Roe—"roe" means red, and the river does run a dusky crimson-brown. You can see it at its most spectacular just south of Limavady in the **Roe Valley Country Park** (tel 028 7772 2074), a 3-mile (5 km) stretch of gorge and valley. Preserved remnants of Londonderry's prosperous linenmaking industry are scattered along the park—scutch mills where the flax fibers were separated for weaving, bleaching meadows in which the coarse woven cloth was spread to dry, and beetling mills where water-powered wooden hammers beat the linen to flatten and smooth it.

South to Maghera

The B68 leads south from Roe Valley Country Park to **Dungiven.** Just south of the town, off the A6 Maghera road,

the impressive ruins of the early 12th-century Augustinian **Dungiven Priory** perch on a bluff above the River Roe. In the church, you'll find one of the best tombs in Ireland—that of "Cooey of the Foreigners," Cooey-na-Gal O'Cahan (died 1385), who lies ready for battle in his armor, guarded by carvings of six soldiers in kilts—"gallowglasses," or mercenaries, from Scotland, whose hire gave Cooey his nickname.

The A6 leads southeast to **Maghera,** where you can head north for 2 miles (3 km) on the A29 before turning left on the Grillagh road. In 1.5 miles (2.5 km), bear left after Rockfield Farm on a track to a parking lot, the entrance to **Drumlamph Wood.** This is one of Northern Ireland's few remaining pieces of ancient woodland—45 acres (18 ha) of hazel and oak, rustling with red squirrels, where walkways lead through a mosaic of bog, river, and rushy pasture. ■

Downhill Demesne & Mussenden Temple

▲ 277 D5

✉ Mussenden Rd., Castlerock, Co. Londonderry

☎ 028 2073 1582

🕑 Temple closed Oct.–April, & weekdays May–June & September

Limavady

▲ 277 D4

Visitor Information

✉ 7 Connell St., Limavady, Co. Londonderry

☎ 028 7776 0307

www.limavady.org

Bellaghy Bawn

Lovers of poetry should continue from Maghera, via the A42 and the B182, to Bellaghy. There, the fortified farmhouse of Bellaghy Bawn (Castle St., Bellaghy, Co. Londonderry, tel 028 7938 6812, closed Sun., Oct.–Easter, $), built in 1613, contains a display on the life and work of Seamus Heaney, Ireland's greatest living poet and the recipient of the 1995 Nobel Prize for Poetry. Born in 1939, Heaney grew up at nearby Mossbawn Farm. At Bellaghy Bawn, you can see first editions and manuscripts of Heaney's work.

EXPERIENCE: Visiting Seamus Heaney Country

It is quite remarkable how many poets such a small island has produced—and continues to produce. For lovers of Irish literature, exploring Seamus Heaney country is a must. Heaney, who won the Nobel Prize for Literature in 1995, is Ireland's most celebrated and widely read living poet. You can visit the places that inspired his works, attend creative writing classes at the Seamus Heaney Centre for Poetry in Belfast, or maybe even meet the great man himself.

Laurel Villa

Laurel Villa Townhouse

(60 Church St., Magherafelt, Co. Derry, tel 028 7930 1459, www .laurel-villa.com; see also p. 377), a bed-and-breakfast on the outskirts of Magherafelt, is a mecca for poetry lovers in the heart of Seamus Heaney country. You'll notice the photographs and paintings lining the walls: James Joyce, Samuel Beckett, Seamus Heaney. There are poems printed on linen, first editions in glass cases. Upstairs you pass the bedroom doors: the Kavanagh Room, the MacNeice Room, the Heaney Room. Laurel Villa is a genuine house of poetry.

Proprietor Gerardine Kielt keeps things immaculate and cooks quite wonderful breakfasts, too. Her husband, Eugene, organizes poetry readings at Laurel Villa and maintains contact with poets far and wide—including Seamus Heaney himself.

Heaney, a local boy born on a farm a few miles from Magherafelt, has a great admiration for the Kielts' love and respect for poetry and has himself come to the unassuming Magherafelt house to give a reading of his poetry in front of an audience of 50. Although Seamus Heaney may not be on the menu in person when you visit, you can be sure of a rich and varied program of readings by poets from across Ireland, and sometimes beyond.

INSIDER TIP:

It's not only about poetry in Seamus Heaney country. Just a 10-minute drive from Laurel Villa is the River Bann [*www.riverbann ireland.com*], one of the best coarse fishing rivers in Europe.

—STEPHANIE ROBICHAUX
National Geographic contributor

Guided Tours

Readings are not the only poetical happenings associated with Laurel Villa. Eugene Kielt also offers guided tours around Seamus Heaney country, taking visitors to places that inspired the Nobel Prize winner and that feature in some of his best known poems. Along with Heaney's Bellaghy Bawn (see sidebar p. 309), these locations include **Barney Devlin's** **forge** at the Hillhead near Magherafelt ("The Forge"), the **old railway** cutting in the townland of Broagh ("The Railway Children"), **Church Island** on the shores of Lough Beg ("The Strand at Lough Beg," Heaney's eulogy for his second cousin, Colm McCartney, murdered by sectarian killers in 1975), **Anahorish,** where Heaney went to school ("Testimony"), and the graveyard where the poet's brother, Christopher Heaney, lies buried near Colm McCartney. Tours are of variable length, depending on the interest of those taking part. Transportation and copies of poems are included. Group rates can be negotiated.

Seamus Heaney Summer School

Every July, the **Seamus Heaney Centre for Poetry** (*www.qub.ac.uk/schools/ SeamusHeaneyCentreforPoetry*) at Queen's University in Belfast (see p. 284) holds a week-long summer school session meant to foster interest in creative writing and contemporary literature. The program typically includes lectures and workshops with leading poets and authors, a tour of Belfast, readings, and a concert. Check the website for application procedures.

Ulster-American Folk Park

South across the Londonderry border in County Tyrone, this admirable collection of buildings gives an authentic flavor of life in bygone rural Ulster, while exploring the poverty and insecurity of tenure that forced families to emigrate. Another area of the park shows the kinds of houses that emigrants built for themselves in America and the life they took up there.

History brought to life: Authentic costumes and props help re-create scenes from Irish history.

Thomas Mellon was five years old when he emigrated with his family from the simple house at Camphill, just north of Omagh, around which the Ulster-American Folk Park has grown since its inauguration in 1976. The young emigrant grew up to be Judge Thomas Mellon, whose son, Andrew, founded the steel industry in Pittsburgh. His descendants wanted to create a memorial to him, and to millions like him, forced from their native land by poverty and lack of opportunity.

The main benefactor, Dr. Matthew T. Mellon, flew over for the opening of the park's visitor center in 1980. He delighted everyone by recounting the tales he had heard his great-grandfather, Judge Thomas Mellon, tell of the Atlantic crossing he made in 1818, a dreadful three-month voyage.

Old World Collection

The **Mellon house** is typical of 19th-century peasant dwellings—dark and low with smoke-pickled yellow walls and creaky wooden beds, smelling of turf smoke and damp. Women in period costume bake and offer bread; ducks and hens quack and cluck around the door. It's a good introduction to this bucolic way of life, though the brisk waft of sanitization remains. An earlier house, of the kind lived in by most peasants in

Ulster-American Folk Park

- 🅰 276 C3
- ✉ 2 Mellon Rd., Castletown, Omagh, Co. Tyrone
- ☎ 028 8224 3292
- 🕐 Closed Oct.–Easter
- 💲 $$

www.nmni.com/uafp

the 18th century, is a single-room cabin into which parents and their children would have crammed.

Most of the buildings of the Old World collection were rescued from demolition and brought here. There's a dark, cobwebby **blacksmith's forge,** piled with bricks of turf, and a **weaver's cottage,** where a costumed spinner sits outside the door, busy at her wheel. Inside is one of the big looms that made possible the cottage weaving

that sustained Ulster's linen industry until industrialization.

Nearby is the **Hughes house,** birthplace of John Joseph Hughes, who emigrated in 1817 as a child. Hughes rose to become the first Catholic Archbishop of New York, and he founded St. Patrick's Cathedral there in 1858.

The **National School from Castletown** is a great favorite with visiting school parties. Lessons are put on twice a day under the "firm but fair" schoolmarm, who instructs the children as they sit at cramped wooden desks.

Cunningham Springhouse

Springhouse

Western Pennsylvania Log House

Smokehouse

Corncrib (hidden)

Log Cabin

Samuel Fulton Stone House

Herb Garden

Pennsylvania Log Farmhouse

Pennsylvania Log Barn

Ship and Dockside Gallery

American Street

Ulster Street

Mountjoy Post Office

Schoolhouse

Ulster-American Folk Park

A complete 19th-century **street** has been created from small-town premises all over Ulster—the little Mountjoy post office, a saddler's shop, a printer and stationer, Devlin the pawnbroker, Murray the draper, Hill the chemist (drugstore), and a pub brought from Newtownbutler.

The street leads to a dark and gloomy dockside with a ticket office, where at a cobbled quay hosts a full-size reproduction of the central section of an **emigrant sailing ship.** You pass down a gangway into the ship's hold, with its low beams, tables, and wooden box berths 4 feet (1.2 m) wide and 5 feet (1.5 m) long into which a whole family would have squeezed.

A mockup of a **New World dockside,** with tumbledown houses advertising "Cheap Logins" and plenty of cheats and sharpers ready to exploit the exhausted emigrants, reinforces a sense of the struggle most of them had when they did get to the other side.

New World Collection

The New World collection shows the kinds of log cabin built by those emigrant settlers who tried their luck in the huge open spaces of the Midwest. ∎

Hughes House

Tullyallen Field

Tullyallen Mass House

Mellon Homestead

Viewpoint

Cambell House

Blacksmith's Forge

Weaver's Cottage

Single-Room Cabin

Presbyterian Meeting House

Vestry

Drive: Sperrin Mountains

The Sperrin Mountains are wild, lonely, and beautiful. They rise in a series of waves on the Tyrone/Londonderry border, seamed with the parallel east–west valleys of the Owen-killew and Glenelly Rivers. Settlements are tiny, views far and wide. This is the haunt of birds of prey, mountain hares, and the occasional hiker.

The rolling landscape of County Tyrone's beautifully untamed Sperrin Mountains

From Omagh, take the B48 north toward Gortin. In 6 miles (10 km), the road enters Gortin Glen between heavily wooded slopes. A 5-mile (8 km) track along the marked scenic drive of the **Gortin Glen Forest Park** ❶ *(tel 028 8167 0666)* takes you to beautiful corners of this coniferous forest.

There are splendid views ahead as the B48 dips into **Gortin** ❷, a small village at the foot of the **Owenkillew Valley**. The **Badoney Tavern** is a walkers' hangout, and the owners can answer your questions about the locality.

From Gortin, take the B46 eastward for 4 miles (6 km); a mile (1.6 km) beyond Drum-lea Bridge, bear left on a twisty mountain road along the south side of the valley. In 4.5 miles (7 km), at Monanameal, the road bends right for Greencastle; keep straight instead. After a mile (1.6 km), you'll pass a field on your left with two ancient stones; one is a fine standing stone, the other a pillar known as the **Aghascrebagh Ogham Stone** ❸, with an inscription at least

NOT TO BE MISSED:

Gortin Glen Forest Park • Aghascre-bagh Ogham Stone • Views from Barnes Gap • Sperrin Heritage Centre

1,500 years old in the ancient Irish writing called Ogham—the only specimen in County Tyrone.

At Crouck Bridge, 10 miles (16 km) from Gortin, bear left and left again to return up the Owenkillew Valley on the north side of the river. In 6 miles (11 km), bear right at Scotch Town on a road through the spectacular viewpoint of **Barnes Gap** ❹, with fabulous views ahead across the Glenelly Valley to the highest Sperrin peaks—**Sawel Mountain** (2,225 feet/678 m) to the right, with its satellite **Dart Mountain** (2,030 feet/619 m), and straight ahead, the bulge of **Mullaghclogha** (2,080 feet/635 m).

Down in **Glenelly Valley,** turn right onto the road that keeps to the south side of the valley.

EXPERIENCE:
Walking the Sperrins

County Tyrone boasts one of the most beautiful hill ranges in Ireland, the Sperrins. To get the best out of them, consult **Martin McGuigan** *(137 Don-aghanie Rd., Omagh, Co. Tyrone, tel 028 8075 8452, www.walkwithmarty.com).* A local man born and bred, McGuigan is a mountaineer and hill walker who knows the Sperrins like the back of his hand and delights in leading strangers through their wild landscape.

See area map pp. 276–277
Omagh
70 miles (112 km)
Half a day
Omagh

In 3.5 miles (5.5 km), turn left to descend and cross the river at Oughtboy Bridge. Bear right on the B47 along the north side of the valley.

In 1 mile (1.6 km), you'll pass the **Sperrin Heritage Centre** ⑤ *(tel 028 8164 8142, closed Nov.–Easter, $)*, where the staff will fill you in on the folklore, wildlife, and geological history of these hills. In another 1.5 miles (2.5 km), turn left at Sperrin village and cross the moorland

heart of the hills on a road that takes you right under the eastern flank of Sawel Mountain.

On the far side of the hills, the mountain road descends to meet the B44 at Park. Just before the B44, bear sharply left to return over the Sperrins into the Glenelly Valley. At Cranagh, turn right along the B47 for the lovely 7-mile (11 km) run to Plumbridge, from where the B48 returns you to Gortin and Omagh.

An Creagan & the Tyrone Bogland

To the south of the Sperrin Mountains, the waist of County Tyrone wears a thick belt of blanket bog—a peat bog mostly composed of dead grasses and dependent on high rainfall. Hauntingly beautiful, it hides a marvelous archaeological treasure—a vast Stone Age and Bronze Age landscape only now beginning to emerge.

The mysterious stone circles and avenue at Beaghmore

An Creagan
🅰 277 D3

Start your trip around the blanket bogs of Tyrone at **An Creagan Visitor Centre** *(tel 028 8076 1112)*, on the A505 road, midway between Omagh and Cookstown. The center gives an excellent overview of the area—its culture and traditions, the bogs themselves, the way they were formed, their great variety of wildlife, and the rare archaeological landscape that surrounds An Creagan. You can also get a meal here and pick up pamphlets that will direct you to the best sites within a 5-mile (8 km) radius of the center,

some reachable on foot and others by recommended cycling routes. To rent bikes, inquire at the Omagh visitor information office *(tel 028 8224 7831)*.

History of the Bogs

The blanket bogs began to develop during a cold and wet climatic phase around 1000 B.C. They crept in on a partly wooded landscape of birch, oak, hazel, and alder, much of it already cleared for farming thousands of years before. Stone Age farmers had erected standing stones, field walls, wedge tombs, and court tombs, and the Bronze Age people who followed them circa 2000 B.C. added stone circles, cist cairns, and artificial crannog islets in the bog lakes. The bog smothered all these and a moody landscape came into being: heathery and grassy bog and oily pools undulating to the horizon.

Farming ceased until dispossessed Catholics were forced to make the best of the boglands during the 18th and 19th centuries. Their attempts to cultivate the peat can be seen in the ruins of lime kilns and telltale ridges of earth beneath which potatoes were stored. The bog turf proved more useful for fuel, and turf cutters unearthed treasures like the Beaghmore Stone Circles.

Beaghmore

Beaghmore is the best known of the Tyrone archaeological sites, lying northeast of the center. The site contains an extraordinary number of stone alignments set up between 2000 and 1200 B.C.—three pairs of circles formed of stones varying from craggy chest-high boulders to prone chunks of rock, one solo circle filled with more than 800 little stone lumps, a dozen or so round cairns, and several stone rows running off to various unfathomable destinations.

Around An Creagan

Due north of An Creagan lies **Peadar Joe Haughey's Cottage,** the restored home of one of Tyrone's last native Gaelic speakers and the large patch of

raised bog known as the **Black Bog.** Much deeper than the surrounding blanket bog, it formed over the remains of a deep lake. North again is **Dun Ruadh,** the Red Fort, a horseshoe-shaped cairn in which Bronze Age people buried 13 of their number.

South of the A505 lie several sites, pride of which are three remarkable tombs. Most westerly is **Loughmacrory wedge tomb,** built around 2000 B.C. with great capstones perched on curbstones. Southeast of An Creagan Visitor Centre, overlooking lonely Lough Mallon, **Creggandevesky court tomb** predates Loughmacross

INSIDER TIP:

The bar at the An Creagan Visitor Centre [*www.an-creagan .com*] features live traditional Irish music every weekend.

—MEREDITH WILCOX
National Geographic Books

by at least 1,500 years and is one of Ireland's finest examples of its type. About 60 feet (18 m) long and composed of tons of tiny stones, it has three chambers. The burned bones of 21 people were excavated here.

Two miles (3 km) east, up a gravelly lane beyond a farmhouse, lies **Cregganconroe court tomb.** A giant capstone stands tilted to the sky among its curbstones and the remains of two sizable galleries and two small side chambers. ■

Beaghmore
🄼 277 D3

Peader Joe Haughey's Cottage
🄼 277 D3

Dun Ruadh
🄼 277 D3

Loughmacrory wedge tomb
🄼 276 C3

Creggandevesky court tomb
🄼 277 D3

Cregganconroe court tomb
🄼 277 D3

County Fermanagh

According to legend, the whole of County Fermanagh used to be dry plain. At its center was a well that the locals kept covered for fear that fairies had cursed it. One day, a girl and her lover happened by. Feeling thirsty, they took a drink from the well but forgot to replace the lid. Next dawn, as the rising sun hit the well, the water overflowed and would not stop. Soon much of Fermanagh was filled with water, and that's how things still stand today.

Belleek
🅐 276 A2

Belleek Pottery
✉ Belleek, Co. Fermanagh
☎ 028 0865 8501
🕐 Closed weekends Nov.–March
💲 $$
www.belleek.ie

Almost all the water in the county belongs to the great twin lake system known as **Lower** and **Upper Lough Erne.** Together, the two lakes stretch for some 50 miles (80 km), hinged together by the isthmus on which stands Fermanagh's county town of Enniskillen. Lower Lough Erne is one mighty sheet of water, while Upper Lough Erne is more like a complicated system of small rivers

winding around tiny islands, peninsulas, and headlands.

From here, via the Ballynamore and Ballyconnell Canal (renamed the Shannon-Erne Waterway; see p. 231), it is possible to cruise all the way south to the Shannon Estuary. As for the two lakes themselves, providing cruising and fishing for visitors is their economic lifeblood.

Belleek

At the westernmost end of the Lower Lough sits Belleek (Beleek), a lively village right on the border between County Fermanagh in Northern Ireland and County Donegal in the Republic. Belleek is a pretty place, with cast-iron street furniture and renovated wooden shop fronts. Its claim to fame is the glittering white parian ware that has been turned out since the 1850s by **Belleek Pottery.**

A tour around the factory shows you the process, in which a mixture of Cornish china clay and glass is beaten with wooden paddles to squeeze out air bubbles. Then, craftsmen shape the mixture into various forms—basketware is the most popular—before decorating them, perhaps with minute birds or flowers. The craftsmen tend to use homemade tools; they say a humble 5-inch

Nothing but the finest craftsmanship at Belleek Pottery

EXPERIENCE: Fishing in Ireland

Ireland is justly famed for its fishing. Atlantic waters, warmed by the Gulf Stream, yield a variety of marine fish species, from Mediterranean to North Atlantic, while the abundant lakes and brisk, highly oxygenated rivers give great trout and coarse fishing.

Information on regulations and fishing sites in Northern Ireland can be found at *www.dcal-fishingni.gov.uk*. South of the border, the **Central Fisheries Board** *(tel 01 884 2600, www.cfb.ie)* is a superb one-stop shop for anyone interested in fishing in Ireland, from coarse and sea fishing to pike, trout, and salmon. The board maintains a list of fishing tackle shops, guides and ghillies, and charter boats. Check the website for regulations and licenses, information on regional boards, maps, and announcements of festivals and one-time events.

(13 cm) nail with one end flattened is the key to success.

Naturally, you can buy examples of Belleek ware in the pottery showroom, though your pockets will need to be deep to afford the best basketware. Some pieces are decorated with lucky shamrocks, although it's doubtful whether these will bring you the kind of good fortune that attended one of the men who helped build the pottery. During construction, he slipped and fell from the roof to the ground but somehow landed on his feet, unharmed. He was given a stiff tot of whiskey and a pat on the back and sent straight back up to carry on with the job.

At Belleek, you can rent a cruiser for the Lower Lough and also visit the **ExplorErne Museum,** an excellent introduction to the world of the lakes.

South of Lower Lough Erne

A long ridge of hills crowned and collared by two big forests—Lough Navar Forest and Big Dog Forest—dominate the wide, hilly area south of Lower Lough Erne.

Lough Navar Forest is well set out for forest driving and for waymarked walking. Most paths and tracks seem to lead eventually to the big panoramic map at **Lough Navar Forest viewpoint,** right on the dramatic bluffs of the **Cliffs of Magho,** where you can see not only the islands and straggly peninsulas of Lower Lough Erne but also Benbulben in County Sligo, 25 miles (40 km) to the west, and the pale 2,467-foot (750 m) triangle of Mount Errigal rising northward, 40 miles (60 km) away in northwest Donegal.

Two fine castles from the early 17th-century plantation days stand to the south: Tully Castle, beside the lough shore, and Monea Castle, on a rocky bluff farther inland. **Tully Castle** was built around 1610 by the Scottish Hume family. In 1641, Roderick Maguire, whose Catholic clan had had all their Fermanagh land confiscated after Hugh O'Neill's disastrous 1601 rising (see p. 26), enthusiastically joined in a general rebellion and burned Tully. Its garrison perished, in spite of Maguire's assurances

ExplorErne Museum

✉ Erne Gateway Centre, Corry, Belleek, Co. Fermanagh

☎ 028 6865 8866

🕐 Closed Oct.–May

💲 $

Tully Castle

🅰 277 B2

✉ Derrygonnelly, on Enniskillen–Belleek road, Co. Fermanagh

☎ 028 6862 1588

🕐 Closed Mon.–Tues. & July–Aug.

of safe conduct to Enniskillen. The tall, gaunt ruins still have the turreted walls of their *bawn*, or defensive enclosure, and a delightful herb garden with a clipped hedge has been laid out in early 17th-century style.

Monea Castle, with its tall, baronial drum towers, looks as if it has been transported from the Scottish Highlands. It, too, was burned in 1641 and again by Jacobite troops in 1689 during their abortive attempts to take Enniskillen. After another fire in 1750, it was finally left to decay.

North of Lower Lough Erne

The north side of Lower Lough Erne possesses two fine forest parks, both with extensive shorelines. **Castle Caldwell Forest** *(tel 028 6632 3110),* 4 miles (6 km) east of Belleek, has beautiful walks along two long wooded lake peninsulas. There's excellent bird-watching here. By the lodge at the park entrance on the A47 is a **memorial stone,** shaped like an outsize violin, to Denis McCabe, a fiddle player who drowned on August 13, 1779, after falling off Sir James Caldwell's barge into the lough while drunk.

Castle Archdale Forest Park, halfway down the lough, has a herd of red deer, a marina where boats can be rented, and more walks.

Five miles (8 km) south, toward Enniskillen, it's worth turning aside into the village

Journey into the depths of the Earth—the wonders of Marble Arch Caves are viewed by boat.

Marble Arch Caves

The southern border of Fermanagh bulges into the panhandle of northwest County Cavan. Down here, south of lovely Lough Macnean Lower, the hills are riddled with caves.

In the northern flank of Cuilcagh Mountain, you can visit Marble Arch Caves (5 miles/8 km W of Florence Court,

off the A4 Enniskillen–Sligo road, tel 028 6634 8855, closed Oct.–mid-March, $$). The exciting tour—which starts with a boat ride along an underground river—ends with a walk among stalagmites, stalactites, and other weird calcite formations, an unforgettable experience not to be missed.

---

churchyard at Killadeas to look at the **Bishop's Stone.** This memorial stone, probably carved around the eighth century, commemorates an abbot with a profile portrait on one side. On the other side of the stone, a very pagan-looking face stares out fixedly. It is as if the carver was reflecting the contemporary changeover (or maybe the early Celtic church's live-and-let-live policy) between paganism and Christianity.

Enniskillen

Both the north and south routes along the shores of Lower Lough Erne converge at **Enniskillen,** on the narrow isthmus separating the lower from the upper lake. Fermanagh's chief town sits right at the heart of the county, socially and economically as well as geographically. There's an excellent tourist office here, several decent hotels, and all the main facilities of a sizable town. The straggling main street—which changes name six times in its mile-long (1.6 km) course—contains a gem of a watering hole in the unreconstructed Victorian pub known as **Blake's**

of the Hollow *(tel 028 6632 0918).* From the whiskey tuns and wood-paneled snugs to the excellent Guinness and frequent traditional music sessions, this is a treasure of a place.

Along the River Erne, you'll find **Enniskillen Castle,** with its handsome twin-towered water gate; a regimental museum here deals with the history of the Inniskilling Fusiliers, and a good heritage center covers Fermanagh history. You can buy local crafts in the converted Buttermarket and watch Fermanagh dealers and farmers in the lively cattle market.

The town's **war memorial** commemorating World Wars I and II, at the top of East Bridge Street, gained worldwide notoriety as the scene of the murder of 11 people by the IRA in a bomb explosion on Remembrance Day, November 11, 1987.

North of the memorial is Forthill Park, where **Cole's Monument** rises from the center of a star-shaped 17th-century fort. The fluted column, erected in 1857, honors Gen. Sir Galbraith Lowry Cole (1772–1842), brother of the 2nd Earl of Enniskillen and one of the Duke of Wellington's generals

Enniskillen
276 B2

Enniskillen Castle
✉ Castle Barracks, Enniskillen, Co. Fermanagh
☎ 028 6632 5000
🕐 Closed Sat.–Sun. Oct.–April; closed Sun. May–June & Sept.
💲 $
www.enniskillen castle.co.uk

The Tudor water gate of Enniskillen Castle, looking out over the River Erne

Crom Estate

🅰 276 C1

✉ 3 miles
(5 km) W of
Newtownbutler
off A34,
Co. Fermanagh

☎ 028 6773 8118

🕐 Closed Oct.–
mid-March

💲 $$

in the Napoleonic Wars. Climb the 108 spiral steps inside the column for a wonderful view over Enniskillen and Lough Erne.

Around Upper Lough Erne

South of Enniskillen the landscape explodes into a crazed maze of water and land as the River Erne wriggles through the countless windings and backwaters of Upper Lough Erne. **Derrylin** ("the friendliest place in Fermanagh"), on the south side of the Upper Lough, and **Lisnaskea,** on the north side, are two pleasant small towns where you can catch your breath.

In the south part of the lough, near the Cavan border and 3 miles (5 km) west of Newtownbutler, the National Trust administers the **Crom Estate** on

INSIDER TIP:

Foodies should pick up a "Taste of Ulster" brochure at any local tourist office. It lists all the province's restaurants and cafés that use local produce and traditional cooking.

–ALLY THOMPSON
National Geographic contributor

the east shore of the lake (note: New Crom Castle is a private residence). The 1611 plantation castle is a picturesque ruin by the lakeshore, with two giant and gnarled 17th-century yews growing in the garden. There are woodland and lough shore walks, deer, and pine martens. ■

EXPERIENCE: Cruising Lough Erne

Though you can catch many charming glimpses of the Upper and Lower Loughs from the shore, you can only enjoy the full picture by cruising their island-dotted waters. The two main boating centers are Belleek (see pp. 318–319) and Enniskillen (see pp. 321–322).

There are reputed to be 93 islands in Lower Lough Erne (or is it 97?) and 152 (or is that 177?) in Upper Lough Erne. No one's counting too carefully—but there are plenty of options from to choose.

Lower Lough Erne

The Lower Lough's best known island is **Devenish,** just downstream of Enniskillen *(ferry from Trory Point, signed off the A32, tel 028 6862 1588, closed mid-Sept.–Easter, $),* with its superb round tower, ruins of monastic churches, and finely carved high cross.

In Caldragh Cemetery, on **Boa Island** *(causeway bridges on the A47),* you'll find the enigmatic fifth- or sixth-century Janus Figure, its two pagan faces staring wildly in opposite directions.

On **White Island** *(ferry from Castle Archdale Country Park, tel 028 6862 1588, park open all year, ring for visitor center summer hours)* stand seven stone carvings that experts have puzzled over. Look for a *sheela-na-gig* (the figure of a grinning woman holding open her vulva), a figure with a book, two probable representations of Christ, a scowling head, along with a bishop and someone who may be King David. The carvings—which seem both Christian and

pagan in character—may date back to the sixth century.

Upper Lough Erne

In Upper Lough Erne, three islands with ancient pagan or monastic carvings are easily reached by either car or boat. **Inishkeen** *(causeway off the A4 just S of Enniskillen)* has strange carved stones in the cemetery of St. Fergus's Church—an antlered head and someone in a vessel. On **Cleenish,** reached by a bridge 2 miles (3 km) east of Bellanaleck, several finely carved gravestones can be found, while in the south, on **Galloon** *(causeway from Landbrock crossroads, 2 miles/3 km S of Newtownbutler),* are more macabre 18th-century graveslabs with designs that include

skull-and-crossbones and hourglass motifs.

Boat Rentals and Cruises

Enniskillen:
Guided cruises and day-boat rentals on Lower Lough Erne are offered by **Erne Tours Ltd.** *(www.ernetoursltd.com);* contact **Lochside Cruisers** *(tel 028 6632 4368)* for cruiser rentals.

Belleek (Beleek):
Contact the **Beleek Angling Centre** *(tel 028 6865 8181)* for day-boat rentals and **Beleek Charter Cruising** *(tel 028 6865 8027)* for cruisers.

Lisaskea:
Share Centre *(tel 028 6772 2122)* offers guided cruises on Upper Lough Erne.

The round tower and monastic buildings on Devenish Island are one of the chief attractions for boaters on Lough Erne.

Two Great Fermanagh Houses

The 18th century was the golden age of grand landscaping and domestic architecture in Ireland. The rich commissioned the very biggest and best country houses that money could buy. County Fermanagh boasts two of the most enchanting.

Florence Court stretches its arcaded wings wide, as if embracing its beautiful parkland.

Florence Court

🏛 276 B1

✉ Signed off the A32 Enniskillen–Swanlinbar road, 8 miles (13 km) SW of Enniskillen

☎ 028 6634 8249

🕐 House: Seasonal; call ahead for hours. Grounds: Open year-round

💲 $$

www.nationaltrust.org.uk

Florence Court

Florence Court is a secluded 18th-century house, tucked away in beautiful wooded grounds looking southwest to the jagged ridge of Cuilcagh Mountain. The Cole family (later Earls of Enniskillen) built it in stages from the 1750s—first the three-story central block and then the arcaded wings.

In the summer, these grounds provide the setting for various outdoor events, from Victorian garden parties and country fairs to a children's teddy bear picnic. One interesting feature is the **sawmill** that was established by the 3rd Earl of Enniskillen during the Great Famine to give paid work to some of his destitute tenants.

Among various lovely woodland walks, one leads toward Cuilcagh Mountain. It passes the **Florence Court Yew,** a tattered old thing shaped like a rocket that was found growing on Cuilcagh in the mid-18th century. Its offspring cuttings have established a distinct species, the Irish yew.

In 1955, the National Trust had to completely restore the house interior—only five years after it acquired the property—following a fire. Wonderful rococo plasterwork can be seen on the staircase walls and the dining ceiling, where puff-cheeked cherubs represent the Four Winds of Heaven and birds flies among flowers.

Upstairs, family prints, drawings, and photographs are displayed. In the bedside table beside the elegant four-poster in the Countess's bedroom is a rare piece of Belleek Pottery (see p. 319)—a chamberpot with a picture of 19th-century British Prime Minister William Gladstone strategically placed on the bottom. Gladstone forfeited the allegiance—indeed, inspired the hatred—of many Irish Ascendancy families (those with British backgrounds who lived and owned land in Ireland) with his support for the Home Rule Bill that threatened to destroy their comfortable supremacy.

Castle Coole

The Lowry-Corry family, Earls of Belmore, built Castle Coole at the end of the 18th century. A flock of greylag geese has been resident in the park for at least 300 years, and legend says that the Belmores will remain at Castle Coole as long as the geese do. The present earl lives in another house on the estate.

Regency architectural supremo James Wyatt designed the great Palladian mansion. Completed in 1798, it is reckoned to be the finest neoclassic house in Ireland. It was commissioned by Armar

Lowry-Corry, a country squire who got lucky in 1741 when he inherited the estate along with streams of money, property, and lands throughout Fermanagh, Tyrone, and Donegal. The house was built as a grand statement of his capacity to exercise power and influence over the Irish political scene. He was created 1st Earl of Belmore in 1797, but vicissitudes of life brought him no joy—his dark-haired beauty of a wife ran off and left him miserable. He died in 1802, so much in debt that his son, the 2nd Earl, had to wait 20 years before finishing the decorations and furnishings.

The house with its **portico** of four immense columns stands on a ridge on 1,500 acres (600 ha) of beautiful parkland. Almost all the original furnishings are here, still in the rooms for which they were designed and built. The oval **saloon,** with its elaborate cast-iron stoves, the **dining room,** and the **drawing room** are floored with Irish oak and opulently furnished. The canopied bed in the **State Bedroom** was created for a visit by King George IV in 1821 (he never showed up, reportedly because he was dallying elsewhere with one of his mistresses). ■

Castle Coole
- 276 B2
- On the A4 Enniskillen–Belfast road, 1.5 miles (2.5 km) SE of Enniskillen
- 028 6632 2690
- House: Seasonal; call ahead for hours. Grounds: Open year-round
- $$

www.nationaltrust.org.uk

Florence Court Mill

It is the Victorian domestic details that bring the heyday of the grand country houses vividly to life. In the gardens of Florence Court, a dripping wooden aqueduct or headrace feeds a big cast-iron waterwheel. In the shed alongside, a wicked-looking circular saw whirrs around. Roughly sawn planks lie nearby. Lingering here and savoring the resinous smell of sawdust, the quiet clanking of the wheel, and the rattle of the slack old driving belt, one can easily imagine it is the 19th rather than the 21st century.

County Armagh

County Armagh, with its oppressive republican reputation, is few people's idea of a visitor destination. Yet historic houses and towns, landscape beauty, and local friendliness are to be found in plenty in this most maligned of the six counties.

At the Armagh Planetarium *(www.armaghplanet.com)* on College Hill in Armagh city

Oxford Island

🗺 277 E2

✉ Oxford Island, Lough Neagh, Craigavon, Co. Armagh

☎ 028 3832 2205

www.oxfordisland .com

The Argory

🗺 277 D2

✉ Derrycaw Rd., Moy, Dungannon, Co. Armagh

☎ 028 8778 4753

🕐 House closed Oct.–Easter & Mon.–Fri. April–May & Sept. Grounds open year-round

💲 $$

Oxford Island

The southern shore of Lough Neagh closes the northern boundary of County Armagh, and here, at the **Lough Neagh Discovery Centre** on Oxford Island, you can learn about the natural history and traditions of the biggest lake in the British Isles. From the bird-watching blinds, you can enjoy the sight of dozens of bird species.

The Argory & Ardress House

South of the M1 Dungannon–Belfast motorway stands **The Argory,** signed from junctions 13 and 14. Built in 1820, the house has an atmosphere and furnishings that have remained frozen in the year 1900. **Ardress House,** 3 miles (5 km) southeast of the Argory, is a 17th-century farmhouse swollen into an 18th-century mansion. Children love the working farmyard attached to the house.

Armagh City

The ancient capital of Ulster and seat of both Catholic and Anglican Bishops of Ireland, Armagh city has two cathedrals, one for each denomination, on opposite hills—symbolic, many think, of their intransigent positions during the recent Troubles.

Fionn MacCumhaill on Slieve Gullion

When you climb to the top of Slieve Gullion in South Armagh, you'll find a dark little lake, the Calliagh Beara Lough, just by the north cairn. Legend has it that Fionn MacCumhaill met Miluchra, an enchantress in the shape of a beautiful young woman, here. She begged him to dive into the lake to retrieve her gold ring. Gallant Fionn did as the maiden asked, but on climbing out of the water, the hero found himself transformed into a feeble old man. The damsel, meanwhile, had turned into a withered hag, the Calliagh Beara.

Some say it was Fionn's men who found the Calliagh Beara hiding in the summit cairn and forced her to undo the mischief. Others tell of how Fionn's dog, Bran, fetched the hero's grandson Oscar, who caught a fairy man who gave Fionn a drink of youth to revitalize him.

The building of the Gothic **Catholic Cathedral of St. Patrick** began in 1838, stopped during the famine, and was completed in 1873. Standing proud at the top of a long flight of steps, it's a marvel of ornate marble and mosaic, with gold-winged angels soaring high in the vaulted nave roof.

Across the valley, the **Anglican cathedral**—also dedicated to St. Patrick—is lower, smaller, and far older than its Catholic counterpart. Built in medieval times and restored in 1765, it holds fine monuments, including the splendid Tandragee Idol, an Iron Age effigy grinning under his fat cheeks and clutching one arm. He might be a representation of Nuada the Silver-handed (see p. 262). Outside, on the west wall of the north transept, is a memorial to Brian Boroimhe or Boru, mightiest of all Ireland's High Kings, who died in 1014 at the Battle of Clontarf, the final victory over the Vikings. Brian lies buried "in the north side of the great church," according to contemporary accounts.

Armagh's **public library** (tel 028 3752 3142), on Abbey Street near the Anglican cathedral, is an antiquarian's dream of old leather books in a solemn and splendid room. The **County Museum,** in the Mall East, has a fabulous collection of artifacts, wooden drinking cups, Bronze Age jewelry, and tools. Just off the Mall, the heritage center of **St. Patrick's Trian** (tel 028 3752 1801) has tableaux of monks and warriors and a treat for children in its "Land of Lilliput."

Two miles (3 km) west of Armagh is **Navan hill fort,** the ancient Eamhain Mhacha, or Queen Mhacha's Palace. The Kings of Ulster ruled from this great mound for 1,000 years. Many of the Ulster hero Cúchulainn's mighty deeds are set here.

South Armagh

In South Armagh, you will find regular music and storytelling at the **Tí Chulainn Cultural Activity Centre** (see p. 45), in Mullaghbane. The **Slieve Gullion Forest Park** is signed off the B113 between Meigh and Forkhill; from here you can drive or walk. The final scramble to the Bronze Age cairns on the summit of Slieve Gullion is short but steep, the view spectacular. ■

Armagh
🅰 277 D2

Armagh County Museum
✉ The Mall East, Armagh, Co. Armagh
☎ 028 3752 3070
🕘 Closed Sun.
www.nmni.com

Ardress House
🅰 277 E2
✉ Annaghmore, Co. Armagh, on B28, 7 miles (11 km) W of Portadown
☎ 028 8778 4753
🕘 Open weekends only mid-March–Sept.
💲 $

Slieve Gullion Forest Park
🅰 277 E1
✉ On B113, 5 miles (8 km) SW of Newry, Co. Armagh
☎ 028 3755 1277
🕘 Closed Sept.–Easter

Walk: Trassey Track to Hare's Gap, Mourne Mountains

The Mountains of Mourne sweep down to the sea at the southern extremity of County Down—beautifully shaped pink-gray granite peaks, 12 of them over 2,000 feet (610 m), all packed into an area measuring 15 by 8 miles (24 by 13 km). Lakes hide in the heart of the Mournes, and there are famous beauty spots such as the narrow and dramatic Spelga Pass. These are accessible by car, but the Mournes are above all walkers' country.

The spectacular views from the high places of the Mourne Mountains make the climb worthwhile.

You need to dress in suitable hill-walking gear and take with you a map, a compass, and food and drink. Weather conditions can change quickly, and though the highest peak, Slieve Donard, is only 2,788 feet (850 m), these are proper mountains. Once on the peaks, though, it's hard to get lost, thanks to the Mourne Wall, a 22-mile (35 km) circuit of drystone wall that links the main inner summits. It was built between 1904 and 1922 to help poverty-stricken, hungry men earn enough to feed their families.

The walk to Hare's Gap starts from the

NOT TO BE MISSED:

Views back from the Trassey Track
• Views forward from Hare's Gap

little parking lot under the forest-covered Clonachullion Hill. From the entrance, walk left along the road, and after about 70 yards (64 m), bear left over a stile and join the **Trassey Track,** a well-trodden path that climbs gradually up, keeping the large **forestry**

Walking in the Mourne Mountains

There are two essentials you should take with you on your walk in the Mournes. The first is *The Mournes*, Ordnance Survey map of Northern Ireland 1:50,000 Discoverer Series No. 29. The second is a card (Walk No. 10) that details the walk. The card is available as part of a pack sold at bookstores, outdoor shops, the Mourne Heritage Trust's **Countryside Centre** in Newcastle *(87 Central Promenade, tel 028 4372 4059)*, and the **Newcastle Tourist Office** *(10–14 Central Promenade, tel 028 4372 2222)*.

Just after the track crosses the river by a footbridge, bear left away from paths going up to the old **quarries ❸** behind the naked cliffs of Spellack. Soon you recross the river. From here, it is a straightforward climb, aiming between converging rock cliffs to reach the **Mourne Wall ❹** in **Hare's Gap.** Take plenty of time to walk forward and admire the stunning views over the end of Ben Crom Reservoir to the bulk of Slieve Commedagh (2,515 feet/767 m) and Slieve Donard.

From here, retrace your steps back down to the parking lot, with still more wonderful views in prospect.

plantation ❶ on your left. At the top edge of the trees, the Ulster Way long-distance footpath bends away to the right. But you should keep walking straight ahead, swinging a little to the left and then straightening to climb on steepening ground, with the Trassey River on your right.

The section of the track you are on now is known as the **Brandy Pad ❷,** with good reason: It is part of an old smuggler's path by which contraband goods (including brandy) were brought by pack pony through the heart of the Mournes from the coast south of Newcastle. Once down in the lowlands on the inland side of the mountains, they could be hidden around any number of farms before onward transportation.

🅰 See area map p. 277 F1

► Parking lot just NE of Trassey Bridge, below Clonachullion Hill (1 mile/1.6 km off the B180, 4 miles/6 km W of Newcastle), Co. Down

↔ 4 miles (6 km), with 850 feet (260 m) of ascent

🕒 3 hours

► Parking lot just NE of Trassey Bridge

St. Patrick's Country

The spirit of Ireland's patron saint infuses the region known as St. Patrick's Country. For it was in this lovely but rather overlooked corner of County Down, between Strangford Lough and the Mourne Mountains, that St. Patrick landed in 432 to begin his great mission of converting Ireland to Christianity.

The Life of St. Patrick

Did St. Patrick even exist? The answers to this question vary depending on who you talk to, but it is most probable that he

Each spring, fresh daffodils are placed on the great incised graveslab of St. Patrick outside Downpatrick Cathedral.

did. The best guess is that he was born in Scotland or Wales, perhaps the son of a Roman centurion at the end of the Roman Empire's tenure in the British Isles. At the age of about 16, he was captured by Irish marauders and taken to County Antrim, where he was put to work herding sheep on Slemish Mountain for six years or so. It seems that some pioneer missionary converted him to Christianity during this period of enslavement.

Patrick finally escaped on a ship that was carrying a cargo of wolfhounds and made his way to Gaul (France). Perhaps a quarter of a century of wandering and preaching across the Continent followed. Then, in 431, Patrick was appointed bishop and, the following year, made his landing in County Down. He probably sailed up the estuary of the Slaney River and landed at Ringbane near Saul, which is located just east of present-day **Downpatrick.**

Patrick, always a practical missionary, hastened to convert the local chief, Dichu, the man with the greatest on-the-spot influence, and Dichu gave Patrick use of a barn (*sabhal* in Irish, hence "Saul") as a temporary base. Though the saint was to move on and travel all through the north

West of Downpatrick

Two more ecclesiastical sites a little to the west of Downpatrick are well worth visiting. **Inch Abbey** *(tel 028 9181 1491)*, off the A7 just beyond the river bridge, is a Cistercian monastery with a fine triple-lancet east window that is beautifully sited beside the River Quoile.

At Loughinisland *(take the B2, then the Loughinisland road)*, three old churches stand on a drumlin island in a lake cradled by hills. You can cross via a causeway to explore these churches. The most notable of the three is **MacCartan's Chapel** with its tiny door, inscribed PMC (for its builder, Phelim MacCartan), and dated 1636—a time when to build a Catholic church was to invite persecution, and maybe even death.

of Ireland, it was to Saul that he returned to die in 461, in the monastery he had founded there.

In 1932, the 1,500th anniversary of Patrick's arrival, a church and round tower in traditional Gaelic style were built on the spot. The **Saint Patrick Centre** contains a very good exhibition about the saint's life and work, with emphasis on local Patrick-related sites. You can climb the purgatorial Stations of the Cross path up the nearby hill of Slieve Patrick to the altar and 30-foot (9 m) cross on top. From the summit there are great views over Strangford Lough and the Lecale Peninsula.

Sites Associated with St. Patrick

In common with all early Christian missionaries, Patrick was a great mortifier of the flesh. At **Struell Wells** *(information from Downpatrick visitor information)*, 2 miles (3 km) south of Saul *(signed off the Downpatrick–Ardglass road)*, the saint tested his own fortitude by immersing himself in freezing water and spending "a great part of the night, stark naked, singing psalms and spiritual songs." The wells in their green valley gained a great reputation for healing powers and were developed in the 18th century into a pilgrimage complex.

Today you can explore the roofless women's bathhouse and the men's bathhouse, with its benches and dark, cold bathing tank under a heavy stone roof. Look, too, for the well whose water cures eye disease, and the domed drinking well—long known as the Tub—in which St. Patrick spent his prayerful night of immersion.

Downpatrick Cathedral, on its rise of ground, is mostly 19th- and 20th-century work. In the shadow of its walls lies the vast slab of rock, inscribed "Patric," that was laid over St. Patrick's grave in 1901 to stop pilgrims removing the sacred earth. Late 12th-century Norman lord Sir John de Courcy vowed he had reburied Patrick's bones here, along with those of St. Columba, who died on Iona in 597, and St. Brigid, who died in Kildare in 523. Whether all or any of them really lie under the great rock is open to question. ■

Downpatrick
🅰 277 F2

Visitor Information Centre & Saint Patrick Centre
✉ 53a Market St., Downpatrick, Co. Down
☎ 028 4461 2233
🕐 Closed Sept.–April, also Sun. in June
💲 $$

www.saintpatrick centre.com

Strangford Lough & the Ards Peninsula

East of Belfast lies one of Ireland's most beautiful and haunting landscapes—the long south-ward-curving arm of the Ards Peninsula and the great bird-thronged sea inlet of Strangford Lough. Two fine National Trust houses, a spatter of islands, and some dramatic coastline complete the picture of County Down.

House and garden form a fine composition at Mount Stewart on the shores of Strangford Lough.

Bangor
🅜 277 F3
Visitor Information
✉ 34 Quay St., Bangor, Co. Down
☎ 028 9127 0069

Strangford Lough
🅜 277 F3–G2
Strangford Lough Office
✉ 13 The Strand, Portaferry, Co. Down
☎ 028 4272 8886

The Ards Peninsula begins at the seaside town of **Bangor,** in northern County Down, and runs south for some 25 miles (40 km). Its coast looks east to the Irish Sea, over splendid sandy beaches often heaped with seaweed and interspersed with rocky coves and fishing villages. At the southern tip, a glorious 5-mile (8 km) coastal walk leads around the hamlet of **Kearney** (*tel 028 4488 1411 or 028 4488 1668*). The National Trust maintains both village and coast.

Strangford Lough

The inner coastline of Ards is entirely different; Strangford

Lough, onto which it looks, has a muddy, mysterious, estuarine feel. The lough is 19 miles (30 km) from innermost corner to the peninsula tip, a great tidal inlet full of drumlin islands, whose waters recede at low tide to expose mighty mudflats and sandbanks.

The bird-watching here is unequaled in Northern Ireland (see sidebar opposite); some 12,000 light-bellied brent geese fly from Greenland to overwinter here, and regular gatherings occur of huge numbers of golden plover, lapwing, curlew, godwit, and redshank, as well as vast clouds of ducks.

Mount Stewart: The Stewarts have their seat at Mount Stewart, a beautiful country house on the east shore of the lough now in the care of the National Trust. There's a family feel to the house, with original bird paintings by English artist and humorist Edward Lear casually stuck to a firescreen and copies of playwright Sean O'Casey's works dedicated in his own hand to Edith, wife of the 7th Marquis of Londonderry. Edith laid out the superb gardens and the Dodo Terrace, with animal statues dedicated to members of her informal "Ark Club" of politicians and soldiers.

Grey Abbey, 4 miles (6 km) farther south, is a fine 12th-century ruin by the shore.

Around Strangford Lough

At Portaferry, an attractive waterside village, catch a ferry to reach Strangford village and the southern and western shores of Strangford Lough. In two miles (3 km), a signed right turn leads to the National Trust property of **Castle Ward** (on A25, 1.25 miles/2 km W of Strangford, Co. Down, tel 028 4488 1204, closed Oct.–March and Mon.–Fri. April–June & Sept., $$), beautifully set on wooded parkland at the southern end of the lough.

The house is an architectural oddity, with the front half in sober Palladian style and the back half all exuberant Gothic. The 18th-century owners, Bernard and Lady Anne Ward, disagreed bitterly over the design of the house, so each took half. Bernard's front half is a model of classical restraint on the outside with wonderful plasterwork within; Lady Anne's rear half features pointed windows and doorframes, fan vaulting, and Moorish decorations.

There are fine river and wetland walks at **Quoile Countryside Centre** (tel 028 4461 5520, closed weekdays Sept.–March), just north of Downpatrick, and far up the western lough shore is some excellent bird-watching at **Castle Espie Wildfowl and Wetlands Trust** (tel 028 9187 4146).

Between the two lies **Mahee Island** (signed), a lonely islet at the end of several causeways. St. Patrick preached here at the monastery of St. Mochaoi. Ancient stone walls, ruins of a round tower and church, and rugged monastic graveslabs are all that remain. ∎

Mount Stewart
- 🅰 277 G3
- ✉ 5 miles (8 km) SW of Newtownards on A20, Co. Down
- ☎ 028 4278 8387
- 🕐 House open mid-March–April & Oct. Sat.–Sun. p.m.; May–June & Sept. Wed.–Mon. p.m. July–Aug. daily p.m. Grounds open year-round.
- 💲 $$

Grey Abbey
- 🅰 277 G3
- ✉ Grey Abbey, Co. Down
- ☎ 028 9054 6552
- 🕐 Closed weekdays Oct.–March; & Mon. April–Sept.

EXPERIENCE: Bird-watching

Ireland has about 400 bird species, roughly three-quarters of the number in mainland Britain. Raptors include peregrine, merlin, and the reintroduced golden eagle. Some species—such as blackcap, stonechat, and goldfinch—are on the increase, while others, like the skylark, robin, and wheatear, are declining. Be sure to take your binoculars wherever you go! Consult the **Birds of Ireland News Service** (www.birdsireland.com) for information on tours, recent sightings, and the rare birds of Ireland. Other valuable sources of information are the **Royal Society for the Protection of Birds** (www.rspb.org.uk) and **Birdwatch Ireland** (www.birdwatchireland.ie).

Cúchulainn, Ulster's Warrior Hero

The ancient kingdom of Ulster, of which Northern Ireland comprises a major part, is steeped in colorful legend. Much of it revolves around the indomitable warrior Cúchulainn, the only hero who might have given that other Irish mythical daredevil, Fionn MacCumhaill (Finn McCool), a run for his money.

Son of the god Lugh the Long-handed, Cúchulainn was given the birth name Setanta. At the age of seven, he slew a ferocious hound that had attacked him on the slopes of Slieve Gullion by jamming his *sliotar* (hurling ball) into its jaws and then beating it with his *camán* (hurley stick). The hound's owner, Culainn the Smith, was not pleased, so Setanta offered to guard his house until he had trained another dog. Thus he acquired his proper name: Cúchulainn, the Hound of Culainn.

Cúchulainn, in his warrior glory, strides toward the Shadow Land.

Haughty but beautiful Emer set him impossible tasks in order to win her hand: to leap the salmon leap, to slay eight men with a single blow—not once, but three times over—and to carry off two women along with their weight in gold and silver. He accomplished all with ease. Before battle, fearsome changes came upon him. He would swell to giant stature and turn different colors, while one eye bulged to enormous size and his body burned so hot that snow melted, sparks showered from his mouth, and a mist of blood spurted from the crown of his head.

The Cattle Raid of Cooley

Cúchulainn's finest hour came when treacherous Queen Medb of Connacht launched the Cattle Raid of Cooley upon Ulster. Envious of a fabulous bull, the White-horned One, that belonged to her husband King Ailill, she was determined to steal a beast that would match it—Ulster's famed Brown Bull of Cooley. The men of Ulster were under an enchantment that made them weak, so the 17-year-old Cúchulainn defended Ulster single-handedly. With sword, slingshot, and the dreaded spear Gae, he defeated Medb's armies. The wicked queen did manage to get back to Connacht with the Brown Bull of Cooley, only to have her prize kill the White-horned One and rampage through Ireland before dropping dead of sheer rage.

Queen Medb's Revenge

Queen Medb had the last laugh, though. Ten years after the Cattle Raid of Cooley, she enlisted three witches—their enchanter father had been killed by Cúchulainn—to put the warrior hero under a spell. Believing that Ulster was being attacked, Cúchulainn set out to defend his homeland.

Soon he met the sons of the Kings of Munster and Leinster. Unfortunately, Cúchulainn had killed those kings, too. In the ensuing

Cúchulainn rides his war chariot into battle.

battle, the hero was mortally pierced with a spear thrust. Binding himself for support to a standing stone, he wielded his sword until he died. But even then the Hound of Culainn was not quite finished. As young King Lughaidh of Munster stepped up and sliced off Cúchulainn's head, the sword fell from the hero's grasp and cut off his enemy's right hand. So passed Ulster's doughtiest champion, a mighty warrior to the last.

EXPERIENCE: In the Footsteps of Legends

The name and fame of Cúchulainn are known to every person who grows up in Ireland, but the Ulster hero is only one of dozens of mythical figures around which the early history and fireside stories of Ireland were built. Centuries of Ireland's storytellers have preserved the mighty adventures and sayings of not only Cúchulainn but also Fionn MacCumhaill, Deirdre of the Sorrows, Diarmuid and Gráinne, Queen Medb of Connacht, Lugh the Long-handed, and many more.

You can hear these and other myths and legends told aloud at **Tí Chulainn**

Cultural Activity Centre (see sidebar p. 45) in Mullaghbane, County Armagh. Or consult **Storytellers of Ireland** (www .storytellersofireland.org), which maintains a directory of expert traditional storytellers throughout Ireland, as well as a list of upcoming events. To hear the ancient stories recounted in Dublin, check online at www.legendarytours.com.

If you want to see the sites that figure in Irish myth, book a tour of the Boyne Valley or the area around Newgrange with **Mythical Ireland** (www.mythicalireland .com). You can also create your own tour.

More Places to Visit in Northern Ireland

Barrontop Fun Farm

With all the sounds, sights, and smells of the farm, this is the perfect place for children. They get the opportunity to hold fluffy chicks, feed the goats, lambs, and ducks, cuddle a friendly puppy or a baby rabbit, and go up close to llamas, deer, and pot-bellied pigs.

For those with a lot of energy to burn, there is an adventure playground and a bouncy castle. Cart rides are another attraction. There are picnic areas and a tearoom—and also plenty of indoor facilities if it's raining. *www.barrontop.co.uk* 276 C3 35 Barron Road., Donemana, Strabane, Co. Tyrone 028 7139 8649 Closed Christmas–mid-March $$

Castlederg

It's worth taking a drive on the B72 out to Castlederg in the west of County Tyrone because, while it has no spectacular visitor attractions, it's a good example of a friendly working village that's still dependent on agriculture. The Tuesday morning sheep sales in Forbes Livestock Mart out on the Killen road are a great gathering place for hill farmers, whose weatherbeaten faces ring the auctioneer with his machine-gun patter. West of Castlederg, County Tyrone makes a bulging salient into County Donegal. There's great walking and leisurely motoring here along the quiet and lonely back roads and lanes around **Killeter Forest** on the border. 276 B3 **Visitor Information** 26 Lower Strabane Rd., Castlederg, Co. Tyrone 028 8167 0795

Knockmany Chambered Cairn

Southeast of Omagh, not far from the border with County Monaghan, the Clogher Valley is a forested, secret glen. Signposted at the summit of a steep wooded hill here is Knockmany chambered cairn, a Bronze Age passage tomb whose pink stones are carved with wonderful whorls and spiral patterns, parallel lines like Ogham script, and maze-like shapes. The view from here over miles

Wrinkled rocks of Ardglass overlook the uncrowded sands of the Lecale Peninsula.

Ancient Architecture

Ireland is particularly rich in the architecture of the ancients. Stone and Bronze Age peoples left us few artifacts to judge and understand them by, but their massive monuments in stone are markers that the passage of many millennia has failed to erase. Most notable are the court tombs from around 4000 B.C., with their partly enclosed courts or ritual spaces fronting the burial chambers. Wedge tombs (wedge-shaped court tombs) were built perhaps a thousand years later. Hard on their heels came the passage graves, man-made mounds with a passage leading to central chambers; these could be any size, with the largest—such as Newgrange (see pp. 264–267)—being as big as a small hill.

Stone circles were erected by both Stone Age and Bronze Age people, some as boundary markers around burial sites, others apparently to form enclosed spaces for rituals. Some possess much larger stones that seem to have had a guardian role.

of forest and hilly country is superb.
🔺 276 C2 **Omagh Visitor Information** (see p. 338)

Lecale Peninsula

The blunt-nosed Lecale Peninsula, east of Downpatrick, has plenty of delights and surprises. The 22-mile (35 km) coast drive, starting at Strangford village, turns south through **Kilclief,** where there is a fine 15th-century tower house. It was built by a naughty Bishop of Down, John Cely—he was defrocked in 1443 for living with Lettice Savage, a married woman, in the tower.

In 5 miles (8 km) you reach **Ardglass,** a lively fishing town that in its day was the most important fishing port in Ulster—hence the large number of towers, minicastles, and other fortified buildings. **Killough,** 3 miles (5 km) on, was laid out neatly in the 18th century by Lord Bangor of Castle Ward as a port to ship out lead and farm produce from his estate. The rule-straight 8-mile (13 km) road he made to connect port and estate is still there. From Killough you can drive or walk the couple of miles (3 km) to the ruined tenth-century chapel on **St. John's Point.** From the tip of the point awaits a fabulous view of the Mourne Mountains. 🔺 277 F2–G2 ✉ East of Downpatrick, Co. Down **Downpatrick Visitor**

Information ✉ 53a Market St., Downpatrick, Co. Down ☎ 028 4461 2233

Lough Neagh

On the eastern border of Tyrone, Lough Neagh stretches its vast, flat shore. Coarse fishing for lough eels, bream, roach, perch, and pike is superb: The Sperrin Tourism Partnership issues a pamphlet guide.

On the shores of Lough Neagh east of Cookstown stands the **Ardboe high cross,** a magnificently carved tenth-century cross 18.5 feet (5.5 m) tall featuring the Judgment of Solomon, Cain bashing Abel with a flail, and Daniel with two lions. Nearby stands a wishing tree, poisoned to death by thousands of votive coins pushed into its trunk. www.discoverlough neagh.com 🔺 276 E3 **Magherafelt Visitor Information,** www.magherafelt.gov.uk/tourism ✉ 6 Church St., Magherafelt, Co. Londonderry ☎ 028 7963 1510

Murlough Bay

This is a glorious bay, and though it lies between the popular Antrim Coast Road and the Giant's Causeway area, it remains unspoiled because of the absence of a major road along this shoulder of the Antrim coast.

Rocks and silvery sand lie under cliffs and slopes clothed in silver birch and mountain ash.

Sailboats prepare for a good night's sleep on Lough Neagh.

From the upper parking lot, various walks are indicated; one of them goes along the cliffs to Fair Head and a wonderful view north to Rathlin Island. From the lower parking lot, there is a choice of beautiful beach and hill slope rambles. 🏔 277 E5–F5 ✉ 5 miles (8 km) E of Ballycastle, off the coast road between Fair Head and Torr Head, Co. Antrim **Ballycastle Visitor Information,** *www.moyle-council.org* ✉ 7 Mary St., Ballycastle, Co. Antrim ☎ 028 2076 2024

Omagh

Tyrone's county town of Omagh was known only as a shopping and local business center until the infamous day of August 15, 1998. Then a republican splinter group opposed to the Good Friday Agreement (see pp. 288–289) and calling itself the Real IRA exploded a car bomb in a street crowded with Saturday shoppers; 29 people were killed. This appalling act brought condemnation across the board, and paradoxically sealed determination to make the peace process work. *www.omagh.gov.uk* 🏔 276 C3 **Visitor Information** ✉ 1 Market St., Omagh, Co. Tyrone ☎ 028 8224 7831

President Wilson Ancestral Home

In the northwest of County Tyrone, 2 miles (3 km) east of Strabane, the President Wilson Ancestral Home is well signposted. The whitewashed cottage that Woodrow Wilson's grandfather James Wilson left in 1807 is kept

---

Ulster's Presidential Ancestral Homes

Along with Woodrow Wilson, several other U.S. Presidents could trace their lineage to Northern Ireland. There are several associated sites worth visiting:

The ancestral home of 21st U.S. President (1881–1885) Chester Alan Arthur can be found at **Arthur Cottage** *(Dreen, Cullybackey, Co. Antrim, tel 028 2563 5900).* Arthur's father emigrated in 1815.

The parents of Andrew Jackson, seventh U.S. President (1829–1837), left Carrickfergus for America in 1765. The

Andrew Jackson Cottage *(Boneybefore, Carrickfergus, Co. Antrim, tel 028 9335 8049),* a traditional cottage of the period, is beautifully restored and furnished with various Jackson exhibits and displays.

John Simpson, the maternal great-grandfather of Ulysses S. Grant, 18th U.S. President (1869–1877), was born in the mud-floored **Grant Ancestral Home** *(Dergina, Ballygawley, Co. Tyrone, tel 028-8555-7133)* in 1738 and emigrated to the U.S. at the age of 22.

by the curators, who are members of the Wilson family, still farming the ancestral land.

Inside are a kitchen and a living room with a press (storage cupboard) and fancy iron fireplace. A ladder leads through the ceiling to an upper room under the smoke-blackened thatch. In this little house with its tiny windows and thick stone walls, each generation of Wilson parents raised swarms of children, often 12 or more. James Wilson married Annie Adams, a girl he met on the boat to America; his grandson Woodrow served as U.S. President from 1913 to 1921. ⓜ 276 C3 ✉ Spout Rd., Dergalt, 2 miles (3.2 km) SE of Strabane, Co. Tyrone ☎ 028 7138 2204 🕐 Open July & Aug. Tues.–Sun., at other times by arrangement

INSIDER TIP:

The very best time to visit County Down's Rowallane Garden is in the spring, when you'll see thousands of rhododendrons and azaleas in full bloom. The colors are amazing—it's a glorious sight.

—ALLY THOMPSON
National Geographic contributor

Rowallane Garden

This is a gorgeous, natural-looking garden on a 50-acre (20 ha) site with no artificial landscaping whatsoever. The Rowallane estate was bequeathed to Hugh Armytage Moore by his uncle, the Reverend John Moore, in 1903, and he tended it for the next half century, planting specimens from all over the world.

You can wander through the walled garden full of azaleas—gorgeous in May—and down to the natural outcrop rock garden by way of the shallow glen of New Ground between banks

of orange, scarlet, pink, yellow, purple, and white rhododendrons. ⓜ 277 F2 ✉ Signed off the A7 Belfast–Downpatrick road near Saintfield, 11 miles (18 km) from both Belfast & Downpatrick, Co. Down ☎ 028 9751 1031 🅂 $

Scrabo Tower

An eye-catching landmark for many miles around, Scrabo Tower rises 135 feet (41 m) from the summit of Scrabo Hill, at the northern end of **Strangford Lough** (also see pp. 332–333). It was erected in 1857 as a gesture of thanks to the 3rd Marquis of Londonderry for his efforts to relieve the suffering of his tenants during the Great Famine.

Nowadays, the tower houses an exhibition about the natural and social history of the area, including Strangford Lough, and if you have the energy to climb up the 122 steps to the top of the tower, it is definitely worth it. The view is wonderful, one of the most impressive in Northern Ireland, taking in the Mountains of Mourne, the hills of the Antrim Coast, Belfast, the great swath of Strangford Lough itself, and the Ards Peninsula. On particularly clear days, you might even be able to get a glimpse of the Isle of Man and the hills of Scotland across the Irish Sea.

The tower is at the heart of the Scrabo Hill Country Park, where woodland gives way to open areas where the dark volcanic rock that overlies the sandstone makes dramatic shapes of outcrops and quarry scars in the green surroundings. ⓜ 277 F3 ✉ Just over a mile (1.6 km) SW of Newtownards, Co. Down ☎ 028 9182 0695 🕐 Closed Oct.–Easter, and Fri. Easter–Sept.; Country Park open year-round

Springhill

Springhill is an excellent example of a plantation house. Built by the Conyngham family from Scotland around 1690, the house was enlarged with two wings in the

Colors, shapes, and sizes of plants blend and contrast at Rowallane Garden.

18th century. Inside is a well-stocked 18th-century library; some splendid 18th- and 19th-century furniture, including ladderback chairs and delicately crafted cabinets; a gun room with some historic weapons displayed (flintlock muskets used by defenders at the Siege of Derry and some pikes captured at the Battle of Vinegar Hill, County Wexford, in 1798); and a costume exhibition. Outside is a walled garden and well-marked walks through park and woodland. ⚠ 277 D3 ✉ Signed on the B18 Moneymore–Coagh road, 5 miles (8 km) NE of Cookstown, Co. Londonderry ☎ 028 8674 8210 🕐 House closed Oct.–Easter and Mon.–Fri. April–June & Sept. 💲 $$

Toomebridge Eel Fishery

Call in on this fishery in the west of County Antrim, near County Londonderry, and enjoy the astonishing sight of eels in the millions. It's a commercial concern, but you are welcome to drop in and visit. The fishery, at the point where the River Bann flows out of the northernmost point of Lough Neagh, is a prime site for eel catching—mostly for export, since Ulster people seem not too fond of these wriggly delicacies. Lough Neagh eel fishermen make their living from the trade, however, and lower along the Bann in summer eel-fishing for sport is a very popular pastime. ⚠ 277 E3 ✉ Lough Neagh Fishermen's Cooperative Society, Toomebridge, Co. Antrim ☎ 028 7965 0618 🕐 Closed Sat. & Sun.

Wellbrook Beetling Mill

The mill was one of six built in this narrow valley from 1767 onward. Their function was to beat linen cloth to a fine sheen with water-powered wooden hammers. You can admire the noisy "beetles," or hammers; the waterwheel; and the rest of the original machinery, and also learn about Ulster's once thriving linen industry in the drying loft display. ⚠ 277 D3 ✉ Signed off the A505 Cookstown–Omagh road at Kildress, 4 miles (6.5 km) W of Cookstown, Co. Tyrone ☎ 028 8674 8210 or 028 8674 1735 🕐 Closed Oct.–mid-March; Mon.–Fri. mid-March–June & Sept. (except bank holiday Mon.) 💲 $

Travelwise

A modern Dublin tram

TRAVELWISE

PLANNING YOUR TRIP

When to Go

The best time of year to visit Ireland is spring and early summer. April to June tend to be the sunniest and mildest months, the population is not yet suffering from tourist overload, and the countryside is green and fresh from the winter rain. Visitor numbers have not yet peaked, so the roads are quiet, but most attractions have opened after the winter layoff.

However, the biggest concentration of the festivals for which Ireland is famous are in summer. The Cork and Dingle Regattas, Galway Arts Festival and Races, Dublin Horse Show and Connemara Pony Show, International Rose of Tralee Festival, and Fleadh Cheoil na h'Éireann (All-Ireland Music Festival) all take place in July or August.

The months of September and October tend to see better weather and beautiful colors in woods and moors; prices are on the way down by October, too. Winter weather is generally mild but can be dark and gloomy. This is the season of low prices and indoor fun—many attractions have closed, but fire-warmed pubs come into their own.

What to Take

Pack clothes that take account of the informal, mostly outdoor nature of a holiday in Ireland. It's certainly wise to take good waterproof clothing, a hat, and an umbrella, as it's bound to rain at least some of the time during your visit. As for other clothing, the keynote is informality unless you intend to stay or dine at the very classiest 5-star places.

Camera and camcorder film is widely available in the larger towns. An English-Irish dictionary or phrase book will help you appreciate the place-names. You may also find bird and flower identification books to be helpful. You can buy these in leading towns and cities across the country.

If you want to join in with the music, a couple of harmonicas or a tin whistle (keys G and D) will fit easily into your suitcase. These are the best instruments for unobtrusively "faking it." And bring a couple of songs, too, in case someone invites you to oblige the company in the pub. There's no better ice-breaker, even if your voice is itself a rusty instrument.

A wide range of over-the-counter and prescription medicines is available in Irish pharmacies (sometimes called chemists), but you should seriously consider bringing any specialized medication with you.

HOW TO GET TO IRELAND

By Air

Flying time between the U.S. and Ireland is between six and nine hours. Scheduled flights link many North American airports to Dublin, Shannon, Cork, Knock (Co. Mayo), and Belfast. The Republic's national carrier (operating to Belfast, too) is Aer Lingus (tel 800/223 6537).

Arrival by air in the Irish Republic is most likely to be at either Dublin or Shannon airport; in Northern Ireland, either Belfast International or Belfast City airport. All have foreign exchange bureaus (generally open by 7 a.m.), the major car rental firms, and taxi ranks—fares are about five times the bus fares.

Getting to the City Centers

Journeys to city centers all take about 0.5–1 hour, depending on traffic. From Belfast City airport, allow 10–15 minutes to reach the city.

Dublin Airport to Dublin
By car—take the M1 south
By bus—Airlink bus every 20 minutes (moderate fare) via central bus station and Connolly railway station to Heuston railway station
By taxi—expensive

Shannon Airport to Limerick
By car—take the N18 east
By bus—Bus Eireann runs a frequent, inexpensive airport–Limerick service
By taxi—moderate/expensive

Belfast International Airport to Belfast
By car—take the A52 east
By bus—Airbus service (moderate fare, children free) runs to the city center every half hour
By taxi—expensive

Belfast City Airport to Central Belfast
By car—follow city-center signs
By taxi—moderate

GETTING AROUND

Getting Around in Dublin

By Bus

Dublin Bus (tel 01 873 4222, www.dublinbus.ie) runs bus services in Greater Dublin (extends to the outskirts of Counties Meath, Kildare, and Wicklow).

Tickets—Buy cheaper prepaid tickets en bloc from the CIE information desk in Dublin Airport, from the Dublin Bus head office at 59 Upper O'Connell Street, or from several hundred ticket outlets across the city.

By Rail

DART (www.dublin.ie/transport/dart.htm) is an efficient rail service connecting outer Dublin with the city center. There are 25 stations—the three most central are Connolly (north of the river, a 10-minute walk to O'Connell Street), and Tara Street and Pearse Street (both south of the river, 5 minutes to Trinity College). Buy tickets at any DART station. The **LUAS** (www.luas.ie) tram system's Green Line goes southeast from St. Stephen's Green to Sandyford; the Red Line goes west from Connolly station to Heuston station, then southwest to Tallaght. (Note: There are no subways in Ireland.)

By Taxi
The main city-center taxi ranks are at St. Stephen's Green, College Green, O'Connell Street, and Westland Row to the east of the Trinity College grounds. Dublin taxis are mostly metered; agree on fares in advance with drivers of those that are not.

Leaving Dublin by Car
Dublin is ringed by the M50 motorway. Main roads out of the city are:

M1 to Dublin Airport, Drogheda, Dundalk, and Belfast
N2 to Slane, Monaghan, and Derry
N3 to Navan, Cavan, Enniskillen, and Donegal
N4 to Kinnegad (where the N6 leaves for Galway), Longford (where the N5 leaves for Westport), and on to Sligo
N7/M7 to Naas (where the N9 leaves for Waterford), Portlaoise (where the N8 branches off for Cork), and Kildare
N11 to Bray, Wicklow, Wexford, and Rosslare car ferry

Traveling around the Republic
By Air
Aer Lingus, Ireland's national airline (U.S. tel 800/474-7424, Ireland tel 0845 084 4444,

www.aerlingus.com) flies from Dublin to Shannon.
Aer Arann (tel 0800 587 2324, www.aerarann.com) flies from Dublin to Cork, Donegal, Kerry, Knock, Galway, and Sligo.

By Car Ferry
Two short car ferry trips that will save you hours on the road are:
Across the Shannon (20-minute crossing, every hour) between Killimer, County Clare, and Tarbert, County Kerry (tel 065 90 53124)
Across Waterford Harbour (10-minute crossing, continuous operation) between Ballyhack, County Wexford, and Passage East, County Waterford (tel 051 382 488)

By Public Transportation
CIE (www.cie.ie) is the company that runs bus and train services in the Republic of Ireland through its subsidiaries Irish Rail (Iarnród Eireann), Irish Bus (Bus Eireann), and Dublin Bus (Bus Átha Cliath).

By Bus
Irish Bus (tel 01 836 6111, www .buseireann.ie), with its distinctive Red Setter logo, services all towns and cities and many rural villages. The daily express buses between Dublin and Belfast are good value and can beat the train for time if traffic conditions permit.

By Train
Irish Rail (tel 01 836 6222, www.irishrail.ie) runs the Republic's train services—efficient north and south of Dublin, slow and in need of investment farther west. Major cities are all connected by rail. The excellent Dublin–Belfast express (eight per day) takes two hours. Reserve in the peak holiday season and for traveling on the very crowded last trains on Friday and Sunday nights.

Tickets
Buy them from any train or bus station. Under-16s and other concessions are up to half-off. There are various good ticket deals on offer, many of them including bus and train, e.g.:
Irish Explorer (5- or 8-day), valid on bus or train; **Emerald Card,** valid on Irish Rail, Irish Bus, Dublin Bus, Northern Irish Railways, and Ulsterbus; and **Irish Rover,** for rail travel in the Republic and Northern Ireland.

Student Discounts
The **Student Travelsave Stamp** gives good discounts on mainline rail, long-distance bus, and ferry tickets. Get it from USIT (19/21 Aston Quay, O'Connell Bridge, Dublin 2, tel 01 602 1904; open Mon.–Fri. 9:30 a.m.–6 p.m., Sat. 9:30 a.m.–5 p.m.) or Bus Eireann Travel Centre (Central Bus Station, Store Street, Dublin 1).

Driving
Car Rental
You'll need a full valid driver's license from your home country, held for two years without endorsement. Age limits are generally 23–70. A deposit is payable before you drive away.

Fly-drive or rail/sail-drive deals offer the best prices. Reservations are essential for mid-July to mid-August. High-season prices are much higher than in low season; they usually include third-party, fire, theft, and passenger indemnity insurance, unlimited mileage, and VAT.

Driving in the Irish Republic
Driving in the Republic, generally speaking, is still a pleasure. Out of the big towns, the roads are uncrowded and most drivers observe the courtesies. The farther west you go, the more roads get narrow, steep, and twisty. Distances on signposts take some getting used to—essentially,

Irish Eurocrats have switched to kilometers (shown on green-and-white signs) and the other 99 percent of the population still operates on miles (black-and-white signs).

Drive on the left; overtake on the right.

Don't park illegally in Dublin; you'll be wheel clamped.

Drivers and front-seat passengers must wear seat belts.

Speed limits: 30 mph (48 kph) in towns, 60 mph (96 kph) on other roads, 70 mph (112 kph) on motorways.

Drink limit: 80 mg of alcohol per 100 ml of blood, i.e., one pint of Guinness.

What to Do in the Event of a Car Accident

1. Dial 999 for fire, police, or ambulance services.
2. Remain at the scene.
3. Exchange names, addresses, and insurance details with anyone else involved.
4. Do not admit liability, whatever the circumstances.
5. Most car-rental firms detail in their documentation the steps they require. These may include a requirement to use a specified towing and repair service; use of another service may invalidate your insurance coverage, so check up.

Maps

Ordnance Survey of Ireland 1:50,000 Discovery Series covers all of Ireland in 89 sheets, good for exploring and walking. Information offices and car rental firms supply general road maps.

Getting around in Belfast

By Bus

Metro (tel 028 9066 6630, www.translink.co.uk/metro.asp) operates buses within Belfast. Buy tickets on the bus or from Europa Bus Centre (Glengall Street) or

Laganside Bus Centre (Oxford Street near Central Station). Cheap multiple tickets/concessions are available.

Free bus connects the Central train station with the two main bus stations and the Youth Hostel; Rail-link bus connects Central and Yorkgate train stations.

By Taxi

Black "London" cabs with yellow identifying discs are metered; others may not be. City-center taxi ranks are at Yorkgate and Central train stations, at bus stations, and at City Hall. Taxi firms are listed in the Yellow Pages.

Leaving Belfast by Car

Main routes are:

A2 north up the coast to Antrim and the Giant's Causeway, east through Bangor and around the Ards Peninsula
M2/A6 to Derry
M1 to Dungannon/A4 to Enniskillen
M1 to Jct7/A1 to Dundalk and Dublin.

Getting around Northern Ireland

By Bus

Ulsterbus (tel 028 9066 6630, www.translink.co.uk/atulsterbus.asp) operates to all towns and most villages across Northern Ireland. Buy tickets at bus stations or on-board buses. Cheap day returns, unlimited travel tickets, bus/rail options, or child/student/OAP discounts are available.

By Rail

Northern Ireland Railways (tel 028 9066 6630, www.translink.co.uk/nir.asp) runs trains from Belfast to Larne (Yorkgate station, tel 028 9074 1700) and to Derry, Bangor, and Dublin (Central Station, tel 028 9089 9400). Buy tickets at train stations.

Driving

Car Rental

Requirements are the same as for the Republic except that the driver's license need only have been held for one year. If you plan to drive in both the Republic and Northern Ireland, ensure the insurance covers you.

The roads in Northern Ireland are uncrowded and drivers are generally relaxed and courteous. Road surfaces are good, and signpost distances are given in miles. Rules and laws apply as in the Republic.

Maps

Ordnance Survey of Northern Ireland 1:50,000 series of 18 sheets covers all of Northern Ireland (along with Donegal and parts of Counties Cavan, Leitrim, Louth, Monaghan, and Roscommon). Ireland North at 1:250,000 is a useful driving map, available from visitor information centers.

PRACTICAL ADVICE

Children

Well-behaved children are made welcome everywhere. In practice, pubs operate individual admittance policies—just ask.

Discounts on transport and entrance fees are usually available.

Communications

Postal Service

The Republic's mailboxes and post vans are green. You can buy stamps from a post office or machine. Letters take roughly two days to reach the United Kingdom, three to four days to get to the United States. In the North, the postboxes and vans are red; British stamps are used.

Telephones

Republic: Phone booths in the Republic tend to be either gray or green and white. You'll find them at train and bus stations, near post offices, and on street corners.

Hotels, pubs, and larger shops usually have a payphone. You'll need plenty of coins, but about half the phone booths use phone-cards, sold by newsagents, post offices, and bigger shops such as supermarkets. You can phone anywhere in the world.

The international code for the Republic of Ireland is 353.

Dial 10 for the domestic operator, 114 for the international operator.

To call Northern Ireland from the Republic, dial 048, then the local number.

Northern Ireland: Northern Ireland has red telephone boxes, along with a plethora of flimsy plastic ones.

The international code for Northern Ireland is 44. Dial 100 for the domestic operator, 155 for the international operator.

Conversions

Distance	multiply by
kilometers to miles	0.62
miles to kilometers	1.6

Length	multiply by
centimeters to inches	0.39
inches to centimeters	2.54
meters to feet	3.28
feet to meters	0.30
meters to yards	1.09
yards to meters	0.91

Area	multiply by
hectares to acres	2.47
acres to hectares	0.40

Weight	multiply by
kilograms to pounds	2.21
pounds to kilograms	0.45
kilograms to U.S. tons	0.001
U.S. tons to kilograms	907

Volume	multiply by
liters to U.S. gallons	0.26
U.S. gallons to liters	3.79

Temperature
°C to °F multiply by 1.8, add 32

°F to °C subtract 32, multiply by 0.55

Currency Restrictions

You can bring as much money as you like into Ireland, but amounts of Irish or other currency taken out of the country are restricted. It is a good idea to complete a currency declaration upon arrival.

Customs

The usual prohibited goods, including illegal drugs, are forbidden in Ireland. Travelers in the EU can carry, duty-paid, up to 110 liters of beer, 90 liters of wine, and 800 cigarettes in and out of Ireland. Duty-free goods allowances (Republic only) include 200 cigarettes, 1 liter of spirits, and 2 liters of fortified wine.

Electricity

Electricity is at a standard 230-volt AC (50 cycles). Wall sockets are for plugs with either three flat or two round pins. U.S. visitors will need a transformer/adaptor.

Embassies & Consulates

Canada: Fourth Floor, 65–68 St. Stephen's Green, Dublin 2, tel 01 417 4100

United States: U.S. Consulate General, Danesfort House, 223 Stranmillis Rd., Belfast BT9 5GR, tel 028 9038 6100

U.S. Embassy, 42 Elgin Rd., Dublin 4, tel 01 668 6770

Entry Formalities

All non-EU nationals need a passport to enter Ireland. U.S. citizens do not need a visa. No ID is needed to cross between southern and Northern Ireland.

Etiquette & Local Customs

There are no formal rules of etiquette in Ireland. Irish people love to talk, banter, sound off, give forth, and take part in the great game of conversation, and the more you join in, the better it all goes round. The Irish love to include strangers and find out all about them. This isn't nosiness, just genuine warmth and curiosity. Such personal interest may be less evident in crowded tourist spots in the high season or in cities in big towns, where, like everywhere else these days, busy inhabitants tend to skip over such an enjoyable way of passing the time.

Don't be afraid to join in with a session of music in a pub. Sing along with the chorus if everyone else is doing so, and if you want to join in with your own instrument, don't forget that it's good manners to ask first! Be sure that you can keep up with (and not spoil) the tune. Don't forget, too, that smoking has been banned in pubs and every other sort of public room.

The old adage about not initiating conversations about sex, politics, and religion is a good one to have in mind, particularly in some areas of the North. In Northern Ireland, you need to be especially sensitive about offering your own ideas on religion and politics unless you have been invited to do so. But nowadays many northerners are keen to talk about the past, present, and future of their troubled country with anyone who is interested. Once the topics are on the table, it's usually best just to listen.

Health

No inoculations are necessary. Tap water is safe to drink. Insurance: see below.

Holidays

January 1 (New Year's Day)
March 17 (St. Patrick's Day)
March/April (Good Friday–Easter Monday)
First Monday in May (May Holiday)

Last Monday in May (Spring Holiday–Northern Ireland)

First Monday in June (June Holiday–Republic)

July 12 (Orangemen's Day–Northern Ireland; nearest Monday is a holiday; parades take place on nearest Saturday)

First Monday in August (August Holiday–Republic)

Last Monday in August (Late Summer Holiday–Northern Ireland)

Last Monday in October (October Holiday–Republic)

December 25 (Christmas Day)

December 26 (Boxing Day/St. Stephen's Day)

Most businesses are closed on national holidays.

Insurance

Medical and dental treatment are available on the Irish health service for nationals of EU countries and certain others on production of a European Health Insurance Card (EHIC), but U.S. and most other nationals should arrange comprehensive health and travel insurance before traveling to Ireland.

Liquor Laws

Licensing hours are rapidly changing to reflect demand, and 24-hour drinking may be just around the corner. Already in Dublin and Belfast there are plenty of places with late licenses, up to 1 a.m. or later. Technically, you can buy alcohol in the Republic between 10:30 a.m. and 11:30 p.m, Monday–Wednesday; 10:30 a.m.–12:30 a.m., Thursday–Saturday; and 12:30–11 p.m. on Sunday.

In Northern Ireland, pubs can open whenever they choose, but alcohol can only be served between 11:30 a.m. and 11 p.m. (12:30 p.m–10:30 p.m. on Sun.) unless the pub has a special extension license and offers food and/or entertainment.

Lost Property

If you lose something, report it to the nearest police station. Don't forget to ask for a signed and dated acknowledgment that you have reported the loss, to show your insurance company.

Media

Among the Republic's serious national papers, two stand out: the *Irish Times* (www.irishtimes.com) and the *Irish Independent* (www.independent.ie). There's one authoritative regional paper, the southwest's *Irish Examiner* (www.examiner.ie), as well as dozens of local papers.

RTE (www.rte.ie), the state broadcasting corporation, has two television channels in English and one in Irish, and four radio stations (one in Irish).

Northern Ireland receives some of the Republic's transmissions and is served with mainland British newspapers, television, and radio, as well as its own regional varieties. It's instructive to read the opposing views of the two strongly aligned Belfast daily papers, the pro-Unionist *News Letter* (www.newsletter.co.uk) and the nationalist *Irish News* (www.irishnews.com).

Money Matters

The currency in the Republic is the euro. There are 100 cents to 1 euro. Bills come in denominations of 5, 10, 20, 50, 100, 200, and 500 euros, although the latter two are seldom seen. The coins come in 1 and 2 euros and 1, 2, 5, 10, 20, and 50 cents.

In Northern Ireland, the British pound is used, with 100 pence to the pound. Coin and note denominations are the same as for euros.

The two currencies are not interchangeable, although a number of Northern Ireland attractions will accept euros for admission fees, especially close to the border, and vice versa, but don't depend on it.

Most major international credit cards and many debit cards are generally accepted and usable in ATMs. The smaller and more rural the establishment, the more prudent it is to have cash at hand.

Opening Times

Republic: Banks are generally open Monday–Friday 10 a.m.–4:30 p.m. In smaller towns, they may close for lunch. Bigger banks in Dublin are open until 5 p.m. on Thursdays and on Saturday mornings.

Shops are generally open Monday to Saturday 9 a.m.–6 p.m.; in central Dublin, many stay open later. On Sundays, supermarkets and some big stores open from noon to 5 or 6 p.m. Shopping centers often stay open until 8 or 9 p.m. Shops in smaller towns may close at 1 p.m. on Wednesdays or Thursdays.

Northern Ireland: Banks are generally open Monday–Friday 9:30 a.m.–4:30 p.m. **Shops** are generall open during the same hours as in the Republic.

Pharmacies

All large towns and many small ones have pharmacies (sometimes called chemists); they should all display a notice on the door giving directions to nearby chemists scheduled to be open after hours.

Places of Worship & Religion

Church of Ireland (Protestant) and Roman Catholic churches abound in Ireland. Methodist, Baptist, and other nonconformist congregations are scarce, as are Jewish, Sikh, Muslim, and Hindu places of worship.

Rest Rooms

You'll find public rest rooms in all the places you'd expect—airports, train and bus stations, and city centers. Some are free; in others, you gain entry with a small coin. There are always facilities in hotels and public places. Rest rooms are generally kept in a reasonable state—though in more rural locations things may be a bit Spartan.

Senior Citizens

Discounts on transport and entrance fees are usually available to senior citizens.

Time Differences

Ireland is on Greenwich Mean Time (e.g., at noon in Ireland, it is 7 a.m. in New York and 4 a.m. in Los Angeles). Clocks are set forward 1 hour between late March and late October.

Tipping

Tipping is very much a matter for you to decide. Generally speaking, the only people who will be upset at the lack of a tip are restaurant waiters and waitresses and cab drivers.

The owners and/or management of some establishments have developed the regrettable habit of keeping a proportion—or all—of a tip for themselves if the customer includes it when paying the bill with a credit or debit card. Don't be afraid to ask your waiter or waitress if that is the case. If it is, then consider paying the tip directly to the server in cash.

Visitor Information

Republic of Ireland

Faílte ("Fawl-che") Ireland (Welcome to Ireland) is the Irish Republic's tourist board (*Baggot St. Bridge, Baggot St., Dublin 2, tel 01 602 4000, www.discoverireland.ie*).

Principal Faílte Ireland offices are:
Dublin: Dublin Tourism, Suffolk St., tel 01 605 7700, *information@dublintourism.ie, www.visitdublin.com*
Kilkenny: Rose Inn St., tel 056 77 51500

Waterford: 41 The Quay, tel 051 875788
Cork: Tourist House, Grand Parade, tel 021 425 5100
Killarney: Beech Road, tel 064 31633
Limerick: Arthur's Quay, tel 061 317522
Shannon Airport: Arrivals Hall, tel 061 471664
Athlone: Athlone Castle, tel 090 649 4630
Galway: Aras Faílte, Forster St., tel 091 537700
Westport: James St., tel 098 25711
Sligo: Áras Reddan, Temple St., tel 071 916 1201

Northern Ireland

The **Northern Ireland Tourist Board** has welcome centers in Belfast (*47 Donegall Place, Belfast BT1 5AD, tel 028 9024 6609, www.discovernorthernireland.com*) and in Dublin (*16 Nassau St., Dublin 2, tel 01 679 1977, or 01 850 230230 if telephoning in Ireland*).

Principal Northern Ireland Tourist Board offices in Northern Ireland are:
Antrim: Giant's Causeway, 44 Causeway Rd., tel 028 2073 1855
Armagh: Old Bank Building, 40 English St., tel 028 3752 1800
Londonderry: 44 Foyle St., tel 028 7126 7284
Down: 34 Quay St., Bangor, tel 028 9127 0069
Fermanagh: Wellington Rd., Enniskillen, tel 028 6632 3110
Tyrone: 1 Market St., Omagh, tel 028 8224 7831

Visitors with Disabilities

Increasing numbers of hotels and other public buildings are being adapted or built to cater to travelers with disabilities. Helpful sources of information are the **National Disability Authority** (*Republic of Ireland; tel 00 353 1 608 0400, www.nda.ie*)

and **Disability Action** (*Northern Ireland; tel 028 9029 7880, www.disabilityaction.org*).

Women

Women travelers are as safe in Ireland as anywhere in the world, provided standard commonsense rules are followed. Serious harassment is extremely rare, and behavior such as wolf-whistling has all but died out.

EMERGENCIES

For all emergencies in Ireland, telephone 999.

Crime & Police

The Republic of Ireland has a well-deserved reputation for being one of the safest countries in Europe. Northern Ireland earned a name for violent disruption during the Troubles, but even then the vast majority of incidents occurred far from anyplace a visitor was likely to be. These days no one need be especially concerned about safety issues in the North.

The kind of crime likely to affect visitors—petty theft, pocket-picking—is largely confined to the more disadvantaged areas of Dublin and Belfast. Outside of these enclaves, the usual general precautions are all you need to observe. If you do get into trouble, help and support are available from the **Irish Tourist Assistance Service** (*Mon.–Fri.: 1a Lower Grand Canal St., Dublin 2, tel 01 661 0562; Weekends & holidays: Store St. Garda Station, Dublin 2, tel 01 666 8109; www.itas.ie*).

In the Republic, the police are known as the *Gardai* (pronounced "Gard-EE"; *www.garda.ie*) or the "gards"; they normally work unarmed. In Northern Ireland, the police force is called the **Police Service of Northern Ireland** (PSNI; *www.psni.police.uk*). They tend to be less forbidding-looking in recent years since shedding their semiautomatic rifles and flak jackets. Both sets of officers will do their best to help any visitor in trouble.

Hotels & Restaurants

Time was—and not so long ago—when the traveler outside Dublin would need to look long and hard for a good place to stay. The norm, especially in small towns, was a run-down hotel with bad beds. But things have changed, and today there is an enormous range of accommodations, from magnificent castles on beautiful grounds to simple hostels, and standards rarely fall below what's acceptable.

HOTELS

In the Republic, tourist offices have lists of accommodations approved by Bord Fáilte (Irish Tourist Board); north of the border, tourist offices have the same, with establishments approved by the NITB (Northern Ireland Tourist Board). You can also book ahead (paying a small supplement): telephone 1800 668668 within the Republic, 0800 6686 6866 within Northern Ireland.

Converted castles and stately homes can be very atmospheric and great fun, though the quality is variable and you may have to put up with some of the inconveniences (lack of elevators, odd-shaped rooms, steep staircases) that come with a rambling old building. Large, very well-organized country houses and golf hotels are another option at the luxury end. There is also a growing number of small, owner-run hotels with very high standards of care and attention.

Bed-and-Breakfast

It is the famous Irish bed-and-breakfast (B&B), though, that for most visitors offers the most enjoyable accommodations, where you are welcomed with true Irish warmth. Generally the owners are only too pleased to share their insiders' knowledge about the best attractions, music pubs, and places to eat. Those approved by Bord Fáilte display a shamrock sign; you can expect very high standards at these places.

Another trustworthy organization is **Town and Country Homes** (tel 071 982 2222, www.townand country.ie), which has more than 1,600 properties. And there are thousands of nonaffiliated B&Bs, where standards are very high. The village pub, shop, or post office is a good place to make inquiries.

One word of caution—many small businesses are closed in the winter, so it is always best to make a reservation. And one more word—the Irish breakfast (in the North known as the Ulster Fry) is an enormous, artery-unfriendly cholesterol blast, absolutely irresistibly bad for you. But you are on holiday, and, in any case, with one of those on board, you won't want lunch.

RESTAURANTS

It used to be a thankless task trying to find a decent place to eat in Ireland, but as with hotels, things have changed. Demand has created supply, and now you'll find a huge range of really good restaurants in every corner.

Although menus and cooking styles across Ireland, the claims of the top Irish restaurants to be among the best in Europe have solid foundations—fresh produce from the land and sea.

Meat has been the mainstay of Irish cooking for the past hundred years; Irish-reared beef, lamb, and pork are excellent, the art of the sausage flourishes, and there has been a cautious but now snowballing welcome of the organic meat movement.

Many places grow their own, or buy in, organic vegetables and herbs nowadays, too, and Irish cheeseboards, long confined to soapy cheddar, have taken on a rapidly growing selection of delicious Irish cheeses.

As for seafood, Ireland is, of course, an island, and there are any number of excellent fish and seafood specialists making diners happy from Kinsale to Portrush.

The Irish cellar has kept up with the improvements in the kitchen, though market-town hotel restaurants can still serve up some pretty execrable plonk under the guise of "house wine."

Don't neglect the café at afternoon teatime for Irish baking. Don't spurn the pub for an inexpensive meal—many pubs now put on a range of dishes that can outclass the local restaurants. And don't forget that your B&B may offer a home-cooked evening meal that might well be more enjoyable than the fanciest restaurant in town.

PRICES

HOTELS

An indication of the cost of a double room in the high season is given by $ signs.

$$$$$	Over $280
$$$$	$200–$280
$$$	$120–$200
$$	$80–$120
$	Under $80

RESTAURANTS

An indication of the cost of a three-course meal without drinks is given by $ signs.

$$$$$	Over $80
$$$$	$50–$80
$$$	$35–$50
$$	$20–$35
$	Under $20

ORGANIZATION & ABBREVIATIONS

All sites are listed first by price, then in alphabetical order.

The abbreviations used are:
L = lunch   D = dinner
AE = American Express;
DC = Diner's Club;
MC = MasterCard; V = Visa

■ DUBLIN

HOTELS

🏨 D4 BERKELEY HOTEL
$$$$$
LANSDOWNE RD.
BALLSBRIDGE, DUBLIN 4
TEL 01 665 3200
FAX 01 661 7238
www.d4hotels.ie
This highly polished and pro-
fessional operation offers the
service and facilities expected
from a 5-star hotel.
ⓘ 188 🅿 130 😊 🈂️
🈂️ All major cards

🏨 THE MERRION
🍴 $$$$$
UPPER MERRION ST.
DUBLIN 2
TEL 01 603 0600
FAX 01 603 0700
www.merrionhotel.com
Deceptively modest, this
Georgian building surrounding a garden offers first-class
cuisine, immaculate service,
and the likelihood of rubbing
shoulders with stellar person-
alities. The Mornington's
Brasserie is less breathless,
while **Restaurant Patrick Guil-
baud** (see p. 353) provides a
grand setting for fine food
rooted in French tradition.
ⓘ 145 🅿 60 😊 🈂️ 🈂️
🈂️ All major cards

🏨 RADISSON BLU
ST. HELEN'S HOTEL
$$$$$
4A STILLORGAN RD.

BLACKROCK, DUBLIN 4
TEL 01 218 6000
FAX 01 218 6010
www.radissonblu.ie
This hotel is located in an
elegant and luxurious Georgian
out-of-town house, overlooking terraced gardens, which
retains many of its original
18th-century features.
ⓘ 151 🅿 230 😊 🈂️ 🈂️ All
major cards

SOMETHING SPECIAL

🏨 RENAISSANCE
SHELBOURNE
$$$$–$$$$$
27 ST. STEPHEN'S GREEN
DUBLIN 2
TEL 01 663 4500
FAX 01 661 6006
www.marriott.com
The Shelbourne, an elegant
Georgian on St. Stephen's
Green, oozes atmosphere, as
befits a hotel that played a part
in the 1916 Easter Rising (see
pp. 30–32). Staying here, in the
centuries-old heart of Dublin,
you'll eat, drink, and sleep with
the shades of everyone who
was anyone in Ireland's historic
and literary life.
ⓘ 190 🅿 45 😊 🈂️ 🈂️ All
major cards

🏨 BURLINGTON
HOTEL
$$$$
UPPER LEESON ST.
DUBLIN 4
TEL 01 618 5600
FAX 01 618 5693
www.burlingtonhotel.ie
This traditional, comfortable
hotel is located within a few
minutes' walk of St. Stephen's
Green and the city's main
Southside attractions.
ⓘ 500 🅿 700 😊 🈂️ All
major cards

🏨 BUSWELLS HOTEL
$$$$
23–25 MOLESWORTH ST.

DUBLIN 2
TEL 01 614 6500
FAX 01 676 2090
www.buswells.ie
Located very close to the
National Museum (see pp.
56–59), just north of St.
Stephen's Green, this 18th-
century town house has been
stylishly converted into a comfortable hotel in a surprisingly
peaceful location.
ⓘ 69 🕐 Closed Christmas
😊 🈂️ All major cards

🏨 THE CLARENCE
$$$$
6–8 WELLINGTON QUAY
DUBLIN 2
TEL 01 407 0800
FAX 01 407 0820
www.theclarence.ie
Owned by members of the
rock band U2, this beautifully
refurbished hotel looks out on
the River Liffey, with Temple
Bar at its back door. The hotel
also hosts the renowned **Tea
Room** (see p. 353).
ⓘ 49 🅿 15 🕐 Closed Christmas 😊 🈂️ 🈂️ All major cards

🏨 FITZWILLIAM HOTEL
$$$$
ST. STEPHENS GREEN
DUBLIN 2
TEL 01 478 7000
FAX 01 478 7878
www.fitzwilliamhotel.com
This luxurious hotel in Dublin's
most favored location has
elegant modern decor and a
notably helpful staff. **Thornton's Restaurant** (see p. 352)
also is housed in the hotel.
ⓘ 130 🅿 85 😊 🈂️ 🈂️ All
major cards

🏨 PREMIER SUITES
DUBLIN
$$$$
STEPHENS HALL
14–17 LOWER LEESON ST.
DUBLIN 2
TEL 01 638 1111
FAX 01 638 1122
www.premiersuitesdublin.com

😊 Elevator 🈂️ Air-conditioning 🈂️ Indoor Pool 🈂️ Outdoor Pool 🈂️ Credit Cards

Located near St. Stephen's Green, this is an interesting idea that works well—a hotel containing several types of accommodations ranging from penthouses and suites to studios, all of them very well appointed.
[i] 34 [P] 40 [⇄] [✦] All major cards

SCHOOLHOUSE HOTEL
$$$$
2–8 NORTHUMBERLAND RD.
BALLSBRIDGE, DUBLIN 4
TEL 01 667 5014
FAX 01 667 5015
www.schoolhousehotel.com
School phobics have no cause to be alarmed! The enjoyably atmospheric decor does indeed reflect the building's original incarnation as a Victorian school, but there's nothing at all Spartan about the well-appointed bedrooms.
[i] 31 [P] 21 [⊕] Closed Christmas [⇄] [✦] All major cards

MARINE HOTEL
$$$–$$$$
SUTTON CROSS
DUBLIN 13
TEL 01 839 0000
FAX 01 839 0442
www.marinehotel.ie
This comfortable gabled hotel, built in a traditional seaside style, is on the north side of Dublin Bay and situated only a few minutes from central Dublin by DART railway.
[i] 48 [P] 150 [⊕] Closed Christmas [⇄] [✦] All major cards

MERCER HOTEL
$$$–$$$$
LOWER MERCER ST.
DUBLIN 2
TEL 01 478 2179
FAX 01 475 6524
www.mercerhotel.ie
You'll find nicely furnished guest rooms and capable staff at this centrally placed hotel near St. Stephen's Green.

[i] 41 [⊕] Closed Christmas
[⇄] [✦] [✦] AE, MC, V

MOUNT HERBERT HOTEL
$$$–$$$$
HERBERT RD.
LANSDOWNE, DUBLIN 4
TEL 01 614 2000
FAX 01 660 7077
www.mountherberthotel.ie
Located to the southeast of the city center, this pleasant hotel is a minute's walk from Lansdowne DART station.
[i] 185 [P] 90 [⇄]
[✦] All major cards

WESTBURY HOTEL
$$$–$$$$
2 GRAFTON ST.
DUBLIN 2
TEL 01 679 1122
www.doylecollection.com
This luxury city-center hotel offers chandeliers, valet parking, and tea on the terrace around the grand piano.
[i] 205 [P] 100 [⇄] [✦]
[✦] All major cards

ABERDEEN LODGE
$$$
53–55 PARK AVE.
BALLSBRIDGE, DUBLIN 4
TEL 01 283 8155
FAX 01 283 7877
www.aberdeen-lodge.com
A classy Edwardian building houses one of Dublin's best private hotels, where high standards of comfort and efficiency are not allowed to get in the way of friendly service.
[i] 20 [P] 16 [✦] All major cards

BLAKES HOTEL & SPA
$$$
50 MERRION RD.
BALLSBRIDGE, DUBLIN 4
TEL 01 668 8324
FAX 01 668 4280
www.blakeshotelandspa.com
Four-poster beds, garden balconies, air-conditioning—the accommodations at Blakes are

both luxurious and tasteful.
[i] 13 [P] 6 [✦] [✦] All major cards

CLONTARF CASTLE
$$$
CASTLE AVENUE
CLONTARF, DUBLIN 3
TEL 01 833 2321
www.clontarfcastle.ie
There is something a little preposterous, but endearing, about the unashamed extravagance of Clontarf Castle, where stone lions and suits of armor greet you.
[i] 180 [P] 134 [⇄] [✦] [✦] All major cards

THE MORRISON
$$$
ORMOND QUAY
DUBLIN 1
TEL 01 887 2400
FAX 01 878 3185
www.morrisonhotel.ie
Cool, chic, and stylish, this is one of the nicest places to stay in the city center.
[i] 90 [⇄] [✦] [✦] All major cards

NUMBER 31
$$$
31 LEESON CLOSE
DUBLIN 2
TEL 01 676 5011
FAX 01 676 2929
www.number31.ie
Located beside St. Stephen's Green, this Georgian residence and coach house is ideally placed for exploring Dublin. It offers a lovely green garden, beautiful fresh food at breakfast, and a typically warm Irish welcome.
[i] 21 [P] 20 [✦] All major cards

REDBANK HOUSE
$$$
5–7 CHURCH ST.
SKERRIES, CO. DUBLIN
TEL 01 849 1005
FAX 01 849 1598
www.redbank.ie
Redbank House is famed for its fresh fish and vegetables,

elegance, and super-comfortable rooms with headboards
of carved wood.
🛏 18 🕐 Closed Christmas
🏧 All major cards

🏨 HAMPTON HOTEL
$$-$$$$
19–29 MOREHAMPTON RD.
DONNYBROOK, DUBLIN 4
TEL 01 668 0995
FAX 01 667 6126
www.hamptonhotel.ie
Located in a desirable district
of the city, the Hampton is
one of Dublin's newest and
nicest boutique hotels. Decor
is stylish, staff are friendly,
and the atmosphere is chic
but warm.
🛏 24 🅿 30 ⬆ 🅢 🏧 All
major cards

🏨 ARIEL HOUSE
$$-$$$
50–54 LANSDOWNE RD.
BALLSBRIDGE, DUBLIN 4
TEL 01 668 5512
FAX 01 668 5845
www.ariel-house.net
This beautifully kept period
Victorian house, which is
located near the Lansdowne
DART station, is run to very
high standards.
🛏 37 🅿 30 🕐 Closed Christ-
mas 🏧 MC, V

🏨 MERRION HALL
$$-$$$
54 MERRION RD.
BALLSBRIDGE, DUBLIN 4
TEL 01 283 8155
FAX 01 283 7877
www.merrionhall.com
Edwardian elegance, modern
comforts, and fine food
combine in this award-win-
ning guesthouse located next
to the RDS and close to the
city center. Four-poster beds
and Jacuzzis are just some of
the features.
🛏 34 🅿 20 🅢 🏧 AE, M, V

🏨 WATERLOO HOUSE
$$-$$$

8–10 WATERLOO RD.
BALLSBRIDGE, DUBLIN 4
TEL 01 660 1888
FAX 01 667 1955
www.waterloohouse.ie
Behind the handsome brick
facade of this luxury town
house, on a quiet street, you'll
find an elegant and peaceful
haven. Wonderful breakfasts
set you up for the fray.
🛏 17 🅿 8 🕐 Closed Christ-
mas 🏧 All major cards

🏨 BEWLEY'S HOTEL
$$
MERRION RD.
BALLSBRIDGE, DUBLIN 4
TEL 01 668 1111
FAX 01 668 1999
www.bewleyshotels.com
Bewley's prides itself on its
relaxed ambience, with staff
striking a welcoming note from
the outset.
🛏 304 🅿 240 ⬆ 🏧 All
major cards

🏨 THE GRESHAM
$$
23 UPPER O'CONNELL ST.
DUBLIN 1
TEL 01 874 6881
FAX 01 878 7175
www.gresham-hotels.com
Just north of the River Liffey,
the Gresham offers comfort
and a high standard of service.
🛏 288 🅿 150 ⬆ 🅢 🏧 All
major cards

🏨 TEMPLE BAR HOTEL
$$
FLEET ST.
TEMPLE BAR, DUBLIN 2
TEL 01 677 3333
FAX 01 677 3088
www.templebarhotel.com
This cozy, centrally located
hideaway shares its name
and location with Dublin's
trendiest quarter—right on
the doorstep—for ambling
around by day and living it
up by night.
🛏 129 🕐 Closed Christmas
⬆ 🏧 All major cards

🏨 CHARLEVILLE LODGE
$-$$$
268–272 NORTH CIRCULAR RD.
PHIBSBOROUGH, DUBLIN 7
TEL 01 838 6633
FAX 01 838 5854
www.charlevillelodge.ie
A short terrace of fine Victorian
houses has been skillfully com-
bined to create this congenial
bolt-hole near the northern
perimeter of Phoenix Park.
🛏 30 🅿 18 🕐 Closed Christ-
mas 🏧 All major cards

🏨 DONNYBROOK LODGE
$
131 STILLORGAN RD.
DONNYBROOK, DUBLIN 4
TEL 01 283 7333
FAX 01 260 4770
www.donnybrooklodge.net
In an exclusive area of Dublin,
this is a charming modern home
set in lovely gardens. It's on
direct bus routes from the city
center, airport, and ferry termi-
nal. The proprietors are friendly,
and breakfast is included. Special
diet options are available. Air-
port or ferry pickup available.
🛏 7 🅿 8 🏧 MC, V

RESTAURANTS

🍴 RESTAURANT PATRICK
GUILBAUD
$$$$$
21 UPPER MERRION ST.
DUBLIN 2
TEL 01 676 4192
FAX 01 661 0052
www.restaurantpatrick
guilbaud.ie
Faultless French cuisine and
immaculate service have
won Patrick Guilbaud more
awards than any other res-
taurant in Ireland. Impeccable
culinary creations here include
succulent Connemara lobster
ravioli and sole and duck confit.
Housed in the Merrion Hotel
(see p. 349), with a fine col-
lection of original Irish art, the
restaurant is an upscale dining

experience with considerable Irish charm.
🕐 Closed Sun.–Mon. 💳 All major cards

🍴 THORNTON'S RESTAURANT
$$$$$
FITZWILLIAM HOTEL
128 ST. STEPHEN'S GREEN
DUBLIN 2
TEL 01 478 7008
FAX 01 478 7009
www.thorntonsrestaurant.com
Kevin Thornton is the chef that everyone keeps on raving about, year after year. Here's your chance to see why—if you manage to get a table. It's worth making a reservation before you leave home to sample the wonderful combinations of flavors and textures and to experience for yourself the perfectionism and flair, and then some. Open pre-theater by arrangement.
🕐 Closed Sun.–Mon. 💳 All major cards

🍴 KING SITRIC
$$$$
EAST PIER, HOWTH
CO. DUBLIN
TEL 01 832 5235
FAX 01 839 2442
www.kingsitric.ie
Right on the harbor, this is a first-class fish restaurant, with lobster and crab caught by its own fishermen, fresh fish landed daily on Howth Pier, and oysters and mussels rushed in from the west coast. As well as traditional Irish and French-influenced dishes, there are Oriental touches.
♿ 🕐 Closed Mon.–Tues. Oct.–April 💳 All major cards

🍴 MV CILL AIRNE
$$$$
QUAY 16, NORTH WALL QUAY
DUBLIN 1
TEL 087 952 4006
www.mvcillairne.com
A short stroll from the O2 concert arena, this beautifully

restored training vessel, with its gleaming wooden floors and bar, makes a characterful place to eat and drink, before or after a show. Dine in style in the Quay 16 Restaurant, or snack in the laid-back bistro
🕐 Closed Sun. & L Sat.

🍴 CHAPTER ONE
$$$
18–19 PARNELL SQ.
DUBLIN 1
TEL 01 873 2266
FAX 01 873 3330
www.chapteronerestaurant.com
The Dublin Writers' Museum sits on top of this excellent north-of-the-Liffey eatery, which uses both French and Irish influences in its cooking to great effect.
♿ 🕐 Closed Sun.–Mon. 💳 AE, DC, V

🍴 EDEN
$$$
MEETING HOUSE SQ.
TEMPLE BAR
DUBLIN 2
TEL 01 670 5372
FAX 01 670 3330
www.edenrestaurant.ie
Right at the hub of happening Temple Bar, Eden does throw its cap definitively into the modern cookery ring, but with no flim-flam. The flavors of quality ingredients sensitively handled speak for themselves, in spicy Thai soup, perhaps, or monkfish and peppers, or tangy balls of finely minced lamb.
💳 All major cards

🍴 HUGO'S
$$$
6 MERRION ROW
DUBLIN 2
TEL 01 676 5955
FAX 01 676 1999
www.hugos.ie
With its awning and bright colors, Hugo's puts you in mind of a small restaurant in a French provincial town. And

the French/Irish/touch-of-the-Mediterranean cooking doesn't disappoint. A good selection of wines complements a menu that's not overlong. Two favorites are the Mediterranean fish soup, with crispy croutons and garlicky rouille, and the slow-cooked duck with Toulouse sausage, *pommes salardaises*, and bacon.
💳 All major cards

🍴 KITES
$$$
15–17 BALLSBRIDGE TERRACE
BALLSBRIDGE, DUBLIN 4
TEL 01 660 7415
A very good Chinese restaurant with a pleasant, low-key atmosphere, serving a wide variety of dishes.
🕐 Closed Sat., Sun. L, Good Fri., Dec. 25–26 💳 All major cards

🍴 L'ECRIVAIN
$$$
109A LOWER BAGGOT ST.
DUBLIN 2
TEL 01 661 1919
FAX 01 661 0617
www.lecrivain.com
A deservedly famous Dublin restaurant, full of good culinary ideas based on the best fresh ingredients, executed brilliantly but without bravado. Monkfish, oysters, prawns, and scallops are all wonderful, and meat-lovers will love the Irish lamb and beef. As a bonus: a particularly interesting wine list.
♿ 🕐 Closed Sun.–Tues. 💳 All major cards

🍴 NOSH
$$$
111 COLIEMORE RD.
DALKEY, CO. DUBLIN
TEL 01 284 0666
www.nosh.ie
The vibe here is young and fresh. Fantastic seafood and other local produce.
🕐 Closed Mon. 💳 All major cards

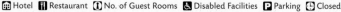

ROLY'S RESTAURANT & CAFÉ

$$$

7 BALLSBRIDGE TERRACE
BALLSBRIDGE, DUBLIN 4
TEL 01 668 2611
www.rolysbistro.ie

A tremendous atmosphere of Dubliners enjoying themselves, and an unfussy approach to food (notably the Dublin Bay prawns and the hearty "keep-out-the-cold" puddings) that lets basic flavors and textures speak for themselves.
All major cards

SHANAHAN'S ON THE GREEN

$$$

119 ST. STEPHEN'S GREEN
DUBLIN 2
TEL 01 407 0939
www.shanahans.ie

Behind the very Irish name is very American cooking: huge steaks done to perfection—a rare art. There's something for everyone on the menu, but carnivores with heroic appetites will think they have died and gone to Dallas.
Closed L Sat.–Thurs. & Sun. All major cards

THE TEA ROOM

$$$

THE CLARENCE HOTEL
6–8 WELLINGTON QUAY
DUBLIN 2
TEL 01 407 0813
FAX 01 407 0826
www.theclarence.ie

You can just drink tea here, if you must, but the Tea Room is really about fine dining in style. The modern cooking, including excellent fresh sea bass, or oysters in a crab sauce, for example, is enjoyed in a light and lively room that's paneled in pale wood, art deco fashion.
Closed Sat. & Sun. L All major cards

BON APPÉTIT

$$–$$$$

9 JAMES TERRACE
MALAHIDE, CO. DUBLIN
TEL 01 845 0314
www.bonappetit.ie

A proper fine-dining experience in trendy Malahide. The set menus are pricey yet still good value for beautifully cooked lobster and prawns, Irish beef and rabbit, and superbly flavorsome vegetables, all meticulously presented. Excellent value downstairs in the Café Bon brasserie, too.
Closed L Mon.–Thurs. & Sat. AE, MC, V

PINTXO

$$–$$$

12 EUSTACE ST.
TEMPLE BAR, DUBLIN 2
TEL 01 672 8590

This lively tapas bar in the heart of bouncing Temple Bar has an open kitchen and more racked wine bottles than you can count. Offerings include paella, patatas bravas, sausage, and octopus, along with Spanish and Portuguese wines, beers, and sherries.
MC, V

101 TALBOT

$$

100–102 TALBOT ST.
DUBLIN 1
TEL 01 874 5011
www.101talbot.ie

Far East (vegetable coconut curry), Middle East (spanakopita), and Near East (Clonakilty black pudding) collide to all-encompassing effect on the menu of this Northside restaurant. It's very convenient for pretheater fueling—both the Abbey and the Gate theaters are within strolling distance.
Closed Sun.–Mon., L All major cards

BELLA CUBA

$$

11 BALLSBRIDGE TERRACE
BALLSBRIDGE, DUBLIN 4
TEL/FAX 01 660 5539
www.bella-cuba.com

Fabulous Cuban cuisine, meaty and fishy with bursts of flavor from combinations of spices and herbs.
Closed L AE, MC, V

CAVISTONS

$$

58–59 GLASTHULE RD.
SANDYCOVE, CO. DUBLIN
TEL 01 280 9245
FAX 01 284 4054
www.cavistons.com

Quite simply, an unpretentious, family-run restaurant whose Irish-style seafood and other cooking is so superb that connoisseurs will visit Ireland specifically to eat here. Yet everyone feels welcome, and no one feels excluded.
Closed D Tues.–Thurs. & Sun.–Mon. All major cards

ELEPHANT & CASTLE

$$

18 TEMPLE BAR
DUBLIN 2
TEL 01 679 3121
www.elephantandcastle.ie

The Elephant & Castle opens early and closes late, so you could eat three (or four) square meals a day here. And why not, when the food's good from breakfast to dinner (enormous baskets of chicken wings, homemade hamburgers with an array of sauces, and a mighty Caesar salad) and the atmosphere is so enjoyable?
All major cards

GOOD WORLD

$$

18 S. GREAT GEORGE'S ST.
DUBLIN 2
TEL/FAX 01 677 5373

Handy for Grafton Street shoppers or visitors to St. Patrick's Cathedral, this is the Chinese restaurant where the Dublin Chinese themselves prefer to eat. All the variations on noodles and beanshoots that you would expect, all beautifully cooked, plus Dublin's best and widest choice of dim sum. ⏱ Closed Dec. 25–26 💳 All major cards

🍴 HO SEN
$$
6 COPE ST.
DUBLIN 2
TEL/FAX 01 671 8181
Wonderful Thai cuisine in a nice, relaxed atmosphere, right in bustling Temple Bar. ⏱ Closed Mon.–Wed. L, Mon. D 💳 All major cards

SOMETHING SPECIAL

🍴 O'CONNELL'S
$$
BALLSBRIDGE COURT HOTEL
LANSDOWNE RD.
BALLSBRIDGE, DUBLIN 4
TEL 01 645 5940
FAX 01 665 5943
www.oconnellsballsbridge.com
What a great idea—this admirable place (at the Ballsbridge Court Hotel) obtains all its ingredients and its wine from top-class sources (organic, free-range, fresh almost goes without saying), and the menu lets you know exactly who and where it all came from. It adds a certain something to your enjoyment of salmon, for example, if you can visualize the cold blue waters off magical green Clare Island where the fish was raised. 💳 All major cards

🍴 POPPADOM RESTAURANT
$$
91A RATHGAR RD.
DUBLIN 6
TEL 01 490 2383
Yes, the poppadoms are admirable—the real thing, properly made—but so is all the authentic Indian food. Really good Indian restaurants

are rarer than hen's teeth in Ireland, but here's one. ♿ ⏱ Closed L 💳 All major cards

🍴 THE WINDING STAIR
$$
40 ORMOND QUAY
DUBLIN 1
TEL 01 872 7320
www.winding-stair.com
This combination eatery and bookshop overlooks Ha'penny Bridge. Read or watch the crowds over Connemara lamb, smoked Cork sausage, or traditional bacon and cabbage. ⏱ Closed Christmas 💳 MC, V

🍴 BUTLER'S CHOCOLATE CAFÉ
$
9 CHATHAM STREET
DUBLIN 2
TEL 01 672 6333
www.butlerschocolates.com
Butler's has done for hot chocolate what Seattle did for coffee, and you can either drink it neat or add one of a variety of flavored syrups. There's great coffee, too, along with freshly baked cakes and croissants and a selection of handmade chocolates. Savory gourmet sandwiches are also available. 💳 All major cards

■ EAST IRELAND

COUNTY KILDARE

ATHY

🏨 COURSETOWN COUNTRY HOUSE
$$
STRADBALLY RD.
TEL 059 863 1101
FAX 059 863 2740
www.coursetown.com
This is a luxurious country-house hotel set on a 250-acre (100 ha) farm, which is also a wildlife sanctuary. The own-

ers are only too happy to share their knowledge with their guests. Lovely walks. ⓘ 5 🅿 22 ⏱ Closed mid-Nov.–mid-Feb. 💳 MC, V

BALLYMORE EUSTACE

🍴 BALLYMORE INN
$$
BALLYMORE EUSTACE
TEL 0458 64585
www.ballymoreinn.com
From tempting starters to the excellent cheeseboard, this pub-style restaurant and bar offers top-quality fare, based on carefully selected ingredients—all served, of course, with a welcoming smile. 💳 AE, MC, V

KILDARE

🏨 MARTINSTOWN HOUSE
$$$
THE CURRAGH, CO. KILDARE
TEL 0454 41269

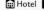

FAX 0454 41208
www.martinstownhouse.com
This upmarket, but comfortable and relaxed, family-run haven is located close to the Curragh and the heart of Ireland's horse-racing world.
i 4 ⊕ Closed Christmas
⊗ AE, MC, V

LEIXLIP

LEIXLIP HOUSE HOTEL
¶¶ $$$–$$$$
CAPTAINS HILL, LEIXLIP
TEL 01 624 2268
FAX 01 624 4177
www.leixliphouse.com
In this fine Georgian house, the enjoyable ambience is more than matched by the cooking, Irish style. With great attention to locally sourced seasonal produce, it sets the standard for other hotel restaurants in the area.
i 19 **P** 64 ⊗ All major cards

STRAFFAN

THE K CLUB
$$$$$
STRAFFAN
TEL 01 601 7200
FAX 01 601 7297
www.kclub.com
A top-notch, 5-star hotel with its own Arnold Palmer–designed golf course—the 2005 Ryder Cup was contested here. Efficient staff offers polished, attentive service. A luxury stopover for those who need not count the cents—nor the dollars.
i 69 plus 10 annex **P** 205
⊟ ⊠ ⊗ All major cards

COUNTY WICKLOW

ASHFORD

BALLYKNOCKEN HOUSE
$$–$$$
GLENEALY, ASHFORD
TEL 0404 44627
FAX 0404 44696

www.ballyknocken.com
This first-class guesthouse makes a convenient base for visiting the Wicklow Mountains. Ask for one of the rooms with the vast Victorian baths. There is also an excellent cooking school.
i 10 ⊕ Closed mid-Dec–Jan.
⊗ MC, V

BRAY

¶¶ CAMPO DE FIORI
$$
1 ALBERT AVENUE
TEL 01 276 4257
The seaside town of Bray has been looking for something like this—an Italian restaurant that is thoroughly proud of its nationality, from the gesticulating and voluble waiters wielding outsize pepper grinders to the delicious smells of garlic and tomatoes wafting from the kitchen. Pasta is properly chunky; pizzas are thin of base and big on authentic flavors.
⊕ Closed L & Christmas

GLENDALOUGH

SOMETHING SPECIAL

BROOKLODGE &
¶¶ WELLS SPA
$$$$
MACREDDIN VILLAGE
TEL 0402 36444
FAX 0402 36580
www.brooklodge.com
A luxury hotel within easy reach of the Wicklow Mountains. De-stress in the sauna, then savor organic, locally sourced food in the **Strawberry Tree** restaurant.
i 90 ⊗ AE, MC, V

TUDOR LODGE
$
LARAGH
TEL 0404 45554
tudorlodgeireland@eircom.net
An exceptionally hospitable

house only a mile (1.6 km) from the beautiful valley and historic monastic site of Glendalough. The owners treat you as if you are a personal friend, rooms are very comfortable and well appointed, there's a cozy sitting room with a fire, and the breakfasts are so gargantuan that you can skip lunch and still wear a smile.
i 6 **P** 8 ⊗ MC, V

KILMACANOGUE

¶¶ AVOCA HANDWEAVERS
$
KILMACANOGUE
TEL 01 286 7466
FAX 01 286 2367
www.avoca.ie
What real food is all about—fresh ingredients, combined into uncomplicated dishes, and served with charm. The restaurant is attached to the famous knitwear store.
⊛ ⊕ Closed D ⊗ All major cards

RATHNEW

TINAKILLY COUNTRY HOUSE HOTEL
$$$$–$$$$$
RATHNEW
TEL 0404 69274
FAX 0404 67806
www.tinakilly.ie
A Victorian house in terraced gardens, with beautiful sea views on this unfrequented coast north of Wicklow town.
i 51 **P** 60 ⊕ Closed Christmas ⊟ ⊗ All major cards

HUNTER'S HOTEL
$$$
NEWRATH BRIDGE
TEL 0404 40106
FAX 0404 40338
www.hunters.ie
A long-established, family-run coaching inn set in beautiful gardens. Wood beams, open fires, beautiful old staircases, and a wealth of antique furni-

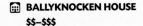

ture set a lovely scene.
🕐 Closed Christmas 💳 All major cards

WOODENBRIDGE

🏨 **WOODENBRIDGE**
$$–$$$
WOODENBRIDGE
TEL 0402 35146
FAX 0402 35573
www.woodenbridgehotel.com
A friendly hotel at the foot of the delectable Vale of Avoca in the south Wicklow Mountains. Some of the rooms date to the 17th century, others are new; all are very comfortable.
ℹ️ 23 🅿️ 100 💳 AE, MC, V

COUNTY CARLOW

BAGENALSTOWN

🏨 **LORUM OLD RECTORY**
$$$
KILGRANEY
TEL 059 977 5282
FAX 059 977 5455
www.lorum.com
A stylish and welcoming place famous for its wonderful home cooking. Fresh flowers throughout the house, croquet and peacocks on the lawn.
ℹ️ 5 🕐 Closed Dec.–Feb.
💳 All major cards

CARLOW

🏨 **AVLON HOUSE**
🍴 **$$**
GREEN LANE, DUBLIN RD.
TEL 059 917 4222
FAX 059 917 3829
www.carlowbedandbreakfast.com
Gerard McCormack and Tom Donagher have created exactly what Carlow needed, a top-notch B&B. Everything is kept in immaculate order, and the mighty breakfasts include fresh fruit and all the trimmings.
ℹ️ 5 🅿️ 7

🏨 **DOLMEN HOTEL**
🍴 **$$**
KILKENNY RD.
TEL 059 914 2002
FAX 059 914 2375
reservations@ dolmenhotel.ie
The Dolmen prides itself on re-creating the comfort and spaciousness of a bygone era, exemplified in its beautiful rooms. Try coarse fishing or stroll in 20 acres (8 ha) of landscaped grounds along the river. You can eat in the formal **Belmont Restaurant,** the laid-back Barrow Grill, or the lunchtime carvery.
ℹ️ 40 plus 12 annex 🅿️ 300
💳 💳 All major cards

COUNTY KILKENNY

KILKENNY

🏨 **BUTLER HOUSE**
$$–$$$$
16 PATRICK ST.
TEL 056 772 2828
FAX 056 776 5626
www.butler.ie
The former Dower House of Kilkenny Castle provides elegant accommodations right in the heart of the town. It has magnificent marble fireplaces and sweeping staircases, and the larger rooms have views over the peaceful garden and the castle. Breakfast is included in the price, either a Continental, served in the rooms, or full hot breakfast provided just across the garden.
ℹ️ 13 🅿️ 24 💳 All major cards

🏨 **LANGTONS HOUSE HOTEL**
$$–$$$
69 JOHN ST.
TEL 056 776 5133
www.langtons.ie
Four times national pub of the year, Langtons now has a stylish hotel extension with the same high standards and attention to detail that won accolades for

the bar and restaurant.
ℹ️ 30 🅿️ 80 🅿️ All major cards

🏨 **KILKENNY ORMONDE HOTEL**
$–$$$
ORMONDE ST.
TEL 056 772 3900
FAX 056 772 3977
www.kilkennyormonde.com
Consistently good food is on offer in both restaurants of this new hotel with large lounge and reception areas.
ℹ️ 118 💳 All major cards

🍴 **CAMPAGNE**
$$$$
THE ARCHES, 5 GASHOUSE LN.
TEL 056 777 2858
www.campagne.ie
The fish, meat, and vegetables of this bright, modern restaurant come from local suppliers. Try the creamy Knockdrinna goat's cheese.
🕐 Closed Mon.–Tues. & D Sun. Sept.–May 💳 MC, V

THOMASTOWN

🏨 **MOUNT JULIET**
$$$$–$$$$$
THOMASTOWN
TEL 056 777 3000
FAX 056 777 3019
www.mountjuliet.ie
Fine stucco, Adam fireplaces, 18th-century furniture, and objets d'art feature within this handsome Palladian mansion. Jack Nicklaus designed the hotel's golf course, and there are 1,500 acres (600 ha) of parkland to explore.
ℹ️ 32 plus 27 annex 🅿️ 200
💳 💳 All major cards

COUNTY WEXFORD

ARTHURSTOWN

🏨 **DUNBRODY COUNTRY**
🍴 **HOUSE HOTEL &**
RESTAURANT
$$$$–$$$$$

ARTHURSTOWN
TEL 051 389600
FAX 051 389601
www.dunbrodyhouse.com
Individually styled bedrooms
with marble bathrooms in
a Georgian country house
set in parkland near the sea.
Award-winning cuisine in the
most beautiful surroundings
on Waterford Harbour.
🛏 22 🅿 40 🕐 Closed Christmas 🆑 All major cards

ENNISCORTHY

🏨 **BALLINKEELE HOUSE**
$$$$
BALLYMUN
TEL 053 913 8105
FAX 053 913 8468
www.ballinkeele.ie
Bedrooms are extremely
comfortable, the ambience
relaxed at this upscale Victorian
farmhouse at the heart of a
working farm.
🛏 5 🅿 20 🕐 Closed Dec.–
Jan. 🆑 MC, V

GOREY

🏨 **MARLFIELD HOUSE**
$$$$$
COURTOWN RD.
TEL 053 942 1124
FAX 053 942 1572
www.marlfieldhouse.com
This luxurious hotel, once a
fine Regency house, was home
to the Earl of Courtown. The
conservatory looks out on
lovely gardens.
🛏 20 🅿 50 🕐 Closed mid-
Dec.–Jan. 🆑 All major cards

ROSSLARE

🏨 **KELLY'S RESORT HOTEL**
🍴 **& SPA**
$$$
TEL 053 913 2114
FAX 053 913 2222
www.kellys.ie
A seafront hotel with a stylish
modern approach, down to
its imported French zinc bar.

The same goes for the food, as
superbly tasty as really direct
contemporary cooking should
be. The seafood chowder and
the Wexford beef hot off the
grill are outstanding.
🛏 118 🅿 99 🕐 Closed mid-
Dec.–late Feb. 🆑 AE,
MC, V

COUNTY TIPPERARY

BALLINDERRY

SOMETHING SPECIAL

🍴 **BROCKA-ON-THE-
WATER**
$$$
KILGARVAN QUAY
TEL 067 22038
Forget the whistles and bells of
more pretentious restaurants.
This one concentrates on the
three things that matter—
atmosphere, location and,
oh yes, food. Brocka-on-
the-Water is a relaxed and
delightful place beside Lough
Derg in northernmost County
Tipperary. The freshest fish
and meat are complemented
by herbs and vegetables from
the restaurant's own garden.
🕐 Closed Sun.–Mon. & Wed.
🆑 No credit cards accepted

CASHEL

🏨 **CASHEL PALACE HOTEL**
$$$$–$$$$$
CASHEL
TEL 062 62707
FAX 062 61521
www.cashel-palace.ie
This hotel is the former palace
of the Bishops of Cashel, with
the spectacular backdrop of
the Rock of Cashel (floodlit at
night). Luxury bedrooms in
the palace itself; family or
group needs are catered for
in mews accommodations
alongside.
🛏 13 plus 10 annex 🅿 35
🕐 Closed Christmas 🆑 All
major cards

CLONMEL

🏨 **HOTEL MINELLA**
$$$
COLEVILLE RD.
TEL 052 612 2388
www.hotelminella.ie
This is a cozy, family-run hotel
with tastefully decorated bed-
rooms (some have Jacuzzis) in
its own extensive grounds by
the River Suir.
🛏 70 🅿 100 🕐 Closed
Christmas 🆑 All major
cards

COUNTY WATERFORD

BALLYMACARBRY

🏨 **GLASHA FARMHOUSE**
$$$
BALLYMACARBRY, VIA CLONMEL
TEL 052 36108
www.glashafarmhouse.com
Paddy and Olive O'Gorman
have made a country haven in
their dairy farmhouse. With
pretty cottage-style furnishings, Glasha is well placed for
exploring the Comeragh and
Knockmealdown Mountains.
🛏 8 🅿 10 🕐 Closed Christ-
mas 🆑 MC, V

🏨 **HONORA'S COTTAGE**
$$–$$$
NIRE VALLEY
TEL 052 613 6134
FAX 052 613 6540
www.hanorascottage
Guests feel like friends here,
where the cooking is superb
and Mary Wall, her son Eoin,
and his wife Judith offer a
warm welcome and all the
advice you need on walking in
the Comeragh Mountains.
🛏 10 🅿 15 🕐 Closed Christmas 🆑 MC, V

DUNGARVAN

🍴 **TANNERY RESTAURANT**
$$$
10 QUAY ST.
TEL 058 45420

FAX 058 45814
www.tannery.ie
A creative approach gives an imaginative twist to everything from old favorites, like grilled plaice with chorizo and shoulder of lamb with Tuscan vegetable stew, to innovations such as hoisin duck with sesame and Bleu d'Auvergne with grilled figs.
🕒 Closed Sun.–Mon. 🕮 All major cards

GLENCAIRN

🍴 PASTIS FRENCH BISTRO
$$
AT THE GLENCAIRN INN
NEAR LISMORE
TEL 058 56232
www.glencairninn.com
An Irish institution, where uncomplicated treatment of extremely fresh ingredients—notably the fish, which is caught locally—produces fabulously tasty dishes.
♿ 🕒 Closed Mon.–Wed. Oct.–April, mid-Nov.–mid-Jan. 🕮 MC, V

WATERFORD

🏨 WATERFORD CASTLE
$$$$–$$$$$
THE ISLAND
TEL 051 878 203
FAX 051 879 316
www.waterfordcastle.com
A chance to stay in a Norman castle, reached by ferry and set up to ensure the most romantic of sojourns. Realists will enjoy the 18-hole golf course, clay shooting, and other outdoor activities.
🛏 19 🅿 50 🔌 🕮 All major cards

🍴 HARLEQUIN CAFÉ & WINE BAR
$–$$
37 STEPHEN ST.
TEL 051 877 552
www.harlequin-cafe.com
Run by an Italian couple, this

is a great place to pop in for pungent coffee to wake you up or some pasta later in the day.
🕒 Closed Sun. & Christmas
🕮 MC, V

■ SOUTHWEST IRELAND

CORK CITY

🏨 HAYFIELD MANOR
$$$$$
PERROTT AVE., COLLEGE RD.
TEL 021 484 5900
FAX 021 431 6839
www.hayfieldmanor.ie
A snug retreat where you can shut the world away (and work on your fitness in the exclusive health club), Hayfield Manor is a comfortable, upscale hotel toward the western outskirts of Cork city. 🛏 88 🅿 100
🔌 ♨ 🏊 🕮 All major cards

🏨 CAFE PARADISO
🍴 $$$
16 LANCASTER QUAY
TEL 021 427 7939
www.cafeparadiso.ie
This vegetarian café with rooms is great for pretheater dining, with such delicacies as caramelized beetroot tart or a cake of couscous, feta cheese, and pistachio.
🛏 3 🕒 Closed D Mon., L Sun.–Fri., & Christmas 🕮 All major cards

🏨 KINGSLEY HOTEL
$$$
VICTORIA CROSS
TEL 021 480 0555
FAX 021 480 0526
www.kingsleyhotel.com
A luxury hotel beside the River Lee, with an agreeably relaxed atmosphere. Big, airy bedrooms have safes, trouser presses, air-conditioning, interactive TVs with messaging —and there's a same-day laundry service, too.
🛏 69 🅿 250 🔌 ♨
🕮 All major cards

🏨 IMPERIAL HOTEL
$$–$$$$
SOUTH MALL
TEL 021 427 4040
FAX 021 427 5375
www.flynnhotels.com
The individually styled en suite rooms of this chic hotel offer comfort and a quiet atmosphere in central Cork.
🛏 125 🅿 40 🕒 Closed Christmas 🔌 🕮 All major cards

🍴 JACOB'S ON THE MALL
$$$
30A SOUTH MALL
TEL 021 425 1530
FAX 021 125 1531
www.jacobsonthemall.com
Sophisticated cuisine such as roast cod with champ—mashed potato with a touch of magic—or oysters with shallots are served in a relaxed atmosphere in the heart of Cork city.
♿ 🕒 Closed Sun. 🕮 AE, MC, V

🍴 JACQUES
$$$
PHOENIX ST.
TEL 021 427 7387
FAX 021 427 0634
www.jacquesrestaurant.ie
Dishes from around the world, each treated with care and attention to detail—Spanish salads, Mediterranean swordfish, Thai green chicken curry, boeuf Bordelaise, and many more.
🕒 Closed Sun. L 🕮 AE, MC, V

🍴 CRAWFORD ART GALLERY CAFÉ
$$
CRAWFORD ART GALLERY
EMMET PLACE
TEL 021 427 4415
www.crawfordartgallery.ie
You wouldn't necessarily expect to find a fabulous eating experience in an art gallery's café, but that's what this is—largely because the celebrated Ballymaloe House kitchens, gardens, and bakery

supply most of what's on offer.
That could mean local lamb
and fish with intriguing herbs,
a big vegetarian stew, or just a
pile of freshly baked bread, the
house chutney, and some Cork
farmhouse cheese.
🕐 Closed Sun. 🚫 MC, V

🍴 **NAKON THAI**
$$
TRAMWAY HOUSE, DOUGLAS
TEL 021 436 9900
FAX 021 488 8002
nakonthai@eircom.net
Superb Thai cooking from
either an à la carte menu or one
of a number of set menus, in
which fresh authentic ingredi-
ents are the watchword.
🕐 Closed Christmas week
🚫 All major cards

🍴 **CAFÉ GUSTO**
$
3 WASHINGTON ST.
TEL 021 425 4446
www.cafegusto.com
Far more than a simple café,
the Gusto whips up sandwiches
made in heaven. If you want
something a little fancier, try the
mezze, antipasti plates, or a good
chunky Moroccan lamb stew.

COUNTY CORK

BALTIMORE

🍴 **CHEZ YOUEN SEAFOOD
RESTAURANT**
$$$
THE WATERFRONT, THE SQUARE
TEL 028 20136 OR 20600
FAX 353 20495
www.waterfronthotel.ie
A slice of pure Brittany in
southwest Cork, developed
with loving care by Breton chef
Youen Jacob and family. Superb
fish dishes, as well as lobster and
crab. Hungry hunters go for the
shellfish platter: crab, crayfish,
lobster, mussels, oysters, and
more.
🕐 Closed Sun.–Mon., Sun.–
Thurs. in winter 🚫 MC, V

BANTRY

🏨 **BANTRY HOUSE &
GARDENS**
$$$$–$$$$$
BANTRY
TEL 027 50047
FAX 027 50795
www.bantryhouse.com
Guests of the B&B, ten
minutes from Bantry town,
have full access to the famous
gardens and historic house
and its impressive collections
of furniture and art. Guest
rooms overlook the gardens
and Hundred Steps, worth the
climb for the breathtaking view
over the house and to the bay.
A self-catering house is also
available year-round.
🛈 7 plus guesthouse 🅿
🕐 B&B closed Nov.–mid-May
🚫 MC, V

🍴 **BLAIR'S COVE HOUSE &
RESTAURANT**
$$$$
DURRUS
TEL 027 62913
FAX 027 61487
www.blairscove.ie
A free-and-easy ambience
allied to beautifully tasty but
unfussy cooking.
🕐 Closed L Mon.–Sat., D
Sun.–Mon.; also early Jan.–
mid-Feb. 🚫 All major cards

🍴 **O'CONNOR'S SEAFOOD
RESTAURANT**
$$$
THE SQUARE
TEL 027 50221
FAX 027 51094
www.oconnorseafood.com
This was the first restaurant in
Ireland to specialize in mussels,
and all the seafood is excellent.
The long menu includes start-
ers such as seafood chowder
or spicy fishcakes with chili
and coriander jam, and main
courses might include scallop
and monkfish gratin or local
mountain lamb. Good old

fish and chips is enhanced by
the use of stout in the batter.
♿ 🕐 Closed L Sat.–Wed., D
Sun., & Sun. Oct.–May (call for
off-season hours) 🚫 MC, V

FERMOY

🏨 **BALLYVOLANE HOUSE**
$$$
CASTLELYONS
TEL 025 36349
FAX 025 36781
www.ballyvolanehouse.ie
You will enjoy an exceptionally
warm welcome at this fine
18th-century Italianate country
house, set in famous gardens
within parkland. Stroll around
the lakes; one has been stocked
for fishing and might yield you
a brown trout.
🛈 6 🅿 25 🕐 Closed Christ-
mas week 🚫 All major cards

🍴 **LA BIGOUDENNE**
$$
28 MACCURTAIN ST.
TEL 025 32832
Breton, Belgian, and northern
French dishes served with
imaginative flair in a very
unfussy setup. Vegetarians
welcome with advance notice.
♿ 🕐 Closed Mon. & L
(except Thurs.) 🚫 AE, MC, V

FOTA ISLAND

🏨 **FOTA ISLAND HOTEL &
SPA**
$$$$$
FOTA ISLAND
TEL 021 467 3000
FAX 021 467 3456
www.fotaisland.ie
This full-scale luxury operation
comprises a wooded estate
on a private island, extremely
comfortable and carefully
furnished rooms with subtle
modern lighting, suites with
private terrace balconies, and
a spa with a hydrotherapy
suite that boasts more than
60 treatments. Outside is a
championship standard golf

course and golf academy.
ⓘ 131 **🕘** Closed Christmas
⬥ All major cards

KILBRITTAIN

🍴 CASINO HOUSE
$$$
COOLMAIN HARBOUR
TEL 023 884 9944
FAX 023 884 9945
www.casinohouse.ie
Stylish and innovative, Casino
House offers invention and a
smack of originality (saddle of
rabbit stuffed with pistachio
nuts, monkfish with beetroot
mousse) to spice up familiar
staples of sophisticated cooking.
🕘 Closed Wed. & Sun. D,
Jan.–mid-March **⬥** DC, MC, V

KINSALE

🏨 OLD BANK HOUSE
$$$–$$$$
11 PEARSE ST.
TEL 021 477 2209
FAX 021 477 4268
www.oldbankhousekinsale
.com
A hospitable Georgian house
meticulously restored by the
owners, who can arrange sea
fishing, riding, and sailing for
guests. Bedrooms are country
house in character, furnished
with fine antiques.
ⓘ 17 **🕘** Closed Christmas
week **😎 ⬥** AE, MC, V

🍴 CRACKPOTS
$$$
3 CORK ST.
TEL 021 477 2847
FAX 021 477 3517
crackpots@iol.ie
A really enjoyable place in
the heart of fish-worshipping
country where carnivores can
subversively enjoy Moroccan
chicken and other beautifully
cooked meat dishes (and—yes—
fresh local fish as well) and then
buy the plates their dinner was
served on; like everything on
the menu, these too are made

on site. (Early dinner, 6–8 p.m.)
🕘 Closed D Sun. **⬥** All major
cards

🍴 FISHY FISHY CAFÉ
$$
GUARDWELL
TEL 021 470 0415
As you'd expect from the
name, fish is king here. Choose
what you like from the fish slab
and it will be cooked exactly
to your liking, or trust the chef
and go for seafood chowder,
fresh prawns, crayfish, hake,
or any of half a dozen other
delights from the menu. In
2006, a second Fishy Fishy Café
opened on Crowley's Quay
in Kinsale—just as good and
popular as the original.
🕘 Closed D

MACROOM

🏨 GOUGANE BARRA HOTEL
$$$
GOUGANE BARRA, BALLINGEARY
TEL 026 47069
www.gouganebarrahotel.com
Neil Lucey and his team have
got a really good thing going
here: a family-run hotel in a
superb lakeside location. The
watchword is comfort and a
relaxed, friendly atmosphere.
Hidden in the nearby forests is
a clutch of wonderful walks.
ⓘ 26 **🕘** Closed late Oct.–
early April **⬥** All major cards

MALLOW

🏨 LONGUEVILLE HOUSE HOTEL
$$$–$$$$$
MALLOW
TEL 022 47156
FAX 022 47459
www.longuevillehouse.ie
A very handsome and elegant
Georgian house with Italian
stucco and many other
original features. Upscale
accommodation in lovely
secluded parkland.

ⓘ 20 **Ⓟ** 30 **🕘** Closed early
Jan.–mid-Mar. **⬥** All major cards

MIDLETON

🏨 BALLYMALOE HOUSE
🍴 $$$$–$$$$$
SHANAGARRY
TEL 021 465 2531
FAX 021 465 2021
www.ballymaloe.ie
Probably the best known res-
taurant in the south of Ireland.
Homemade paté, Cobh smoked
fish, local beef with original
sauces, fabulous Cork cheeses
as a complement to the famous
Ballymaloe bread—everything is
exactly right.
ⓘ 22 plus 10 annex **Ⓟ** 30
🕘 Closed Christmas & 2 weeks
in Jan. **🐾 ⬥** All major cards

ROSSCARBERY

🍴 O'CALLAGHAN WALSHE
$$$
NORTH SQUARE
TEL 023 884 8125

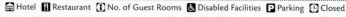

www.ocallaghanwalshe.com
Oysters, mussels, and lobster to
turbot, cod, and Dover sole—all
salty-fresh and served in a cozy
environment. (No children
under 12 after 7:30 p.m. during
the summer.)
🕐 Closed Mon., L; also Fri. in
winter 💳 MC, V

SCHULL

 MOSSIE'S RESTAURANT
🍴 **& ULUSKER HOUSE**
$$
ADRIGOLE, BEARA
TEL 027 60606
www.mossiesrestaurant.com
This delightful place, a beauti-
fully restored 17th-century
house in a charming garden,
is just the setting for tapas in
the conservatory, an evening
meal based around fresh fish or
local meat, or just a strawberry
cream tea on the lawn.
ⓘ 4 🕐 Closed L & Jan. 💳 All
major cards

🍴 **NEW HAVEN**
$$
MAIN ST.
TEL 028 28642
Once the upscale La Coquille,
it's now rebranded as New
Haven, with a broader menu.
The French onion soup and
fresh fish are still wonderful.
💳 AE, DC, MC

SKIBBEREEN

SOMETHING SPECIAL

🍴 **ISLAND COTTAGE**
$$
HARE (HEIR) ISLAND
TEL 028 38102
www.islandcottage.com
A romantic boat ride to an
island restaurant—sounds
good? Island Cottage is entirely
idiosyncratic, but in a good way.
There's no choice of menu,
because you don't need one
with such out of this world

source material (all local,
most organic) and beautiful,
uncomplicated cooking. You'll
eat what you're given and like
it, d'you hear? Telephone well
in advance, though, and note
there's a separate charge for
the boat trip.
🕐 Closed L, Mon.–Tues. mid-
Sept.–mid-May 💳 No credit
cards accepted

YOUGHAL

 AHERNE'S
🍴 **$$$–$$$$**
163 N. MAIN ST.
TEL 024 92424
FAX 024 93633
www.ahernes.net
Family-run for several gen-
erations, this is a place that
simply exudes traditional Irish
hospitality, from the warm
welcome to the fond farewell.
The restaurant is very strong
on fresh seafood and meats.
ⓘ 13 ♿ 🅿 20 🕐 Closed
Christmas 💳 All major cards

COUNTY KERRY

BALLYDAVID

🍴 **OLD PIER RESTAURANT**
$$
FEOTHANACH
TEL 066 915 5242
www.oldpier.com
In a wonderful location
on the north shore of the
Dingle Peninsula, with a big
bay window overlooking the
sea, this is a stylish modern
restaurant (and guesthouse).
The extensive menu includes
plenty of wonderfully fresh and
tasty local seafood.
♿ 🕐 Closed L; Tues. Nov.–
Feb. 💳 MC, V

DINGLE

🏨 **GREENMOUNT HOUSE**
$$$

UPPER JOHN ST., GORTONORA
TEL 066 915 1414
www.greenmount-house.com
Set on beautiful Dingle
Harbour, Greenmount House
offers warm hospitality and a
relaxed atmosphere.
ⓘ 14 🅿 12 🕐 Closed Dec.
💳 MC, V

🍴 **OUT OF THE BLUE**
$$$
WATERSIDE
TEL 066 915 0811
www.outoftheblue.ie
Out of the Blue only serves
fresh fish and only when local
fishermen have fish to sell—
Atlantic salmon, cod, turbot,
monkfish; oysters, mussels,
scallops; crab, crayfish, lobster.
The décor is simple, the cooking superb.
🕐 Closed L Wed. & when
fresh fish is unavailable, Nov.–
Feb. 💳 MC, V

GLENBEIGH

🏨 **KERRY OCEAN LODGE**
$–$$
GLENBEIGH
TEL 066 976 9666
FAX 066 976 9667
www.kerryoceanlodge.com
You don't have to be a walker
to stay here, but it helps. With
the famed Macgillycuddy's
Reeks nearby, the lodge offers
friendly, warm service and
delicious breakfasts.
ⓘ 20

KENMARE

SOMETHING SPECIAL

🏨 **PARK HOTEL KENMARE**
$$$$$
KENMARE
TEL 064 664 1200
FAX 064 664 1402
www.parkkenmare.com
A smart and luxurious Victorian country-house hotel that
is set in landscaped gardens,
where strollers enjoy superb

views over the Kenmare River's broad estuary. The staff is competent and cheerful.
🛈 46 🅿 60 🕐 Closed Nov.– April; open two weeks around Christmas & New Year's
🔁 🚫 All major cards

🍴 PACKIE'S
$$$
HENRY ST.
TEL 064 664 1508
FAX 064 664 2135
martinhallissey@yahoo.com
Desserts are rich and delicious here, particularly the homemade ice cream—but make sure you leave room for the main courses, which marry first-class ingredients to unpretentious cooking. The menu includes such dishes as potato cakes with garlic butter.
🕐 Closed Mon & mid-Jan.– Feb. 🚫 MC, V

KILLARNEY

🏨 AGHADOE HEIGHTS HOTEL & SPA
$$$$$
AGHADOE
TEL 064 663 1766
FAX 064 663 1345
www.aghadoeheights.com
This luxury hotel commands stunning views of the lakes and mountains of Killarney National Park. Service is personal, friendly, and helpful, and the hotel is superbly appointed. The stylish bedrooms are air-conditioned, and many have their own sundecks.
🛈 73 🅿 120 🔁 🚫 🚫 All major cards

🏨 KILLARNEY PARK
$$$$–$$$$$
KENMARE PLACE
TEL 064 663 5555
FAX 064 663 5266
www.killarneyparkhotel.ie
Purpose-built for the luxury end of the Killarney visitor market, the Killarney Park gives

you a soft landing and a stylish ride all the way.
🛈 71 🅿 70 🕐 Closed Christmas 🔁 🚫 🚫 🚫 All major cards

🍴 BEAUFORT BAR & RESTAURANT
$$
TEL 064 664 4032
www.beaufortbar.com
This historic bar has been run by the O'Sullivan family since it opened in 1841, and from 1911 to 1914 it was the base of the American Kalem Film Company, which shot about 70 movies in the area (still photographs hang on the walls here). The restaurant is a more recent addition, but soon acquired a reputation for excellent cuisine.
🕐 Closed Nov. & Christmas 🚫 All major cards

KILLORGLIN

🍴 NICK'S SEAFOOD RESTAURANT & PIANO BAR
$$$
LOWER BRIDGE ST.
TEL 066 976 1219
A restaurant that would run a hundred miles rather than take itself too seriously, Nick's fills your ears with music, your mouth with rollicking choruses, and your belly with good tucker. The menu leans cheerily on local meat and fish—Kerry-reared beef, say, or local shellfish such as mussels done in a superb Franco-Irish style.
🕐 Closed Mon.; Tues. Dec.–March; Nov., Christmas, & 2 weeks in Jan. 🚫 All major cards

SHEEP'S HEAD PENINSULA

🏨 HILLCREST FARM
$
AHAKISTA, DURRUS
TEL 027 67045
www.ahakista.com

Agnes Hegarty offers the warmest of welcomes, and this delightful farmhouse is very well placed for exploring the superb Sheep's Head Way footpath.
🛈 4 🕐 Closed Nov.–March 🚫 MC, V

WATERVILLE

🏨 BUTLER ARMS HOTEL
$$$–$$$$
WATERVILLE
TEL 066 947 4144
FAX 066 947 4520
www.butlerarms.com
A spacious hotel that occupies a splendid location overlooking the sea. Most of the bedrooms have sea views, and all have en suite marble bathrooms.
🛈 40 🅿 50 🕐 Closed Oct.–March 🔁 🚫 All major cards

COUNTY LIMERICK

ADARE

🏨 DUNRAVEN ARMS
$$$–$$$$
ADARE
TEL 061 605 900
FAX 061 396 541
www.dunravenhotel.com
Relax in the easygoing atmosphere of this traditional country inn in Adare, one of Ireland's most attractive preserved estate villages.
🛈 86 🅿 90 🔁 🚫 🚫 All major cards

🍴 WILD GEESE RESTAURANT
$$$
ROSE COTTAGE
TEL 061 396 451
www.thewild-geese.com
A gorgeous cottage is the setting for this extremely well-regarded restaurant, where first-class ingredients are used to please a discerning and enthusiastic clientele. Light lunches only in summer.
🕐 Closed Mon.; Sun. Oct.–

April; Christmas; 2 weeks in
Jan. 🚫 AE, MC, V

BALLINGARRY

🍴 THE MUSTARD SEED
$$$
BALLINGARRY
TEL 069 68508
www.mustardseed.ie
Fine cooking based on local,
organic, and seasonal produce,
for example, pheasant and ven-
ison or a rack of Irish mountain
lamb—all done with a warmly
hospitable touch.
🚹 🚫 All major cards

KILMALLOCK

🏨 FLEMINGSTOWN HOUSE
$$
KILMALLOCK
TEL 063 98093
FAX 063 98546
www.flemingstown.com
Just outside the country town
of Killmallock, the Georgian
farmhouse of Flemingstown
House offers a winning combination of elegance and style—
antiques in the drawing room,
stained-glass windows in the
dining room—together with
the warmth and helpfulness of
the staff and the owner.
🛏 5 🅿 12 🕐 Closed Nov.–
March 🚫 MC, V

LIMERICK

🏨 NO. 1 PERY SQUARE
HOTEL & SPA
$$$–$$$$
PERY SQUARE
TEL 061 402 402
FAX 061 313 060
www.oneperysquare.com
This boutique hotel in a
beautiful Georgian townhouse
has huge beds and luxurious
furnishings. Eat and drink in
the first-floor brasserie, and
bask in the spa's herb and
seaweed treatments.
🛏 20 🕐 Closed Christmas
🛗 🚫 All major cards

🏨 CASTLETROY PARK
HOTEL
$$$
DUBLIN RD.
TEL 061 335 566
FAX 061 331 117
www.castletroy-park.ie
A fine modern hotel with
extensive leisure and banqueting facilities.
🛏 188 🅿 160 🏊 🚫 All
major cards

🍴 RIVER BISTRO
$$$
4 GEORGE'S QUAY
TEL 061 400 990
www.theriverbistro.ie
Discreetly lit and nicely placed
overlooking the River Shan-
non, this quayside restaurant
is big on flavor—spicy chicken,
roast cod, or pork belly with
delicious crispy tripe, all served
with seasonal vegetables.
🕐 Closed L. & Sun.–Mon.
🚫 AE, MC, V

◼ WEST IRELAND

COUNTY CLARE

BALLYVAUGHAN

🏨 GREGAN'S CASTLE
$$$$
BALLYVAUGHAN
TEL 065 707 7005
FAX 065 707 7111
www.gregans.ie
In a superb location in the
heart of Clare's Burren region,
the medieval tower house
of Gregan's Castle stands at
the foot of the famous Cork-
screw Hill. Accommodations
are up to date in amenities,
however. Each bedroom is
individually furnished in
country-house style—all have
wonderful countryside views,
and some have their own pri-
vate gardens. The emphasis is
very much on peace and quiet;
bedroom televisions
are conspicuous by their
absence.

🛏 22 🅿 25 🕐 Closed mid-
Dec.–mid-Feb. 🚫 AE, MC, V

BUNRATTY

🏨 FITZPATRICK
BUNRATTY
$$$$
BUNRATTY
TEL 061 361177
FAX 061 471252
reservations@bunratty
.fitzpatricks.com
A modern, ranch-style hotel
with all modern facilities,
conveniently close to Shannon
Airport and to the castle and
folk park at Bunratty.
🛏 119 🅿 300 🕐 Closed
Christmas 🏊 🚫 All major cards

COROFIN

🏨 FERGUS VIEW
GUESTHOUSE
$
KILNABOY
TEL 065 683 7606
FAX 065 683 7192
www.fergusview.com
An excellent family-run guest-
house, where Mary Kelleher's
cooking of local meat and fish
and homegrown vegetables is
scrumptiously set off by her
amazing puddings. Very well
positioned for exploring the
Burren or the coast.
🛏 6 🅿 8 🕐 Closed Nov.–
Easter

DOOLIN

🏨 ARAN VIEW HOUSE
HOTEL
$$$
COAST RD.
TEL 065 707 4061 OR 4420
FAX 065 707 4540
www.aranview.com
A friendly hotel. Each bedroom
is beautifully furnished,
equipped with TV, en suite
bathrooms, and superb views
out across Galway Bay to the
Aran Islands from this snug

hotel. Traditional music is laid on at the Aran View several times a week.

🛈 13 plus 6 annex 🅿 40
🕓 Closed Nov.–March 🚫 All major cards

🍴 BALLINALACKEN COUNTRY HOUSE & RESTAURANT
$$$
BALLINALACKEN CASTLE
TEL 065 707 4025
www.ballinalackencastle.com
Ballinalacken Castle is a famous local landmark with a restaurant that is popular with locals who appreciate good food from the sea and land nearby. Dishes include crab cakes, fresh cod, monkfish, and lamb.
🕓 Closed Nov.–mid-April

ENNIS

🏨 WOODSTOCK
$$$$
SHANAWAY RD.
TEL 081 836 5036
FAX 065 689 3371
www.woodstockhotelennis.com
A championship golf course, Jacuzzi, sauna, solarium, swimming pool, and gym are some of the facilities available at this well-equipped modern hotel set in woodland. The bedrooms are beautifully furnished in restrained good taste.
🛈 67 🕓 Closed Christmas
🔄 🎵 🚫 All major cards

KILFENORA

🍴 VAUGHAN'S
$
KILFENORA
TEL 065 708 8004
www.vaughanspub.ie
Vaughan's is a most delightful pub where the Guinness is great, the music is brilliant, and the "plain Irish cooking" uses the best local ingredients for local dishes (bacon and cabbage, beef and stout pie) that

locals eat with relish.
🕓 Closed Good Fri., Christmas
🚫 MC, V

KILLALOE

🍴 CHERRY TREE RESTAURANT
$$$
BALLINA ST.
TEL 061 375 688
FAX 061 375 689
www.cherrytreerestaurant.ie
On the shores of Lough Derg in southeasternmost Clare, you'll find expert cuisine that delights without overwhelming. Such dishes as Parma ham enwrapping asparagus with sage and wild mushroom, or local, dry-aged beef retain all the essential flavors of the ingredients.
♿ 🕓 Closed L; Sun.; Mon.–Tues. in winter; Christmas; last week Jan.–first week Feb.
🚫 All major cards

KILRUSH

🏨 HILLCREST VIEW
$
DOONBEG RD. (OFF N67)
TEL 065 905 1986
FAX 065 905 1900
www.hillcrestview.com
This is a family house with a hospitable atmosphere and clean, comfortable rooms
🛈 6 🅿 7 🚫 AE, MC, V

LAHINCH

🍴 BARRTRÁ SEAFOOD RESTAURANT
$$
BARRTRÁ
TEL 065 708 1280
www.barrtra.com
If the local boats have taken it out of the sea that day, the chances are it'll be on the table at Barrtrá, looking and tasting even better thanks to the fabulous sea views.
🕓 Closed Sun.–Thurs. March–May; Thurs. in Jun.; Mon.–Fri. Oct.–Dec. (call for off-season

hours); & Jan.–Feb. 🚫 AE, MC, V

LISDOONVARNA

SOMETHING SPECIAL

🏨 DROMOLAND CASTLE
$$$$–$$$$$
NEWMARKET-ON-FERGUS
TEL 061 368 144
FAX 061 363 355
www.dromoland.ie
This is every multimillionaire's dream of a Gothic revival castle with turrets, irregular rooflines, and battlements. It may have been built many centuries after such defenses were actually necessary, but this fairy-tale pile is not about grim reality. It is about escapism and enjoying excellent modern facilities in a fantastical setting.
🛈 100 🅿 120 🏊 🚫 All major cards

🏨 SHEEDY'S COUNTRY
🍴 HOUSE HOTEL
$$$
LISDOONVARNA
TEL 065 707 4026
FAX 065 707 4555
www.sheedys.com
Comfortable and friendly, this small, family-run hotel is attached to an excellent restaurant (try the succulent casserole of local lamb with rosemary and organic vegetables) in one of Clare's most characterful towns.
🛈 11 🅿 40 🕓 Closed mid-Oct.–mid-March 🚫 AE, MC, V

TULLA

🍴 FLAPPERS
$$
MAIN ST.
TEL 065 683 5711
Excellent small restaurant, equally good for light-to-medium lunches or for full-blooded dinners. Even the

🏨 Hotel 🍴 Restaurant 🛈 No. of Guest Rooms ♿ Disabled Facilities 🅿 Parking 🕓 Closed simplest salads, fish pies, and breast of chicken are superb. 🚹 🕑 Closed 2 weeks Nov. & Jan. 🅰️ MC, V

COUNTY GALWAY

ARAN ISLANDS

🏨 **MAN OF ARAN COTTAGE**
$$
KILMURVEY, INISHMORE
TEL 099 61301
FAX 099 61324
www.manofarancottage.com
If you're visiting the Aran Islands, don't miss this gem of a thatched, whitewashed cottage B&B and restaurant on Inishmore. Maura Wolfe does simple, aromatic home cooking with local ingredients, expecially her husband Joe's organic vegetables and herbs. 🛏️ 3 🕑 Closed Nov.–Feb. 🅰️ No credit cards

BALLYNAHINCH

🏨 **BALLYNAHINCH**
🍴 **CASTLE**
$$$–$$$$$
BALLYNAHINCH
TEL 095 31006
FAX 095 31085
www.ballynahinch-castle.com
A cheery, outdoorsy place on the banks of a famous sporting river (most of the comfortable bedrooms enjoy river views). You don't have to catch your own dinner here—though the chef will be only too delighted to cook anything you do bring in from lake, river, or sea. Otherwise, just settle back to enjoy one of Ireland's most agreeable castle settings. 🛏️ 40 🅿️ 🕑 Closed Feb., Christmas 🅰️ All major cards

BUSHYPARK

🏨 **GLENLO ABBEY**
$$$$$
BUSHYPARK

TEL 091 526 666
FAX 091 527 800
www.glenlo.com
A hotel full of character, incorporating a restored church and early Georgian abbey buildings, on the shores of Lough Corrib. A modern wing houses the very comfortable bedrooms, many of which have fabulous lough views. 🛏️ 46 🅿️ 150 🕑 Closed Christmas 🍽️ 🅰️ All major cards

CASHEL

🏨 **CASHEL HOUSE HOTEL**
$$$$–$$$$$
CASHEL
TEL 095 31001
FAX 095 31077
www.cashel-house-hotel.com
Stunningly set in 50 acres (20 ha) of superb gardens on one of Connemara's most beautiful bays, Cashel House offers elegant, luxurious accommodation. 🛏️ 32 🅿️ 40 🕑 Closed Jan.–early Feb. 🅰️ All major cards

🍴 **ZETLAND COUNTRY HOUSE**
$$$
CASHEL BAY
TEL 095 31111
FAX 095 31117
www.zetland.com
Unpretentiously delicious cooking in a beautifully appointed room with one of Connemara's classic sea and coastal views to aid digestion. 🕑 Closed L, Dec.–Jan. 🅰️ All major cards

CLARENBRIDGE

🍴 **PADDY BURKE'S**
$$
CLARENBRIDGE
TEL 091 796226
FAX 091 796016
www.paddyburkesgalway.com
Simply the most famous oyster house in Ireland, *fons et origo* of the Clarenbridge Oyster Fes-

tival, where the glitterati and the literati rub shoulders with denizens of the real world over excellent seafood and stout. 🕑 Closed Good Fri., Christmas 🅰️ All major cards

CLIFDEN

🏨 **ABBEYGLEN CASTLE HOTEL**
$$$$
SKY RD.
TEL 095 21201
FAX 095 21797
www.abbeyglen.ie
Abbeyglen Castle is just west of Clifden on the fabulously scenic Sky Road. A highly dedicated family team puts both comfort and cuisine in the top bracket, but also with antennae tuned to what might please the guests—hence many music sessions in the bar. 🛏️ 45 🅿️ 50 🕑 Closed early Jan.–early Feb. 🅰️ All major cards

🏨 **ARDAGH HOTEL**
$$$–$$$$
BALLYCONNEELY RD.
TEL 095 21384
FAX 095 21314
www.ardaghhotel.com
Beautifully located on Ardbear Bay near Clifden, this is a well-run family setup where guests' comfort and well-being come first. Well-furnished bedrooms with either sea or country views. 🛏️ 19 🅿️ 35 🅰️ All major cards

🏨 **MALLMORE COUNTRY HOUSE**
$$
BALLYCONNEELY RD.
TEL 095 21460
www.mallmore.com
A very stylish house, complete with pillared portico, beautiful furnishings, and wonderful views. Amid all this, owners Kathleen and Alan Hardman have not forgotten the essential

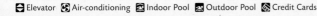
🛗 Elevator 🅰️ Air-conditioning 🏊 Indoor Pool 🏊 Outdoor Pool 🅰️ Credit Cards

ingredient of any Irish B&B—a warm, welcoming atmosphere. ⓘ 6 ⌚ Closed Nov.–Feb. 🚫 No credit cards

🍽 MITCHELL'S RESTAURANT
$$$
MARKET ST.
TEL 095 21867
This friendly, family-run restaurant on Clifden's main street has many loyal devotees—and no wonder, with mouth-watering favorites such as fish and chips, shepherd's pie, mussels, and fish cakes. ⌚ Closed Nov.–Dec. 🚫 All major cards

GALWAY CITY

🏨 HARBOUR HOTEL
$$$–$$$$$
NEW DOCK RD.
TEL 091 894 800
FAX 091 589 455
www.harbour.ie
Forming part of development of Galway's harbor frontage, this hotel may be modern in design, but it offers all the traditional comfort of open fires and plush furnishings. ⓘ 96 🅿 64 ♿ 🚫 All major cards

🏨 ALMARA HOUSE
$–$$
2 MERLIN GATE, DUBLIN RD.
TEL 091 755 345
FAX 091 771 585
www.almarahouse.com
The proprietors of Almara House also own a butcher's shop, so fresh bacon and sausages for breakfast are guaranteed. Cozy bedrooms and a warm welcome are assured, and there's a bus stop for city-center services right outside. ⓘ 4 🅿 8 🚫 All major cards

🍽 K. C. BLAKES BRASSERIE
$$$
10 QUAY ST.

TEL 091 561 826
Dine royally in Blakes Castle, a restored 15th-century tower house, in Galway's "Latin Quarter." It's a beautiful medieval building that has been given a stylish modern décor. The menu combines global cuisine with classic French dishes. ⌚ Closed Christmas 🚫 AE, MC, V

🍽 TIGH NEACHTAIN & ARTISAN RESTAURANT
$$
CROSS STREET
TEL 091 568 820
This smallish restaurant does things with a Gallic twist and is all the better for it. Meat comes from local sources and fish out of Galway Bay. Excellent organic vegetables. ⌚ Closed Christmas 🚫 All major cards

🍽 GOYA'S
$
2–3 KIRWANS LANE
TEL 091 567 010
www.goyas.ie
Stickies, slices, and sweet nothings to ruin your waistline and keep out the cold—even if it's a Galway heatwave. ⌚ Closed Sun., D 🚫 MC, V

LETTERFRACK

SOMETHING SPECIAL

🏨 ROSLEAGUE MANOR
$$$$$
LETTERFRACK
TEL 095 41101
FAX 095 41168
www.rosleague.com
Rosleague Manor preserves remarkably the atmosphere of a highly relaxed, slightly eccentric country house. The house looks out over beautifully kept gardens, mature trees, and a lake-like sea inlet to a memorable prospect of the Connemara mountains. There are four-poster beds, huge baths, antique furniture,

PRICES

HOTELS
An indication of the cost of a double room in the high season is given by **$** signs.

$$$$$	Over $280
$$$$	$200–$280
$$$	$120–$200
$$	$80–$120
$	Under $80

RESTAURANTS
An indication of the cost of a three-course meal without drinks is given by **$** signs.

$$$$$	Over $80
$$$$	$50–$80
$$$	$35–$50
$$	$20–$35
$	Under $20

and sumptuous breakfasts. ⓘ 20 ⌚ Closed mid-Nov.–mid-March 🚫 MC, V

OUGHTERARD

🏨 ROSS LAKE HOUSE
$$$–$$$$$
ROSSCAHILL
TEL 091 550109
FAX 091 550184
www.rosslakehotel.com
A handsome Georgian house in a quiet setting among the miles of beautiful woodland. Rooms are furnished in keeping with the elegant 18th-century ambience, including comfortable beds and big fireplaces. Rowing, sailing, and fishing on Ross Lake are easily arranged. ⓘ 13 🅿 150 ⌚ Closed Nov.–mid-March 🚫 All major cards

RECESS

🏨 LOUGH INAGH LODGE
$$$–$$$$

INAGH VALLEY
TEL 095 34706
FAX 095 34708
www.loughinaghlodgehotel.ie
A delightful lakeside retreat, formerly a 19th-century hunting lodge, set in a beautiful valley with the Twelve Bens rising mystically on one side and the Maumturk Mountains the other. All bedrooms have lovely views, and five are deluxe standard.
🛏 12 🅿 16 🕘 Closed mid-Dec.–mid-March 🎦 🅲 All major cards

COUNTY MAYO

ACHILL ISLAND

🏨 ACHILL CLIFF HOUSE
$$–$$$
KEEL
TEL 098 43400
FAX 098 43007
www.achillcliff.com
Breathtaking views of the mountains and seacoasts of Achill Island from this comfortable modern guesthouse, run by a warm and hospitable hostess who is full of good ideas and insider knowledge.
🛏 10 🅿 20 🕘 Closed Christmas 🅲 AE, MC, V

CASTLEBAR

🏨 LYNCH BREAFFY HOUSE HOTEL & SPA
$$$$
CASTLEBAR
TEL 094 902 2033
FAX 094 683 3759
www.lynchotels.com
A 19th-century house among 100 acres (40 ha) of woods; old house public rooms, while a whole wing is given over to well-appointed bedrooms with modern amenities. Entertainment organized for guests during the summer.
🛏 62 🅿 300 🎦 🅲 AE, MC, V

🍴 BAR ONE
$$
RUSH ST.
TEL 094 903 4800
www.barone.ie
Up-to-the-minute décor and atmosphere with a menu far removed from the usual gastro-pub fare. Try the flavorsome and tangy fisherman's pie or the beer-battered fish, chips, and mushy peas.
🕘 Closed Sun. 🅲 MC, V

CONG

🏨 BALLYWARREN COUNTRY HOUSE
$$$
BALLYMACGIBBON N.
CROSS
TEL/FAX 094 954 6989
www.ballywarrenhouse.com
Ballywarren House is located in an inland, rural area of County Mayo; an elegant house painstakingly converted into a stylish and welcoming country hotel.
🛏 3 🅿 4 🅲 AE, MC, V

SOMETHING SPECIAL

🍴 ASHFORD CASTLE
$$$–$$$$$
CONG
TEL 094 954 6003
FAX 094 954 6260
www.ashford.ie
To push the boat as far out as it'll go while in Cong, lie back and enjoy the Connaught Room's spot-on service and cuisine—one of a handful of absolutely top-drawer Irish restaurants, set in the surroundings of the country's grandest castle. The George V Dining Room—the Connaught's brother restaurant at the castle—offers equally exalted standards in a slightly less rarified atmosphere.
🅲 All major cards

WESTPORT

🏨 HOTEL WESTPORT

$$$$
NEWPORT RD.
TEL 098 25122
FAX 098 26739
www.hotelwestport.ie
A smart modern hotel with facilities that include a gym, sauna, and pool—and a staff that makes it all run efficiently.
🛏 129 🅿 220 🎦 🎦 🅲 All major cards

🏨 ARDMORE COUNTRY HOUSE
$$$–$$$$$
THE QUAY
TEL 098 25994
FAX 098 27795
www.ardmorecountryhouse.com
With superb views over Westport Quay, Clew Bay, and Croagh Patrick, Ardmore Country House is a relaxed and enjoyable place to stay close to the town center.
🛏 13 🅿 40 🕘 Closed Jan.–Feb. 🅲 AE, MC, V

🍴 THE LEMON PEEL
$$
THE OCTAGON
TEL 098 26929
FAX 098 26965
robbie@lemonpeel.ie
Everyone likes this friendly place, where the food comes served with a pleasant greeting. If you are a mashed potato connoisseur, look no further—though everything on the menu is delicious.
🕘 Closed L & Sun.–Mon. in off-season 🅲 All major cards

▥ NORTHWEST IRELAND

COUNTY SLIGO

BALLYSADARE

🏨 SEASHORE COUNTRY HOUSE
$
OFF BALLINA RD. (N59)

LISDUFF
TEL/FAX 071 916 7827
www.seashoreguests.com
A bungalow guesthouse with a conservatory dining room looking out over sea and mountains, in a beautifully quiet spot on the seashore of tidal Ballysadare Bay.
[i] 5 [P] 6 [S] MC, V

CASTLEBALDWIN

🍴 CROMLEACH LODGE COUNTRY HOUSE
$$$$
CASTLEBALDWIN, NEAR BOYLE
TEL 071 916 5155
FAX 071 916 5455
www.cromleach.com
Truly fabulous food that comes in interesting combinations—pureed sweet potato around a slice of local beef, for instance. Delectable deserts such as poached pears or banana nougats round off the meal.
[🕐] Closed L [S] All major cards

COLLOONEY

🏨 MARKREE CASTLE
$$$$
COLLOONEY
TEL 071 916 7800
FAX 071 916 7840
www.markreecastle.ie
You could probably eat a boiled boot and enjoy it in surroundings like these—a gorgeous old castle now turned into a fine hotel, with en suite luxury rooms and its own riding stables. It's run by a family who has owned it since Methuselah was a lad.
[i] 30 [P] 60 [🕐] Closed Christmas [⊟] [S] All major cards

GRANGE

🏨 ROWANVILLE LODGE
$
MONEYGOLD
TEL 071 916 3958
www.rowanville.com
Beautifully situated within full

view of W. B. Yeats's magnificent mountain of Benbulben, this cheerful and very friendly house makes an excellent base for exploring Yeats Country (see pp. 212–217).
[i] 3 [P] 8 [🕐] Closed Oct.–Feb. [S] MC, V

SLIGO TOWN

🏨 SLIGO CITY HOTEL
$$$
QUAY ST.
TEL 071 914 4000
FAX 071 914 6888
www.sligocityhotel.com
This pleasantly relaxed hotel is conveniently located on the old quays in the center of Sligo town. All of the bedrooms are comfortable and smartly furnished in a modern style; some are of luxury standard with plenty of space and huge beds, and some have been adapted to suit wheelchair users.
[i] 58 [P] 20 [🕐] Closed Christmas [⊟] [S] All major cards

🏨 SLIGO PARK HOTEL
$$$
PEARSE RD.
TEL 071 919 0400
FAX 071 916 9556
www.sligoparkhotel.com
Standing in 7 acres (3 ha) of beautiful parkland on the southern outskirts of Sligo town, the Sligo Park is well placed for exploring the countryside associated with the Yeats brothers. This is a well-appointed, smartly run hotel with big en suite bedrooms furnished in a straightforward, modern style.
[i] 135 [P] 200 [🕐] Closed Christmas [⊟] [S] All major cards

🏨 CHESTNUT LAWN
$
CUMMEEN, STRANDHILL RD.
TEL/FAX 071 916 2781
www.chestnutlawn.com
A comfortable, carefully

maintained house with modern, attractively furnished bedrooms on the way out from Sligo town to Strandhill—within a short distance of the Sligo Bay beaches, Knocknarea Mountain, and the megalithic cemetery at Carrowmore.
[i] 3 [P] 4 [🕐] Closed Nov.–Feb. [S] MC, V

🍴 MONTMARTRE
$$
MARKET YARD
TEL 071 916 9901
FAX 071 914 0065
montmartre@eircom.net
A dash of Gallic flair, zest, and ambience gives va-va-voom to dinner here; the accent's on all things French, but much of the menu (especially the shellfish) has only had to travel across the bay to the kitchen.
[🕐] Closed Mon., Dec. 24–26 [S] AE, MC, V

🍴 HARGADON'S
$
4–5 O'CONNELL ST.
TEL 071 916 5370
www.hargadons.com
The food in Hargadon's is fine, from good steaks to traditional bacon and cabbage—but this remarkable town-center pub, famous throughout the northwest, is really about relaxation and great conversation in one of the private snugs or up at the characterful old bar.
[🕐] Closed Good Fri., Dec. 25

COUNTY DONEGAL

ANNAGARY

SOMETHING SPECIAL
🍴 DANNY MINNIE'S
$$
ANNAGARY, THE ROSSES
TEL 074 954 8201
FAX 074 954 8809
www.dannyminnies.com
A superb refuge from wind, weather, and wild country out in Donegal's western

margins, Danny Minnie's offers warm hospitality and a menu that makes the most of local produce. Examples are delicious local lobster and tender mountain lamb specialty.
🔆 Closed Christmas; Sun., call for opening times Sept.–May 💳 DC, MC, V

ARDARA

🏨 NESBITT ARMS
$–$$$$
THE DIAMOND
TEL 074 954 1103
FAX 074 954 1895
www.nesbittarms.com
A very characterful, central hotel offering comfortable en suite accommodations, with friendly staff and some great musical sessions.
ℹ️ 19 💳 MC, V

BALLYBOFEY

🏨 KEE'S
🍴 $$$
STRANORLAR
TEL 074 913 1018
FAX 074 913 1917
www.keeshotel.ie
A family-run hotel with a good reputation for solid, competent cooking. In spite of the fact that there's a mountain or two between Stranorlar and the sea, the fish is great—try Kee's pan-fried cod or smoked haddock chowder for a delicious smack of the briny.
ℹ️ 53 🅿️ 90 🏊 💳 All major cards

BALLYLIFFIN

SOMETHING SPECIAL

🏨 OSTAN GWEEDORE
$$$
BUNBEG
TEL 074 953 1177
FAX 074 953 1726
www.ostangweedore.com
Right on the sea near Bunbeg,

with fresh seafood daily, this is the place from which to get acquainted with Donegal's most far-out coasts. A haven of comfort in a truly wild region.
ℹ️ 69 🅿️ 80 🔆 Closed Dec.–Jan. 🏊 💳 AE, MC, V

🏨 STRAND HOTEL
$$
CLONMANY
TEL 074 937 6107
FAX 074 937 6486
www.ballyliffin.com
This family-run hotel, attractively set in well-maintained gardens, has lovely views to Pollan Strand and Malin Head. It offers music and dancing nights and there is golf nearby.
ℹ️ 38 🅿️ 50 🔆 Closed Christmas 💳 MC, V

DONEGAL TOWN

🏨 HARVEY'S POINT
🍴 COUNTRY HOTEL
$$$
LOUGH ESKE
TEL 074 972 2208
FAX 074 972 2352
www.harveyspoint.com
Enjoying a very peaceful and beautiful location just outside Donegal town, by the sheltered shores of Lough Eske, Harvey's Point is a modern hotel with all the creature comforts. Bedrooms are furnished in Swiss mode, and big windows overlook the lake. Fairly formal dining features classic cooking —baked salmon fillet, roast venison with truffle sauce.
ℹ️ 20 🅿️ 300 💳 All major cards

DUNFANAGHY

🍴 MILL RESTAURANT
$$$
FIGART
TEL/FAX 074 913 6985
www.themillrestaurant.com
A wonderful lakeside location for excellent stylish, cooking

based on the best of local ingredients—Donegal lamb, beef, and pork, locally caught fish and shellfish—and really decent artwork on the walls, too, all done by members of the owner's family.
♿ 🔆 Closed mid-Dec.–mid-March 💳 All major cards

GREENCASTLE

🍴 KEALY'S SEAFOOD BAR
$$$
THE HARBOUR
TEL/FAX 074 938 1010
kealys@iol.ie
This is a great restaurant for those who like a laid-back atmosphere in which to enjoy unfussy but perfectly cooked and presented food—not just seafood, but that's what Kealy's particularly shines at.
♿ 🔆 Closed Mon.–Tues.; L Wed.–Thurs.; 2 weeks Nov. 💳 All major cards

LAGHEY

🍴 COXTOWN MANOR
$$$
DONEGAL
TEL 074 973 4575
FAX 074 973 4576
www.coxtownmanor.com
If you're hungry in south Donegal, this is the place to go. Local produce combines with Belgian influences—rich-flavored sausages, hearty soups, veal cutlets, fried fish—all in a very pleasant, warm atmosphere. The beer and the chocolate are both Belgian, too, hence irresistible.
🔆 Closed Nov.–Feb. 💳 All major cards

RATHMULLAN

🏨 RATHMULLAN HOUSE
$$$$$
RATHMULLAN
TEL 074 915 8188
FAX 074 915 8200
www.rathmullanhouse.com

Whether a game of tennis, a dip in the pool, a massage with herbal essences, or a stroll on the beach, Rathmullan House, overlooking beautiful Lough Swilly, guarantees relaxation.
🛏 32 🕒 Closed Christmas 🏧 All major cards

🛏 FORT ROYAL
🍴 $$$–$$$$
RATHMULLAN
TEL 074 915 8100
www.fortroyalhotel.com
A country house with a fabulous position overlooking Lough Swilly from the Fanad Peninsula. Cooking is free of pretension, but has modern twists and turns. Abundant fresh produce from the hotel's garden goes into superb vegetable and herb soups.
🛏 11 plus 4 annex 🅿 40
🕒 Closed Nov.–Easter 🏧 All major cards

ROSSNOWLAGH

🛏 SANDHOUSE HOTEL
$$$–$$$$
ROSSNOWLAGH, DONEGAL BAY
TEL 071 985 1777
FAX 071 985 2100
www.sandhouse-hotel.ie
The welcoming, easy-paced Sandhouse commands one of southwest Donegal's best sea views, around the bay at Rossnowlagh. Bedrooms are in classical country-house style, and some have four-poster beds and sea views.
🛏 55 🅿 40 🕒 Closed Dec.–Jan. 🏧 All major cards

COUNTY LEITRIM

CARRICK-ON-SHANNON

🛏 THE LANDMARK
$$$$
CARRICK-ON-SHANNON
TEL 071 962 2222
FAX 071 962 2233
www.landmarkhotel.com

A very luxurious and elegant hotel overlooking the River Shannon at the heart of this prime boating and angling area; cruising, fishing, riding, and golf can be arranged.
🛏 50 🅿 60 🍽 🏧 All major cards

■ CENTRAL IRELAND

COUNTY ROSCOMMON

BALLINLOUGH

🛏 WHITE HOUSE HOTEL
$$
BALLINLOUGH
TEL 094 964 0112
FAX 094 964 0993
info@white-house-hotel.com
Near the Roscommon/Mayo border, this agreeable hotel is convenient for Knock shrine and airport, for the fishing lakes of the border country, and for Tuam and north Galway.
🛏 19 🕒 Closed Christmas 🍽 🍽 🏧 All major cards

ROSCOMMON TOWN

🛏 ABBEY HOTEL
🍴 $$$
GALWAY RD.
TEL 090 662 6240
FAX 090 662 6021
www.abbeyhotel.ie
In this 19th-century house just outside of Roscommon, you can choose between contemporary bedrooms in a modern wing or Victorian style in the original building. Locals out to enjoy a good dinner in a friendly atmosphere gravitate to the restaurant.
🛏 50 🅿 150 🕒 Closed Christmas 🍽 🍽 🏧 All major cards

COUNTY LONGFORD

DRUMLISH

🛏 LONGFORD COUNTRY HOUSE

$
ENNYBEGS
TEL 043 23320
FAX 043 23516
kc@iol.ie
A large mock-Tudor house with several unusual features, including a spiral staircase from the parlor to the upstairs library, Longford Country House offers turf fires, pleasant rooms, and a warm welcome.
🛏 6 🅿 20 🏧 MC, V

GRANARD

SOMETHING SPECIAL

🛏 TOBERPHELIM HOUSE
$–$$
GRANARD
TEL/FAX 043 668 6568
info@toberphelimhouse.com
A very child-friendly setup, with a separate family sitting room, private playground, and plenty of farm animals to fawn over on a 200-acre (80 ha) working farm. The hotel is in a Georgian country house, located in the lake country near Longford's border with Counties Meath, Westmeath, and Cavan.
🛏 3 🅿 10 🕒 Closed late Sept.–April 🏧 No credit cards

COUNTY CAVAN

BAILIEBOROUGH

🛏 BAILIE HOTEL
$$$
MAIN ST.
TEL 042 966 5334
FAX 042 966 6506
www.bailiehotel.com
Bailieborough is a neat, proud little town, and the Bailie Hotel is right in that tradition—well run, friendly, efficient, and welcoming with a plasant and helpful staff.
🛏 18

BALLYCONNELL

🏨 SLIEVE RUSSELL HOTEL
$$$$

BALLYCONNELL
TEL 049 952 6444
FAX 049 952 6046
www.slieverussell.ie
A grand hotel with a championship golf course, attentive service, and all the modern amenities.
ⓘ 219 🅿 600 ⮂ 🏊 🆑 All major cards

BLACKLION

SOMETHING SPECIAL

🍽 MACNEAN HOUSE & RESTAURANT
$$

BLACKLION
TEL 071 985 3022
FAX 071 985 3404
www.macneanrestaurant.com
In the MacNeans' small family-run restaurant in a village on the North/South border is a 5-star culinary experience from the young maestro, Irish master chef Neven Maguire. Perish the day he moves on to bigger—though not necessarily better—surroundings.
🕒 Closed Jan.–early Feb.
🆑 MC, V

KINGSCOURT

🏨 CABRA CASTLE
$$–$$$$

KINGSCOURT
TEL 042 966 7030
FAX 042 966 7039
www.cabracastle.com
Fish, golf, or practice your archery at this refurbished castle amid 100 acres (40 ha) of parkland and let the friendly but well-drilled staff help you to enjoy a stylish few nights. Bedrooms are all decorated in keeping with the Georgian surroundings—chandeliers, luxurious furnishings, and all.
ⓘ 80 🅿 200 🕒 Closed Christmas 🆑 All major cards

COUNTY MONAGHAN

CARRICKMACROSS

🏨 NUREMORE HOTEL
🍽 **$$$$–$$$$$**

CARRICKMACROSS
TEL 042 966 1438
FAX 042 966 1853
www.nuremore.com
A large Victorian mansion skillfully brought up to date: deluxe demisuites with separate sitting areas, extremely comfortable single bedrooms, or large family rooms. The ambience in the restaurant is rather formal, though perfectly friendly. Cooking is excellent throughout the menu (quails' eggs, duck, locally gathered mushrooms) with plenty of style. There also are sports facilities, including an 18-hole golf course, in a peaceful country setting.
ⓘ 72 🅿 200 ⮂ 🏊 🆑 All major cards

MONAGHAN

🏨 HILLGROVE HOTEL
$$$–$$$$

OLD ARMAGH RD.
TEL 047 81288
FAX 047 84951
www.hillgrovehotel.com
Just beside the cathedral and overlooking the town, the Hillgrove has a long-established reputation for comfort and a welcoming atmosphere.
ⓘ 44 🅿 430 🕒 Closed Christmas ⮂ 🅐 🆑 All major cards

🍽 ANDY'S BAR & RESTAURANT
$$$

12 MARKET ST.
TEL 047 82277
www.andysmonaghan.com
This is where the locals go to eat fine pub grub in the bar downstairs. The menu here might feature dishes such as sausages and mashed potato, or bacon and cabbage. There's also a decent middlebrow restaurant upstairs, where a more upscale selection could run to fish and steaks.
🕒 Closed Sun. L, Mon. D, early July, Good Fri., Christmas 🆑 MC, V

COUNTY WESTMEATH

ATHLONE

🏨 HODSON BAY HOTEL
$$$–$$$$

HODSON BAY
TEL 090 644 2000
FAX 090 644 2020
www.hodsonbayhotel.com
Commanding a wonderful panorama of Lough Ree, the Hodson Bay Hotel has been refurbished and extended to provide high levels of comfort and service. Some of the bedrooms overlook the lake, and the views from their big picture windows are absolutely stunning. The hotel has its own golf course and lake marina.
ⓘ 133 🅿 300 ⮂ 🏊 🆑 All major cards

🏨 PRINCE OF WALES HOTEL
$$

CHURCH ST.
TEL 090 647 6666
FAX 090 649 1750
www.theprinceofwales.ie
An unpretentious family-run hotel with clean and comfortable bedrooms, conveniently positioned right in the center of Athlone.
ⓘ 73 🅿 35 🆑 All major cards

🍽 WINEPORT LODGE
$$$

GLASSON
TEL 090 643 9010
www.wineport.ie
One of the great restaurants of

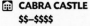
⮂ Elevator 🅐 Air-conditioning 🏊 Indoor Pool 🅿 Outdoor Pool 🆑 Credit Cards

Ireland, in an area not exactly oversupplied with them. Wonderful lake views sharpen the appetite for a menu that's dictated by what's available locally, fresh and with regard to the season, e.g. all sorts of game, newly picked mush-rooms, smoked eels; also Irish beef and delicious farmhouse cheeses. Ask about lakeside accommodations.
🕑 Closed L & Christmas
💳 All major cards

🍴 LEFT BANK BISTRO
$$
FRY PLACE
TEL 090 649 4446
www.leftbankbistro.com
Veggies in Ireland have traditionally fared about as well as sun-worshippers, but here's one place where the art of the vegetable is understood. Not that carnivores are left unsatisfied; sharp modern ideas shine a light on every corner of the menu at the Left Bank. Children welcome before 7 p.m.
♿ 🕑 Closed Christmas
💳 AE, MC, V

MULLINGAR

🏨 WOODLANDS FARM HOUSE
$$
STREAMSTOWN (N6)
NEAR HORSELEAP
TEL 044 922 6414
maxwells.woodlandsfarm@
gmail.com
If you're looking for one of the friendliest Be&Bs in Ireland, in one of the quietest spots, then Woodlands is exactly what you're after. The rooms in this ivy-hung old house are immac-ulately kept. There's a pot of tea and a snack waiting no matter what time you arrive, and the mighty breakfast will keep you going all day.
🛏 4 🕑 Closed mid-Oct.–Feb.
💳 No credit cards

COUNTY OFFALY

BANAGHER

🏨 HARBOUR MASTER'S HOUSE
$$
SHANNON HARBOUR
TEL 057 915 1532
Open fires, splendid breakfasts, and a warm welcome, not to mention a great pub a short stroll away—this is a haven in the bleakly beautiful boglands, right on the Grand Canal.
🛏 5 🕑 Closed Christmas
💳 MC, V

BIRR

🍴 THE THATCH
$$
CRINKLE
TEL 050 972 0682
FAX 050 972 1847
A great pub, bursting with atmosphere. The menu here caters to those looking for a zest of the exotic (kangaroo steaks, anyone?), devotees of local game (rabbit, pigeon), and those who just want good traditional pub grub.
🕑 Closed Good Fri., Christmas
💳 DC, MC, V

KINNITTY

🏨 ARDMORE COUNTRY HOUSE
$$
THE WALK
TEL 057 913 7009
FAX 086 278 9147
www.kinnitty.com
You haven't tasted potato cakes until you've sampled Chris Byrne's. But that's not the only talent of the hospitable hostess of Ardmore House—she is a stalwart of the local walking club, knows all the best walks in the Slieve Blooms, and plays the fiddle like a demon, too!
🛏 5 🕑 Closed Christmas
💳 No credit cards

PRICES

HOTELS
An indication of the cost of a double room in the high season is given by $ signs.

$$$$$	Over $280
$$$$	$200–$280
$$$	$120–$200
$$	$80–$120
$	Under $80

RESTAURANTS
An indication of the cost of a three-course meal without drinks is given by $ signs.

$$$$$	Over $80
$$$$	$50–$80
$$$	$35–$50
$$	$20–$35
$	Under $20

COUNTY LAOIS

DURROW

🏨 CASTLE DURROW HOTEL
$$$–$$$$
DURROW
TEL 057 873 6555
FAX 057 873 6559
www.castledurrow.com
This fabulous 300-year-old country-house hotel is set in beautiful gardens and grounds offering woodlands and riverbank strolls. A relaxed and friendly atmosphere, with luxury rooms in the house or something a bit simpler in the converted stable block.
🛏 60 🕑 Closed first 2 weeks Jan. 💳 All major cards

PORTLAOISE

🏨 IVYLEIGH HOUSE
$$
BANK PLACE, CHURCH ST.

🏨 Hotel 🍴 Restaurant 🛏 No. of Guest Rooms ♿ Disabled Facilities 🅿 Parking 🕑 Closed

TEL 057 862 2081
FAX 057 866 3346
www.ivyleigh.com
A friendly welcome awaits at
this Georgian house, which is
meticulously maintained and
efficiently run, making it a very
comfortable stopover in Portlaoise. The bedrooms are light
and airy, with a striking decor
of bright color schemes.
🛏 6 🅿 6 🕐 mid-Dec.–early
Jan. 💳 MC, V

🍴 KINGFISHER
RESTAURANT
$
OLD AIB BANK, MAIN ST.
TEL 057 866 2500
www.kingfisherrestaurant
.com
The Kingfisher does things
exceptionally well, employing
fresh herbs and spices as well as
high-quality meats and vegetables. The menu include dozens
of tasty Indian dishes—some old
favorites, others to tempt the
experimentally inclined.
🕐 Closed Christmas 💳 AE,
MC, V

COUNTY MEATH

KELLS

🍴 VANILLA POD
RESTAURANT
$$$
HEADFORT ARMS HOTEL
TEL 081 822 2800
www.headfortarms.ie
Although it's housed in the
same building as the Headfort
Arms Hotel, the Vanilla Pod is
a separate setup and attracts
a large following for its wine
nights as well as great food,
including the best charcoal-
grilled steaks in the region.
🕐 Closed L except Sun.;
Christmas 💳 All major cards

NAVAN

🏨 BELLINTER HOUSE
$$$$$

NAVAN
TEL 046 903 0900
www.bellinterhouse.com
Very elegant 18th-century
house with varied accommo-
dations, from grand bedrooms
to cozy couple-friendly
hideaways and bedroom-plus-
living-room apartments in
the stable block, perfect for
families.
🛏 34 💳 All major cards

🏨 ARDBOYNE HOTEL
$$$
DUBLIN RD.
TEL 046 902 3119
www.ardboynehotel.com
An efficiently run, well-
equipped hotel on the edge
of town that offers comfort
and good service in a relaxed
atmosphere. The pleasantly
upbeat bedrooms are well lit
and have garden views.
🛏 29 🅿 186 🕐 Closed
Christmas 💳 All major cards

SLANE

🏨 TANKARDSTOWN
HOUSE
$$$$$
RATHKENNY
TEL 041 982 4621
www.tankardstown.ie
Tankardstown House aims to
be a home away from home—
and indeed it is, if your home
happens to be a magnificent
country house set on 80 acres
(32 ha) of tree-lined parkland.
Luxury bedrooms, courtyard
cottages, spa treatments, an
outdoor hot tub, and iPod-
friendly trees (ask when you
get there).
🛏 18 💳 All major cards

COUNTY LOUTH

BETTYSTOWN

🍴 BACCHUS AT THE
COASTGUARD
$$$
BAYVIEW

TEL 041 982 8251
This restaurant enjoys a
wonderful setting, right on
the bay, but it's not just the
view that's the attraction. The
excellent menu features a wide
range of choices, though fish
is the thing here: prawns, crab,
fresh seasonal lobster, sea bass,
salmon, whitefish, and shellfish.
🕐 Closed Mon., L (except
Sun.), Sun. D

CARLINGFORD

🏨 GHAN HOUSE
🍴 $$$–$$$$$
CARLINGFORD
TEL 042 937 3682
FAX 042 937 3772
www.ghanhouse.com
Famous for its hospitality,
Ghan House sits on Carlingford
Lough between mountains
and the sea. This quiet but very
social retreat features open
fires and super-comfortable
bedrooms. The food is
superbly prepared, from local
beef and lamb to Carlingford
Lough fish and free-range eggs.
🛏 12 🕐 Closed L except Sun.;
Christmas 💳 All major cards

🏨 BEAUFORT HOUSE
$$$
GHAN RD.
TEL 042 937 3879
www.beauforthouse.net
This comfortable B&B boasts
stunning views out over Car-
lingford Lough to the Mourne
Mountains. The welcoming
hosts are very keen sailors who
can tell you everything about
boating and sailing locally.
🛏 5 🕐 Closed Christmas
💳 MC, V

🍴 P. J. O'HARE'S BAR &
RESTAURANT
$$
THOLSEL ST.
TEL 042 937 3106
www.pjoharescarlingford.com
A genuine "black and white"
pub, with low ceilings, beams,

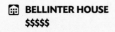
🛗 Elevator 🅰 Air-conditioning 🏊 Indoor Pool 🏊 Outdoor Pool 💳 Credit Cards

black woodwork, white walls, open fires, llive music, and a wonderful atmosphere. Great Guinness and seafood pie.
All major cards

DROGHEDA

⊞ BEST WESTERN BOYNE VALLEY HOTEL & COUNTRY CLUB
$$$
STAMEEN, DUBLIN RD.
TEL 041 983 7737
FAX 041 983 9188
www.boyne-valley-hotel.ie
A leisure center, tennis court, gym, and putting green are just some of the attractions of this well-run hotel, with pleasant modern guest rooms.
73 200 All major cards

⊞ WESTCOURT HOTEL
$$$
WEST ST.
TEL 041 983 0965
FAX 041 983 0970
www.westcourt.ie
One of those traditional hotels at the heart of the community where you can drink, eat, dance, meet, or get married.
29 All major cards

⊞ TRIPLE HOUSE
$$
TERMONFECKIN
TEL/ FAX 041 982 2616
If you're staying in Drogheda, head out to the village of Termonfeckin for dinner—this is a friendly house, with a neat hand with the local fish.
Closed Mon., L Tues.–Sat., Christmas week MC, V

■ NORTHERN IRELAND

BELFAST

⊞ MALMAISON BELFAST
$$$
34–38 VICTORIA ST.

BELFAST, BT1 3GH
TEL 028 9022 0200
www.malmaison-belfast.com
All Malmaison hotels have started life in a different role; this handsome building was once a grand seed warehouse. Rooms are and done out in black, cream, and red. There's a bar and a brasserie offering such delights as salmon, wood pigeon, and smoked haddock.
62 All major cards

⊞ MALONE LODGE
$$$
60 EGLANTINE AVE.
BELFAST, BT9 6DY
TEL 028 9038 8000
FAX 028 9038 8088
www.malonelodgehotel belfast.com
In a quiet, leafy street south of the city center, Malone Lodge offers a warm welcome, a friendly atmosphere, and very pleasant surroundings. This is one of the nicest hotels in the city, with extremely comfortable guest rooms.
51 35 All major cards

⊞ BALMORAL HOTEL
$$–$$$
BLACKS RD.
BELFAST, BT10 0NF
TEL 028 9030 1234
FAX 028 9060 1455
www.balmoralhotelbelfast.co.uk
Just 4 miles (6 km) south of the city, this is a stylish modern hotel with well equipped rooms. There's a choice of spacious lounges, a restaurant, and a bar.
43 300 All major cards

⊞ CRESCENT TOWNHOUSE HOTEL
$$–$$$
13 LOWER CRESCENT
BELFAST, BT7 1NR
TEL 028 9032 3349
FAX 028 9032 0646

www.crescenttownhouse.com
A decent, comfortable hotel where the welcome is warm and staff are friendly and efficient. It's a stylish Regency townhouse next to the Botanic Gardens station; lively bars below, smart bedrooms above.
17 Closed part July & Christmas All major cards

⊞ CAMERA
$–$$
44 WELLINGTON PARK
BELFAST, BT9 6PD
TEL 028 9066 0026
FAX 028 9066 7856
www.cameraguesthouse.com
A stylish guesthouse with bright, airy, modern rooms in the peaceful, well-maintained area close to the university.
9 All major cards

⊞ RESTAURANT MICHAEL DEANE
$$$$
34–40 HOWARD ST.
BELFAST, BT1 6PD
TEL 028 9033 1134
FAX 028 9056 0001
www.michaeldeane.co.uk
If you are out to catch the real formal dining tiger by the tail, there's only one place north of the border to go hunting, and that's at Michael Deane's. Far and away the most accomplished cook in the North, Deane has set out every detail—room, service, wine list—to complement his marvelous skills at the stove. You can really blow out the walls on his great eight-course Menu Prestige, or go for impeccable fish (monkfish, scallops) or meat (Irish mountain lamb, local beef). Closed Mon.–Tues., Christmas, 2 days in July
AE, MC, V

⊞ JAMES STREET SOUTH
$$$
21 JAMES ST. SOUTH
BELFAST, BT2 7GA

⊞ Hotel ⊞ Restaurant No. of Guest Rooms Disabled Facilities Parking Closed

TEL/FAX 028 9043 4310
www.jamesstreetsouth.co.uk
There's a timeless and very
welcoming atmosphere to
this former linen mill. The
menu includes local fruit and
vegetables, Antrim-reared beef
and lamb, game from nearby
estates, and fish out of the Irish
Sea—all complemented by a
well-balanced wine list.
🕐 Closed L Sun. & Christmas
💳 AE, MC, V

🍴 NICK'S WAREHOUSE
$$$
35–39 HILL ST.
BELFAST, BT1 2LB
TEL 028 9043 9690
www.nickswarehouse.co.uk
An enjoyable experience, for
vegetarians as much as for carni-
vores, with more than a nod to
Irish traditions of cuisine—local
pork with red wine and deli-
cious champ (mashed potatoes
for angels) and a cheeseboard
full of Irish produce.
♿ 🕐 Closed Sun.–Mon.,
Christmas 💳 All major cards

🍴 NO. 27 TALBOT STREET
$$$
27 TALBOT ST.
BELFAST, BT1 2LD
TEL 028 9031 2884
www.no27.co.uk
Girders and brickwork hint at
linen mill origins. You can nibble
away or go the whole trencher-
man from a varied menu that
is strong on local ingredients.
Irresistible desserts.
🕐 Closed Sun., D Mon., L Sat.
💳 MC, V

🍴 SHU
$$$
253 LISBURN RD.
BELFAST, BT9 7EN
TEL 028 9038 1655
www.shu-restaurant.com
Excellent brasserie-style cooking,
where traditional values of first-
class ingredients and true flavors
are what matter. Try their duck
confit or a tasty dish of smoked

hake with special chips.
♿ 🕐 Closed Sun., Christmas
💳 AE, MC, V

🍴 ALDEN'S
$$
229 UPPER NEWTOWNARDS RD.
BELFAST, BT4 3JF
TEL 028 9065 0079
www.aldensrestaurant.com
Alden's is one of Belfast's best
and brightest; warm welcome,
warm atmosphere, and a touch
of southern warmth in the
cooking. Southern Europe,
that is: Roast sea bass or some
fritters of goat cheese with
sweet red peppers. All on the
unfashionable east side of the
city, too.
♿ 🕐 Closed Sat. L, Sun.
💳 All major cards

🍴 BEATRICE KENNEDY
$$
44 UNIVERSITY RD.
BELFAST, BT7 1NJ
TEL 028 9020 2290
www.beatricekennedy.co.uk
In an elegant 1920s row house
right next to Queen's Uni-
versity, this stylish restaurant
features modern fusion dishes
that are prepared with creative
flair—chili salt squid with
coriander salad, for instance,
or seared scallops with Thai
curry and sweet potato broth.
Service is friendly and attentive.
🕐 Closed Mon., L (except
Sun.), Christmas week, Easter
💳 MC, V

🍴 CAYENNE
$$
7 ASCOT HOUSE
SHAFTESBURY SQ.
BELFAST, BT2 7DB
TEL 028 9033 1532
FAX 028 9026 1575
www.cayenne-restaurant
.co.uk
A long, narrow dining room.
run by celebrity chef Paul
Rankin and his wife, Jeanne.
Thai pork and crab, Mediter-
ranean vegetable terrine,

Japanese oysters, Far Eastern
fishcakes, all shored up with
the best of British cuisine. It's
an animated environment,
too—it has to be, with so many
wanting to eat here.
♿ 🕐 Closed Sat.–Wed. &
Christmas 💳 All major cards

🍴 CROWN LIQUOR SALOON
$
46 GREAT VICTORIA ST.
BELFAST, BT2 7BA
TEL 028 9027 9901
www.crownbar.com
The Crown is a Belfast
institution, and so firmly on
the tourist trail that it must
be superglued there. And it's
no wonder—this fabulously
ornate pub, impeccably cared
for by the National Trust, is the
best example anywhere in the
city of an authentic Victorian
imbibing emporium. The
food is great, and most of it
is traditional Irish cuisine—eat
sausages and champ here
before you leave Ireland, and
you'll pine until you're back in
the Crown once more.
💳 DC, MC, V

SOMETHING SPECIAL

🍴 ERRIGLE INN
$
312–320 ORMEAU RD.
BELFAST, BT7 2GE
TEL 028 9064 1410
www.errigle.com
A 1930s Belfast pub well
known as a music hotspot with
good plain food.
💳 All major cards

🍴 OLIVE TREE COMPANY
$
353 ORMEAU RD.
BELFAST, BT7 5GL
TEL 028 9064 8898
Eat hot (Irish fish stew) or
cold (French pastries), lightly
(cheese and olives) or substan-
tially (duck salad), at this café,

but always deliciously. And if you really like what you've had, you can buy the ingredients of the dish on site—for the Olive Tree also shelters Belfast's finest delicatessen.

🕒 Closed D 🚫 No credit cards accepted

COUNTY ANTRIM

BALLYCASTLE

🍴 CENTRAL WINE BAR
$$–$$$
12 ANN ST.
BALLYCASTLE, BT54 6AD
TEL 028 2076 3877
www.centralwinebar.com
An absolutely fabulous place, and a bit of a surprise to find such a snappy atmosphere and general excellence in a sleepy seaside town. Family-run with wonderful food and a cheerful, personal air about the service.
🚗 All major cards

BALLYMENA

🏨 GALGORM RESORT & SPA
$$$
BALLYMENA, BT42 1EA
TEL 028 2588 1001
FAX 028 2588 0080
www.galgorm.com
Horseback riding, water-skiing, and fishing are some of the activities you can enjoy at this handsome Victorian manor-house hotel, set on 85 acres (35 ha) beside the River Maine—with river views from comfortable guest rooms.
ⓘ 24 🅿 170 🚗 All major cards

🏨 MARLAGH LODGE
$–$$
71 MOORFIELDS RD.
BALLYMENA, BT42 3BU
TEL 028 2563 1505
FAX 028 2564 1590
www.marlaghlodge.com
Musicians Rachel and Robert Thompson rescued Marlagh

Lodge from dereliction. It's lovingly presented, from the prime ingredients in your breakfast to the books in your bedroom bookcase.
ⓘ 3 🕒 Call during off-season 🚗 MC, V

BUSHMILLS

🏨 BUSHMILLS INN
🍴 $$$$
9 DUNLUCE RD.
BUSHMILLS, BT57 8QG
TEL 028 2073 3000
www.bushmillsinn.com
The Bushmills Inn has a great reputation for character, whether it's the wonky old floors, the real coal and turf fires, or the individually decorated bedrooms. The perfect stopover for your tour of the Old Bushmills Distillery.
ⓘ 41 🚗 All major cards

CARNLOUGH

🏨 LONDONDERRY ARMS
🍴 $$$
20 HARBOUR RD.
BT44 0EU
TEL 028 2888 5255
FAX 028 2888 5263
www.glensofantrim.com
A comfortable old Georgian inn in a fishing village on the spectacular Antrim coast. Paintings of local scenes by Ulster artists and antique furnishings combine to make this hotel—once owned by Sir Winston Churchill—a memorable place to stay. A relaxed approach and plenty of skill in the kitchen makes this a good place to stop for dinner on your way up the Antrim Coast Road.
ⓘ 35 🅿 50 🕒 Closed Christmas 🔁 🚗 All major cards

PORTRUSH

🍴 RAMORE WINE BAR
$$
THE HARBOUR
PORTRUSH, BT56 8BN

TEL 028 7082 4313
www.ramorerestaurant.com
The Ramore made its name as an upscale place for sophisticated dining, but it has turned into a cheap(ish) and very cheerful place serving superior grills, steaks, and pasta to a relatively young crowd.
🚗 MC, V

COUNTY LONDONDERRY

COLERAINE

🏨 GREENHILL HOUSE
$$
24 GREENHILL RD.
AGHADOWEY, BT51 4EU
TEL 028 7086 8241
FAX 028 7086 8365
www.greenhill-house.co.uk
Comfort and a touch of elegance but not at the expense of its warmth or hospitality—and that's what brings people back to this handsome Georgian house in beautiful gardens in the valley of the River Bann.
ⓘ 6 🅿 10 🕒 Closed Nov.–Feb. 🚗 MC, V

COOKSTOWN

🏨 TULLYLAGAN COUNTRY HOUSE HOTEL
$$–$$$
40B TULLYLAGAN RD.
COOKSTOWN, BT80 8UP
TEL 028 8676 5100
FAX 028 8676 1715
www.tullylagan.com
This is a very handsome country-house hotel set in 30 acres (12 ha) of gardens and grounds, with all the comfort and service you'd expect. A great base for exploring the nearby Sperrin Mountains.
ⓘ 15 🕒 Closed Christmas 🚗 All major cards

GARVAGH

🏨 GORTIN GLEN HOUSE
$

52 BALLYAGAN RD.
GARVAGH, BT51 4ES
TEL 028 7086 8260
FAX 028 7086 8176
www.gortinglen.co.uk
Bedrooms are located in carefully converted outbuildings at Gortin Glen House, situated in the beautiful rolling countryside of east Derry.
[i] 3 [P] 6

LIMAVADY

RADISSON BLU ROE PARK RESORT
$$
LIMAVADY, BT49 9LB
TEL 028 7772 2222
FAX 028 7772 2313
www.radissonroepark.com
A very well-appointed hotel in a beautiful location. Golfing fiends will find an 18-hole course, floodlit driving range, putting green, and a golf-training academy. Others will enjoy the wooded grounds, health and exercise facilities, and excellent fishing.
[i] 118 [P] 300 🔽 🏊 All major cards

THE LIME TREE
$$
60 CATHERINE ST.
LIMAVADY, BT49 9DB
TEL 028 7776 4300
www.limetreerest.com
A hospitable house where the cooking is solidly spot-on. The menu might include sirloin steaks in peppercorn sauce or perhaps a plate of sensational crab cakes.
Closed L, Sun. AE, MC, V

LONDONDERRY

BEECH HILL COUNTRY HOUSE HOTEL
$$$
32 ARDMORE RD.
LONDONDERRY, BT47 3QP
TEL 028 7134 9279
FAX 028 7134 5366
www.beech-hill.com

An early Georgian mansion in wooded grounds, gardens, and waterfalls, offering well-furnished rooms and a stylish yet relaxed atmosphere.
[i] 17 plus 10 annex [P] 75
Closed Christmas
All major cards

TOWER HOTEL DERRY
$$–$$$
BUTCHER ST.
LONDONDERRY, BT48 6HL
TEL 028 7137 1000
FAX 028 7137 1234
www.towerhotelderry.com
This is a new and very stylish hotel, with great views over the city from the upper floors. The public areas, which include a popular bistro and contemporary bar, are minimalistic, but there's no shortage of Irish hospitality from the staff.
[i] 93 [P] 25 Closed Christmas week All major cards

MAGHERAFELT

SOMETHING SPECIAL

LAUREL VILLA
$$
60 CHURCH ST.
MAGHERAFELT, BT45 6AW
TEL/FAX 028 7930 1459
www.laurel-villa.com
An absolute delight. Charming Gerardine Kielt supervises the immaculate bedrooms and cooks heavenly breakfasts, while her husband, Eugene, organizes poetry readings and tours of nearby Seamus Heaney Country (the Nobel Laureate poet is a local boy).
[i] 5 Call in off-season MC, V

COUNTY TYRONE

DUNGANNON

GRANGE LODGE
$$

7 GRANGE RD.
DUNGANNON, BT71 7EJ
TEL 028 8778 4212
FAX 028 8778 4313
www.grangelodgecountryhouse.com
This is one of the friendliest and most comfortable guesthouses in Ireland. Nothing is too much trouble for the hospitable Browns, and the home cooking is superb.
[i] 5 [P] 12 Closed mid-Dec.–Jan. MC, V

GORTIN

BADONEY TAVERN
$
16 MAIN ST.
GORTIN, BT79 8PH
TEL 028 8164 8157
pksmckenna@aol.com
Very friendly pub where Peter McKenna "will cook you whatever you like, as long as I *can* cook it."
All major cards

OMAGH

HAWTHORN HOUSE
$
72 OLD MOUNTFIELD RD.
OMAGH, BT79 7EN
TEL/FAX 028 8225 2005
info@hawthornhouse.co.uk
This handsome Victorian house offers warm hospitality, comfortable rooms, and a high standard of cooking. Salmon, sole, and steaks are all good, and for vegetarians there are such delights as mushrooms with spinach and goat's cheese.
[i] 5 [P] 65 All major cards

COUNTY FERMANAGH

ENNISKILLEN

KILLYHEVLIN HOTEL & HEALTH CLUB
$$$
ENNISKILLEN, BT74 6RW
TEL 028 6632 3481
www.killyhevlin.com

A cozy modern hotel on the outskirts of Fermanagh's county town.
🛈 70 🅿 500 🕐 Closed Christmas 💳 All major cards

🏨 ARCH HOUSE
$–$$
TULLYHONA, FLORENCECOURT
ENNISKILLEN, BT92 1DE
TEL 028 6634 8452
www.archhouse.com
This welcoming place offers superb mountain views and is a convenient base for visiting Florence Court House and Marble Arch Caves. Breakfast on kippers, homemade bread and scones, or a mighty fry.
🛈 6 💳 MC, V

🏨 AGHNACARRA HOUSE
$
CARRYBRIDGE
LISBELLAW, BT94 5HX
TEL 028 6638 7077
FAX 028 6638 5811
normaensor@talk21.com
Right on the peaceful shores of Upper Lough Erne south of town, this friendly guesthouse enjoys its own lake fishing.
🛈 7 🅿 8 🕐 Closed Nov.–March 💳 MC, V

🏨 DROMARD HOUSE
$
ENNISKILLEN, BT74 4HR
TEL 028 6638 7250
www.dromardhouse.com
Based in a beautiful old house, with bedrooms in a converted stable block. Dromard House stands in extensive grounds, and there are paths through the woods down to Lough Erne where you can fish.
🛈 4 🅿 4 🕐 Closed Christmas 💳 No credit cards

IRVINESTOWN

🏨 MAHON'S HOTEL
$$
MILL ST.
IRVINESTOWN, BT74 1GS
TEL 028 6862 1656
www.mahonshotel.com
Handy for Enniskillen, the islands of Lower Lough Erne, and the beautiful hilly country of southwest Tyrone, Mahon's is a friendly family-run hotel with comfortable, airy rooms.
🛈 24 🅿 40 💳 All major cards

COUNTY ARMAGH

ARMAGH CITY

🏨 NEWFORGE HOUSE
$$$$
58 NEWFORGE RD.
MAGHERALIN, BT67 0QL
TEL 028 9261 1255
FAX 028 9261 2823
www.newforgehouse.com
Hosts John and Louise Mathers are the latest in six generations of the family at Newforge House, and there's an air of settled comfort and confidence about the place. Lovely grounds and fabulous cooking, with local ingredients and home-grown vegetables.
🛈 6 🕐 Closed Christmas 💳 All major cards

KEADY

🏨 DUNDRUM HOUSE
$
116 DUNDRUM RD.
TASSAGH, BT60 2NG
TEL 028 3753 1257
www.dundrumhouse.com
Surrounded by 80 acres (32 ha) of its own farmland, this is a charming early 18th-century farmhouse with some splendid original features. It has been creatively restored, and the friendly hosts offer unlimited choices for breakfast—at whatever time you choose.
🛈 3 🅿 5 💳 MC, V

NEWRY

🏨 CANAL COURT HOTEL
$$$–$$$$
MERCHANT'S QUAY

<hr>

PRICES

HOTELS
An indication of the cost of a double room in the high season is given by **$** signs.

$$$$$	Over $280
$$$$	$200–$280
$$$	$120–$200
$$	$80–$120
$	Under $80

RESTAURANTS
An indication of the cost of a three-course meal without drinks is given by **$** signs.

$$$$$	Over $80
$$$$	$50–$80
$$$	$35–$50
$$	$20–$35
$	Under $20

<hr>

NEWRY, BT35 8HF
TEL 028 3025 1234
www.canalcourthotel.com
With its dramatic frontage and lobby, this new hotel announces its status as a high-class place to stay. But there's an intimacy about it, and an emphasis on old-fashioned hospitality. Rooms have classic décor and king-size beds, the restaurant offers fine dining, and there's entertainment in the bar.
🛈 51 🅿 60 🕐 Closed Christmas 🛗 💳 All major cards

COUNTY DOWN

COMBER

🏨 OLD
🍴 SCHOOLHOUSE INN
$$–$$$
100 BALLYDRAIN RD., COMBER
NEWTOWNARDS, BT23 6EA
TEL 028 9754 1182
FAX 028 9754 2583
www.theoldschoolhouseinn.com

There are 12 bedrooms, each named after an American president of Ulster descent, in this welcoming guesthouse. Enjoy a candlelit dinner of local specialties.

🛗 🌀 Closed Mon.–Sat. L, Sun.–Mon. D, Christmas
💳 AE, MC, V

DOWNPATRICK

🏨 🍴 **THE MILL AT BALLYDUGAN**
$$
DRUMCULLEN RD.
BALLYDUGAN
DOWNPATRICK, BT30 8HZ
TEL 028 4461 3654
www.ballyduganmill.com
A really unusual place to stay—a lovingly restored flour mill eight floors high, offering characterful rooms and excellent food in either the wheelhouse café or beamed restaurant.
🛗 12 💳 All major cards

🏨 **PHEASANTS' HILL**
$$
37 KILLYLEAGH RD.
DOWNPATRICK, BT30 9BL
TEL/FAX 028 4461 7246
www.pheasantshill.co.uk
In a superb rural location north of Downpatrick near Quoile Pondage nature reserve, this is an organic farm offering a warm welcome and well-appointed accommodations.
🛗 3 🅿 10 🌀 Closed Nov.–mid-Mar. 💳 All major cards

HOLYWOOD

🏨 **BEECH HILL COUNTRY HOUSE**
$$–$$$
23 BALLYMONEY RD.
CRAIGANTLET
NEWTOWNARDS, BT23 4TG
TEL/FAX 028 9042 5892
www.beech-hill.net
Georgina Campbell's "Best B&B 2010" and "Best Breakfast 2010" are thoroughly deserved. The local farm shop supplies

most ingredients for the memorable breakfasts—you won't need lunch!
🛗 3 💳 All major cards

KILLINCHY

🍴 **BALLOO HOUSE**
$$$
1 COMBER RD.
KILLINCHY
NEWTOWNARDS, BT23 6PA
TEL 028 9754 1210
www.balloohouse.com
A real treat. You can dine in style on langoustine and crab from Strangford Lough or venison from nearby Finnebrogue, or in more casual bistro style on daily special dishes.
🌀 Closed Sun.–Mon.
💳 MC, V

KILLYLEAGH

🍴 **THE DUFFERIN ARMS**
$$$
35 HIGH ST.
KILLYLEAGH, BT30 9QF
TEL 028 4482 1182
www.dufferinarms.co.uk
With its castle and wonderful setting by Strangford Lough, Killyleagh makes a perfect escape from Belfast (half an hour away). This restaurant serves local produce with warmth and flair.
💳 All major cards

NEWTOWNARDS

🏨 **BALLYNESTER HOUSE**
$$
1A CARDY RD.
GREYABBEY
NEWTOWNARDS, BT22 2LS
TEL 028 4278 8386
FAX 028 4278 8986
www.ballynesterhouse.com
A welcoming guesthouse in a beautiful location in the hills above Strangford Lough, with fine views. Choose from airy, comfortable bedrooms in the house, or the pitch pine beams and wooden ambience of the

self-catering lodge next door.
🛗 3 🅿 9 💳 MC, V

🏨 **EDENVALE HOUSE**
$$
130 PORTAFERRY RD.
NEWTOWNARDS, BT22 2AH
TEL 028 9181 4881
www.edenvalehouse.com
Peace and quiet are the keynotes at this Georgian hideaway with its large gardens and views over Strangford Lough. Bedrooms are decorated and furnished in period style.
🛗 3 🅿 10 🌀 Closed Christmas
💳 MC, V

PORTAFERRY

🏨 🍴 **PORTAFERRY HOTEL**
$$$
10 THE STRAND
PORTAFERRY, BT22 1PE
TEL 028 4272 8231
www.portaferryhotel.com
A very well-run hotel right on the waterfront of charming Portaferry, overlooking the Narrows of Strangford Lough. The staff here is exceptionally pleasant, and the rooms with lough views are wonderful. As at the Narrows (below), it's the fish—especially the scallops—that bring people to the restaurant here from all over the neighborhood.
🛗 14 🅿 6 🌀 Closed Christmas
💳 All major cards

🍴 **THE NARROWS**
$$$
8 SHORE RD.
PORTAFERRY, BT22 1JY
TEL 028 4272 8148
Good cooking with a light touch (fresh fish don't have to travel far). A friendly atmosphere, and a great loughside position.
💳 AE, MC, V

 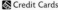

Shopping

Think of shopping in Ireland, and the first things that spring to mind are usually superb crafts: Waterford crystal, Aran knitwear, Donegal tweed, Belleek pottery, Claddagh rings, Connemara marble, and Ulster linen, among others. Kilkenny is an acknowledged center of the best in Irish craftsmanship, and the major tourist information centers around the country usually have a good selection on sale. An excellent reminder of a trip to Ireland is some recorded traditional music, evoking happy evenings spent in pubs or at a *ceilidh*, or perhaps some poems by Yeats, a copy of *The Islandman* by Tomás O'Crohan, or an anthology of humorous articles by Flann O'Brien.

Irish food and drink specialties include Bailey's liqueur, Cork gin, and the famous Irish whiskeys (Bushmills, Powers, Jamesons, Paddy)—sure, you can buy all of these just about anywhere, but touring the distillery first makes it a very special shopping experience. There are also tasty farmhouse cheeses (try the Cashel Blue), smoked salmon, and delicious soda bread. More of an acquired taste, but certainly worth trying, is dulse, an interesting kind of dried seaweed snack.

For those visitors with a taste for kitsch, there are still plenty of outlets full of bright green, shamrock-encrusted souvenirs, shilelaghs, and dancing leprechauns, along with various items of clothing that will declare in no uncertain terms to friends and neighbors back home that you have indeed been to the Emerald Isle.

You will also find plenty of religious memorabilia, from gaudy plastic Virgin Marys to tasteful and artistic replicas of Celtic crosses; these reach peak proportions in places where storekeepers can trade on various stories of visions and miracles, such as at Knock in County Mayo.

Visitors in search of their Irish roots will also find plenty of genealogy centers, many with computerized research facilities, offering documents to take home that give information about your family name.

◼ DUBLIN

Dublin has long been a good place to shop, particularly fashionable south of the river, and there is apparently no limit to the choices available. Clothing includes classics, trendy designer innovations, and the latest streetwise and club-wear. Some of the finest arts and crafts in the world, and all manner of high-tech gadgetry, can be found here. Traditional-style department stores, reflecting a bygone age, stand alongside glittering malls and one-of-a-kind stores run by people who really know their stuff and don't mind how long it takes to tell you about it.

Grafton Street is undoubtedly the best place to start, full of character and bustling with shoppers and buskers. It leads to **Stephen's Green Shopping Centre** (www.stephensgreen.com), a bright and spacious mall. Side streets in the area have plenty of places to eat and interesting stores.

Powerscourt Centre (www.powerscourtcentre.com) is a unique mall, converted from a large town house, containing upscale stores and eating places.

The maze of narrow, cobbled lanes that comprise **Temple Bar** is a treasure trove of unique stores and galleries, interspersed with pubs and restaurants.

North of the river is not quite so glitzy, but it's been getting a facelift, and wide **O'Connell Street** is full of character. The new **Liffey Boardwalks** are worth a browse, and the street markets here give a true flavor of old Dublin.

There are a number of big shopping malls on the outskirts of the city—**Tallaght,** to the south, is the biggest.

Antiques

One of the best areas to shop for antiques is on and around **Francis St.** There are also regular antiques fairs in the city, notably at **Newman House** (*85–86 St. Stephen's Green*) on alternate Sundays year-round.

Car Boot Shop (*21 Eden Quay, tel 086 679 8849, www.thecarboot shop.com*) has a huge selection of silver, china, and curios.

Gerald Kenyon (*6 Great Strand St., tel 087 908 1639*) specializes in the sale and restoration of fine furniture.

Books

Books Upstairs (*36 College Green, tel 01 679 6687*), across from Trinity College, has a terrific selection of Irish literature and drama, minority interest works, and popular fiction.

Eason's (*40 O'Connell St., tel 01 858 3800, www.eason.ie*) stocks some Irish books but mostly offers run-of-the-mill fiction, along with stationery and art supplies.

Hodges Figgis (*56–58 Dawson St., tel 01 677 4754*) is the largest bookstore in Dublin, a historic emporium that was mentioned by James Joyce in *Ulysses*. It has a huge range of books and there's a coffee shop upstairs.

Crafts

Design Yard (48–49 Nassau St., tel 01 474 1011, www.designyard gallery.com) is one of Ireland's leading showcases for modern quality arts, including an exceptional range of jewelry.

Irish Celtic Craftshop (10–12 Lord Edward St., tel 01 679 9912) has a variety of crafts, including jewelry, knitwear, ceramics, and T-shirts with Celtic designs.

Kilkenny Shop (6 Nassau St., tel 01 677 7066, www.kilkennyshop .com) has a very upscale selection of quality knitwear, woven goods, designer clothing, and pottery.

Department Stores

Arnotts (12 Henry St., tel 01 805 0400), a long-established institution, has three floors of clothing, home wares, sporting goods, and other items.

Brown Thomas (88–95 Grafton St., tel 01 605 6666) is by far the best and most exclusive department store in the city, with an aura of quality and class. Products include designer fashion, perfumes, crystal, and home wares.

Clery & Co. (18–27 Lower O'Connell St., tel 01 878 6000, www.clerys.com) was once the place to shop in Dublin and is still interesting to wander around. It offers conservative fashions, household goods, etc.

Fashion

BT2 (28–29 Grafton St., tel 01 605 6666, www.bt2.ie) is the new-generation Brown Thomas, located opposite its parent store (above); it sells designer labels for the sons and daughters of the original store's customers.

Design Centre (Powerscourt Shopping Centre, 59 S. William St., tel 01 679 5718, www.designcentre.ie) is home to the best Irish designers, including Louise Kennedy (see below) and Therese McKeone.

Louis Copeland (39–41 Capel St., tel 01 872 1600, www.louiscopeland .com) is the outlet for one of Europe's most renowned tailors, providing suits for the rich and famous, including some U.S. presidents.

Louise Kennedy (56 Merrion Sq., tel 01 662 0056, www.louiseken nedy.com) offers exclusive designs for women such as Enya and Gwyneth Paltrow.

Jewelry

Appleby (5–6 Johnson's Court, Grafton St., tel 01 679 9572, www .appleby.ie) is an exclusive jeweler with an excellent selection.

Weir & Sons (96 Grafton St., tel 01 677 9678, www.weirandsons.ie) has quality jewelry and watches, silver, and leather goods.

Markets

Wandering around the markets of Dublin offers a great insight into the day-to-day life of the city. Try the artisan food market on **Meeting House Square** in Temple Bar (Saturdays) which has a great selection of cheeses, organic vegetables, fish, meat, and cakes; **Moore Street** market (Monday to Saturday) is famous for fruit, vegetables, and footwear; **Georges Arcade** (Monday to Saturday) has the same, plus clothing (new and secondhand) and fresh bread. There's a **book market** in Temple Bar Square on weekends; **Mother Redcap's Market** (Friday to Sunday), in Christ Church Place and Winetavern St., is famous for antiques and bric-a-brac.

Music

Celtic Note (12 Nassau St., tel 01 670 4157, www.celticnote.com) has a huge range of Celtic music—traditional, pop and rock, ballads, classical—as well as videos and instruments.

Claddagh Records (2 Cecilia St., Temple Bar, tel 01 677 0262, www.claddaghrecords.com) is an Aladdin's cave full of CDs, tapes, and vinyl. It carries traditional Irish music, including some rare recordings, bluegrass, blues, and world music.

■ EAST IRELAND

Antiques

Granny's Attic (33 North Main St., Naas, Co. Kildare, tel 045 876 988) is a treasure trove of antiques and curios.

Tara Antiques of Grennan Watermill (Thomastown, Co. Kilkenny, tel 056 775 4077) specializes in English and Irish furniture, art, clocks, and mirrors.

Books

Bridge Street Books (Bridge St., Wicklow, tel 04 046 2240) has a fine, wide selection of books.

Byrne's Kilkenny Bookshop (82 High St., Kilkenny, tel 056 772 3400) has a wide range of books, as well as toys and games. There's a café upstairs.

Clothing

Padmore & Barnes of Kilkenny (Wolf Tone St., Kilkenny, tel 056 772 1037, www.padmore-barnes .com) specializes in handmade Irish shoes, exporting to the U.S., Canada, Japan, and Europe.

Crafts

Ardmore Pottery & Craft Shop (The Cliff, Ardmore, Co. Waterford, tel 024 94152, www.ardmorepottery .com) sells spotted, striped, clever, and irresistible ware in gorgeous blues, reds, and yellows.

Avoca Handweavers (Kilmacanogue, Co. Wicklow, tel 01 286 7466, www.avoca.ie) sends their quality woven goods to craft outlets all over Ireland and have established themselves as the

country's leading brand.
Irish Pewter Mill *(Timolin,
near Moone, Co. Kildare, tel 059
862 4164)* has pewter jewelry,
tableware, and gift items that
are made here, in the mill of a
1,000-year-old nunnery.

Kilkenny is Ireland's principal
center for top-quality original
crafts, with many artists and
artisans working in the area.
The **Kilkenny Design Centre**
*(tel 056 772 2118, www.kilken
nydesign.com)*, in the Castle Yard,
is their showcase, with all kinds
of wares, including ceramics,
carving, jewelry, and fabrics.
Lace Gallery *(Carrigslaney,
Kilbride, Co. Carlow, tel 059 915
5676, www.irishcarrickmacrosslace
.com)* is where Mary O'Neill
makes, shows, and sells fine
handmade lace.
Waterford Crystal *(on the N25/
Cork road, tel 051 332500, www
.waterford.com)* is world-famous
for its glittering goblets, glasses,
and chandeliers. You can buy
them from the showroom here.

Jewelry
Murphy Jewellers of Kilkenny
*(High St., tel 056 772 1127, www
.murphyjewellers.com)* has Irish-
made Celtic gold and silver
designs, diamond-set jewelry,
and watches.

Markets
Kilkenny Market, in Market
Yard on Friday and Saturday
mornings, has home produce,
home baking, crafts, and plants.

■ SOUTHWEST IRELAND
This area is home to some of the
finest craftspeople and some of
the longest-established craft businesses, including Blarney Woollen
Mills (see below). Cork city has
plenty of outlets, as does Killarney, farther north, and there are

little craft communities in various
out-of-the-way places, like Ballydehob and Kinsale.

Antiques
Georgian Antiques
*(21 Lavitt's Quay, Cork, tel 021
427 8153)* as its name implies,
specializes in Georgian-era
furniture, clocks, porcelain, silver,
writing boxes, and more.

Books
Bookstór *(1 Newman's Mall,
Kinsale, Co. Cork, tel 021 477 4966,
www.bookstor.ie)* is an admirable
independent bookshop, with
a huge bargain selection and a
children's book club, Kidzaminer
(www.kidzaminer.com).
Killarney Bookshop *(32 Main
St., Killarney, tel 064 34108, www
.killarneybookshop.ie)* specializes
in books of Irish interest but has
thousands of others to choose
from, too.

Crafts
Blarney Woollen Mills *(Blarney,
Co. Cork, tel 021 451 6111, www
.blarney.com)* has one of the largest craft shops in Ireland, stock-
ing not only the said woolens
but also Waterford crystal, Royal
Tara china, Belleek Pottery, Irish
Dresden, and other crafts.
Kinsale Crystal *(tel 021 477 4493,
www.kinsalecrystal.ie)* is run by
Gerry Dale, ex-Waterford Crystal
craftsman, who has a worldwide
reputation.
Ladies View Industries *(Ladies
View, near Killarney, Co. Kerry, tel
064 663 3430, www.ladiesview
.com)* has a superb selection of
lace and other crafts, and a wonderful view.
Shandon Craft Centre *(Buttermarket, Shandon, Co. Cork, tel 021 450
3936)* has various crafts on sale,
plus the chance to see jewelry,
pottery, sculpture, and musical
instruments being made.
Weavers Shop *(Green St., Dingle,*

*Co. Kerry, tel 066 915 1688, www
.lisbethmulcahy.com)* has a range of
Lisbeth Mulcahy's designs in woven
scarves, wall hangings, and designer
clothing, and you can watch
handloom-weaving in action.

Food
West Cork **cheese** is well-known,
and makers of quality include
Carrigaline Farmhouse Cheese
(www.carrigalinecheese.com), **Durrus
Cheese** *(www.durruscheese.com)*
from just west of Bantry, and
Milleens *(www.milleenscheese.com)*,
from the Beara Peninsula. And if
you are in Clonakilty, Co. Cork,
drop in at **Edward Twomey's**
celebrated butcher store on
Pearse St. and pick up a link or
two of his tasty **black pudding**
(blood pudding), made from a
family recipe that dates back to
the 1800s. **Mussels** are cultivated
in Bantry Bay.

Jewelry
Brian de Staic *(www.briandestaic
.com)* is a craftsman who produces
beautiful pieces of Celtic jewelry.
He has outlets in Dingle *(Green St.,
Dingle, Co. Kerry, tel 066 915 1298)*
and Killarney *(18 High St., Killarney,
Co. Kerry, tel 064 33822)*.

Markets
The best shopping fun you are
likely to have in Cork city is in
the enclosed **English Market**
(www.corkenglishmarket.ie), with
entrances off Grand Parade,
Patrick St., and Princes St. It's
an atmospheric place, brim-
ming with goodies that include
crafts, a delicatessen, and more
mundane household items—with
some good chat.

Most towns of any size in this
area will have a general market once
or twice a week. A particular highlight is the weekly **farmer's market
at Skibbereen** *(www.skibbereen
market.com)*.

Music

Serious electric guitar fans should check out **Crowley's Music Centre** (29 MacCurtain St., Cork, tel 021 450 3426), where R&B hero Rory Gallagher bought his iconic Fender Stratocaster in 1963.

■ WEST IRELAND

Galway is the main city, with the **Eyre Square Shopping Centre** (www.eyresquarecentre.com) at its heart and a cluster of shopping streets with lots of character. Country towns in this area, with their easy pace of life, no-pressure sales staff, and ready conversation, are a delight to stroll around: try the narrow streets of **Ennis** in Co. Clare, or the Georgian thoroughfares of **Westport** in Co. Mayo.

A different shopping experience is to be found at **Bunratty Village Mills** (tel 061 364321) in Co. Clare village—a big, modern complex, catering to the tourists who flock here for the castle and folk park. Stores range from tasteful and expensive to kitschy.

If you're flying out of Shannon Airport, don't forget its **duty-free store** for souvenirs and gifts.

Antiques

Arcadia Antiques (Castle St., Galway, tel 091 561861) is a characterful place, full of ornaments, pictures, and a large range of antique jewelry.

Long Acre (Bridge St., Westport, Co. Mayo, tel 098 28718, www.thelongacre.com) is a fine family-run emporium stuffed with collectibles, antique and just elderly.

Books

Since the famous Kenny's Bookshop moved out to an industrial estate, bookworms get their browsing at **Charlie Byrne's Bookshop** (Cornstore Mall, Middle St., Galway, tel 091 561 766,

www.charliebyrne.com), a rambling secondhand treasure cave.

Clothing

The Co-op (Inishmaan, tel 099 73010) produces Aran garments made by local knitters that are exported worldwide.

Mairéad Sharry (Lurgan Village, Inis Oirr, Aran Islands, Co. Galway, tel 099 75101) is a designer who incorporates traditional Aran stitches into gorgeous modern garments. Her shop also has Aran yarn, vintage tweed clothes, and books. Learning vacations and workshops are available as well.

Crafts

Connemara Marble Industries (at their quarry at Moycullen, Co. Galway, tel 091 555 102 or 555 746) produces beautiful craft and household items, including jewelry and gifts.

Kylemore Abbey Pottery (Kylemore Abbey, near Letterfrack, Co. Galway, tel 095 41437, www.kylemoreabbey.com) has plenty going for it—a beautiful location, friendly workers, and its own gorgeous trademark fuschia design.

Dive & Watersports

Burren Adventures Dive Centre (Aughinish, Kinvara, Co. Galway, tel 065 707 7921, www.burrenadventures.com) is a state-of-the-art dive and watersport shop offering clothing, equipment, courses, expeditions, and advice.

Food

Connemara Smokehouse (Ballyconneely in western Connemara, tel 095 23739, www.smokehouse.ie) is the place to buy wild, organic, smoked, or marinated salmon and other fish for your picnic or take-home present.

Jewelry

The big item in Galway, of course, is the famous Claddagh ring, with its charming and distinctive motif of two hands encircling a heart, topped by a crown. Its long history is explained at the little museum behind **Dillon's Claddagh Ring Shop** (1 Quay St., Galway, tel 091 566365, www.claddaghring.ie), where you can buy rings in gold, silver, or platinum.

Markets

Every Saturday morning, **Galway** hosts a market near St. Nicholas Collegiate Church that is particularly strong on organic produce and homemade breads.

Music

Custy's Traditional Music Shop (Cookes Ln., Ennis, Co. Clare, tel 065 682 1727, www.custysmusic.com) has traditional instruments, including whistles, fiddles, and squeeze boxes.

Powells (The Four Corners, Williams St., Galway, tel 091 562295) sells Irish music tapes and CDs, plus instruments and sheet music.

Roundstone Musical Instruments (IDA Craft Centre, Roundstone, Co. Galway, tel 095 35808, www.bodhran.com) is most famous for the bodhráns (traditional Irish drums) that are made here. It also sells traditional music tapes and CDs.

■ NORTHWEST IRELAND

Sligo and **Donegal** towns have an enjoyable mix of upscale stores aimed at visitors and more down-to-earth shopping for locals, such as old-fashioned drapers and clothing stores (this is the home of Donegal tweed), plus traditional grocers and hardware stores with carved, wooden storefronts.

Antiques

The Gallery (Dunfanaghy, Co. Donegal, tel 074 913 6224), in a former fever hospital, has two stories of antiques, paintings, and crafts.

Mourne Antiques (8 Port Rd., Letterkenny, Co. Donegal, tel 074 912 6457, www.mourneantiques. com) is crammed full of china, jewelry, silver, furniture, and other collectibles.

Crafts

Donegal Craft Village (tel 074 972 2225, www.donegalcraftvil lage.com), just outside Donegal on the Sligo road, comprises a cluster of workshops where you can see artisans at work and buy unique items: metalwork, jewelry, sculpture, and batik, as well as uilleann pipes.

Glencolumbkille Folk Village Shop (tel 074 973 0017, www .glenfolkvillage.com) makes a good stop-in for its range of knitted, crocheted, and other textile goods, and also crafts, jewelry, etc.—all made by locals.

Leitrim Design House (Market House Centre, Carrick-on-Shannon, Co. Leitrim, tel 071 965 0550, www.intoleitrim.com) is a retail showroom and gallery for Leitrim craftspeople and artists.

Department Stores

Magee's (The Diamond, Donegal town, tel 074 922 2660) is the place for tweed. You can watch a weaver at work before buying top-quality jackets and other tweed items

McElhinney's (Main St., Ballybofey, tel 074 913 1217, www.mcelhinneys .com) is the largest department store in the northwest, with a wide selection of quality goods.

Food

The Organic Centre (Rossinver, tel 071 985 4338, www.theorganic centre.ie) sells organic cheese, meat, herbs, vegetables, fruit, and candy.

Jewelry

The Cat and the Moon (4 Castle St., Sligo, tel 071 914 3377, www .thecatandthemoon.com) is an all-encompassing craft and gift shop, including Celtic jewelry.

■ CENTRAL IRELAND

Books

Bookwise Bookshop (Metges Lane, Kennedy Rd., Navan, tel 046 902 7722, www.bookwisebookshop .com) has a good selection, including Irish interest, local history, maps, and guides.

Crafts

Carna Craft (Baltrasna, Ash-bourne, Co. Meath, tel 01 835 0273) sells Michael Mulkerrin's sculptural figurines made of horseshoe nails.

Carrickmacross Lace Gallery (Market Square, Carrickmacross, Co. Monaghan, tel 042 966 4176, www.carrickmacrosslace.ie) has lace made in the traditional way; a lace-making demonstration is given by appointment.

Cavan Crystal Visitor Centre (Dublin Rd. in Cavan, tel 049 433 1800) is one of the oldest glassworks in Ireland, and you can see the master glassblowers and cutters in action before you buy.

Celtic Clays Workshop (Riverside, Carlingford, Co. Louth, tel 042 938 3996) is one of Ireland's leading studio potteries, producing stoneware with rich, earthy glazes.

Jewelry

Coldrick Jewellers (8 Trimgate St., Navan, Co. Meath, tel 046 902 3836) has top-quality items, including Celtic designs.

■ NORTHERN IRELAND

Once, stores in Northern Ireland were reckoned bigger and better than any south of the border, but the Troubles saw the province's shopping facilities stagnate. Now, there is a welcome revival, though there is still some way to go to match the kind of upscale visitor stores of the Republic. Typical souvenirs and collectibles here include Belleek pottery, Tyrone and Fermanagh crystal, Irish linen, and Bushmills whiskey.

Belfast

The city has a number of vast Victorian stores, dating back to its real boom time. At the other end of the spectrum is the bright, ultramodern **Castle-Court Shopping Centre** (tel 028 9023 4591, http://uk.westfield .com/castlecourt), which encompasses 8.5 acres (3.5 ha) in the heart of the city.

Antiques

Donegall Pass is the center of the antiques area of Belfast.

Oakland Antiques (135–137 Donegall Pass, tel 028 9023 0176) is the city's largest antiques store, with Georgian, Victorian, and Edwardian furniture, silver, glass, porcelain, paintings, and many other items for sale.

Books

The Bookshop at Queen's (91 University Rd., tel 028 9066 6302, www.queensbookshop.co.uk) is a general and academic bookstore that also includes a varied selection of poetry.

Another choice is **Waterstone's** (Queen's Buildings, 8 Royal Ave., tel 028 9024 7355, and 44–46 Fountain St., tel 028 9024 0159, www.waterstones.com).

Crafts

Conway Mill Craft Shop and Exhibition Centre (5–7 Conway St., tel 028 9032 6452), within a restored historic flax mill, displays the work of the 22 craft workshops on site.
Workshops Collective for Arts and Crafts (1a Lawrence St., tel 028 9023 4993) has 12 workshops, a showroom, and a coffee shop in an old stable block off Botanic Avenue.

Fashion

The Bureau (46–50 Howard St., tel 028 9043 9800, www.the bureaubelfast.com), once strictly a male preserve, now also has women's clothes for sale. Notable designers include Calvin Klein, Dries Van Noten, Katherine Hamnet, Miu-Miu, and others.
Carter Clothing (11 Upper Queen St., tel 028 9024 3412, and 555 Lisburn Rd., tel 028 9066 9335, www.carterclothing.com) offers very cool jackets and jeans, William Hunt boots, Sand, and Turet Kneufermann.
Office (2 High St., tel 028 9023 5189) is great for shoes that are a little bit naughty, a little bit nice.

Food

Aunt Sandra's Candy Factory (60 Castlereagh Rd., tel 028 9073 2868, www.auntsandras.com) sells handcrafted candy that you can watch being made.
Sawyers (Unit 7 beneath the Fountain Centre, tel 028 9032 2021) is the best deli in town, with a huge range of cheeses, salamis, exotic meats (such as wild boar and ostrich), and patés, as well as fresh dulse (seaweed).

Jewelry

Lauren May Jewellery (10 Queens Arcade, tel 028 9023 2681, tel laurenmay.co.uk) has quality pieces by young designers.

Music

Golden Discs (29 Donegall Pl., tel 028 9032 2653) specializes in Irish folk, rock, and country artists. It also stocks chart toppers, plus blues, dance, and classical recordings.
Knight's (33 Botanic Ave., tel 028 9032 2925), which specializes in traditional jazz, is a great antidote to the chain stores. You will find very little new stuff here, but it does offer a lot of secondhand vinyl and CDs.

Northern Ireland Counties

You'll find historic towns with traditional high streets, but there are also modern shopping facilities, such as the **Foyleside Shopping Centre** (www.foyleside .co.uk) in Derry, anchored by **Dunnes** (www.dunnesstores.ie) and **Marks & Spencer** (www .marksandspencer.com).

Antiques

Crannog Antiques (5 The Brook, Enniskillen, Co. Fermanagh, tel 028 6632 5850) has a lovely selection, including glass, china, furniture, jewelry, brass, and silver.

Books

As in the rest of Ireland, you'll find branches of **Eason's** in all the major towns and cities. Those listed below are alternatives that have good selections, including Irish and local interest.
Bell's Corner (2 High St., Carrickfergus, Co. Antrim, tel 028 9335 1486).
Bookworm Community Bookshop (18–20 Bishop St., Derry, Co. Londonderry, tel 028 7128 2727).
Cameron's (23–29 Broughshane St., Ballymena, Co. Antrim, tel 028 2564 8821).
L. Hall (34–36 Darling St., Enniskillen, Co. Fermanagh, tel 028 6632 2275).

Crafts

Belleek Pottery (Belleek, Co. Fermanagh, tel 028 6865 8501, www. belleek.ie) is one of Ireland's top visitor attractions and is known worldwide for its delicate porcelain (see pp. 318–319).
Buttermarket Craft & Design Centre (Down St., Enniskillen, Co. Fermanagh, tel 028 6632 4499) has 16 workshops, producing pottery, fishing flies, carvings, sculptures, and fine art. There's also a showroom and café.
Irish Linen Centre (Market Sq., Lisburn, Co. Down, tel 028 9266 3377) has an exhibition about the production of Irish linen, as well as a shop and café.
Island Turf Crafts (25 Coalisland Enterprise Centre, 51 Dungannon Rd., Coalisland, Co. Tyrone, tel 028 8774 9041, www.islandturfcrafts .com) makes statues, Celtic crosses, jewelry, and more out of Irish turf (peat).
Tyrone Crystal (115 Coalisland Rd., Dungannon, Co. Tyrone, tel 028 8772 5335, www.tyronecrystal.com) has a glittering array of crystal, and you can see it being made. The showroom also stocks cutlery, tableware, and gifts.

Jewelry

Faller the Jeweller (12 Strand Rd., Derry, Co. Londonderry, tel 028 7136 2710, www.faller.com) is a family-run store with designer jewelry, watches, and gifts, including items made in their own workshop.
Inisor Jewellery (59 Molesworth St., Cookstown, Co. Tyrone, tel 028 8676 1606, www.inisor.com) produces handcrafted jewelry. You can watch the jeweler at work.

Entertainment & Activities

Anyone who spends time in Ireland needs no persuading that the Irish are natural entertainers—not in the "cap-and-bells" sense, but as a people absolutely in love with conversation, music, song, curiosity, argument, joking, and nonsense, the famous Irish *craic* (pronounced "crack"). And every town and village has a stage where anyone can be the star and everyone is part of the enthusiastically participating audience: the pub. There is so much recreation value in the pub that many don't bother looking elsewhere for their entertainment. An even more traditional venue for this kind of informal, come-all-ye gathering is the *ceilidh* (meeting) house, a cornerstone of community life before television when neighbors and strangers would gather to chat, play music, and dance in some house known to be a venue for such goings-on. Ceilidh houses are enjoying something of a revival, and it's worth asking whether there is one in your locality.

The theater is extremely strong in Ireland, opera is gaining ground in the wake of the success of the annual Wexford Festival Opera, and Irish cinema has had extraordinary popularity in the past couple of decades.

Traditional culture is perpetuated in many forms, and apart from the informal music sessions in pubs, you'll find it in stage shows and tourist-oriented banquets.

Almost anywhere you look, there's some kind of festival going on: guzzling seaweed in Antrim or oysters in Galway; hooker (a kind of boat) racing in Connemara; poetry in Sligo; storytelling in Cork.

Nightlife in the big cities—Dublin, Belfast, Cork, Limerick, Galway—has kept pace with its European counterparts in the shape of extreme-noise dance clubs, comedy venues, and late-license bars. But in the smaller communities that make up Ireland's country towns and villages, where the majority of visitors spend most of their time, it is still the pub that offers the best of music, dancing, talk, and laughter.

When it comes to sports, a day at the racetrack (horses or greyhounds) is a long-established and dearly cherished form of entertainment in Ireland, and Gaelic football, hurling, and soccer draw big crowds. Golf, fishing, boating, and horseback riding are popular activities, and walking is gaining ground, so to speak. The **Irish Heart Foundation** (www.irishheart.ie) lists around 70 walking clubs in the Republic.

■ DUBLIN

As the capital and a seedbed of a great literary tradition, Dublin is a cultured city with a long history of entertaining foreigners, vacationers, countryfolk, and Dubliners themselves. There are plenty of places where you can party until dawn. But Dublin has a lot more to offer than that.

Bars

Cool bars south of the river include **Café en Seine** (40 Dawson St.), a three-story art nouveau hive of bars and coffee hangouts; **Whelan's** (25 Wexford St., tel 01 478 0766, www.whelanslive.com), a relaxed lounge with a DJ; the hip, dark, and moody **Dakota** (9 South William St.); and in Temple Bar, the chic **Morgan Bar** (Morgan Hotel, 10 Fleet St., tel 01 643 7000, www.themorgan.com).

North of the river, you could check out the African-themed **Zanzibar** (Lower Ormond Quay) and the amusing Russian Communist-chic décor of **Pravda** (35 Lower Liffey St., tel 01 874 0090, www.pravda.ie).

City Walks

Podcasts of walks around the city, from "Viking & Medieval Dublin" to one based on James Joyce's *Ulysses*, are available to download from **Dublin Tourism** (tel 1850 230 330 or 066 979 2083, www.visitdublin.com/iwalks).

Nightlife

Pure modern club dance is great at **POD** (Harcourt St., tel 01 478 0166, www.pod.ie); gentler Latin sounds are not too far away at **Gaiety Theatre** (South King St., tel 01 677 1717, www.gaietytheatre.com). Across in Temple Bar, an excellent dance club is **Club M** (Cope St., tel 01 671 5274, www.clubm.ie).

As far as other nightlife, if you're under 50 and looking for a lively time, you can scarcely escape the lure of **Temple Bar**. This is where stag and hen parties contest the cobbles with students, Celtic Tiger cubs, and cohorts of youngsters in from the suburbs—all good fun mostly, but things can get a bit silly in the early hours. Clubs, pubs, sidewalk cafés, and other fun destinations seem to occupy all the buildings that don't house avant-garde or retro stores. Drinking and dancing places can change place overnight in the trendiness pecking order, but currently the cool **Fitzsimons** (www.fitzsimons.com) and the **Turk's Head** (www.turkshead.ie), both on Parliament St., are up in the popularity mix—as is **The Porterhouse** (16–18 Parliament St., tel 01 679 8495, www.porterhousebrewco.com), a microbrewery that provides live music every night. There's more music at the **Viperoom Theatre Bar and Club** on Aston Quay.

Pubs

Enjoy the art at the pub immortalized in James Joyce's *Ulysses*, **Davy Byrne's** *(21 Duke St., www .davybyrnes.com)* very fine establishment. You can eavesdrop on conspiratorial politicians and other city heavyweights in the Victorian comfort of **Doheny & Nesbitt's** on Lower Baggot St. **Mulligan's** *(Poolbeg St., www.mulligans.ie)* has long claimed to serve the best Guinness in Ireland. The theatrical but fun **Dublin Literary Pub Crawl** *(nightly in summer; Thurs.–Sun. in winter; tel 01 670 5602, www .dublinpubcrawl.com)* starts at the Duke pub on Duke St. and tours famous literary pubs, with guides who offer information about the authors and act out scenes from their work.

Theater
Three of Dublin's many theaters well worth making an effort to get to include the sometimes experimental, always interesting **Project Arts Centre** *(39 East Essex St., tel 01 881 9613, www.projectartscentre .ie)* and the well-regarded **Gate Theatre** *(Cavendish Row, Parnell Sq., tel 01 874 4085, www.gate-theatre .ie)*. And, of course, there's the one founded by W. B. Yeats, J. M. Synge, Lady Gregory, and others— the famous **Abbey Theatre** *(26 Lower Abbey St., tel 01 878 7222, www.abbeytheatre.ie)*, still putting on works by the great classic playwrights as well as newcomers.

Traditional Music
When it comes to finding the best session of traditional music, the city's *In Dublin* magazine lists what's where. One really excellent, reliable venue is the unpretentious but friendly **Cobblestone Bar** *(North King St., tel 01 872 1799)*, north of the river, where the nightly sessions (all day Sundays) are memorable. Also up there in the ratings is the **Brazen Head** *(20 Lower Bridge St., tel 01 677 9549, www.brazenhead.com)*, an ancient

pub (probably the city's oldest) with great beer and an exceptional atmosphere.

■ EAST IRELAND
Car Touring
Follow the **Gordon Bennett Touring Route** *(www.gordonbennettroute .com)*, a signposted trail of 104 miles (167 km) that takes you along quiet back roads through Counties Carlow, Kildare, and Laois.

Golf
The east of Ireland, with its large areas of level ground and low-lying coasts, is great for golf, and as in the rest of the country, there are many championship courses. Down on the coast of County Waterford, there's the **Tramore Golf Club** *(tel 051 386 170, www. tramoregolfclub.com)*, 10 miles (16 km) south of Waterford town and open seven days a week.

Horse Racing
Kildare is horse-racing country, home to the **National Stud** (see pp. 93–94) and the foremost racetrack—**The Curragh** *(tel 045 441 205, www.curragh.ie)*. Northeast of Kildare town, off the N7, it's where most of Ireland's classic races are run. There are two tracks at Naas, Co. Kildare—the **Punchestown** track *(www.punchestown.com)* and the **Naas** town track *(www. naasracecourse.com)*–and one in **Leopardstown** *(www.leopardstown. com)* in County Dublin. Not quite so prominent, but just as much fun, are the **Waterford & Tramore** *(www.tramore-racecourse.com)* and **Wexford** *(www.wexfordraces.ie)* tracks.

Irish Culture
The **Bru Boru Heritage Centre** *(tel 062 61122)*, in Cashel, is a cultural enclave in the shadow of the Rock of Cashel, set up to study and portray Irish music, song, dance,

storytelling, and theater. Its resident group of musicians and artists are world-famous.

Opera
Don't miss **Wexford Festival Opera** (see p. 114) if you like your opera a little obscure and a lot of fun.

Theater
The **Backstage Theatre & Centre for the Arts** *(Farneyhoogan, Longford, Co. Longford, tel 043 47888, www .backstage.ie)* is a small, custom-built theater that offers an excellent, varied program, including touring international theater companies, Irish drama, comedy, and music.

The **Theatre Royal** *(The Mall, Co. Waterford, tel 051 874 402, www .theatreroyal.ie)* is housed in the Georgian City Hall and offers high-quality drama, music, and dance from Irish and international companies.

Wexford Arts Centre *(tel 053 912 3764, www.wexfordartscentre.ie)*, in the Cornmarket, has a rich program of music, theater, and film.

The **Watergate Theatre** *(Parliament St., Kilkenny, Co. Kilkenny, tel 056 776 1674, www.watergatetheatre.com)* has a lovely, intimate auditorium and a very interesting program of quality drama, music, and children's theater.

In Carlow, the new **Centre for Contemporary Art** *(Old Dublin Rd., tel 059 917 2400, www.visualcarlow .ie)* has a wide range of events, from ballet and comedy to drama and storytelling.

Traditional Music
There are countless pubs for good traditional music. In St. Celbridge in County Kildare, an enjoyable session takes place on Thursday nights in the Kitchen Bar of the **Celbridge House** *(Maynooth Rd., tel 01 627 2729, www. celbridgehouse.com)*. The pub also offers live music on Friday nights and Saturday lunch in the lounge bar.

In the beautiful Vale of Avoca in County Wicklow, **The Meetings** *(tel 040 235 226, www.themeetingsavoca.*

com) has music every weekend—every night April–September—and has a traditional Irish *ceilidh* outdoors on summer Sunday afternoons.

In the north of County Tipperary, on the shores of Lough Derg, you'll find traditional music every night from June to October in **Larkin's** *(tel 067 23232, www.larkinspub.com),* at Garrykennedy near Portroe.

If you're down in Wexford town, try **The Sky and the Ground** *(tel 053 912 1273),* an excellent pub with a great atmosphere—sessions (Mon. & Wed.) are often heavy on the songs.

One of the most famous places (so it's often crowded) is **Johnny Fox's** *(tel 01 295 5647, www.jfp.ie)* in Glencullen, high up in the Wicklow Mountains, where there is live music seven nights a week and on weekend afternoons, too (and also a dinner show with traditional dancers).

◼ SOUTHWEST IRELAND
Concerts
The **National Events Centre** *(Gleneagle Hotel, Muchross Rd., Killarney, Co. Kerry, tel 064 667 1555, www.inec.ie)* is the largest venue in Ireland and hosts concerts, shows, and theater.

Gaelic Football
Purely Irish entertainment! You may well be the only foreigner in attendance if you turn up on Sunday to **Austin Stack Park** on John Joe Sheehy Rd. (soon to move to Tralee Racecourse) in Tralee, Co. Kerry, to watch a blisteringly exciting game of Gaelic football—like soccer, but with more thrills per minute *(tel 066 712 6490 for match details).*

Golf
Golf fiends can cosset their addiction in Kerry on several notable courses, all agreeably scenic, some spectacularly so—try **Ballybunion Golf Club** on www

.ballybuniongolfclub.ie), **Tralee Golf Club** *(tel 066 713 6379, www.traleegolfclub.com),* **Beaufort Golf Resort** *(tel 064 664 4440, www.beaufortgolfclub.com),* or **Ross Golf Club** *(tel 064 663 1125)*—the latter two near Killarney—or **Waterville Golf Links** on the Iveragh Peninsula's Ring of Kerry *(tel 066 947 4102, www.watervillegolfclub.ie).* You could try two sports in one place at the **Killarney Golf and Fishing Club** *(tel 064 663 1034, www.killarney-golf.com).*

Greyhound Racing
Be prepared to stand up and shout your head off at the dogs on an evening out with a wallet of flutter money at **Cork Greyhound Stadium** *(tel 01890 269969 or 061 448 040)* in Curaheen Park on Curaheen Rd.

Horse Racing
There are tracks at **Mallow**, Co. Cork *(www.corkracecourse.ie),* and at **Killarney** and **Tralee** *(www.traleehorseracing.com),* Co. Kerry, where you can enjoy the thrill of the sport among like-minded countryfolk.

Irish Culture
Tralee, in northern Co. Kerry, is where you'll find **Siamsa Tíre**, the National Folk Theatre of Ireland *(Ivy Terrace, tel 066 712 3055, www.siamsatire.com).* From May to October, the theater offers a program of entertainment based around Ireland's rich culture of music, dance, and folklore.

Pubs
For that longed-for relaxing pint and conversation (firelit on chilly days), you can't do better than the cozy little first-floor **Hi-B Bar** opposite Cork city post office on Oliver Plunkett Street. Near Killarney, Co. Kerry, **Kate Kearney's Cottage** *(tel 064 44146, www.katekearneyscottage.com),* at

the entrance to the Gap of Dunloe beauty spot, is a nice old pub.

Theater
Belltable *(69 O'Connell St., Limerick, tel 061 319866, www.belltable.ie)* offers a program that ranges from plays and concerts to dance, mime, poetry readings, and exhibitions. **Cork Opera House** *(Emmet Pl., Cork, tel 021 427 0022, www.corkoperahouse.ie)* is a handsome city-center theater that can seat 1,000 for opera, dance, and drama. The well-known **Everyman Palace Theatre** *(15 MacCurtain St., Cork, tel 021 450 1673, www. everymanpalace.com)* is a restored 630-seat Victorian theater with a varied program, majoring in Irish drama during the summer.

Traditional Music
An Spailpín Fanach on South Main St., Cork, opposite the Beamish brewery, is great for music—often traditional, but just about anything might emerge.

Music lovers are spoiled for choice in west Cork: **De Barra** *(www.debarra.ie)* in Clonakilty, **McCarthy's** in Baltimore, **The Shanakee** in Kinsale, and **Barry Murphy's** pub in Bantry are good options.

In Co. Kerry, traditional music in pubs is plentiful in Tralee—try **Paddy Mac's** on the Mall, **Baily's** on Ashe St., **Kirby's Brogue Inn** *(www.kirbysbrogue.com)* on Rock Street, or **Turner's** on Castle Street.

In Dingle town, head for **The Small Bridge** *(www.thesmallbridge.com),* **Dick Mack's** *(www.dickmacks.homestead.com),* or the apparently tongue-tangling **Ua Flaithbheartaigh's** (don't panic—it's O'Flaherty's).

In Killarney, on High St., **O'Connor's Traditional Pub** puts on traditional music, as does the **Laurels** *(www.thelaurelspub.com)* on Main St.

In Limerick city, there's **Dolan's Pub & Restaurant** *(www.dolanspub.com)* on Dock Rd., **Nancy Blakes** on Denmark St., or **An Sibín** at the Royal George on O'Connell St.

WEST IRELAND

Clubbing
If you're an over-21 clubber, the short trip west out of Galway to the **Warwick** (*Salthill, Co. Galway, tel 091 521 244, www.thewarwick .com, open from 10 p.m.*) could be worth your while.

Greyhound Racing
Enjoy a bet on the dogs at **Galway Greyhound Track** (*tel 091 562 273*) on College Rd.

Horse Racing & Horseback Riding
Galway has **racing festivals** in July and September each year, when the racing world mingles with enthusiasts and visitors for a memorable Irish experience.

If you want to explore Connemara on a Connemara pony, there are plenty of places. Try **Errislannan Manor** (*tel 095 21134, www.errislannan manor.com*) on the west coast, just south of Clifden, which offers riding and trekking for adults and children.

Medieval Banquets
In the west, especially in Co. Clare, there are lots of banquets, with groups of musicians and actors dressed in historical costume, often in castles and country houses. You really have to be in the mood, but when the craic and the company are right, they can be very good fun. Try **Bunratty Castle** (*tel 061 360 788*), where you feast (eating with your fingers) with the "Earl of Thomond," or take in a Riverdance-style show in the Corn Barn at **Knappogue Castle** (*tel 061 360 788*) near Quin (eating irons provided here). Reservations advised.

Theater
In Galway city, theater lovers will make for the **Town Hall Theatre** (*tel 091 569 777, www.tht.ie*), in Court House Square, or for the more adventurous, **Druid Theatre** (*tel 091 568 660, www.druidtheatre .com*) nearby on Courthouse Lane.

Traditional Music
The **Glór Irish Music Centre** (*tel 065 684 3103, www.glor.ie*) in Ennis, Co. Clare, puts on performances of traditional Irish music with some of the country's top musicians. If you prefer to take your chances in a Clare pub—and Clare is renowned for it—get down to Doolin and **McGann's** (mostly tunes; *www.mcgannspubdoolin.com*) and **O'Connor's** (more songs), or the pubs in Kilfenora, Ennistymon, Lisdoonvarna, and many another town and village.

In Galway city, settle down with a pint at **Taaffe's** of Shop St., **O'Malley's** on Prospect Hill, the **Róisín Dubh** (*www.roisindubh.net*) on Upper Dominick St., or the atmospheric **Crane Bar** (*www.thecranebar .com*) on Sea Road on the west bank of the river, where you might find an Irish dancing session upstairs.

Co. Mayo is great for music, too—Westport is probably the cream of the crop, with really lively sessions in **Matt Molloy's** (the flautist with the Chieftains; *www.mattmolloy.com*), **Hoban's**, or **McHale's**.

NORTHWEST IRELAND

Boating
Little Co. Leitrim depends on its lakes and waterways to attract visitors, and there are a couple of enjoyable cruises to take: **Moon River Cruise** (*tel 071 962 1777, www.moonriver.ie*) on Main St., Carrick-on-Shannon (floating bar and live music), and **Sliabh an Iarainn Sunset Riverbus and Davy's BBQ** (*tel 071 964 4079*) on Railway Rd., Ballinamore (live music on board, then a barbecue and more entertainment on land).

Golf
For sheer scenic beauty, not to mention a respectable challenge, the **County Sligo Golf Club** (*tel 071 917 7134, www.countysligogolfclub.ie*), known here as Rosses Point, is hard to beat—it was even immortalized by W. B. Yeats, who dedicated a poem to the view from the third tee.

Irish culture
Teac Jack (*tel 074 953 1173, www .teacjack.com*) is a cultural center at Derrybeg out by Gweedore in northwest Co. Donegal, where there are music sessions and ceilidh dancing. Sligo town gains tone from its associations with the famous Yeats brothers, hence its **Yeats International Summer School** (see p. 208) and **Sligo Live Music Festival** (*www.sligolive.ie*).

Seaweed Baths
If you want a unique experience, go to Enniscrone on the Sligo coast for a sloppy and refreshing slither in **Kilcullen's Seaweed Baths** (see p. 211; *tel 096 36238, www.kilcullensea weedbaths.com*).

Theater
High-quality musicals, classical concerts, and dramas are staged at the **Hawk's Well Theatre** (*tel 071 916 1526, www.hawkswell.com*) on Temple St., Sligo. Letterkenny, Co. Donegal, offers **An Grianán Theatre** (*tel 074 912 0777, www.angrianan. com*) on Port Rd., with regular music and drama.

Traditional Music
Furey's (*www.fureysofsligo.com*) on the bridge is the best music pub in Sligo town (it's owned by the Sligo band Dervish). In Co. Donegal, the friendliest, most spontaneous spot is the **Scotsman** on Bridge Street. **Peter Oliver's** in Ardara, **An Teach Ceoil** at Fintown, and the **Central Bar** on Upper Main Street, Letterkenny, are great for music, too.

CENTRAL IRELAND
Entertainment tends to be less tourist-oriented here than in the

rest of Ireland—for the simple reason that this dairying and bog area sees fewer visitors.

Fishing

In Co. Meath, you can fish in any of a hundred lakes and rivers— **Anglers World** *(Balmoral Business Park, Kells Rd., Navan, tel 046 907 1866)* offers permits and advice.

Golf

Meath is a great golfing county. Try the **Royal Tara Golf Club** *(Bellinter near Navan, tel 046 902 5508, www.royaltaragolfclub.com)*, **Headfort Golf Club** *(Navan Rd., Kells, tel 046 924 0146, www .headfortgolfclub.ie)*, or **County Meath Golf Club** *(Newtownmoy ragh, Trim, tel 046 943 1463, www .countymeathgolfclubtrim.ie)*.

Greyhound Racing

In Co. Westmeath, small-town Ireland's passion for dog racing finds a noisy and enjoyable outlet in **Mullingar Greyhound Stadium** *(tel 044 934 8348)* at Ballinderry near Mullingar.

Horse Racing & Horseback Riding

In Co. Meath, **Fairyhouse Race-course** *(Ratoath, tel 01 825 6167, www.fairyhouseracecourse.ie)* is one of Ireland's major racetracks. For something less formal, there's a unique meeting at **Laytown** in June in which horses race along the beach while spectators watch from the dunes. If you want to ride, **Kells Equestrian Centre** *(Normanstown, Carlanstown, near Kells, tel 046 924 6998 or 086 849 9201, www.kellsequestrian.com)* is one place to go.

Irish Culture

At Ballyconnell in Co. Cavan, there's the **Ballyhugh Arts and Cultural Centre** *(tel 049 952 6044 or 049 952 6754)* out on the

Belturbet road, where exhibitions, live shows, and ceilidhs explore the native culture of west Cavan.

Theater

Co. Monaghan has the **Garage Theatre** *(St. Davnet's Complex, Monaghan town, tel 047 81597, www.garagetheatre.com)*, where you can catch a wide program of drama, dance, music, and comedy. In Drogheda, Co. Louth, there's the **Droichead Arts Centre** *(tel 041 983 3946, www.droicheadartscentre .com)* on Stockwell Lane. In Dundalk, the **Spirit Store** *(tel 042 935 2697, www.spiritstore.ie)*, on Georges Quay, offers a varied mix of cultural activities.

Traditional Music

There are tremendous music sessions (Sunday lunchtimes and Tuesday and Wednesday nights) in **C. ní Cairbre's** dark and character-ful pub on North Strand, Dundalk, Co. Louth.

Walking the Slieve Bloom Mountains

The Slieve Bloom Mountains rise out of the agricultural plains, straddling the borders of Counties Laois and Offaly. They can't really claim to be mountains; they are more like rounded hills, packed tightly together. But there can't be a hill range in Ireland better provided with keen walkers.

Among other initiatives, the local ramblers have founded the superb springtime **Slieve Bloom Walking Festival** *(early May, www .slievebloom.ie)*. They've also devised a whole scattering of looped walks from trailheads in the skirts of the mountains. Some of these are part of the official National Looped Walks scheme, and some are styled "eco-walks." Others are purely local initiatives. Best of all, the hospitable ramblers of the Slieve Bloom Walk-ing Club are only too happy to have visitors along so they can show

them just what it is they love about these hills.

■ NORTHERN IRELAND
Belfast

After years of apathy, neglect, and lack of investment brought about by the Troubles, Belfast has seized avidly on these more peaceful times to reinvent itself as just as much of a party city as Dublin. Every kind of entertainment is on offer here.

Concerts

The **Waterfront Hall** *(2 Lanyon Pl., tel 028 9033 4455, www.waterfront .co.uk)* shows off its superb acoustics with mega-concerts and shows, while the **Ulster Hall** *(34 Bedford St., tel 028 9032 3900)* and **King's Hall** *(Balmoral, tel 028 9066 5225, www .kingshall.co.uk)* host big pop music shows.

Nightlife

The famed **Golden Mile** between the city center and the university is crammed with bars offering live entertainment.

Pubs

A great way to acquaint yourself with some of Belfast's oldest and most characterful pubs is to turn up outside the Northern Ireland Tour-ist Board's offices at 59 North St. at 2 p.m. on a Saturday and take part in a **Pub Walking Tour** (see p. 292; *tel 028 9268 3665)*.

Theater

Opera, musicals, pantomime, concerts, comedy shows, theater, and ballet can all be enjoyed in truly sumptuous surroundings at the **Grand Opera House** *(tel 028 9024 1919, www.goh.co.uk)* on Great Vic-toria St. There's excellent repertory theater at the **Lyric Theatre** *(tel 028 9038 5673, www.lyrictheatre.co.uk)* on Stranmillis. The **Crescent Arts Centre** in the Golden Mile *(tel 028*

9024 2338, www.crescentarts.org)
offers music, comedy, dance, and
drama in a more intimate space.

Traditional Music

The **Rotterdam** (54 Pilot St., tel
028 9074 6021) is, by general
concensus, the home of live
music in Belfast, and this includes
traditional sessions on Mondays
and Thursdays. Or try **Madden's
Bar** (52–74 Berry St., tel 028 9024
4114, www.maddensbar.com).

Northern Ireland Counties

Clubbing

Kelly's Complex (tel 028 7082
3539, www.kellysportrush.co.uk),
on Bushmills Road at Portrush,
Co. Antrim, has seven bars, three
dance floors, and a popular club
known as **Lush**.

Fishing & Boating

Fermanagh offers fishing or boating
on Lough Erne (tel 028 6632 3110).
Fishermen in Co. Down could try
for a trout in the Mourne Mountains' Shimna River. Obtain permits
from **Four Seasons** (47 Main St.,
Newcastle, tel 028 4372 5078).

Golf

Downpatrick offers golf at the
18-hole **Downpatrick Golf Club**
(Saul Rd., tel 028 4461 5947, www.
downpatrickgolfclub.org.uk) and
at **Ardglass Golf Club** (tel 028
4484 1219, www.ardglassgolfclub.
com). One of the best (and one of
the oldest) courses is the **Royal
County Down Golf Club** (tel 028
4372 3314, www.royalcountydown.
org) at Newcastle, a championship
links course beneath the Mourne
Mountains.

Horse Racing

Co. Down is Northern Ireland's
horse-racing base, with **Down
Royal** (www.downroyal.com) and
Downpatrick (www.downpatrick

racecourse.co.uk), which bills itself
as "the friendliest racecourse in
Ireland."

Irish Culture

Two excellent Co. Tyrone venues
are **Dún Uladh Heritage Centre**
(tel 028 8224 2777) on the
outskirts of Omagh (Sat. evenings
from 10 p.m.) and **An Creagán
Visitor Centre** (tel 028 8076 1112,
www.an-creagan.com), east of
Omagh, on the Cookstown road.
In South Armagh, tradition comes
into its own in the admirable **Tí
Chulainn Cultural Activity Centre**
(see sidebar p. 45; tel 028 3088
8828, www.tichulainn.com), in the
village of Mullaghbane, where the
rich culture of the area is explored
in music, song, and storytelling.

Nightlife

In Derry city, the **Gweedore Bar**
(59–63 Waterloo St., tel 028 7137
2318, www.peadars-gweedorebar.
com) puts on live local bands and
gets packed and sweaty. **Mullan's
Bar** (13 Little James St.), locally
known as **Jackie Mullan's**, is a
popular place, with three bars on
different levels where the music
can be anything from jazz to disco.
In Co. Tyrone, Omagh has plenty
of music pubs and **McElroys Bar**
(24–30 Castle Street, tel 028 8224
0266) for the 18–25 crowd.

If you're out on the town by
night in Co. Down, try Bangor's **Café
Ceol** (tel 028 9146 8830, www.cafeceol-
bangor.com)—hot, hard, and housey.

Theater

Co. Antrim theaters include
Riverside Theatre (tel 028 7032
3232), on the University of Ulster
campus at Coleraine, and the
McNeill Theatre (tel 028 2826
0088), on Tower Rd., Larne. In Co.
Armagh, there's the **Market Place
Theatre** (tel 028 3752 1821, www.
marketplacearmagh.com) in Armagh
city. In Co. Fermanagh, there's
Enniskillen's **Ardhowen Theatre**

(tel 028 6632 5440, www.ardhowen
theatre.com), beside Lough Erne.

Traditional Music

In Co. Antrim, many of the small
towns and villages have music
pubs, in particular **McCol-
lam's** (locally known as **Johnny
Joe's**; www.mccollamsbar.com) in
Cushendall. In Derry city, **Peadar
O'Donnells** (tel 028 7137 2318,
www.peadars-gweedorebar.com) is a
characterful place with the decor
of an old grocery store, and **Henry
Joy McCracken's** (10a Magazine St.)
has sessions and good local bands.

Traditional music and the
delights of the ceilidh house have
revived recently in Co. Tyrone. **Teach
Eoin at Fernagh** (tel 028 8277 1551),
out east of Omagh, is wonderfully
friendly—telephone first. **Teach
Ceoil** (tel 028 8164 8882), in Rous-
key, is another music house in the
foothills of the Sperrin Mountains,
with a session usually held the last
Saturday of every month.

In Enniskillen, Co. Fermanagh,
you'll find live music at the **Crowe's
Nest** in the High Street. "**Blakes
of the Hollow,**" on Church St., is a
gem, and regular sessions here are
among the best. In the village of
Derrygonnelly, on the west side of
Lower Lough Erne, try **McGovern's**
or the **Cosy Bar**.

Co. Down boasts traditional
music pubs in every town—a nice
variant to the breakneck tunes is a
singalong session, which you will
find in the **Fiddlers Green** (10–12
Church St., Portaferry, tel 028 4272
8393, www.fiddlersgreenportaferry
.com).

Walking

The **Ulster Federation of
Rambling Clubs** (www.ufrc-online
.co.uk) can put you in touch with
33 member walking clubs in
Northern Ireland.

INDEX

Bold page numbers indicate
  illustrations.
CAPS indicates thematic categories.

ILLUSTRATIONS CREDITS

National Geographic
TRAVELER
Ireland

Published by the National Geographic Society
John M. Fahey, Jr., *President
  and Chief Executive Officer*
Gilbert M. Grosvenor, *Chairman of the Board*
Tim T. Kelly, *President, Global Media Group*
John Q. Griffin, *Executive Vice President; President,
  Publishing*
Nina D. Hoffman, *Executive Vice President;
  President, Book Publishing Group*

Prepared by the Book Division
Barbara Brownell Grogan, *Vice President
  and Editor in Chief*
Marianne R. Koszorus, *Director of Design*
Barbara A. Noe, *Senior Editor*
Carl Mehler, *Director of Maps*
R. Gary Colbert, *Production Director*
Jennifer A. Thornton, *Managing Editor*
Meredith Wilcox, *Administrative Director, Illustrations*

Staff for This Book
Lawrence M. Porges, *Project Editor*
Kay Kobor Hankins, *Art Director*
Mary Stephanos, *Text Editor*
Connie D. Binder, *Indexer*
Michael McNey, Nicholas P. Rosenbach, and Mapping
  Specialists, *Map Research and Production*
Jack Brostrom, Bridget A. English, Stephanie Robichaux,
  Maura Walsh, *Contributors*
Al Morrow, *Design Assistant*

Manufacturing and Quality Management
Christopher A. Liedel, *Chief Financial Officer*
Phillip L. Schlosser, *Vice President*
Chris Brown, *Technical Director*
Nicole Elliott, *Manager*
Rachel Faulise, *Manager*

First edition: Edited and designed by AA Publishing
(a trading name of Automobile Association Developments Limited, whose registered office is Norfolk House,
Priestley Road, Basingstoke, Hampshire, England RG24
9NY. Registered number: 1878835).

Drive maps drawn by Chris Orr Associates, Southampton,
  England
Cutaway illustrations drawn by Maltings Partnership,
  Derby, England

Founded in 1888, the National Geographic Society is
one of the largest nonprofit scientific and educational
organizations in the world. It reaches more than 285
million people worldwide each month through its
official journal, *National Geographic,* and its four other
magazines; the National Geographic Channel; television documentaries; radio programs; films; books; videos and DVDs; maps; and interactive media. National
Geographic has funded more than 8,000 scientific
research projects and supports an education program
combating geographic illiteracy.

For more information, please call 1-800-NGS LINE
(647-5463) or write to the following address:

National Geographic Society
1145 17th Street N.W.
Washington, D.C. 20036-4688 U.S.A.

Visit us online at www.nationalgeographic.com

For information about special discounts for bulk
purchases, please contact National Geographic
Books Special Sales: ngspecsales@ngs.org

For rights or permissions inquiries, please contact
National Geographic Books Subsidiary Rights:
ngbookrights@ngs.org

Printed in China

ISSN 0-7922-4145-2 (1st ed.)
ISBN: 978-1-4262-0022-9 (2nd ed.)

**National Geographic Traveler:
Ireland (Third Edition) :
ISBN: 978-1-4262-0636-8**

The information in this book has been carefully
checked and to the best of our knowledge is accurate.
However, details are subject to change, and the
National Geographic Society cannot be responsible for
such changes, or for errors or omissions. Assessments
of sites, hotels, and restaurants are based on the
author's subjective opinions, which do not necessarily
reflect the publisher's opinion.